Cervantes in Algiers

A CAPTIVE'S TALE

Cervantes in Algiers

A CAPTIVE'S TALE

María Antonia Garcés

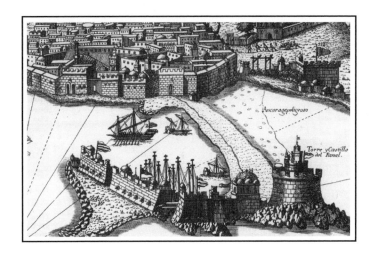

Vanderbilt University Press

NASHVILLE

This book is printed on acid-free paper.
Manufactured in the United States of America

Frontispiece: Detail from *La Ciudad de Argel* [The City of Algiers]
(c. 1700) N.A. Reprinted by permission of Servicio de Publicaciones
de la Agencia Española de Cooperación Internacional.

Text design: Dariel Mayer

Library of Congress Cataloging-in-Publication Data

Garces, Maria Antonia.
Cervantes in Algiers : a captive's tale /
Maria Antonia Garces.— 1st ed.
    p. cm.
    Includes bibliographical references.
    ISBN 0-8265-1406-5 (cloth : alk. paper)
    1. Cervantes Saavedra, Miguel de, 1547-1616—Captivity,
1575–1580. 2. Cervantes Saavedra, Miguel de, 1547–1616—
Knowledge—Algeria. 3. Algeria—History—1516–1830. 4.
Islam—Relations—Christianity   I. Title.
PQ6338.A6G37 2002
863'.3—dc21

                                        2002004335

To the memory of my beloved son
Álvaro José Lloreda Garcés,
December 29, 1962–March 17, 1988

Farewell, thou child of my right hand and joy!
My sin was too much hope of thee, lov'd boy.

—Ben Jonson, "On My First Son"

Contents

Illustrations

Preface and Acknowledgments

THIS BOOK WAS WRITTEN during the difficult period of mourning that followed the death of my beloved son Álvaro José, my firstborn and closest interlocutor. It is ironic that a book on the effects of trauma on Cervantes, one planned before the fatality that took my son's life, ended up being composed in the midst of what may be the worst of traumas: the death of one's child. Like other forms of emotional turmoil, trauma speaks to the encounter with death that marks catastrophic events and to the vicissitudes of the survivor who asks why he or she did not die in the other's place—an additional trauma felt by a parent who feels responsible for the physical and psychological well-being of her children.

During this period of mourning, I have been sustained by the love and support of my family, especially of my other four children, who have often rescued me from grief and have granted me new illusions. Close friends have also comforted me. Teaching has enormously aided the work of healing, imbuing my life with delight and exciting new projects. The most important resource in this process of grieving and recovery, however, has been my writing on Cervantes. More than anyone or anything else, Cervantes has been the great teacher, the healer who has helped me to reattach *"el roto hilo de mi historia"* [the broken thread of my life] as I read, and wrote about, his fictions. Laughing with these fictions, reinterpreting them time and time again, often from different perspectives, pondering the profound questions that emerge from Cervantes's texts, I have been pressured to sound the complexities of literary and psychic constructions, both in Cervantes and in myself. The admiration I have always felt for Cervantes, specifically for his extraordinary capacity for invention, has been deepened as I explored the processes of renewal and recreation mirrored by his works. If wit and humor in Cervantes are a fundamental tribute to life, the remarkable fertility of his creations that swirl around the vortex of trauma has shown me that it is possible to turn trauma into song. I must thank Cervantes, first and foremost, for conspiring with me to transform mourning into a creative endeavor. His festive affirmation of Eros, symbolized by his dictum *"¿quién pondrá riendas a los deseos?"* [who can put a rein on desire?], has enabled me to reassemble the shattered pieces of myself, together with those expressions of joy and grief that assert the continuity of life.

I BEGIN THESE ACKNOWLEDGMENTS by expressing my thanks to my four children—María Lucía, Jorge Alberto, Felipe, and Mariana Lloreda Garcés —who have offered their love and support during the writing of this book, and ever since I began an academic career, as a graduate-student–mom. They know that "children are half of one's soul," as Cervantes wrote in a little-known play entitled *La entretenida ("Mitades son del alma/los hijos")*. I thank them for the respect, not devoid of humor, with which they acknowledge my accomplishments and for the lovely gift of their own children. Her geographical proximity in the United States has allowed my daughter María Lucía to provide much tender loving care and thoughtful insights during this process. After Álvaro José's death, Jorge Alberto was thrust into the difficult position of acting as the mainstay of our family. He has assisted us all with his generosity and has sustained me, in particular, with his enduring love. Felipe has cheered me with his creativity, his wit, and his psychological insights, which have oftentimes afforded a new vision of reality. And Mariana has brightened my days with the enthusiasm she brings to any task she undertakes and with her devoted daughterly affection.

I am deeply grateful to my mother, Mariana Arellano de Garcés, for her support in every phase of my career, one that, to her chagrin, has taken me to another continent. I express my admiration for the grace and courage with which she has faced adversity. My brothers Jorge and Ricardo Garcés have always stood behind me with their affection. My sister María Cristina Garcés teaches me constantly about loyalty and giving; her love has been a source of motivation. My father would have liked to follow this project to its conclusion. His love, assistance, and recognition were essential in the initial stages of my career as a scholar.

I would also like to express my profound gratitude to my daughter-in-law Carolyn Field for the love she gave my son Álvaro José, and for the children she bore him, Alejandro and Juliana, who have brought great joy into my life. She has been a daughter to me since her marriage to Álvaro José, and we are now united by love and death.

More than anyone, Diana de Armas Wilson has helped me to give birth to this book. With her critical vision and extraordinary generosity, she has encouraged me to formulate my hypotheses about Cervantes and Algiers and to weave literary history with trauma theory. I thank her for her friendship and affection, which have been instrumental in the creation of my new life in the United States.

The following friends and scholars have read chapters of this book, often in their earliest versions, and have helped me to assess the tenor of my research. Debra Castillo has often read pieces of my work and offered her sharp insights. John Kronik read a partial manuscript with meticulous attention and provided generic directions. Ciriaco Morón Arroyo read more extensive sections of the manuscript and gave me his valuable input, including his help in deciphering various sixteenth-century documents. The chair of Romance Studies at Cornell University, Mitchell Greenberg, provided invaluable support as well as special funds that enabled me to finish my bibliography on time. Mieke Bal's brilliant reading of two embryonic chapters strengthened my revision of the manuscript. Max Hernández proffered his learned psychoanalytical insights. Kate Bloodgood, editor par excellence, has rehabilitated many passages in this book and has shed light on Islamic determinism. Andrés Lema-Hincapié helped me to tame an unmanageable bibliography. Spanish historian Mercedes García Arenal has offered intellectual stimulation and endless bibliographical suggestions on the sixteenth-century Maghrib and its relations with Spain. I also thank the two readers of my manuscript for Vanderbilt University Press, whose generous comments improved the revision of this study. My special thanks to copyeditor Katharine O'Moore-Klopf for her sensitivity and impeccable work. I am deeply grateful to all of these readers and writers.

Memorable exchanges with María Soledad Carrasco, Edward Dudley, Javier Herrero, Bob ter Horst, and the late Ruth El Safar, as well as with Michel Moner and Augustin Redondo across the Atlantic, have vastly enriched my thinking about Cervantes. Various friends and scholars in Colombia have provided their valuable support. I am indebted to Carlos José Reyes, director of the Biblioteca Nacional de Colombia, for inviting me to speak at the cycle of conferences "Cervantes y El Quijote," which took place in Bogotá, in November 1997. My paper for this conference became the seed of this book, eventually expanding into various chapters on Cervantes and Algiers. Anthony Sampson has supported me with his friendship and his brilliant readings in Lacanian psychoanalysis. The late Montserrat Ordóñez shared her work and her passion for literature with me. Early in my career, my dear friend, the late María Cristina Mera, participated in many conversations with me about Cervantes and other writers. Francisco Piedrahíta, the rector of Universidad Icesi, in Cali, Colombia, invited me to teach a course on *Don Quijote* during the painful period that followed my son's death, a kind gesture that forced me to return to Cervantes for inspiration. My interest in psychoanalysis was enkindled by Libardo Bravo Solarte, who has been a model of ethical values. I am grateful to all for their encouragement.

For their friendship, intellectual support, and generosity, I wish to thank

Birgitte Bönning González-Espitia, Luis Cárcamo Huechante, Mary Jo Dudley, Nelly Furman, Juan Carlos González-Espitia, Guillermo Izabal, Carol Kaske, Bill Kennedy, José Edmundo Paz-Soldán, Richard Klein, Betty Osorio de Negret, Angelika Rauch, María del Mar Ravassa, and Maria Krystyna Nowakowska Stycos. My cousins Elena Garcés Echavarría and Laura Garcés Sarolly have comforted me with their affection in both happy and difficult times. My graduate-school friends and colleagues Nicolás Wey-Gómez and Verónica Salles-Reese have offered their encouragement and inspiration during the years. I owe them all a special debt of gratitude.

In the course of my research for this book, I have been assisted by scholars and librarians from all over the world. I thank Comm. Frá John Edward Critien from the Order of Saint John of Jerusalem of Malta, in Rome, for his kind help in looking for documents in the archives of the Order of Malta. My friend Liliana Tedesco assisted me with inquiries regarding the Order of Malta in Rome. Maroma Camilleri, senior assistant librarian in the Malta National Library, provided valuable indications regarding sources and entries from the Archives of the Order of Malta. I am grateful to Malta historian Joseph Muscat for his data regarding the loss of the galley *San Pablo* from the Order of Malta in 1577. Dr. Theresa M. Vann, the Joseph S. Micallef Curator of the Malta Study Center at the Hill Monastic Manuscript Library, St. John's University, Collegeville, Minnesota, advanced much needed information and microfilm copies of documents from the Archives of the Order of Malta. Concha Lois Cabello, director of the Reference Department at the Biblioteca Nacional in Madrid, obtained copies of letters included in two early modern books housed in this library. Officers from the Archivo General de Simancas in Valladolid efficiently located various documents related to the capture of the galley *San Pablo* from the Order of Malta. Ana Echevarría was kind enough to look for some documents at Simancas. In my own home institution at Cornell, David Block, the Ibero-American Bibliographer at Olin Library, has been a strong supporter who has promptly ordered the books I have needed. Julie Copenhagen and Caitlin Finlay at the Olin Interlibrary Services have granted their efficient and kind assistance. Likewise, Nicole Brown and the reference librarians at Olin Library located early modern books and prints for me across the World Wide Web. I am grateful to these friends, writers, librarians, and institutions for their invaluable help.

The idea for this book emerged during my tenure as a fellow at the Society for the Humanities at Cornell, during the academic year 1997–98, under the theme "Why Trauma, Why Psychoanalysis?" This fellowship enabled me to rehearse many of the ideas developed in my study on Cervantes and Algiers and to exchange ideas on trauma with a group of scholars from around the world. I am especially grateful to Dominick LaCapra, director of the Society for the Humanities, for his steady support, as well as to the fellows who shared spirited discussions with me during the seminars of 1997–98 and afterward: Teresa Brennan, Tom Conley, Jonathan Elmer, Bruce Fink, Max Hernández, Ellis Hanson, Mary Jacobus, Biddy Martin, Tim Murray, Petar Ramadanovic, Herman Rappaport, Annette Schwarz, Mark Seltzer, Suzanne Stewart, and Lindsey Stonebridge. Mary Ahl and the staff at the Society for the Humanities provided a lovely atmosphere for work. I thank them all for their continuous assistance.

I am also grateful to more distant mentors who launched me onto the roads of scholarship. Harry Sieber led me through the twists and turns of early modern Spanish literary history and taught me the importance of meticulous research. Eduardo González showed me how to sail through cultural and geographical spaces, making daring connections along the way. Neil Hertz has provided inspiration and unrelenting support throughout the years. Nancy Struever motivated me with her passion for her work and her impeccable erudition. Even further back, Michael E. Gerli opened the world of Cervantes for me and unknowingly initiated me into an academic career. In various ways, the mentorship and stimulation of these scholars have contributed to this book.

Other literary critics whom I have met only in writing have deeply influenced the composition of this book. I owe my foremost debt to Jean Canavaggio, whose luminous books on Cervantes are cited throughout this work. My study on Cervantes and Algiers is a response to his throwing down the gauntlet to the scholars who would be willing to continue his Cervantine investigations. I have also benefited from the textual dialogue with literary historians in the United States and Spain: Juan Bautista Avalle-Arce, Daniel Eisenberg, Antonio Rey Hazas, Alberto Sánchez, Florencio Sevilla Arroyo, Henry Sullivan, the late Françoise Zmantar, and Stanislav Zimic. Beyond the writings of Fernand Braudel, which have been an inexhaustible source of information, various contemporary historians have left their mark on these pages. José Fernando de la Peña and Emilio Sola awakened my interest in Cervantes and Algiers. I alluded earlier to the stimulating impact of Mercedes García Arenal's work on early modern Spain and the Maghrib. In addition, historians Bartolomé and Lucile Benassar, Miguel Ángel de Bunes, Mikel de Espalza, Andrew Hess, and Dahiru Yahya have influenced my study of the Mediterranean, and of Algiers and the Maghrib in the sixteenth century. Finally, I recognize my indebtedness to such theorists of trauma as Cathy Caruth, Shoshana Felman, Dori Laub, and Robert Jay Lifton. Their meaningful contributions to the study of trauma and its afterlife have illuminated my study of the trauma of captivity in Cervantes. As acknowledged in its dedication, this book is devoted to the memory of my beloved son, Álvaro José Lloreda Garcés, who was a strong and loving supporter of all my scholarly efforts.

VARIOUS CHAPTERS IN THIS BOOK contain pages that have appeared in earlier publications: "*'Cuando llegué cautivo'*: Trauma and Testimony in *El trato de Argel*," in *Cervantes para el siglo XXI/Cervantes for the 21st Century*, Commemorative Collection in Honor of Professor Edward Dudley, ed. Francisco LaRubia-Prado (Newark, DE: Juan de la Cuesta, 2001) 79–105; *"El cautiverio: meollo de la obra cervantina,"* *El Quijote en Colombia ayer y siempre*. Special issue of *Senderos* 9.33 (1998): 1322–35; "Cervantes's Veiled Woman," in Miguel de Cervantes, *Don Quijote*, Norton Critical Edition, trans. Burton Raffel, ed. Diana de Armas Wilson (New York: Norton, 1998) 821–30. I thank the editors for permission to incorporate sections of the above essays into this book.

Publication of this book has been supported by generous grants from the Hull Memorial Publication Fund of Cornell University and the Program for Cultural Cooperation between Spain's Ministry of Education, Culture and Sports and United States Universities.

Cervantes in Algiers

A CAPTIVE'S TALE

Introduction

CERVANTES: TRAUMA AND CAPTIVITY

Since then, at an uncertain hour,
That agony returns;
And till my ghastly tale is told
This heart within me burns.

—Coleridge,
"Rime of the Ancient Mariner"

RETURNING TO SPAIN AFTER FIGHTING in the Battle of Lepanto and other Mediterranean campaigns against the Turks, soldier Miguel de Cervantes was captured by Barbary pirates and taken as a captive to Algiers. The five years he spent in the *baños* [prison houses] of Algiers (1575–80) left an indelible impression on his work. From the first plays and narratives written after his release from captivity, *El trato de Argel [Life in Algiers]* (c. 1581–83) and *La Galatea* (1585), to his posthumously published novel *Los trabajos de Persiles y Sigismunda [The Trials of Persiles and Sigismunda]* (1617), the story of his traumatic experience continuously speaks through Cervantes's fictions. His oeuvre is haunted by images of captivity: cages of all sizes, Christian captives, galley slaves, and female prisoners, some used as translators, others confined to special prisons. All of these figures join the multiple Cervantine characters who literally suffer the pain of human bondage. Even Don Quijote returns home as a prisoner in *Don Quijote*, Part I, and, as the object of multiple sadistic pranks, he is practically held hostage in the palace of the duke and duchess in Part II. Figurative incarcerations abound in Cervantes's fictions, such as that suffered by Don Quijote, a prisoner of his delirium, and by the deranged scholar Vidriera, a captive of his glass-body—that is, of his madness.

One wonders whether Cervantes could have become the great creative writer that he was had he not suffered the traumatic experience of his Algerian captivity. A number of early modern writers, contemporaries of Cervantes, as well as others across the centuries, have acknowledged that catastrophic events were the point of departure for their writing. At the time of Cervantes's imprisonment in Algiers, Portuguese cleric Antonio de Sosa, a captive too in the city, composed a monumental treatise on Algerian history and customs entitled *Topographia, e historia general de Argel* (1612). Writing from his prison, Sosa claimed that he wrote every single day to let the world know about "the great miseries, sufferings, torments and martyrdoms suffered by the Christian captives in the hands of the Moors and Turks, especially in Algiers."[1] Flemish aristocrat Emanuel d'Aranda, captured in 1640 by Turkish corsairs along the coast of Bretagne and enslaved for two years in Algiers, became a writer after his release, evoking time and time again his fortunes and misfortunes in Barbary, *"desquels je confesserai ingénument avoir tiré autant ou peut-être plus de profit en peu de temps que de mes études de plusieurs années"* [from which I would have to confess naively that I obtained equal or perhaps more profit than from my studies during various years].[2] Forty years after his liberation, d'Aranda continued writing about his past experiences, presenting new editions and expanded translations of his *Relation de la captivité & liberté du sieur d'Aranda*, a work that eventually touched on contemporary problems, even while returning constantly to his visions of Barbary.

In the twentieth century, many authors claimed that catastrophic events turned them into writers. Primo Levi, a survivor of Auschwitz and chronicler of the Holocaust, states: "If I hadn't gone to Auschwitz I probably would not have written, or I would have written completely different things—maybe scholarly articles about chemistry. I certainly possessed the capacity to write, I can't deny that [. . .]. But I wouldn't have had—how can I explain it?—the 'raw material' to become a writer."[3] Colombian poet and novelist Álvaro Mutis says something similar regarding his fifteen-month imprisonment in the Mexican penitentiary of Lecumberri:

> gracias a esa experiencia, tan profunda como real e incontrovertible, he logrado escribir siete novelas que reuní con el título de *Empresas y tribulaciones de Maqroll el Gaviero*. Hasta entonces sólo había intentado andar los caminos de la escritura narrativa con algunas historias reunidas bajo el título de *La mansión de Araucaima* [. . .]. En los treinta años anteriores había escrito solo poesía.

> [Thanks to that experience, as profound as real and irrefutable, I have been able to write six novels that I have collected under the title of *Adventures of Maqroll*. Until then I had attempted to tread the paths of narrative writing with some stories collected under the title of *The Mansion of Araucaima* [. . .]. In the thirty years before this event, I had only written poetry].[4]

Mutis ascribes this change of genre to his immersion in the prison world, where pain and horror were conjugated with the warmest human solidarity. Emphasizing the effects of his imprisonment on his fiction, he adds: *"Jamás hubiera conseguido escribir una línea sobre las andanzas de Maqroll el Gaviero, que ya me había acompañado a trechos en mi poesía, de no haber*

vivido esos quince meses en el llamado, con singular acierto, 'El Palacio Ne-
gro' " [Never could I have written a line about the adventures of Maqroll
the mastman, who had already accompanied me here and there in my poetry, had I not lived during those fifteen months in the so-called, with singular correctness, Black Palace] (*Diario de Lecumberri*, 11). We can ask ourselves whether a similar transformation occurred in Cervantes after his
encounter with trauma. Let us recall that as a young man, before leaving
for Italy in 1569, Cervantes had written a number of poems. When he returned to Spain eleven years later, after participating as a soldier in the
Mediterranean wars with the Turks and enduring a long captivity in Barbary, he embarked on a multifaceted career as a writer, one that spanned
all literary genres, from drama to poetry to narrative prose.

Starting with the dramatic circumstances of his Algerian captivity, this
book attempts to explore the afterlife of trauma in Cervantes, especially
its effects on his literary production. The psychoanalytical notion of trauma
alludes to a wound inflicted on the mind, a wound caused by an event
that occurred too soon, too unexpectedly, to be fully known and is therefore not available to consciousness except through the repeated nightmares
and actions that haunt the survivor. The traumatic event of Cervantes's
captivity resonates with the experience of war and other traumas described
by Freud in *Beyond the Pleasure Principle*. Freud rightly emphasizes the
peculiar temporality of the traumatic experience: This "past" experience
continues to intrude on the present, reappearing in the subject as flashbacks, dreams, or reenactments of the catastrophic event (SE 18:12–14). Such
processes speak to the many Cervantine fictions that turn on the motif of
captivity, plays and narratives that disclose their links with the history of
the sixteenth-century Mediterranean and its bloody wars with Islam.

Cervantes in Algiers: A Captive's Tale explores the relation between fiction and memory, between speech and survival in some of Cervantes's most
representative works. By focusing closely on sections of *La Galatea;* the
plays *El trato de Argel, Los baños de Argel [The Dungeons of Algiers]*, and
El gallardo español [The Gallant Spaniard], as well as *La historia del cautivo
[The Captive's Tale]* interpolated in *Don Quijote*, Part I, the novella *La
española inglesa [The English-Spanish Girl]*, and his final *Persiles*, I examine the complex links between figurative language and testimony in the
work of Spain's major author. Yet, as Geoffrey Hartman reminds us, the
literary construction of memory is obviously not a literal recovery but a
construction of a different sort.[5] In Cervantes's case, this reconstruction
relates to the negative moment in experience, to what in experience was
not or could not be adequately experienced. Paradoxically, to paraphrase
Hartman, the traumatic experience becomes "burned into the brain" (540),
like an indelible scar that is not always remembered. These reconstructions,
moreover, question the relations between trauma and creation.

Notwithstanding the prolonged scholarly interest in Cervantes's Algerian captivity, which has been discussed by various articles on and biographies of Cervantes, albeit in a fragmentary way, there is not a single work that offers a comprehensive view of Cervantes's life as a slave, and, particularly, of the lingering effects of this traumatic experience on his literary creations. My book, then, examines the complex frontier world of North Africa, where Cervantes spent five years of his life. This study sets the stage for the analysis of the uncanny recurrence and continual transformation of the catastrophic event into some of the most experimental fictions of Spanish literature. Starting from the dynamic borderline between "the life" and "the work" in Cervantes, I extend the rethinking of trauma theory through a committed engagement with the texts of an early modern historian, Antonio de Sosa, who wrote the most important history of Algiers in the sixteenth century, and a modern cultural historian, Fernand Braudel, who revitalized the history of the Mediterranean in the age of Philip II. My reading also enters into dialogue with a contemporary group of scholars who have renovated the history of North Africa and its complex exchanges with Christian Europe, especially with Spain, such as Bartolomé and Lucile Benassar, Miguel Ángel de Bunes, Mercedes García Arenal, and Andrew Hess, among others. Their work studies the intricate Hispano-Muslim borderland, pushed, after the fall of Granada, to North Africa, where two adjoining yet increasingly different societies clashed and intermingled through political, cultural, and commercial interchanges. Finally, this book attempts to continue the marvelous work of Jean Canavaggio on Cervantes, which has opened new venues into the life and work of the author.

In sum, *Cervantes in Algiers: A Captive's Tale* connects history, cultural studies, and literary testimonies with psychoanalytical literary criticism. Certainly, no writer in Spanish literature seems so insistently to demand a psychoanalytical approach as Cervantes. His profound reflection on madness—so central to *Don Quijote* and other works—converts him into a pioneer in the exploration of the psyche three centuries before Freud, opening the way for such studies of insanity as those conducted by Michel Foucault and Jacques Lacan in the twentieth century. If Cervantes's oeuvre is conceived from the *other shore*, as Juan Goytisolo claims, adding that the writer elaborated his complex vision of Spain while in prison in North Africa,[6] I would argue that Cervantes's explicit interest in the question of madness emerges from the borderline situations he endured as a captive, from the encounter with death that transformed him into a survivor. His inquiry into fantasy and reality would thus arise from the impact of the catastrophic experiences that create other selves, other names for Cervantes, in the immense biographical rubric that aligns trauma with fiction in his work.

The renewed interest in trauma studies, revived after Vietnam and intensified by terrifying events both in the Balkans and in the United States, speaks to the recent explosion of books on trauma across the disciplines: Cathy Caruth's *Unclaimed Experience: Trauma, Narrative, and History* (1996) and Shoshana Felman and Dori Laub's *Testimony: Crisis of Witnessing in Literature, Psychoanalysis and History* (1992) are but two examples that demonstrate the cross-fertilization between field work, clinical perspectives, and academic research.[7] In this vein, my book approaches the human experience and literary creations of Cervantes from the perspective of trauma studies. The Cervantine fictions that turn on the motif of captivity represent a poetic mode of witnessing—of accessing reality—when all other forms of knowledge have been precluded. My research on trauma, moreover, pressures me to explore the frontier between life and death in Cervantes, between limit-experiences and the belated and repeated representations of these traumatic events in fiction.

In addition, I show that trauma in Cervantes functions as a fountain of creation: the reenactment of the traumatic experience in the writer's works generally produces an outburst of fantasy, an escape into another reality that circumvents the traumatic event itself even while functioning as an artistic testimony to trauma. More specifically, the traumatic repetitions that traverse Cervantes's literary production unfold into fantastic images that open the window of creation. This Cervantine paradigm sheds light on Lacan's dictum that "it is in relation with the real that phantasy functions. The real supports the phantasy, the phantasy supports the real."[8] As the most elusive of the three orders, the Lacanian "real" refers to the impossible because it is impossible to imagine and impossible to integrate into the symbolic order—impossible to describe or to attain in any way. It is this characteristic of resistance to symbolization that lends the real its essential traumatic quality, one that permits us to equate the real with trauma, as we shall see shortly. In Cervantes, the interweaving of traumatic repetitions and fantasy leads to an eroticization of the imaginary, what I have called an "erotics of creation" that emerges from the writer's reenactments of his Algerian captivity. This poetic testament not only questions the relationship between trauma and fantasy but also leads to a basic question regarding testimony in Cervantes, such as that asked by Hartman in his brilliant article on trauma and literary studies: "Why literature, story, and not events, history?" (541).

Cathy Caruth's crucial inquiry into trauma and its affinity with history provides one of the frameworks for my book.[9] Following Caruth's reading of *Moses and Monotheism* as a drama of Freud's unconscious, I ask: How does trauma—a traumatic event in the life of the critic—affect literary criticism itself, either in the unconscious identifications and choice of materials made or in the approaches and interpretations used by the theoretician? Such inquiry seems crucial from my own perspective as a literary critic. In December 1983, I was kidnapped by an urban guerrilla group in Cali, Colombia, during the initial kidnapping campaigns that have taken on massive dimensions in present-day Colombia. During my seven-month confinement, I remained locked in a tiny, windowless cell, constantly guarded by armed jailers. My love for literature kept me alive during a long period of physical inactivity paired with feverish mental activity. One book in particular helped me through this ordeal: *El laberinto de la soledad [The Labyrinth of Solitude]* by Octavio Paz. Through his central study of solitude as an essential human experience, Paz helped me search for answers and for hope, while I attempted to think the unthinkable. My raw reflections on this terrifying experience, woven with my reactions to Paz's splendid meditation on Mexico and Latin America, are recorded in a letter I wrote to Paz some months after my liberation.[10] This traumatic event cut my life in half, marking a point of departure for another continent and other experiences—those of a professor of Hispanic studies at Cornell University. Yet the painful exodus that forced me to leave my country after my release from captivity offered me, paradoxically, freedom from the traditions and social constraints that had previously bound me, opening new horizons in my career as a scholar and literary critic.

This traumatic experience first kindled my interest in Cervantes's captivity, an interest fueled by my fascination with Cervantes's creations and my profound understanding of the rigors of human bondage, from that of the early modern prisoners of war, such as Cervantes and Antonio de Sosa, to that of the Holocaust victims and contemporary casualties of kidnapping and terrorist activities in different parts of the world. My own ordeal as a "prisoner of war" in Colombia—as my captors called me during my detention—not only enhanced my capacity to read and listen to Cervantes with another ear but also refined my ability to grasp and respond to the complexities of trauma theory. Having been visited by death, *having lived it in some way* during this unspeakable tribulation, I am also personally aware of the vicissitudes of telling undergone by the survivors who attempt to recount their stories, difficulties eloquently discussed by Dori Laub in various articles. On the other hand, even though I have limited the discussion of my kidnapping in this study, my writing on Cervantes's captivity and correlated fictions has indirectly aided me to work through my own experience in the interminable process of recovering from trauma.

Ceaseless Repetitions and Reenactments

"The real," said Lacan, is "that which always comes back to the same place" (*Four Fundamental Concepts of Psychoanalysis*, 42, 49). Lacan was referring to the Freudian concept of repetition *[Wiederholung]* and its enigmatic relation with the Real, especially in the case of the traumatic neuroses. The above lines introduce Lacan's difficult and inventive discussion of the encounter with the real in the fifth chapter of *The Four Fundamental Concepts of Psychoanalysis*, entitled *"Tuché and Automaton"* [Chance and Spontaneity]. Lacan is referring to the Aristotelian distinction between two kinds of chance to illustrate the differentiation between the Real and the Symbolic. As we might recall, among the three orders envisioned by Lacan—the Symbolic, the Imaginary, and the Real—the Real refers to a realm that falls entirely outside the signifying dimension. Hence, the Real is not only opposed to reality; it is that which falls outside the symbolic process. For Lacan, as it turns out, chance, in the sense of pure contingency, occurs only in the Real.

In the second book of the *Physics*, where the concept of causality is examined, Aristotle explores the role of chance and fortune and causality. He distinguishes between two types of chance: *automaton*, which alludes to chance events in the world at large, and *tyche* [Fr. *tuché*], which designates chance in so far as it affects agents who are capable of moral action. Lacan redefines *automaton* as "the network of signifiers," thus situating it in the symbolic order. The term, in effect, refers to those phenomena which seem to be chance but which are in truth the insistence of the signifier in determining the subject.[11] In turn, Lacan aligns the real with the Aristotelian *tyche*, which he redefines as "the encounter with the real *(as if by chance)*" (*Four Fundamental*, 51–55; Evans, 24). *Tyche* thus refers to the incursion of the Real into the symbolic order, a violent and arbitrary incursion which in Lacan's clever explication resembles a knock on the door that interrupts a dream (*Four Fundamental*, 56). On a more painful level, this violent encounter is trauma. The traumatic event not only is arbitrary and completely unforeseeable for the victim (hence, *as if by chance*) but also, as an encounter with the Real, is extrinsic to signification. As Malcolm Bowie elucidates, trauma "is as intractable and unsymbolizable as objects in their materiality."[12]

At the center of Lacan's text on repetition, then, is the reenactment of the traumatic event proper: "what is repeated, in fact, is always something that occurs—the expression tells us quite a lot about its relation to the *tuché—as if by chance*" (*Four Fundamental*, 54). For this reason, Lacan sees the function of the *tuché*, of the Real as encounter, as that of "the missed encounter" (the *troumatique*, Lacan puns)—that is, trauma. The real as encounter (or missed encounter) presents itself to us "in the form of that which is unassimilable—in the form of the trauma" (*Four Fundamental*, 55). Trauma, in effect, may be described as an unmediated shock, an ungraspable wound, registered rather than experienced. In "the very heart of the primary process," asserts Lacan, we see preserved the insistence of trauma in calling attention to its existence: "The trauma reappears there, indeed, frequently unveiled. How can the dream, the bearer of the subject's desire, produce that which makes the trauma emerge repeatedly—if not its very face, at least the screen that shows us it is still there behind?" (*Four Fundamental*, 55).

This passage announces Lacan's rereading of the "burning child" dream studied by Freud in *The Interpretation of Dreams*. What materializes as pre-eminently real in this text is the dead child himself, who reappears in the father's dream as if he were asleep, still burning with fever and crying out in pain: "Father, don't you see I'm burning!" The unfortunate father, we may recall, had gone to rest in the room next to the one in which his dead child lay, leaving the child in the care of an old man. The father was awakened by the knocking, "a noise made to recall him to the real," but this expresses in his dream the parallel reality of what is happening: "the very reality of an overturned candle setting fire to the bed in which his child lies" (*Four Fundamental*, 57). The traumatic dream that reenacts the scene of the child's death and his cry "Father, don't you see I'm burning!" repeats in its utter brutality the father's confrontation with the death of his own child and, at the same time, the missed reality that caused the death of the child. To use Lacan's words, "is not the dream essentially, one might say an act of homage to the missed reality—the reality that can no longer produce itself except by repeating itself endlessly, in some never attained awakening?" (*Four Fundamental*, 58).

For Lacan, the encounter, forever missed, has occurred between dream and awakening: "the terrible vision of the dead son taking his father by the arm designates a beyond that makes itself heard in the dream" (59). This beyond is that of trauma, which cannot be grasped by conscience, only repeated inexorably in dreams, hallucinations, or other modes of repetition. Studying this scene, Bowie notes that this dream "is an accident that repeats an accident, an irreducible fragment of the Real that speaks of irrecoverable loss, an encounter that is peremptory and brutal and yet that can now never, outside dreams, take place" (106). As an example of traumatic repetition, the dream of the burning child points to the resurgence in actual life of the catastrophic occurrence itself and, simultaneously, to the utter incompressibility of the traumatic event.

Another instance of a traumatic dream is presented by Primo Levi, the post-war chronicler and witness to the Holocaust. In the poem that prefaces *La tregua [The Truce]*, Levi finds himself first in the post-Holocaust world of civilization but then falls back into the world of the Lager as the civilized world crumbles around him.[13] In the camps, Levi reports, he dreamed of "going home, of eating, of telling our story," until he was awakened by the cruel dawn reveille: *Wstawach*. The last world of the dream and the last world of *The Truce* itself is the Polish *Wstawach (alzarsi)*, the command to get up used in the Lager, and from which he could not escape:

Our hunger is quenched.
All our stories have been told.
It is time. Soon we shall hear again
The alien command:
Wstawach.

(*The Truce*, 183)

Speaking of Holocaust survivors, Dori Laub states that the subject of trauma "lives in its grip and unwittingly undergoes its ceaseless repetitions and reenactments."[14] Having taken place outside the parameters of "normal" reality, the traumatic event defies such boundaries as causality, sequence, place, and time. Hence, the trauma is an event that has "no beginning, no ending, no before, no during and no after" ("Bearing Witness," 68–69). This absence of categories that circumscribe trauma lends it not only a quality of "otherness" but also a preeminence, a timelessness, and a ubiquity that places it outside the range of apprehension, of recounting, and of mastery. Trauma survivors, argues Laub, "live not with memories of the past, but with an event that could not and did not proceed through to its completion, has no ending, attained no closure, and therefore, as far as its survivors are concerned, continues into the present and is current in every respect" ("Bearing Witness," 69). Recalling the recurring visions of captivity in Cervantes, this description may shed light on the continual restaging of the traumatic experience by his fictions. Indeed, the corpus of Cervantes's works seems to be haunted by the reenactments of trauma, possessed by the continual images and "dreams" that assault the survivor. If the writer's literary works speak of the urgency to recount the story of his ordeal, the repetitions of the captivity motif mark the efforts of the survivor—the narrator—to assimilate the unthinkable event, to apprehend—*to think*—his Algerian experience.

Such processes, however, turn not only on the repeated return of the traumatic event but also on the therapeutic process set in motion by the reconstruction of a narrative, by the construction of a history and, essentially, by the reexternalization of the event. Referring to Holocaust survivors, Laub indicates that this reexternalization of the event can occur "only when one can articulate and *transmit* the story, literally transfer it to another outside oneself and then take it back again, inside." Telling thus entails a reconfirmation of the power of reality and a reexternalization of the evil that affected and polluted the trauma victim ("Bearing Witness," 69). Again, it is Primo Levi, a writer like Cervantes, who illuminates these issues as he recalls his desperate compulsion to tell the story of the things he had seen and suffered in Auschwitz. Levi felt compelled to force his tale on every passerby: "I told my story to everyone and anyone, at the drop of a hat, from the plant manager to the yard-man [of the paint-factory where he worked] [. . .] just like the Ancient Mariner" (Rodi, "An

Interview with Primo Levi," 356). In *The Periodic Table*, Levi states that he wrote these things down "at breakneck speed, so much so that gradually a book was later born."[15] In the same book, he evokes his need to achieve internal liberation: "It seemed to me that I would be purified by recounting [. . .] by writing I found peace for a while and felt myself become a man again" (*Periodic Table*, 157).

The implicit comparison of early modern Algiers with a concentration camp is not fortuitous. In *El trato de Argel*, Cervantes associates the dungeons of Algiers with Dante's *Inferno*, while literary critic Louise Fothergill-Payne has equated the Algerian *baños* with the brutal reality of a concentration camp.[16] For Cervantes, the process of reconstructing and reaffirming historical reality was founded by the long testimony he composed for the *Información de Argel*, an inquiry that took place in Algiers in 1580, after his liberation. This statement, which bears witness to his Algerian experience, is the first long prose work written by the author, organized, as it were, in episodes or "chapters."[17] The reconstructive process is also constituted by the inquest itself, which attests to the individual and collective testimonies of the witnesses who corroborate and expand Cervantes's affidavit even while testifying to their own sufferings in Barbary. Through this initial testimony, Cervantes enacts a testimonial process similar in nature to the psychoanalytical process itself, in that it is another medium that provides compassionate listeners for the trauma victim, another medium of reexternalization, and thus historicization, of the event, as Laub claims, referring to Holocaust survivors ("Bearing Witness," 70).

Massive trauma, nevertheless, precludes its registration; the observing and recording mechanisms of the human mind are, so to speak, shattered, not functioning. The emergence of the narrative that is being listened to—and heard—is, accordingly, the process and the place wherein the apprehension, the "knowing" of the event is initiated. In this metaphorical delivery, psychoanalyst Laub explains, the listener is "a party to the creation of knowledge *de novo*" ("Bearing Witness," 57). Followed by the innumerable legal and literary testimonies that traverse his life, the first testimony to Cervantes's captivity opens up new narrative avenues, such as those inaugurated by his play *El trato de Argel*.

CHAPTER I OF THIS BOOK sketches the history of the Barbary Coast, from the Spanish conquests of the North African shores following the fall of Granada in 1492, to the arrival of the legendary Barbarossa brothers, founders of the modern State of Algiers, and, in the 1570s, the consolidation of the famous city as the capital of corsair activity par excellence in the early modern Mediterranean. This chapter also examines the question of Muslim and Christian piracy in the Mediterranean together with the ensuing conflicts between the Habsburg and the Ottoman Empires that culminated in the Battle of Lepanto in 1571, including the role of Cervantes in this battle, which left indelible scars. The capture of Cervantes by Barbary corsairs in 1575, his experience as a slave in the *baños* of Algiers, and his four escape attempts, in which he barely avoided death, are studied side by side with archival documents and contemporary accounts of captivity in North Africa. As mentioned earlier, the most relevant of these accounts is the *Topographia, e historia general de Argel* (Valladolid, 1612), composed by the captive Antonio de Sosa in the dungeons of Algiers between 1577 and 1581.

Chapter 2 focuses on the relation between Antonio de Sosa and Cervantes in Algiers. Until recently, little was known of Sosa, not only one of Cervantes's best friends in captivity but also his first biographer and the most authoritative witness in the *Información de Argel*, collected in 1580 by Cervantes himself. I have discovered several documents linking the Portuguese cleric to the Order of St. John of Malta, a military order established in Malta in 1530, after the fall of Rhodes to the Ottomans. My interest in Antonio de Sosa centers on his reading and writing day by day during his captivity, obsessively recording every bit of information obtained from Christian slaves and their captors. Concomitantly, Sosa recounts that throughout almost four years, Cervantes shared numerous conversations on poetry and literature with him and often sent him his compositions for his perusal.

This chapter also brings to life some of the most colorful personages of Cervantes's Algiers, such as rulers Ramadān Pasha, Hasan Veneciano, and 'Abd al-Malik of Morocco, all known to Cervantes. I recreate the atmosphere that surrounded the captives interested in literary endeavors, such as Cervantes and Sosa, among others who composed poems, letters, or extensive works in the *baños*. The rest of chapter 2 recounts Cervantes's ransom through the intervention of the Trinitarian order in 1580. I conclude with the testimonies rendered by various witnesses regarding Cervantes in the *Información de Argel*, including his own affidavit, which is the longest extant text composed in Algiers by the future author. I choose to read Cervantes's own testimony as a fundamental form of action that permits the freed captive to continue the process of survival after liberation. Testimony is the way in which Cervantes—the survivor—initiates the construction of a narrative, the reconstruction of his own history. I would suggest that this first act of attesting to his traumatic experience allows Cervantes to reclaim his own history and to break out of his emotional imprisonment to start a new life in Spain.

Chapter 3 addresses the first literary testimony of Cervantes regarding his Algerian experience, the play *El trato de Argel*, probably composed between 1581 and 1583, soon after his return to Spain. Inaugurating Cervantes's career as a playwright, *El trato de Argel* functions as a denunciation of, and a collective testimony to, captivity in Algiers, a city represented in the play as an actual dungeon. I examine the most relevant episodes of this drama side by side with other scenes from *Los baños de Argel*, another Cervantine play that dramatizes the sufferings of the Christian slaves in North Africa. In addition, I compare the testimonies offered by *El trato de Argel* with those of other captives and survivors across the centuries, from Antonio de Sosa in sixteenth-century Algiers to Primo Levi in twentieth-century Auschwitz. Chapter 3 thus explores the complex autobiographical dimensions of Cervantes's play, which dramatizes for the first time on the Spanish stage the actual experience of captivity in Barbary.

The torment and continuous suffering of the captives, often leading to death, as portrayed in *El trato*, turn this drama into a collective tragedy. Issues of biography and history, however, are neither simply represented nor reflected in this play but are reinscribed, translated, and fundamentally reelaborated by Cervantes. This drama reveals for the first time what will become a paradigm in the writer's literary production: The reenactment of the traumatic experience in his fiction generally elicits an outburst of fantasy in Cervantes. As a fragmented text among the vertiginous scenes that follow one another without respite, *El trato* reflects both the breakdown of understanding and the literal reenactments of traumatic events. Entering into a dialogue between the individual and the collective, these fragmented scenes and discourses render a collective testimony of captivity in Algiers.

That Cervantes would have chosen the theater as a medium to bear witness to his catastrophic experience is intriguing. According to Laub, bearing witness to trauma is a process that encompasses the listener. For the testimonial process to take place, there needs to be a bonding, "the intimate and total presence of an *other*—in the position of one who hears. Testimonies are not monologues; they cannot take place in solitude. The witnesses are talking to somebody: to somebody they have been waiting for, for a long time" ("Bearing Witness," 70–71). The theater, of course, facilitates this encounter between the witness and the listener. The staging of Cervantes's drama thus made possible an encounter between the survivor and the listener (the spectator), so that an individual and a collective testimony could take place.

Even more powerful is *La historia del cautivo*, interpolated in *Don Quijote* I (39–41), which I examine in chapter 4. This tale not only offers a synthesis of Cervantes's soldierly career in the Mediterranean but also provides an extraordinary depiction of the life of Christian slaves in Barbary, one that points to the mysterious frontier that cuts across the life and work of Cervantes. *La historia del cautivo* is doubly signed, first, by a date that permits us to situate the narration in 1589, and then, by Cervantes's own surname, Saavedra. The phantasmatic apparition of the name *Saavedra* in the reenactment of the writer's own captivity presses me to include an analysis of the proper name and of the signature in Cervantes. Moving between autobiography and fiction, I study the appearance of the surname *Saavedra* in Cervantes's life and fictions, from *El trato de Argel*, where this name emerges for the first time, to the author's assumption of the surname *Saavedra* in 1586, to *La historia del cautivo* (1589) and the concurrent *Memorial* addressed to the president of the Council of Indies in 1590, requesting a post in the Indies. Here the writer includes a detailed account of his service to the crown, stressing his captivity, under the name *Miguel de Cervantes Saavedra*. The multiple meanings of the surname *Saavedra* in Cervantes suggest that *Saavedra* incarnates both the limit—experience of the captive who survived the encounter with death, and the fluctuating limit between biography and literary production. It is under the name *Miguel de Cervantes Saavedra* that, fifteen years later, the author of *Don Quijote* would achieve success and then enduring fame.

The astounding conjunction of trauma and fantasy in *La historia del cautivo* leads me to question the associations between trauma and creation in Cervantes and, correspondingly, the odd lack of discussion of these complex relations in trauma theory. If the name *Saavedra* simultaneously delineates a signature, a geography, a body, and a bleeding scar in this tale, it also represents that frontier or tenuous borderline between biography and fiction. It is precisely after the intrusion of Cervantes's name (*Saavedra*) in his narrative that the image of Zoraida, the Moorish woman who brings about the escape of the captive Captain, surfaces in the text. It suffices to say that the dangerous approach to the vortex of trauma—to the reenactment of captivity in this tale—engenders the fabulous fiction of Zoraida, one of the most appealing creations in the Cervantine oeuvre.

As mentioned earlier, the joint appearance of traumatic memories and fantastic inventions constitutes a pattern that traverses Cervantes's works. This paradigm can be noticed in other Cervantine fictions, such as in the plays *El trato de Argel*, *Los baños de Argel*, and the novellas *La española inglesa* [*The English Spanish Girl*], and *El amante Liberal* [*The Liberal Lover*], to cite only a few. The role of the Moorish woman, whose appearance is generally linked to the memories of Algiers in Cervantes, is especially fascinating. Idealized, like Zoraida in *La historia del cautivo*, or ambiguously portrayed, like Zahara and Fátima in *Los tratos de Argel*, the Moorish woman is often the spokeswoman for the author, recounting critical autobiographical events or emerging next to the reenactment of the traumatic experience in Cervantes's texts, thus pointing to the links between trauma and creation. In the second part of this chapter, I study the figure of Zoraida as a "symptom" for the Captive—that is, as an image of the Virgin Mary that functions as the ultimate shield against death, an approach grounded in Freudian and Lacanian psychoanalysis and the theories of Julia Kristeva. In like manner, I show that *La historia del cautivo* represents a turning point in Cervantes's literary creation, an explosion of creativity that opens the way for Cervantes's great invention, *Don Quijote*.

Chapter 5, subtitled "Anudando este roto hilo" [Tying Up This Broken Thread], explores the textual itinerary of recurrent images or tropes that function as testimonies to Cervantes's Algerian ordeal. Reenacting the very moment of the capture, these statements surface initially in *La Galatea* and crisscross other Cervantine works, such as *El trato de Argel, Los baños de Argel,* and *La española inglesa,* ending with *Persiles,* in the final testimony that closes Cervantes's life. Revealing a truth impossible to assimilate, these are the stories of a wound that *cries out,* that addresses us in an attempt to express an indescribable reality. Gradually, however, traumatic truth in Cervantes evolves into shorter testimonies, which are increasingly diffused with his fiction. This is demonstrated by *La española inglesa,* where the memories of Cervantes's captivity are reduced to a few lines that open the way to an infinite sequence of ludic repetitions and, in turn, to new adventures.

In *Persiles,* moreover, the phantoms of Algiers are associated with questions of remembrance and forgetting. The last allusion to Cervantes's captivity in this novel opens up a kind of writing that traces the negatives and residues of the traumatic experience, a writing that begins with *"no me acuerdo"* [I don't remember] and that playfully underscores the loss of memory suffered by those who endure afflictions. Certainly, in Cervantes's later works, the diffused reflections of the phantoms of Algiers reveal both a familiarization with and a simultaneous distancing from the catastrophic scenario through the work of creation. Hence, the literary production of Cervantes opens and closes with the vivid reenactment of his most painful experience. My book thus traces the complex, continuous reelaboration of the effects of captivity in Cervantes since his deliverance from slavery to the moment of his death. In the end, Algiers—*"puerto universal de corsarios, y amparo y refugio de ladrones"* [a universal haven for pirates and a shelter and refuge for thieves], as Cervantes calls the North African city in *Persiles*— remains the core, the texture of the Cervantine *obra*.

I

The Barbary Corsairs

Cuando llegué cautivo, y vi esta tierra
tan nombrada en el mundo, que en su seno
tantos piratas cubre, acoge y cierra
no pude al llanto detener el freno.
　　　　　—Saavedra, *El trato de Argel*[1]

MANY CRITICS HAVE ALLUDED to the marks left on Cervantes's thoughts
and works by his North African captivity. *"Fue el más trascendental hecho*
en su carrera espiritual" [it was the most transcendental event in his spiritual career], says Américo Castro, referring to this catastrophic experience,
while Juan Bautista Avalle-Arce argues that the capture by Barbary pirates
in 1575 *"es el gozne sobre el que se articula fuertemente toda la vida de Cer-*
vantes" [is the hinge which forcefully organizes the entire life of Cervan-
tes].[2] Certainly, Cervantes's Algerian enslavement is the phantasmatic center
to which his writing incessantly returns. In the words of Juan Goytisolo,
Cervantes's captivity is *"ese vacío—hueco, vórtice, remolino—en el núcleo cen-*
tral de la gran invención literaria" [that void—hole, vortex, whirlwind—
in the central nucleus of the great literary invention].[3] This whirling void
speaks to the presence of trauma.

As Hartman reminds us, trauma, on the one hand, is registered rather
than experienced, bypassing, as it were, perception and consciousness; on
the other, it reappears as a kind of memory of the event, "in the form of a
perpetual troping of it by the bypassed or severely split (dissociated) psyche"
(537).[4] In Cervantes, the ungraspable experience of captivity returns relentlessly, as an incessant ritual of concealment and invention that agitates
his fiction in uncanny ways. Such insistent thematic repetitions—the Christian captives and Algerian corsairs that endlessly reappear in his texts—suggest that trauma is localizable not in that violent occurrence situated in
the subject's past but rather in the way it comes back, unassimilated, to
haunt its victim. As it turns out, the recurrence and reenactment of the
traumatic event in his works may even function as a source of creation for
the writer.

As early as 1915, Armando Cotarelo Valledor claimed that the theme of captivity was a fountain of inspiration for Cervantes: "Fue el primero en traer a la dramática española los asuntos de cautivos; [. . .] aportó antes que nadie una fuente copiosísima de inspiración artística [. . .]: la realidad" [He was the first to bring the subject of captivity into Spanish drama (. . .). Before anyone else, he contributed a rich fountain of artistic inspiration (. . .): his own experience] (*Teatro*, 30–31). More recently, George Camamis has cogently argued that *La historia del cautivo* is the first modern novel on the subject of captivity, one that inaugurates the new genre of the contemporary historical novel. Camamis stresses the perplexing connections between captivity and literary invention in Cervantes: "el cautiverio en Cervantes viene a ser un mundo complejo de creación artística" [captivity in Cervantes turns out to be a complex world of artistic creation].[5] This seems to be a Cervantine paradigm—a pattern studied in depth by this book. Not only does Cervantes probe the theme of captivity in almost all his writings but the related issue of freedom is a constant in his work, inspiring Luis Rosales to remark that "la libertad [. . .] ocupa el centro del pensamiento antropológico cervantino" [liberty (. . .) occupies the core of Cervantine anthropological thought].[6]

BASIC TO THE DISCUSSION of Cervantes's captivity in Algiers is the history of the Barbary Coast, from the Spanish conquests of the North African shores following the fall of Granada in 1492 to the arrival of the legendary Barbarossa brothers, founders of the modern State of Algiers, and the consolidation of the famous city in the 1570s—at the time of Cervantes's imprisonment—as the capital of corsair activity par excellence in the early modern Mediterranean. This includes the conflictual events that led to the Battle of Lepanto in 1571, as well as Cervantes's participation and heroism in this campaign, where he lost the use of his left arm. The subsequent capture of Cervantes by Algerian corsairs in 1575, his experience as a slave in the *baños* of Algiers, and his four consecutive escape attempts, in which he barely escaped death, are carefully examined here side by side with archival documents and contemporary accounts of captivity in Barbary. In addition, this chapter focuses on the cruel fate of Christian slaves in Algiers and the punishments perpetrated by their masters on the prisoners who tried to flee, an account that ends with Cervantes's relation to the renegades—Christian converts to Islam. The five years spent by Cervantes in Algiers—a life in the frontier between various worlds—evoke a period in which the undeclared war fought by the expelled Hispano-Muslims who settled in the Maghrib, fueled by the conflicts between the two great powers that fought for control of the Mediterranean, led to the capture of thousands of Christian captives, some of whom were ransomed, while others remained in Barbary forever.

Since the early nineteenth century, the historical experience of captivity and its artistic expression have attracted the attention of biographers and scholars of Cervantes.[7] Of late, the admirable biography of French Hispanist Jean Canavaggio has undertaken an exploration of the writer's soldierly career in the Mediterranean, the tribulations of the captive, and the price of his freedom.[8] Canavaggio's biography, however, raises more questions than it answers in regard to Cervantes's life, especially in regard to his Algerian captivity. Overcome by the silences and lacunae that obscure these years of Cervantes's life, the French critic admonishes that many uncertainties remain: *"¡Cuántas oscuridades todavía!"* (*En busca del perfil*, 10; *Cervantes*, 6). A renewed interest in the five years (1575–1580) spent by Cervantes in Algiers has emerged at the turn of the twenty-first century.[9] Although this is one of the most documented periods of Cervantes's life, it is also, paradoxically, one of the most enigmatic. As Canavaggio suggests, referring to the testimonies of men who shared the experience of captivity with the future author: "However precious they [these testimonies] may be, these sources are virtually silent on what constitutes [. . .] the essential point: How Cervantes lived within that experience; the relationships he established with Muslims and Christians; the way he viewed a civilization different from his own" (*Cervantes*, 79).

Many critics have turned to the literary projections of this ordeal to complete these data. The plays *El trato de Argel [Life in Algiers]*, *Los baños de Argel [The Dungeons of Algiers]*, *El gallardo español [The Gallant Spaniard]*, and other fictions, such as *La historia del cautivo [The Captive's Tale]*, interpolated in *Don Quijote*, and *El amante liberal [The Liberal Lover]*, among other works, offer precious information on the fate of Christian captives in Barbary, even while revealing the personal impressions of the man who suffered these tribulations. Others have proposed that Cervantes's interest in the marginal, his openness toward other cultures, and his respect for difference emerge from his Algerian enslavement.[10] Goytisolo, the contemporary Spanish writer who looks on Cervantes with confessed admiration, offers a synthesis of these ideas: "La summa cervantina [es] concebida desde la otra orilla—la de lo excluido y rechazado por España. [. . .] Cervantes elaboró su compleja y admirable visión de España durante su prisión en tierras africanas, en contraposición al modelo rival con el que contendía" [The Cervantine *obra* is conceived from the other shore—that of the excluded and rejected by Spain. (. . .) Cervantes elaborated his complex and admirable vision of Spain while in prison in the African territory, in opposition to the rival model against which he fought] (*Crónicas*, 60–61). In addition, I propose that the profound reflection on madness—on the meaning of insanity—that traverses the work of Cervantes, converting him into a pioneer in the exploration of the psyche three centuries before Freud, emerges from the borderline situations that he endured as a captive, from the encounter with death that transformed him into a survivor.

Let us begin, then, by adumbrating the background of the writer's captivity in the sixteenth-century Mediterranean.

The Barbary Coast

This section traces the emergence of Algiers, on the Barbary Coast, as a formidable political organization whose growth and prosperity in early modern times portends the gradual decline of the Spanish frontier in North Africa. The first half of the sixteenth century in the western Mediterranean, then, evinced the resurgence of Islam under the outright expansion of the Ottoman power into the central Maghrib. This dynamic event led Spain to commit many lives and resources to fight the growth of another threat to Christian Iberia from Muslim North Africa. Among the many lives lost or caught in these battles was that of soldier Miguel de Cervantes, whose captivity in Algiers must be seen in the framework of the Hispano-Ottoman wars in the Mediterranean.

In 1519, the grandson of Catholic monarchs Ferdinand and Isabella, Charles I of Spain, became Charles V, the emperor of the Holy Roman Empire in Europe. Charles inherited a geographically scattered succession of kingdoms and states whose only element of union, beyond hereditary rights, was a cohesion of beliefs on the part of most of his subjects. Charles's possessions were separated and cut off by enemy states that often declared war to consolidate their position in the face of his excessive power. Under these circumstances, Charles V's life would be burdened by struggles with the Lutherans in the Low Countries, conflicts with France, and the war with the Turks, which took place on two fronts simultaneously: the Danube and the Mediterranean.

The only state capable of confronting Spain in the sixteenth century was the Ottoman Empire, ruled by the formidable Süleymān the Magnificent (1520–1566). Süleymān headed a compact empire that extended from the Mediterranean in the west to the Black Sea and the Indian Ocean in the east, one governed by an iron hand and united by both the homage rendered to the sultan and the religious beliefs of his subjects. The significant title of Leopold Von Ranke's old book, *Die Osmanen und die Spanische Monarchie im 16. und 17. Jahrhundert [The Ottoman and the Spanish Empires in the Sixteenth and Seventeenth Centuries]* (1837), signals the parallelism between the impetuses of these two political monsters, one to the east, the other to the west of the Mediterranean, the Ottoman on one side, the Habsburg on the other.[11] While Charles was mainly interested in maintaining his frontiers and his patrimony, Süleymān strove to expand his empire on all its fronts. The debate regarding which of the two powers would dominate Europe was raging in 1519, when Charles was elected Holy Roman Emperor. Accordingly, while the armies of Charles V battled the Turks in the Mediterranean, Süleymān captured Belgrade in 1521, destroyed the Hungarian army in 1526, and surrounded Vienna in 1529. At the same time, the exiled descendants of the Moors from Granada were engaged in guerrilla warfare against the Christians in the Mediterranean, especially against Spain, their most abhorred enemy.

With the conquest of Granada in 1492 by Ferdinand and Isabella, the Strait of Gibraltar became the southern Spanish frontier, certainly an insufficient boundary between the Christian kingdom of the Iberian peninsula and the Islamic world of North Africa. In this Mediterranean far west, as Fernand Braudel suggests, the coasts of Spain and Africa are so close that a bonfire lit on one shore can be seen from the other. At the turn of the fifteenth century, small boats crossed this western channel daily, making the journey between Vélez de la Gomera and Málaga or, if the winds were favorable, between Valencia and Orán. The fall of Granada gave the Catholic monarchs possession not only of the rich meadows that surround the Moorish city but also of the southern littoral of Andalucía with its excellent ports and watchtowers. Was it not natural, asks Braudel, to continue the war against the infidel on African soil, or even to use the boundless energies liberated by the fall of Granada in the Maghrib, a theater of expansion and adventures (*En torno*, 46)?[12]

Since the end of the fifteenth century, then, Spaniards dedicated themselves to the capture of the Maghribi coastal villages. In 1494, Pope Alexander VI gave his blessing to the African crusade and continued the extraordinary tax, the *cruzada*, that would defray the expenses of such expeditions.[13] The death of Isabella in 1504 confirmed the thrust of the new campaign. Her testament states that Castilians should devote themselves unremittingly to the conquest of Africa and the war against Islam.[14] Soon after, instigated and financed by warrior-priest Cardinal Jiménez de Cisneros and led by celebrated seaman Pedro Navarro, an army of ten thousand men, more than fifteen times the size of the force Cortés used to conquer Mexico ten years later, launched into the conquest of the North African coast (Hess, 39). Between 1508 and 1510, the Spaniards conquered the inaccessible Peñón de Vélez (1508), Orán (1509), Bougie, and Tripoli (1510), where they built *presidios* [fortresses]. The legendary Navarro—a former corsair, known in his old days as *"Roncal el Salteador"* [Roncal the Highwayman]—sacked these cities, distributing the booty among the conquerors and capturing the inhabitants, who were sold as slaves.[15] Spain's endeavors in North Africa were obviously spurred by more than the passion to convert the Muslims to Christianity and to control the frontiers of Islam. The spirit of adventure and the bait of riches lying ahead on the African land had as much influence on the sixteenth-century Spaniards as the preoccupation with eternal salvation. Possessing the coasts of the Maghrib, moreover, helped to bridle Muslim piracy, the great resource of the Maghribi ports. In Tangier and Hone, in Orán, Algiers, Bougie, Bizerta, and Tunis, to cite only a few important posts, Muslim corsairs armed galleys and light vessels that they launched against Christian ships.

Piracy was not new to the Mediterranean. For centuries, Muslims and Christians had practiced it on an equal basis. In the sixteenth century, however, Muslim privateering had been reinforced by the affluence of the Spanish Moriscos expelled by the *Reconquista*. In fact, the Spanish invasion of the Maghrib was also driven by the need to control the activities of these exiles who fled the Peninsula after the fall of Granada in 1492. In the face of increasing persecution by the Old Christians, thousands of Morisco refugees from Granada opted for *"pasar allende"* [passing overseas]—including the dethroned king Boabdil and an important sector of the Grenadine nobility. In 1494, the first revolt of the Alpujarras, on the outskirts of Granada, delivered a new batch of angry Hispano-Muslims to Africa. Established in Barbary—the name used in the sixteenth century to designate the coastal area of northern Africa, roughly from Tripoli to Morocco—the émigrés declared a holy war against Spain. Concurrently, the aggressive Iberian presence in important enclaves of the African coast stimulated the guerrilla warfare waged by Muslim raiders, many of whom were Morisco renegades from Andalucía and Valencia who had fled the peninsula. Aided by other Moriscos who had not yet migrated, they assaulted the Spanish coasts, plundered towns and churches, and captured hostages, who were made slaves.

These corsair activities had their counterpart in the privateering of Christian pirates who launched raids against the Maghribi coasts. A *Memorial* addressed to King Ferdinand around 1506 describes the practice of Spanish privateers, especially from Jerez and the Bay of Cádiz, cruising along the African shore from Bougie to the Atlantic, in single vessels and squadrons sufficiently powerful to occupy fortified towns and carry off between four hundred and eight hundred captives at a time. The Spanish conquest of Melilla (1497) and Mers-el-Kebir (1505) led to large-scale forays perpetrated by soldiers and privateers, such as the raids that Pedro Navarro and his men would carry out at the end of the decade. One example suffices: In 1507, after plundering three neighboring towns, a Spanish expedition from Mers-el-Kebir captured fifteen hundred Moors, four thousand head of cattle, and other booty before encountering a large Muslim force from Tlemcen that killed two thousand Spaniards and carried off four hundred prisoners. In spite of Ferdinand's harsh prohibitions against privateering, dating from 1489, Spanish corsairs flocked to the Maghribi coastal areas, and by 1498, the king was forced to authorize the unrestricted use of privateers in the Mediterranean, apart from his imposition of a strict veto on privateering in Barbary waters.[16]

The Legendary Barbarossa

The conflict between Spain and its émigrés was intensified with the arrival of corsairs Arūj and Khair ad-Dīn [Kheir ed-Din] Barbarossa, founders of the Barbary State in the Algerian coastal region. The story of the Barbarossa brothers must be recounted to shed light on the rise of Algiers as both the greatest corsair city in the Mediterranean and as a highly organized Ottoman province, paradoxically conquered by eastern Mediterranean sailors. Under Khair ad-Dīn Barbarossa's government, Algiers became the dominant maritime power of the western Mare Nostrum, more dreaded by Christian nations and people than its nominal superior, the Ottoman Porte. The Barbarossa brothers turned the province and its capital, Algiers, into the stable, well-organized, and powerful corsair establishment known by Cervantes.

There is agreement that the famous Barbarossa brothers came from the island of Mytilene in Greece, engaged in coastal trade and privateering, and were involved in the Ottoman political struggles of the early sixteenth century.[17] Arūj Barbarossa acquired his political stature in the context of the Iberian conquest of the North African towns. Using the banner of Islam against the Spaniards, Barbarossa obtained the support of Turkish followers and Berber tribes, in addition to that of numerous Morisco colonies from Valencia and Aragon who settled in these regions.[18] In August 1516, Arūj Barbarossa overtook Algiers, killing its ruler, Selim ben Tumi. Various traditions recount the murder in striking ways: The king was either stabbed, strangled with his own turban, or asphyxiated in the royal steam bath by Barbarossa himself, stories that dramatized Barbarossa's cruelty and expanded his fame throughout the Mediterranean. A letter written by Italian humanist Pietro Martire d'Anghiera from the Spanish court on August 31, 1516, reveals the preoccupation of Charles's Hispano-Italian entourage with the triumphs of Barbarossa:

> A certain Copper Beard—vulgarly called Barbarossa—has turned from a pirate into a terrestrial troublemaker in Africa, whose major coastal regions he is deceiving, through the Muslim hermits, who are the priests of the Moors [. . .]. He promises them that, if elected king, he, as a follower of the Islamic law, will liberate them from the Christian yoke and will keep them safe [. . .]. The city of Algiers has already proclaimed him King; thus, Barbarossa already calls himself King in Africa.[19]

Barbarossa's brilliant career in North Africa and the Mediterranean was cut short by the Spaniards in 1518. His valiant defense in the siege of Tlemcen and his death at the hands of a company of Spanish soldiers are eloquently described by Pietro Martire again, in a letter dated July 4, 1518: "Overwhelmed by the majority, Barbarossa finally fell, vanquished. But he gave us too cruel a victory. He killed most of our men and he wounded many [. . .] courageous soldiers. The head of Barbarossa, driven into a stake, was taken to Tlemcen, with great rejoicing of the Moors and joy of our people. Thus finished his days Barbarossa, pirate of Sicily" (Letter 621, *Epistolarium* III: 322–23).[20]

Arūj Barbarossa was succeeded by his brother Khair ad-Dīn, who had the political vision to turn to the Turkish sultan for protection to counteract the menace of an Iberian invasion. In exchange for military help, Khair ad-Dīn Barbarossa placed his conquests under the mantle of the Ottoman Empire. Algiers became a new Ottoman *sancak* [province], with two thousand janissaries and four thousand other Levantine Muslims and corsairs enlisted into the Algerian militia. In 1529, while Charles V was preparing to travel to Italy for his solemn coronation by the pope as emperor of the Holy Roman Empire, Khair ad-Dīn launched a definitive assault on the Peñón of Algiers, a Spanish *presidio* buried deep in the harbor of that city, and captured it after a twenty-day bombardment. A skillful politician and military commander, Khair ad-Dīn imparted to the Algerian Turkish Regency its characteristic form and legitimate existence through his connections with the Ottoman Empire.

In 1529, Süleymān marched on Vienna with an army of four hundred thousand men. His defeat in this campaign induced him to invite Barbarossa to Constantinople to discuss the construction of a great Turkish fleet. The colossal armada, commanded by the *kapudan pasha* [grand admiral] Barbarossa, captured Tunis from the Spaniards in 1534.[21] Leaving Algiers for Constantinople, Barbarossa became the most powerful and richest man of the Ottoman court. In the following years, the Turkish Armada commanded by Barbarossa devastated the Italian coasts and the fortress of Castilnovo (near Kotor, in Yugoslavia), abducting a great number of captives.[22] Charles V then attempted to win the corsair to his side. In the course of the secret negotiations conducted by Andrea Doria, the great admiral of the imperial navy, and Fernando Gonzaga, the viceroy of Sicily, for the release of Spanish captives, the emperor offered to recognize Barbarossa as king of Algiers and Tunis if he broke his alliance with the Turks.[23]

The mythical Barbarossa elicited a biography by contemporary Spanish chronicler Francisco López de Gómara—Hernán Cortés's biographer—who is well known in Spanish American historiography for his *Historia general de las Indias y conquista de México* (1541). Gómara closes his perplexing treatise on the Barbarossa brothers with this eloquent statement: *"Haradin Barbarroja es el mayor corsario y mejor capitán de mar que jamás ha habido y que más y mejores cosas ha hecho sobre el agua"* [Khair ad-Dīn Barbarossa is the greatest corsair and the best sea-captain that there ever was and has accomplished the best and most awesome things on water] (*Barbarroja*, 439). His accomplishments went beyond the water, however, for Barbarossa turned Algiers into an inexpugnable nest of corsairs. The Algerians filled their ranks with numerous Spanish and Italian captives who chose to convert to Islam to obtain their freedom and dedicate themselves to privateering in Barbary.

We can thus say that the modern state of Algiers was inaugurated by the Barbarossa brothers, who established the principles of organization of the Ottoman province. Peopled by innumerable refugees from Granada and other cities from Andalucía and Valencia, as well as by the renegades who started arriving in large numbers from different points in the Mediterranean, Algiers became an invincible bastion of Islam, the corsair-city that confronted Charles V in 1541 with his worst maritime defeat. This catastrophic event would be evoked forty years later by Saavedra, a character in Cervantes's play *El trato de Argel [Life in Algiers]*, who cries while comparing his fate as a slave in Algiers to that of the impotent Charles V on that occasion.

The Emperor's Defeat in Algiers

In 1541, Charles V launched his third and last attack against Algiers with a formidable convoy that prefigured the Armada. In his *Guerras de mar del Emperador Carlos V*, López de Gómara describes the formidable assault of the imperial armada.[24] Conceivably, the failure of the negotiations between Charles V and Khair ad-Dīn (1538–1541) formed the background for the emperor's strike on the North African city. López de Gómara, who was among Charles's entourage along with Hernán Cortés, the conqueror of Mexico, and his two sons, justifies the imperial offensive: *"Quiso [el emperador Don Carlos] probar de tomar á Argel, que era cueva de corsarios y ladrones y lugar fuerte, de donde Barbarroja había hecho tantos daños en España y fuera de ella"* [The Emperor Don Carlos decided to try to take the city of Algiers, which was a dungeon of corsairs and robbers and a strong post, from which Barbarossa had done so much damage inside and outside of Spain] (*Crónica*, 432). Charles did not order an immediate assault but first sent an arrogant ultimatum that the city must surrender instantly to him, the king of kings. The Algerians, led by their *beylerbey*, Hasan Agha, refused.[25] After several assaults by the Algerians and the Berber tribes, on the morning of October 24, 1541, while Christian troops prepared to attack, a terrible tempest completely destroyed the imperial fleet. Gómara reports that four hundred large ships and small vessels were completely shattered by the hail (*Guerras*, 219). A modern historian calculates that the retreat from the Maghribi coast cost the emperor one hundred fifty ships, twelve thousand men, and a significant amount of military equipment and horses (Hess, 74). The magnitude of the disaster is eloquently recounted by Gómara:

Fue gran lástima, que los llantos no se oían con el ruido de las olas, que bramando quebraban en la costa y navíos trastumbados, ver cómo los alárabes lanceaban a los cristianos que salían hechos agua sin armas y las manos juntas pidiendo misericordia. [. . .]. Otros se tornaban a la furiosa mar por miedo de las lanzas jinetas, y otros se ahogaban, no sabiendo ni pudiendo nadar, antes de conocer el mortal peligro de tierra.

[It was a great pity—for the cries were not heard with the noise of the waves, which broke roaring on the coast, breaking the vessels apart—to see how the Berbers lanced the Christians who came out of the water, almost drowned, unarmed, with their palms together asking for mercy. (. . .) Others returned to the furious sea, fearing the lances and spears, and others drowned, not knowing how to swim, preferring this to the mortal danger of the land.]

(*Guerras*, 219)

A Turkish chronicler confirms that the Berber tribes of Algiers fell on the crews of these ships and massacred them all: "This journey alone saw 12,000 Christians perish at the sword of the faithful, and one could say that the shores of North Africa, from Dellys to the east of Algiers, to Cherchel, to the west, were littered with the bodies of men and horses." Another Ottoman historian claims that the Moors came out like ants and fought with the remaining survivors, so that "it seemed that the world was coming down and that the wrath of God had fallen upon the Christians."[26]

On hearing the news, Süleymān sent Hasan Agha a magnificent robe and a diploma, conferring on him the title of vizier (*pasha*) (*Gazavat*, 196; Wolf, 29). The astonished Europeans, for their part, acutely deplored the defeat of their emperor. Lamenting the loss of the beautiful Spanish and Genoese horses that drowned in the high seas while their masters pitifully looked on, the French chronicler Chevalier de Brantôme has Charles V curse the heavens while he asks *"pourquoy Dieu ne l'eust-il favorisé en une si saincte, juste et chrestianne entreprise"* [why God did not favor him in such a saintly, just, and Christian enterprise].[27] In fact, Charles V's response to this devastating loss was silent and stoic. He personally oversaw the boarding of the survivors on the ships that pulled through, forcing the noblemen to throw their horses into the sea, to embark the remaining soldiers. Gómara recapitulates: *"el Emperador, como cristiano piadoso, antepuso la vida del hombre a la del caballo"* [the Emperor, as a pious Christian, put the lives of men before those of horses] (*Guerras*, 222).

A Latin pamphlet, written by Knight of St. John Nicholas Durand de Villegagnon, a witness to the disaster, shows the eloquence of the Christian response to Charles V's defeat. Entitled *Carlo V Emperatoris Expeditio in Africam ad Algeriam*, the pamphlet was immediately translated into various European languages. The subtitle of an English translation, published in 1542, runs: "A lamentable and piteous Treatise verye necessary for everie

Christen Manne to reade: wherin is contayned, not onely the high Entreprise and Valeauntness of th' Emperour Charles the V. and his Army (in his Voyage made to the Towne or Argier [sic] in Affrique, agaynst the Turckes, the Enemyes of the Christen Fayth . . .) but also the myserable Chaunces of Wynde and Wether; with dyverse other Adversities, hable to move a stonye Hearte to bewayle the same, and to pray to God for his Ayde and Succor."[28] The emperor's defeat at Algiers inaugurated the long, intermittent struggle between the Habsburg Mediterranean Empire, ruled by Charles V and then by his son Philip II, and the Ottoman Empire on the eastern border of that sea. Twenty years later, a young soldier named Miguel de Cervantes would find himself at the center of these Mediterranean wars.

At the death of Charles V in 1558, his son Philip II controlled Malta, Sicily, Naples, and the fort of La Goleta in Tunis. Nevertheless, Spain's ascendancy in the Mediterranean was fundamentally weakened. Operating from Algiers, the Barbary corsairs sailed all over the Mediterranean, and even into the Atlantic Ocean, in search of human bounty, while the Ottomans advanced from the east, capturing Tripoli from the Knights of Malta in 1551 and the island of Djerba in 1560. In fact, the 1550s were singularly unfortunate for the Spaniards in their North African enterprise. The Knights of Malta were chased out of Tripoli (1551), al-Mahdiyeh was evacuated, and the count of Alcaudete, governor of Orán, perished in the disaster of Mostaganem (1558). In the next decade, the second revolt of the Alpujarras (1568–1570) exploded in Granada, while the Morisco leaders, pushed into rebellion by laws that forbade many of their Islamic customs, sought the assistance of the Ottomans. Between 1569 and 1570, with the approval of the sultan, Ottoman infantry were recruited by the Moriscos in Barbary, and soldiers and arms were sent to the rebels by Alūj Ali Pasha, the *beylerbey* of Algiers (Hess, 88–89).

Although the insurrection of the Alpujarras was violently crushed in 1570 by Don Juan de Austria and his armies, the Ottoman conquest of Cyprus, the most distant of the Venetian outposts in the same year, heightened the crisis in the Mediterranean. Alarmed by the exploits of Islam, Pope Pius V urged that Venice become the spearhead of a confederation of Christian states. After a year of difficult negotiations, an armada constituted by Venice, Spain, and the Holy See was finally assembled. In 1571, the forces of the Holy League came together in Messina, under the command of the generalissimo Don Juan de Austria. Among the two hundred soldiers of the galley *Marquesa*, captained by Diego de Urbina, was harquebusier Miguel de Cervantes. To borrow Jean Canavaggio's suggestive words: "Having become a soldier of Philip II, the author of *Don Quijote* mounts the stage of history" (*Cervantes*, 53).

The Wounds of Lepanto

The impressive armada of the Holy League, with more than three hundred vessels and about eighty thousand men aboard, confronted the Ottoman fleet in the deep waters of the Gulf of Lepanto, on October 7, 1571.[29] The Turks, led by Ali Pasha, arrived with a fleet of two hundred fifty galleys and ninety thousand men aboard. The *Marquesa*, where Cervantes was fighting, belonged to the contingent of Venetian galleys ascribed to the allied fleet. The testimony of his comrades is noteworthy. In spite of being sick with fever, the soldier appeared on the bridge before the battle began, and, in response to his captain and friends who advised him to take cover because he was sick and in no condition to fight, he exclaimed *"que más quería morir peleando por Dios y por su Rey, que no meterse so cubierta, e que su salud"* [that he would rather die fighting for God and his king than go below the deck and look after his health]. The same eyewitness adds that Cervantes *"peleó como valiente soldado, con los dichos turcos en la dicha batalla, en el lugar del esquife, como su capitán lo mandó"* [fought like a valiant soldier against the aforementioned Turks in the aforementioned battle, by the launch berth, as his captain ordered him to do].[30] As Canavaggio elucidates, the launch emplacement, located at the front of the ship, was an especially vulnerable combat post (*Cervantes*, 36).

There is no doubt, indeed, about Cervantes's courage on this and other occasions. The engagement became a hand-to-hand combat where sixty thousand soldiers clashed against each other in beastly carnage: "The battle was, at that moment, so bloody and horrible—writes an eye-witness—that you would have said the sea and the fire were but a single thing" (quoted by Canavaggio, *Cervantes*, 56). During the repeated attacks of the enemy, the *Marquesa* suffered forty dead—including the captain—and one hundred twenty wounded. Cervantes received three harquebus wounds: two in the chest and a third one in the left hand. He would later say, referring to the hand lost in Lepanto, that although this blunderbuss wound looks ugly, *"él la tiene por hermosa, por haberla cobrado en la más memorable y alta ocasión que vieron los pasados siglos, [. . .] militando debajo de las vencedoras banderas del hijo del rayo de la guerra, Carlos Quinto, de felice memoria"* [He considers it beautiful, since he collected it in the greatest and most memorable event that past centuries have ever seen, (. . .) fighting beneath the victorious banners of the son of that glorious warrior, Charles V, of happy memory].[31]

In this way was born *el manco de Lepanto* [the one-handed soldier from Lepanto], at the very moment when the Christian allies obtained victory over the Ottoman forces, thanks to the force of the Venetian cannons and to the superiority of the Spanish infantry (Braudel, *Mediterranean*, II: 1102). The balance of Ottoman losses was awesome: one hundred ten ships destroyed or sunk, one hundred thirty captured, thirty thousand men dead or wounded, three thousand prisoners, and nearly fifteen thousand slaves freed. As for the Christian allies, twelve thousand men were lost in combat, including those who died from their wounds (Canavaggio, *Cervantes*, 54–59).[32] Although some modern historians have claimed that this was a victory that led nowhere, in the opinion of the Captive, the character in *Don Quijote*, a critical objective was accomplished: *"Aquel día, que fue para la cristiandad tan dichoso, [. . .] se desengañó el mundo y todas las naciones del error en que estaban, creyendo que los turcos eran invencibles por la mar; [. . .] aquel día quedó el orgullo y soberbia otomana quebrantada"* [On that day, which was so fortunate for Christendom, (. . .) all the nations of the earth were disabused of their error in imagining the Turks to be invincible on sea. (. . .) On that day, Ottoman pride and arrogance were broken] (*DQ* I, 40).[33]

Fernand Braudel, who studies the problem from a number of different angles, agrees with the Captive. According to the French historian, the victory can be seen as "the end of a period of profound depression, the end of a genuine inferiority complex on the part of Christendom and a no less real Turkish supremacy." Even though Ottoman naval power was not destroyed, it is the myth of Turkish invincibility—concludes Braudel—that collapsed at Lepanto (*Mediterranean*, II: 1103–05). From then on, Christians felt free to show their galleys everywhere on the sea, as regiments of soldiers and adventurers of every nation began flocking to the south in search of employment on the Mediterranean battlefield.[34] Others concur with Braudel on the psychological effects of this victory over the Turks. John Lynch posits that after Lepanto, even if Cyprus remained under Turkish rule, even if the sultan replaced the lost Ottoman soldiers with astonishing rapidity and the Algerian corsairs were still at large, the spell of Turkish power was broken; Christendom finally gained a moral victory and freed itself from an old sense of insecurity (336).

As for the wounded and feverish soldier Cervantes, he recuperated onboard the *Marquesa* and later at the city hospital of Messina, where he remained for six months. During the following months, the soldier received four consecutive subventions *"para acabar de curar las heridas que sufrió en la batalla"* [to help him cure the wounds he received in the battle]. Some of these supplementary aids are consigned in the notebook of secret and extraordinary expenses of Don Juan de Austria as help bestowed on certain persons *"por lo bien que le habían servido en la jornada del año pasado de mil quinientos setenta y uno"* [for the commendable way in which they had served him in last year's battle of 1571] (Astrana Marín, II: 371; Sliwa, 42–43). Although Cervantes had lost the use of his left hand, he soon resumed active military duty and, in the following years, participated in the disastrous North African campaigns of Navarino (1572), La Goleta (La Goulette) (1574), and Tunis (1574) against the Turks, where the Spaniards were drastically defeated. After the three wounds received at Lepanto, three campaigns against the Turks, and four years in military service, Cervantes decided to return to Spain. Promoted to *soldado aventajado* [elite trooper], he obtained two letters of recommendation from the Duke of Sessa and Don Juan de Austria.[35] During the first week of September 1575, *soldado aventajado* Miguel embarked at Naples, on the galley *Sol,* with his brother Rodrigo, a soldier like him. *Sol* was one of the four vessels making up a Spanish flotilla that set sail for Barcelona, with Cervantes on board, under the command of Don Sancho de Leiva. A few days later, a storm scattered the Spanish galleys. While three of them finally reached port safely, the last one, *Sol,* would not make it. On September 26, 1575, along the Catalan coast, the galley *Sol* was attacked by Barbary corsairs, and its surviving passengers were all taken as captives to Algiers.

The head of the three pirate galleys was an Albanian renegade, Arnaut Mamí; his lieutenant, of Greek origin, was called Dalí Mamí. During the energetic resistance, which lasted for several hours, many Spaniards perished—including the captain of the vessel. The survivors were transported, tied hand and foot, to the Algerian ships. Suddenly, the rest of Leiva's squadron appeared on the horizon, chasing the corsairs, who escaped in haste with their booty. The prestigious signatures on the letters of recommendation found on Miguel de Cervantes led the corsairs to believe that he was an important personage, worthy of a high ransom. While Rodrigo was designated as part of the booty reserved for Ramadān Pasha, the *beylerbey* of Algiers, Miguel fell into the hands of Dalí Mamí, nicknamed *el Cojo* (the cripple), who demanded as the price of ransom the exorbitant sum of five hundred gold *escudos.* The image of his arrival in Algiers would be engraved forever in the memory of the future author of *Don Quijote*:

> Cuando llegué cautivo, y vi esta tierra
> tan nombrada en el mundo, que en su seno
> tantos piratas cubre, acoge y cierra
> no pude al llanto detener el freno.

> [When I arrived a captive, and saw this land,
> Ill-famed in all the world, whose bosom conceals,
> Protects, embraces such a throng of pirates,
> I could not keep from weeping.]

These words belong to Saavedra, a character in *El trato de Argel [Life in Algiers].*[36] His tears evoke the initial shock of the traumatic experience of captivity endured by the young Cervantes. His experience was that of numerous men, women, and children, Christians and Muslims alike, who were captured by the Barbary corsairs or Christian privateers in the Mediterranean.

Privateering: An Undeclared War

A few words about piracy and privateering may be needed here to give insight into the complex sixteenth-century Mediterranean world, where corsair campaigns—prizes and cargoes—and tacit warfare ruled the seas. According to Braudel, between 1574 and 1580—around the period of Cervantes's captivity in Algiers—privateering functioned as a substitute for undeclared war, soon coming to dominate the now less spectacular history of the Mediterranean. The new capitals of warfare were no longer Constantinople, Madrid, and Messina, but Algiers, Valletta (Malta), Leghorn, and Pisa. Distinguishing *piracy* and *pirates* from *privateering* and *privateers,* or *corsairs,* Braudel advances that "privateering is legitimate war, authorized either by a formal declaration of war or by letters of marque, passports, commissions, or instructions" (*Mediterranean,* II: 866). In fact, the terms *pirate* and *piracy* did not exist before the seventeenth century. As opposed to the pirates, who launched operations on their own, robbing those who came into their view, the privateers were backed by letters or passports from a particular government or state, although they sailed at their own risk and gain. "The corsair is properly the individual that, as a private person (authorized with letters or passports from his government), commands an armed vessel, and runs the seas against the enemies of his country, in times of war, at his own risk and gain." On the contrary, the pirates are "a group of outlaws with no other law than the appetites, united only to rob the seas, without a flag or with a false flag, without respect for peace or truce, without papers" (Guglielmotti, III: 49).[37]

As Braudel has demonstrated, in the sixteenth century there was already a form of international law with its own protocols and regulations: the Islamic and Christian states exchanged ambassadors, signed treaties, and often complied with their clauses. Nevertheless, because the entire Mediterranean was an arena of continuous conflict between two bordering and warring civilizations, war was the only abiding reality, one that explained and justified piracy. Privateering—an ancient form of piracy common to the Mediterranean, with its own customs, agreements, and negotiations—was not the exclusive realm of any group or seaport: It was endemic. All—from the most wretched to the most powerful, rich and poor alike—were caught up in a web of operations cast over the whole sea, suggests Braudel (*Mediterranean,* II: 865–66). The notorious fortune of Algiers tends to blind Western historians to the rest of corsair activity in the Mare Nostrum. Godfrey Fisher's classic book *Barbary Legend* illustrates the chauvinism of certain notions that ascribe the hunting of men, robberies, tortures, and atrocious cruelties to the Algerian corsairs only. Both Braudel and Fisher convincingly show that the misery and horror of these early modern practices were widespread throughout the Mediterranean.

In the Mediterranean, the *ponentini*—as Western corsairs were called in the waters of the Levant in early modern times—robbed Turks and Christians alike, seizing Venetian or French vessels or whatever came their way (Braudel, *Mediterranean*, II: 867). French and Venetian corsairs not only attacked and looted Christian ships but also assaulted the coasts of Naples, Genoa, and Sicily, as well as other islands. In 1593, Prince Doria, the commander of Philip II's navy, seized and captured a French ship, the *Jehan Baptiste*, carrying all the necessary certificates and passes issued by the Spanish representative in Nantes, only to sell her cargo and clap her crew in irons. And Sancho de Leiva, the renowned commander of many fleets under Philip II—the same captain of the flotilla that transported Cervantes when he was captured—proposed, in a letter dated November 20, 1563, to sail with a few Sicilian galleys to the Barbary coast to carry prisoners for the row-benches: *"para ver si puede haber algunos esclavos"* (quoted by Braudel, *Mediterranean*, II: 869). A few years later the Marquis of Santa Cruz, commander of Philip II's Armada, went on a "patrolling expedition" along the Tunisian coast, a mission that was nothing less than a pirate raid against the destitute Kerkennah Islands. In Braudel's words, piracy was simply "another form of aggression, preying on men, ships, towns, villages, flocks." It meant "eating the food of others in order to remain strong" (*Mediterranean*, II: 869).

Sixteenth-century privateering was usually instigated by a city acting on its own authority. For instance, the celebrated centers of corsair activity Dieppe and La Rochelle, in the Atlantic, launched their ships even into the Mediterranean. The famous Knights of St. John of Jerusalem from the Order of Malta—established by Charles V on this island in 1530, after the fall of Rhodes to the Turks—cruised the Mediterranean in their powerful galleons, harassing Levantine shipping and the Maghribi ports under Ottoman control and capturing an infinite number of slaves and riches that they sold at Valletta. Their objective was to board and capture Muslim ships and bring them back to sell as prizes: The captives were either held for ransom or sold as galley slaves to the Maltese or other European governments.[38] Under the protection of the order's navy, Maltese privateering came to form a kind of industry that was eventually organized along business lines and made to fit into a moral, social, and economic system (Sire, 90). These corsair activities were represented as a heroic fight led against the enemies of the Christian faith.[39]

Christian privateers often operated in very small ships, brigantines, frigates, and sometimes even the tiniest fishing vessels, in meager operations that have not been fully recorded by historians. Among the stories recounted in his *Diálogo de los mártires de Argel*, Antonio de Sosa depicts the exploits of Valencian corsair Juan Cañete, master of a brigantine with fourteen oar-benches, based at Majorca. An assiduous hunter of the Bar-

bary coast, Cañete was famous for entering the very gates of Algiers during the night and capturing people sleeping under the city walls. In the
spring of 1550, venturing again into the port, Cañete attempted to set fire
to the poorly guarded Algerian galleys. He was caught and, nine years later,
executed in the *baños*.[40] A similar account illustrates the way in which early
modern European governments gave their backing to privateers. Another
corsair from Valencia, Juan Gasco, put himself under the protection of the
king of Spain and offered to launch corsair and warring expeditions against
Algiers. In 1567, he revived Cañete's plan, successfully setting fire to a few
ships in the port of Algiers. Gasco was later captured on the high seas by
Dalí Mamí, Cervantes's future master, who found on him letters of marque
signed by Philip II. The documents not only authorized Gasco to go on
privateering expeditions but also requested the viceroys of Valencia and
Majorca to assist the corsair in his excursions. Brought back to Algiers,
Gasco was tortured and hung by the heel of the foot from a butcher's
hook with the letters of marque endorsed by Philip II. Although he was
rescued by Dalí Mamí and other corsair captains who argued that, as a
corsair, Gasco was subject to the laws of war, which excused his actions,
he was finally impaled by certain Moriscos who asked the Algerian ruler
for his head (*Mártires*, 123–28).

The boldest Christian corsairs in the middle of the sixteenth century
were the Knights of St. John of the Order of Malta, led by Jean de la Valette
between 1557 and 1568, and by the famous Chevalier Romegas, who would
become the general of the order's galleys in the 1570s. Second place went
to the Florentines, who soon challenged the supremacy of the Knights of
St. John. Besides Valletta, Leghorn, and Pisa, there were other famous
privateering centers on the Christian side, such as Naples, Messina, Palermo
and Trapani, Malta, Palma de Majorca, Almería, Valencia, and Fumel. Three
cities, however, stood out among those dedicated to corsair activity: Valletta,
founded by the Knights of Malta in 1566; Leghorn, refounded by Cosimo
de' Medici; and finally, above all, the astonishing city of Algiers, which
functioned as the apotheosis of privateering. This fascinating North African city would leave its indelible mark on Cervantes.

The Apotheosis of Privateering

In 1571, when Cervantes arrived, Algiers was a booming urban center of
about one hundred twenty-five thousand inhabitants, freemen and slaves,
perhaps even more populous than Palermo or Rome (Wolf, 97–98). For-
midably guarded by the military constructions laid by Khair ad-Dīn and
the fortifications later built by the Turks, the city was also a well-planned
center that took full advantage of its natural setting to provide its cosmo-

politan residents with excellent amenities. French geographer Nicholas de
Nicolay, on disembarking in 1551, described his impressions:

> Quant aux édifices, outre le palais royal, il y a plusieurs belles maisons des
> particuliers, davantage grand nombre de bains et cabarets publiques. Et y
> son les places et rues si bien ordonnées que chacune a ses artisans à part; il y
> peu bien avoir trois mille feux. Au bas de la ville que regarde la tramontane,
> joignant les murailles [. . .], en une grande place, est par singulier artifice et
> superbe architecture édifiée leur principale et maîtresse mosquée [. . .]. Cette
> cité est fort marchande à cause qu'elle est située sur la mer, et si est par ce
> moyen merveilleusement peuplée pour sa grandeur.

> [Beyond the Royal Palace are very fair houses belonging to particular men,
> with a great number of baths and restaurants. The places and streets are so
> well ordained that each one has its artisans apart. There may be about three
> thousand hearths. At the bottom of the city, near the defensive ramparts (. . .),
> in a great plaza, is by great artifice and subtle architecture built their princi-
> pal and head Mosque (. . .). This city is very merchant-like in that she is situ-
> ated upon the sea and for this reason marvelously populated for her gran-
> deur].[41]

This sophisticated urban conglomerate was inhabited by a multiethnic lot
constituted by Algerian Muslims, exiled Moriscos, Berbers, Turks, renegade
Christians from every country in Europe, and Jews.[42] As the corsair capital par excellence, where privateers from all over the world found shelter
and supplies, Algiers owed its prosperity to privateering. Each year it wel-
comed thousands of captives and stolen merchandise, abducted in the
assaults on Christian vessels and on the coasts of Spain and Italy. Contemporary sources claim that in the 1570s there were around twenty-five thousand Christian captives in Algiers.[43] Other data reveal that between 1520
and 1660, approximately five hundred thousand to six hundred thousand
Christian slaves were sold in the prosperous city (Wolf, 151), considered by
the Turks their "Indies and Peru" (*Topografía*, II: 88). These war prizes
were traded in the busy market of this commercial center open to Ottoman caravans and ships, vessels bringing ransom for Christian captives, and
Christian merchant galleons—French, Catalan, Valencian, Corsican, Italian, English, or Dutch. In effect, *ra'is (re'is)* [commanders of corsair ves-
sels] of every nation—Muslim or half Muslim, sometimes northerners—
attracted by the affluence of the city, settled in Algiers, bringing with them
their galleys or nimble sailing ships (Braudel, *Mediterranean*, II: 870).[44]
The ample racial and cultural composition of this society, where every adventurer found a place, was described by the captive Antonio de Sosa, who
spent four years as a slave in Algiers in the late 1570s.
    A Portuguese cleric captured in 1577 aboard the galley *San Pablo* from
the Order of Malta, Antonio de Sosa has been identified as the author of

the notable *Topographia, e historia general de Argel* (Valladolid, 1612), attributed to Archbishop Diego de Haedo. George Camamis has conclusively shown that Dr. Antonio de Sosa composed this monumental work between 1577 and 1581, while he was a captive in Algiers. Fray Diego de Haedo was a nephew of the Inquisitor and later archbishop of Palermo, also named Diego de Haedo, known for assisting captives after their liberation.[45] If we are to believe Fray Diego in his dedication, he received the unfinished papers on captivity from his uncle (Haedo #1), who composed them from reports delivered by former captives. Fray Diego (Haedo #2) merely polished these drafts, giving them *"su última forma y esencia"* [their last form and essence] (*Topografía*, I: 10–11).

That Archbishop Haedo would have composed this treatise from accounts provided by Christian captives is highly unlikely. *Topographia, e historia general de Argel* covers hundreds of pages with infinite details about sixteenth-century Algiers—its geography, customs, history, and the ordeals of the Christian captives—while its author speaks on multiple occasions as an eyewitness who offers his personal viewpoint. French historians Ferdinand Denis and H. -D. de Grammont were the first to detect something suspect in the way the work was put together (Camamis, 132–34).[46] In 1902, in his annotations to a letter written to Pope Gregory XIII by various captives, Cristóbal Pérez Pastor suggested that "Dr. Antonio de Sosa, a Portuguese clergyman and a great friend of Cervantes, captured in 1577 and rescued in 1581, [is] the author of this Memorial and of the summaries that helped Archbishop Haedo write the *Historia general de Argel*."[47] Luis Astrana Marín also established in 1949 that the three Dialogues that constitute the third part of Haedo's *Topographia*—*Diálogo de los mártires de Argel, De la captividad,* and *De los morabutos*—were composed by Dr. Antonio de Sosa (Astrana Marín, II: 468). Camamis has finally demonstrated that there is no mention of the Haedos in the work, and, more important, that the freed captives who arrived in Sicily came from Constantinople, not from Algiers.

As it turns out, *Topographia, e historia general de Argel* was composed in the very dungeons of Algiers, between 1577 and 1581, when Antonio de Sosa was a captive in the city. The first book of this treatise, *Topographia,* is dedicated to a minute description of the city of Algiers, its geography and customs, while the second, *Epítome de los reyes de Argel,* is a chronicle of its most recent history, from the foundation of the Barbary State to the last decade of the sixteenth century. The third part of this work contains three *Dialogues* on captivity and theological issues, of which Antonio de Sosa is the unsung protagonist. Reading these pages, one gets the unmistakable feeling that Sosa is the author of the entire work, including its imposing first part.[48] Indeed, Sosa often claims that, since arriving in Algiers, he has been writing day by day what occurs in the city: *"dende el primer día que entré en Argel, tengo escrito con otras cosas, el número de cuantos* *[moriscos] vinieron y aun en qué mes, en qué semana, en qué día y hora* *vinieron, y cómo vinieron"* [from the first day that I entered Algiers, I have written, among other things, the number (of Moriscos) that arrived, and even in what month, in what week, in what day and hour, and how they came] (*Topografía*, III: 253).

The three *Dialogues* contained in the third part of *Topographia* represent the eloquent testimony of an eyewitness who participated in the dramatic experience endured by Christian slaves in Barbary. If this enterprise epitomizes the author's effort to document the sufferings and torments of Christian captives in North Africa, especially in Algiers, the subtitle of *Topografía e historia general de Argel* corroborates the unity of the topic that runs throughout the whole work: *"Do se verán casos extraños, muertes* *espantosas, y tormentos exquisitos que conviene se entiendan en la Chris-* *tiandad"* [Where you will see strange cases, horrifying deaths, and exquisite torments that should be understood by Christianity]. The facts surrounding the creation of *Topographia* should be clearly established, first because Antonio de Sosa was robbed of the authorship of the most important sixteenth-century historiographical treatise on Algiers, one characterized by a modern historian as "the most extensive and more exact of the documents" on the first seventy years of Algiers under Turkish rule (de Grammont, 1881: iii).[49] The second reason that Sosa's work should be reclaimed for its true author regards, as we shall see in chapter 2, the writer's life as a captive in Algiers and his multiple links with Cervantes.[50]

"Turks by Profession"

According to Antonio de Sosa, more than half of the inhabitants of Algiers in the 1570s were "Turks by profession"—that is, renegades: *"Los turcos de* *profesión son todos los renegados que, siendo de sangre y de padres cristianos,* *de su libre voluntad se hicieron turcos [. . .]. Estos y sus hijos, por sí solos, son* *más que todos los otros vecinos moros, turcos y judíos de Argel"* [The Turks by profession are all the renegades who, descending from Christian blood and parents, have voluntarily converted into Turks. (. . .) Both these Turks and their children are more (numerous) than the other inhabitants, the Moors, Turks, and Jews of Algiers] (*Topografía*, I: 52). The extraordinary mosaic of Barbary society is suggestively depicted by Sosa in this long passage worth quoting at length:

No hay nación de cristianos en el mundo de la cual no haya renegado y renegados en Argel. Y comenzando de las remotas provincias de Europa, hallan en Argel renegados moscovitas, rojos, [. . .] búlgaros, polacos, húngaros, bohemios, alemanes, de Dinamarca y Noruega, escoceses, ingleses, irlandeses, flamencos, borgoñones, franceses, navarros, vizcaínos, castellanos, gallegos, portugueses, andaluces, valencianos, aragoneses, catalanes, mallorquines, sardos, corzos, sicilianos, calabreses, napolitanos, romanos, toscanos, genoveses, saboyanos, piamonteses, lombardos, venecianos, esclavones, albaneses [. . .], griegos, candiotas, cretanos, chipriotas, surianos y de Egipto y aun Abejinos del Preste Juan e indios de las Indias de Portugal, del Brasil y de Nueva España.

[There is no Christian nation in the world from which there are no renegades in Algiers. And beginning with the remote provinces of Europe, there are in Algiers renegade Muscovites, Reds (. . .), Bulgarians, Poles, Hungarians, Bohemians, Germans, from Denmark and Norway, Scots, Englishmen, Irishmen, Flemish, Burgundians, Frenchmen, Navarrese, Basques, Castilians, Galicians, Portuguese, Andalusians, Valencians, Aragonese, Catalans, Majorcans, Sardinians, Corsicans, Sicilians, Calabrese, Neapolitans, Romans, Tuscans, Genoese, Savoyans, Piedmontese, Lombards, Venetians, Slaves, Albanians (. . .), Greeks, Candiotas, Cretans, Cypriots, Surianos (from Surinam) and from Egypt, and even Abejinos of Prester John, and Indians from the Indies of Portugal (India), from Brazil and New Spain].

(*Topografía*, I: 52–53)

Certainly, no other European or Mediterranean city at the time could claim to have such an exceptional multicultural conglomerate, which even included Indians from India and Amerindians from Brazil and New Spain (Mexico). Sosa maintains that most of the "renegade" Christians who had abandoned the true path of God had become Muslims either because they rejected the work of slavery or because they favored a life of freedom, marked by the pleasures of the flesh. Evidently, the captives, soldiers, or mercenaries who converted to Islam were thorns in the sides of the Christians, particularly the Spaniards, who saw them as the most blatant representatives of accommodating and pliable morals. These men or women broke not only with their religious creed but also with most of the mental and cultural categories of their society.

The complexities behind these early modern conversions to Islam have been recently explored by various works, such as the suggestive book written by Bartolomé and Lucile Benassar, *Los cristianos de Alá: La fascinate aventura de los renegados* (1989), which examines one thousand five hundred fifty cases of renegades tried by the Spanish and Portuguese Inquisition between 1550 and 1700, and the excellent study coauthored by Mercedes García Arenal and Miguel Ángel de Bunes, *Los españoles y el Norte de África. Siglos XV–XVIII* (1992).[51] The confessions of many renegades, and the depositions of the witnesses who testified in their cases, clearly express the attraction exerted by Islam on numerous Christians in early modern times, even if they did not apostatize. Barbary stood, then, for a land of plenty.

Many of the renegades tried by the Inquisition vowed that they wanted to make a fortune with the Moors, because, in Barbary, "one could live with more abundance" (*Cristianos*, 419).

In effect, through their apostasy and conversion to Islam, those who were mere numbers in the different social strata or classes of their nations acceded to a more egalitarian society in Algiers, where individuals were valued for their wealth and personal qualifications. Even Sosa grudgingly conceded that these apostates might have had more intricate reasons for embracing Islam than the sins of the flesh he constantly denounced. He states that some Turks and renegades had ten, twelve, fifteen, twenty, or more of these Christian renegades, *"a los cuales llaman y tienen por hijos"* [whom they call and treat like sons]. When these men adopted the Muslim religion, their owners generally offered them letters of credit and gave them slaves and money. And later, *"muriendo [los turcos] sin herederos reparten con ellos sus bienes y hacienda como sus hijos y generalmente a todos los que aún no eran libres los dejan libres antes que mueran"* [if the Turks die without heirs, they divide amongst the renegades their possessions and estate as if they were their children, and generally they free all of those who had not been freed before they die] (*Topografía*, I: 53–54).

These renegades or Turks by profession constituted six thousand of the twelve thousand households counted in Algiers between 1577 and 1581, when Sosa turned his discerning eye on the city. Most of them were corsairs who dedicated themselves to privateering in the Mediterranean. In fact, of the thirty-five *ra'is* who lived in Algiers in 1581 and were enumerated by Sosa, ten were Turks, three were sons of renegades, one was a Jewish convert to Islam, and the rest were Christian renegades, of which there were a dozen Italians (*Topografía*, I: 89–91). The proportion is significant. Until the end of the sixteenth century, when renegade seamen from northern Europe began to arrive in Algiers, the majority of corsairs were old Christians from Italy, Spain, and the Mediterranean islands, both from the western and eastern Mare Nostrum. It is not fortuitous that after 1568, the *beylerbeys* of Algiers were all "new Muslims." Those figures who held important positions in the period of Cervantes's captivity included Calabrian Alūj Ali [Euch Alí] (Cervantes's Uchalí, often mentioned in *Don Quijote*), Corsican Ramadān Pasha (owner of Rodrigo Cervantes), and Venetian Hasan Pasha (the cruel Hasan Agá, portrayed by both Sosa and Cervantes), all discussed in the next chapter.

The elaborate ceremonies, both religious and social, surrounding corsair activity in Algiers are minutely detailed by Sosa. The chronicler describes the construction of the ships, privately owned by different *ra'is*, who used their own slaves and those commonly owned by the city in the fabrication of their vessels; and the great feasts and celebrations that followed the return from an expedition, when the *ra'is* of Algiers held open house, in their urban residences or in the villas outside the city, where the gardens were the most beautiful in the world (*Topografía*, I: 79–89). After a few days or weeks on the sea, the "fortunate and happy" corsairs returned to Algiers, *"cargados de infinitas riquezas y cautivos"* [loaded with infinite riches and captives], spoils that were easily multiplied because they sailed three and four times a year—or more—in search of human bounty: *"Navegan todo el verano y invierno, y tan sin temor se pasan por todos los mares de Poniente y Levante burlándose de las galeras cristianas [. . .] como y ni más ni menos si anduviesen a caza de muchas liebres y conejos, matando aquí uno y allí otro"* [They navigate during the whole summer and winter, and they rove with such daring and disregard all over the West and East seas, making fun of the Christian galleys (. . .), as if they were chasing many hares and rabbits, killing one here, another there] (*Topografía*, I: 84). Sosa nevertheless extols the art of the *ra'is*, *"tan pláticos y tan ejercitados"* [so practical and experienced], and the excellence of their vessels, *"tan listas, tan en orden, tan ligeras"* [so ready, so orderly, so light], implicitly contrasting the dexterity of the Algerian corsairs with the incompetency of the Christian seamen, who were hindered by their bulky and heavy galleons (*Topografía*, I: 84).

Sosa's account has been corroborated by contemporary historians, who described the frenetic activities of the Barbary corsairs in the Mediterranean, and even in the north Atlantic, from which a significant number of French, Portuguese, and English slaves (fishermen) came to the *baños* of Algiers. The danger was everywhere, as Sosa suggests. Some of the most dangerous zones included the islands or archipelagos, Madeira, Azores, the Canary Islands, and the Lisbon–Madeira route, where the "Turkish" corsairs scanned the seas for fleets coming from the Indies and Brazil. There were, however, two black zones in this large map of risks: first, the Strait of Gibraltar complex, situated between two imaginary lines, Cartagena–Orán to the east, and Cape St. Vincent–Mazagán to the west, an obligatory route for the Spanish and Portuguese ships that carried provisions for the presidios of Orán, Melilla, Ceuta, Larache, and Mazagán, among others. This route was also a forced transit for the ships that crossed from the Atlantic into the Mediterranean. Roughly one third of the one thousand five hundred fifty renegades studied by the Benassars were caught in this zone. The second area of peril was the Sicilian complex, including the strait on the north coast of Sicily, and the south coast of this island. Corsairs from Algiers, Tunis, Bizerta, and Tripoli, among other centers, dominated the sea of Sicily, often capturing fishing boats close to the trap-net sites and even venturing outside the ports of Trapani, Palermo, and Naples.

A Captive Called Cervantes

Like other captives, Miguel de Cervantes was imprisoned in the *"baño"*[52]—slave house or prison—of the king *[bey]* of Algiers. The Captive tells us that in these *baños "Encierran los cautivos cristianos, así los que son del rey como de algunos particulares, y los que llaman del almacén, que es como decir* cautivos del consejo, *que sirven a la ciudad en las obras públicas [. . .], y estos tales cautivos tienen muy dificultosa su libertad"* [They confine the Christian captives, both those of the king and those belonging to certain private individuals, and also those they call the slaves of the *"Almacén"*—that is to say, slaves of the township who also serve the city in public works and other employment. (. . .) Such slaves as these find it very difficult to obtain their freedom] (*DQ* I, 40; *Captive's Tale*, 79–80). In addition, certain private citizens took their prisoners to these *baños*, especially the ones to be ransomed, because they were kept there in security and at ease until their ransom arrived (*DQ* I, 40).

According to Antonio de Sosa, the common slaves, owned by the city and destined for public labor in Algiers, were confined in the Baño de la Bastarda (Bastard Prison), where four hundred or five hundred men were kept in squalid conditions. The ransomable prisoners, on the other hand, were consigned to the royal *baño*, located in the Street of the Souk, where at the time of Cervantes's enslavement there were between fifteen hundred and two thousand Christian captives who belonged to *beylerbey* Hasan Veneciano. This large prison was rectangular (seventy feet long by forty feet wide) and was two stories high, with many small vaulted chambers and, in the middle, a cistern with fresh water. Sosa describes the Christian oratory or chapel, located to one side, under the galleys, where mass was celebrated every day and where the priests often preached with such crowds that on Sundays or feast days, such as Easter, mass was moved to the open courtyard so that all the slaves who wished to do so could attend after paying an entrance fee to the Turkish and Moorish guards (*Topografía*, I: 195). Emanuel d'Aranda, a Flemish captive in Algiers between 1640 and 1642, claims he heard twenty-two languages in the *baño*, *"la meilleure université [. . .] pour apprendre le monde a vivre"* [the best university (. . .) to teach the world to live] (152).

City slaves assigned to the "warehouse" had more freedom than others because they were allowed to roam the city, dragging their chains after them, when they were not occupied in public works. But the two thousand or more captives enclosed in the royal *baño "están todos encerrados siempre y a buen recaudo, con sus porteros continuos a las puertas y guardas que día y noche a cuartos los velan y guardan"* [are always locked and in safety with their porters continuously at the doors and jailers that watch over them and guard them day and night, on sentry] (*Topografía*, I: 195–

96). According to Fray Melchor de Zuñiga, who described these prisons in the 1630s, the doors of the *baños* closed at six P.M. in the summer, and at five P.M. in the winter. From the middle of the patio, a guard would announce the closing of the prison gates with shouts or loud voices, so that the visitors would leave. Once closed, these gates would not open again until the next morning.[53]

As for the prisoners kept for ransom, the Captive affirms: "*los cautivos del rey que son de rescate no salen al trabajo con la demás chusma, si no es cuando tarda su rescate; que entonces, por hacerlos que escriban por él con más ahínco, les hacen trabajar e ir por leña con los demás, que es un no pequeño trabajo*" [the king's captives that are to be ransomed do not go to work with the rest of the plebes, unless their ransom is delayed, in which case, to make them write for it with greater urgency, they make them work and go for firewood with the rest, which is no small task] (*DQ* I, 40; *Captive's Tale*, 79–80). Like the Captive, the soldier Cervantes was placed next to the gentlemen—the aristocrats. Most of the noblemen, priests, or ship captains who were to be ransomed were treated with a certain consideration. Elite captives were also excused from serving in the galleys. Yet Cervantes was a soldier. If his maimed left hand saved him from becoming a galley slave in the corsair galleons, the letters of recommendation signed by Don Juan of Austria marked him for a long, perhaps eternal captivity. In the Captive's words:

> Yo, pues, era uno de los de rescate; que como se supo que era capitán, puesto que dije mi poca posibilidad y falta de hacienda, no me aprovechó nada para que no me pusiesen en el número de los caballeros y gente de rescate. Pusiéronme una cadena, [. . .] y así pasaba los días en aquel baño, con otros muchos caballeros y gente principal, señalados y tenidos por de rescate.

> [I, then, was one of those to be ransomed. For as it was known that I was a captain, although I told them that I had no wealth and few prospects, nothing could dissuade them from putting me on the list of the gentlemen and others to be ransomed. They put a chain on me, (. . .) and so I spent my time in that *baño* with many other gentlemen and important people who had been singled out and kept for ransom.]

> (*DQ* I, 40; *Captive's Tale*, 81)

The autobiographical overtones of this passage are striking. Although Cervantes was never promoted to captain, his descriptions of the *baño* in *La historia del cautivo*, including the type of prisoners who shared his fate with him, coincide with his own testimony regarding his captivity. According to various witnesses, Cervantes apparently endured the standard treatment given to elite captives during the bargaining over ransoms that inaugurated captivity in Algiers. First handled with courtesy, the captive was then threatened and told his true identity had been discovered—that he was a grandee of Spain, the son of a duke, a cousin to the king, or even a bishop, if he was a priest—only to be finally chained and sometimes beaten and thrown into solitary confinement with more irons. These are Antonio de Sosa's illustrations of the system in his *Diálogo de los mártires de Argel* (*Topografía*, II: 138–243). His declarations regarding the treatment of elite captives are confirmed by various witnesses in a collection of testimonies assembled by Cervantes after his release from captivity. Hernando de Vega, still a slave of Dalí Mamí when he testifies in 1580, says that because their common master had a very high opinion of Cervantes's worth and reputation, *"de ordinario, lo tuvo aherrojado y cargado de hierros y con guardas, siendo vejado y molestado, todo a fin de que se rescatase y le diese buen rescate"* [he ordinarily had him fettered and covered with irons and with guards, subjecting him to various forms of humiliations and discomforts, so that he would rescue himself and provide a good ransom]. The witness reiterates that he knows what he is talking about, for he belonged to the same master and he was present at the time (*Información*, 95). Antonio de Sosa himself attests that Cervantes often complained to him of the high opinion his master had of him, thinking he was one of the principal gentlemen of Spain: *"por esto lo maltrataba con más trabajos, y cadenas y encerramiento"* [because of this he mistreated him with more labors, chains, and confinement] (*Información*, 156). Under such circumstances, knowing that no one in his family had access to the sum of money established for his ransom, and in spite of the difficulties and risks involved, Cervantes would attempt to escape four times during his five years of captivity.

The First Escape Attempt

Only four or five months after his capture, in January or February 1576, Cervantes tried to reach the nearest Spanish fortress in Orán, by walking some four hundred kilometers (two hundred twenty miles) across the desert, an escape evoked in his play *El trato de Argel*. Escape overland was extremely hazardous, as illustrated by the desperate flight of several captives in this drama. Hostile nomad tribes who hunted fugitives for bounty, wild animals—such as lions, hyenas, and cheetahs—and lack of food or drink made it a nightmare. Per Álvarez, a fugitive in *El trato de Argel*, describes the ordeal that tempts him to return to his captors in Algiers:

> Tanto pasar de breñas y montañas
> y el bramido contino
> de fieras alimañas,
> me tienen de tal suerte,
> que pienso de acabarle con mi muerte.

[So much crossing of heath and mountains,
and the continuous roaring
of man-eating beasts
Has put me in such a state,
That I think to end it with my death.]
                              (*El trato de Argel*, IV, 1950–1955)

Escape overland was indeed marked by a high rate of failure. The passage
of an unknown individual or a group of men not attached to a detach-
ment of troops could not go unnoticed by the inhabitants, who generally
reacted in cruel ways. Many fugitives walked by night, which supposed a
superior knowledge of the terrain, and hid themselves during the day. Tortured by fear, hunger, and insufferable thirst, Cervantes's fugitive exclaims:

> Ya la hambre me aqueja,
> ya la sed insufrible me atormenta;
> ya la fuerza me deja;
> ya espero de esta afrenta
> salir con entregarme
> a quien de nuevo quiera cautivarme.

> [Now hunger afflicts me
> and insufferable thirst torments me;
> Already my strength is waning;
> I hope to escape from this ordeal
> By giving myself up
> to whomever may want to recapture me.]
>   (*Trato*, IV, 1962–1965).

The fateful thoughts of the fugitive in this play point to the double bind
represented by slavery in Algiers: If escaping through the desert certainly
meant death for any slave, either being devoured by the wild beasts or mur-
dered by the Berber tribes who captured escapees or tortured to death by
their Algerian masters if caught trying to escape, staying in Algiers as a
captive could also end in death, as we shall see. While Per Álvarez—who
reenacts Cervantes's escape—is miraculously saved in the play, another fugitive in *El trato* is clubbed to death as the pasha watches and orders even
worse torments: "*¡Abridle, desolladle y aun matadle!*" [Open him up, tear
him to shreds, and even kill him!] (*Trato*, IV, 2346–53).

Cervantes's first escape attempt is succinctly retold by various witnesses
in their 1580 deposition. Ensign Diego Castellano claims that

[Estando] siempre encerrado, cargado de cadenas, [. . . Cervantes], deseando
hacer bien y dar libertad a algunos cristianos, buscó a un moro que a él y a
ellos los llevase a Orán, por tierra, y los sacó de Argel; y habiendo caminado

algunas jornadas el moro los desamparó; por lo cual le fue necesario volverse para Argel al propio encerramiento que de antes estaba, y desde entonces fue muy más maltratado que de antes de palos y cadenas.

[Being always locked in jail, loaded with chains, (. . .) Cervantes, wishing to do good and to give liberty to some Christians, found a Moor who could lead him and these Christians to Orán overland. The Moor led them out of Algiers and, after walking for several days, deserted them, so it was necessary to turn back to Algiers, to the same enclosure where he was before; and thereafter, he was more mistreated than before, with more chains, clubs, and imprisonment.]

(*Información de Argel*, 75)[54]

Mercifully for Cervantes, his life is spared. The future writer says only that after his return to prison, *"[fue] muy maltratado de su patrón, y de allí en adelante tenido con mas guardia, y cadenas, y encerramiento"* [he was badly mistreated by his master, and from then on, held under a tighter guard, more chains, and imprisonment] (*Información*, 50). This penalty, in effect, cannot be compared to the tortures and death endured by recaptured slaves and graphically portrayed in Cervantes's *El trato de Argel* and in Sosa's *Topografía*.[55] Speaking of similar offenses during the rule of *beylerbey* Hasan Veneciano, Sosa claims that in one year, between October 1577 and 1578, the pasha cut off the ears of thirteen Christian captives who tried to escape by foot to Orán, while another slave from Majorca had his ears and nose cut off because he was found constructing a boat in his master's garden (*Topografía*, II: 113). The death of an elite prisoner, however, meant losing an enormous amount of money. Canavaggio proposes that the reason Cervantes was not killed or severely tortured after this infraction was the profits his master Dalí Mamí hoped to obtain through the ransom paid for a protégé of Don Juan de Austria (*Cervantes*, 83).

Although Cervantes was spared, the insults, tortures, and cruelties perpetrated against other Christian captives who attempted to flee from Barbary were atrocious. If the conditions of captivity—including those suffered by Muslim captives in Europe—were awesome, the cruelties of many Turkish or Algerian slave owners toward their chained and often shackled captives were appalling. Certainly the lowliest slaves, privately owned by the Turks or held by the municipality of Algiers, suffered the most. The worst fate, however, was that of the slaves destined for the galleys: Chained to their benches, these men often died of hunger or thirst or as a result of the blows and tortures inflicted by many corsairs (*Topografía*, II: 90–93). Indeed, both from the Muslim and, especially, from the Christian point of view, to be sent to the galleys meant a death sentence. To prove this point, it is enough to cite the statistics collected on the galley slaves of Louis XIV's Mediterranean squadrons: One of two slaves died during the voyage, and two thirds of the forced oarsmen perished before completing three years of service.[56]

For many slaves, life in Algiers was a veritable hell, in Cervantes's words: *"Purgatorio en la vida/Infierno puesto en el mundo"* [Purgatory in life/hell situated on earth] (*Trato*, I.5–6). Fifty years later, French priest Pierre Dan, a former captive, confirmed this dictum: *"S'il y a quelque lieu dans le monde que puisse avec raison être appelée l'Enfer des Chrétiens c'est assurément la malheureuse contrée des Turcs et de ceux de Barbarie"* [If there is anywhere in the world that might rightly be called a hell for Christians it is assuredly the wretched country of the Turks and those of Barbary] (411). Sosa asserts that the worst cruelties were inflicted by the renegades who, to prove their loyalty to their Muslim overlords and their genuine conversion to Islam, tortured the Christian slaves with every kind of atrocity (*Topografía*, II: 94). A witness who professed to know and to write day by day what occurred in Algiers, Sosa claims that *"Todo Argel y todas sus plazas, las casas, las calles, los campos, las marinas y sus bajeles no son menos que unas herrerías propias y naturales del demonio"* [All of Algiers and its plazas, houses, streets, its countryside, the marina and its ships are nothing less than natural and proper smithies of the devil]. In this inferno, one continuously hears nothing but *"golpes, tormentos y dolores [. . .] de inhumanos y crueles tormentos [. . .] para matar cristianos"* [beatings, torments, and pains (. . .) from the cruel instruments invented (. . .) to kill Christians] (*Topografía*, II:125).

Some considerations are needed here. If the preceding *mise en scène* is certainly awesome, we must bear in mind that Sosa speaks from the perspective of a Christian suffering the miseries and sorrows of captivity—that is, from hell. He was also a passionately religious man engaged in a sacred crusade against the Turks. His intent, then, was to move European princes to eradicate the scourge of captivity in Barbary. Certainly, the sufferings of the Christian galley slaves in North Africa were emphasized by the majority of Europeans who depicted their tribulations. Some of the most dramatic accounts of the plight of these men came from members of the Orders of Redemption, who needed to move the hearts and pockets of parishioners to increase their collection for rescues. This is not to say that all the descriptions of these ordeals were exaggerations. It is evident that there were corsairs who cut off the arms of some of their oarsmen to intimidate the others to row, or galley-slave drivers who cut open or chopped off the ears of crewmen for diversion, but these were generally exceptions. As García Arenal and de Bunes indicate, in spite of their abundance in early modern times, captives were expensive commodities, and their owners needed to keep them alive for as long as possible to recoup the cost of their investment (*Españoles*, 230).

A study of Sosa's dialogues, moreover, reveals that most of the tortures and executions imposed on Christian captives occurred for a number of reasons: (1) in response to a general rebellion in the city or in any of the Algerian garrisons; (2) as a retaliation against Christian corsairs, such as the cases of Cañete or Gasco, described above; (3) as punishment applied to Christian captives who attempted to escape, a penalty that invariably meant death, if the escapee was a renegade Christian; (4) as a death sentence applied for religious infractions, such as in the case of Muslims who turned Christian. For Sosa, however, the Barbary world was an apocalyptic universe filled with tortures, executions, and bloodshed, torments portrayed with such detail that one might be tempted to compare his three dialogues to a treatise à la Sade. No wonder that his interlocutor, Ramírez, closes their colloquy in *Diálogo de los mártires* with the following words: *"¡Qué tormentos tan exquisitos! ¡Y qué crueldades tan horrendas, tan fieras y tan inhumanas!"* [What exquisite torments! And what horrible, bestial, and inhuman cruelties!] (201).

Although Cervantes never attains the heights of horror displayed by Sosa in his depiction of these tortures, the Captive, referring to Hasan Pasha, the *beylerbey* of Algiers, corroborates Sosa's portrayal of these ordeals:

> Y aunque la hambre y desnudez pudiera fatigarnos a veces, y aun casi siempre, ninguna cosa nos fatigaba tanto como oír y ver a cada paso las jamás vistas ni oídas crueldades que mi amo usaba contra los cristianos. Cada día ahorcaba el suyo, empalaba a éste, desorejaba aquél; y eso, por tan poca ocasión, y tan sin ella, que los turcos conocían que lo hacían más por hacerlo, y por ser natural condición suya ser homicida de todo el género humano.
>
> (*DQ* I, 40)

> [And although hunger and lack of clothes did distress us at times—in fact almost always—nothing distressed us so much as to hear and see, at every turn, the cruelties, never before heard of or seen, which my master inflicted upon the Christians. Every day he hanged someone, impaled another, cut off the ear of another. And this on the slightest pretext, or on none at all, so that even the Turks acknowledged that he did it merely for the sake of doing it and because it was in his nature to be the murderer of the entire human race.]
>
> (*Captive's Tale*, 81; translation slightly modified)

Cervantes, however, did not endure any of the customary punishments assigned to common runaways after his first escape attempt. Alluding to the cruelties of Hasan Pasha, *beylerbey* of Algiers, the Captive, acting as Cervantes's spokesman, affirms that

> Solo libró con él un soldado español llamado tal de Saavedra, el cual, con haber hecho cosas que quedarán en la memoria de aquellas gentes por muchos años, y todas por alcanzar la libertad, jamás le dio palo, ni se lo mandó dar

[. . .]; y por la menor cosas de muchas que hizo temíamos que había de ser empalado, y así lo temió él más de una vez. (*DQ* I, 40)

[The only one who fared at all well with him was a Spanish soldier called something de Saavedra, for although this man had done things which will stay in the memory of those people for many years, things done solely to gain his freedom, his master never struck him, nor ordered another to strike him (. . .). And for the least of many things that Saavedra did we were all afraid that he would be impaled and he himself feared it more than once.]

(*Captive's Tale*, 81; *DQ* I, 40)

Such exploits that would be remembered for years are reported by Antonio de Sosa, as it turns out, in his account of Cervantes's second escape attempt. Indeed, among the thirty stories that constitute Sosa's *Diálogo de los mártires de Argel*—stories that Emilio Sola has aptly called a "martyrology" because they describe the endurance of Christian captives in the face of death (*Mártires*, 32–33)—only one does not end with the execution of the principal culprit. This is Narrative 25, which recounts Cervantes's second escape attempt and summarizes his efforts to organize four collective escapes of Christian slaves from Algiers.

The Second Escape Attempt

The above words spoken by the Captive are strikingly similar to those pronounced by Sosa in his depiction of the second escape attempt enacted by Cervantes in 1577, an episode included in his *Diálogo de los mártires de Argel* (178–81).[57] On this occasion, Cervantes took fourteen of the principal Christian captives of Algiers and, with the help of a Christian gardener from Navarra, hid them in a cave on the outskirts of the city. Cervantes's master, Dalí Mamí, was out on a privateering expedition. The captives presumably spent five months hidden in the cave, nourished and nurtured by Miguel de Cervantes (*Mártires*, 178). Rodrigo de Cervantes had just been liberated in August 1577, thanks to a loan of sixty ducats given to the mother of the Cervantes brothers, and to moneys obtained from the sale of all but the most essential family possessions. These sums, however, were not enough to rescue both brothers, and Miguel convinced the Mercederian monks, who had arrived to ransom captives, to buy Rodrigo's freedom first.

The brothers carefully planned Miguel's escape. An experienced mariner from Majorca named Viana—an expert on the Barbary Coast—had been recently ransomed. He promised to return in a few days to rescue other captives. On arriving in Spain, Rodrigo was to obtain help from the authorities and contact some of those intrepid seamen who crossed the strait at night to pick up captives in Barbary. Let us turn to Cervantes's own testimony in *Información de Argel*:

Deseando servir a Dios y a su Majestad y hacer bien a muchos cristianos principales, caballeros, letrados, sacerdotes, que al presente se hallaban cautivos en Argel, dio orden como un hermano suyo que se llama Rodrigo de Cervantes, que deste Argel fue rescatado el mes de Agosto del mesmo año de los mismos dineros del dicho Miguel de Cervantes, de su rescate, pusiese en orden y enviase de la plaza de Valencia y de Mallorca y de Ibiza, una fragata armada para llevar a España los dichos cristianos.

[Wishing to serve God and his Majesty, and to do good to many principal Christians—gentlemen, learned men, lawyers and priests—who at the time were captives in Algiers, he requested of a brother of his named Rodrigo de Cervantes, who was ransomed from this Algiers in the month of August of the same year (1577) with the same money provided for the ransoms of the said Miguel de Cervantes, that he arrange for and dispatch from Valencia and Majorca and Ibiza an armed frigate to carry the said Christians to Spain.] (*Información*, 50–51)

The plan had important mediators. Don Antonio de Toledo and Don Francisco de Valencia, Knights of St. John of Malta who were captives in Algiers, gave Rodrigo letters for the viceroys of Valencia and Majorca, begging them to favor the transaction (*Información*, 50–51).

Four weeks later, in Majorca, a frigate was armed, with Viana as the commander. On the night of September 28, 1577, Viana was supposed to come for the captives, but he never appeared. For two nights the fugitives waited in vain. Much later, the waiting men learned that the Majorcan sailors who came to get the captives were discovered by some lookouts and forced to weigh anchor. One witness claims that *"la dicha fragata vino conforme a la orden que el dicho Miguel de Cervantes le había dado, en el tiempo señalado para venir; y llegó una noche al mismo puesto, y por faltarles el ánimo a los marineros y no saltar en tierra a darle aviso a los que estaban escondidos, no hubo efecto el dicho negocio"* [the said frigate arrived as ordered by Miguel de Cervantes, and at the time indicated, and having arrived a second night at the same spot, the sailors' courage failed them and, because no one dared to jump ashore to notify the hidden men, the escape failed] (*Información*, 77). Sosa gives a third reason for this failure: *"yo mismo hablé después y lo supe de marineros que con la misma fragata vinieron, que cautivaron después, y me contaron por extenso como vinieron dos veces, y la causa de su temor"* [I personally talked to the sailors who came in the frigate, who were later captured, and they told me extensively how they came twice, and the reason for their fear] (*Información*, 158). Apparently, then, the Majorcan sailors who attempted to rescue the fugitives were discovered, and later captured by the Algerians. In the meantime, the anxious men in the cave were not aware of what was happening.

At the same time, a Spanish renegade nicknamed *El Dorador* (The Gilder), a go-between and supplier of goods for the Spaniards in hiding, lost his nerve and betrayed the fugitives to the new *beylerbey* of Algiers, Hasan Pasha. Eight to ten Turks on horseback and another twenty-four guards on foot, armed to the teeth with shotguns, scimitars, and spears, surrounded the garden and forced the fugitives out of the cave. Sosa sums it all up in his *Diálogo de los mártires*: "*Y los prendieron a todos, y particularmente maniataron a Miguel de Cervantes, un hidalgo de Alcalá de Henares, que fuera autor deste negocio, y era, por lo tanto [el] más culpado*" [And they seized them all, and particularly shackled Miguel de Cervantes, a gentleman from Alcala de Henares, who was the author of this business, and was, therefore, the most to blame] (*Mártires*, 178–81; *Topografía*, III: 162–63).

According to the principal witnesses, Miguel showed incredible courage. At the moment of capture, he told his companions to blame him for everything, promising them he would turn himself in to the Algerians to save them. While the Turks were binding them, Miguel de Cervantes said out loud, so that the Turks and Moors heard him: "*[N]inguno de estos cristianos que aquí están tienen la culpa en este negocio, porque yo solo he sido el autor dél y el que los ha inducido a que se huyesen*" [(N)one of the Christians here are guilty in this business, because I alone was the author of it and the one who persuaded them to flee]. These are Cervantes's own words (*Información*, 52–53). Taken alone before Hasan Pasha, he declared himself the only culprit in this escape attempt so that the rest of the fugitives would be spared. And in spite of the multiple death threats and intimidations—"*amenazas de muerte y tormentos*"—pronounced by the pasha, Cervantes affirmed "*que él era el autor de todo aquel negocio y que suplicaba a su alteza, si había de castigar a alguno, que fuese a él solo, pues él solo tenía la culpa de todo; y por muchas preguntas que le hizo, nunca quiso nombrar a ningún cristiano*" [that he was the author of this business and that he implored his Highness that, if he had to punish anyone, that it be him only, because he was the only guilty one; and in spite of the many questions that he (the Pasha) asked him, he refused to implicate or name any Christian] (*Información*, 53).

Considering Hasan's reputation for cruelty and the appalling punishments administered to recaptured slaves in Barbary, Cervantes's courage was daunting. There was a victim, however. On October 3, 1577, the Christian gardener from Navarra, named Juan, was hung by his foot and tortured in the presence of the fugitives, until he died choking on his own blood (*Mártires*, 180). As for Cervantes, he escaped capital punishment again. Weighted down with manacles and chains, he was imprisoned in the royal *baño* for five months. Sosa concludes his narrative with an allusion to the four aborted escapes of Cervantes, insisting that some of the Christians "*estuvieron encerrados sin ver luz [. . .] por más de siete meses, [. . .] sustentándolos Miguel de Cervantes con gran riesgo de su vida, la cual cuatro veces estuvo a pique de perderla—empalado o enganchado, o abrasado vivo— por cosas que intentó por dar libertad a muchos"* [were shut up without seeing the light (. . .) for more than seven months, (. . .) while Miguel de Cervantes sustained them with a great risk to his life, which he was at the point of losing—impaled or hooked, or burnt alive—for things he attempted to do in order to free many men] (*Mártires*, 180; *Topografía*, III: 160–65).

We might ask ourselves what Cervantes thought when he read Sosa's description of his second escape attempt, included in *Topographia, e historia general de Argel*, edited by Fray Diego de Haedo. As mentioned earlier, the work appeared in Valladolid in 1612, where Cervantes had lived for three years, between 1604 and 1607, and where he still had acquaintances. The first part of *Don Quijote* had been published in 1605, and Cervantes was already celebrated, both in Spain and in Europe. Living in Madrid since 1607, where he attended various literary salons and booksellers, the writer would have certainly heard about a new book on Algiers. The former captive positively knew that *Topographia* had been composed by his friend Dr. Antonio de Sosa in his Algerian house-prison, where Cervantes often came to visit, as we shall see, and where he probably read parts of the work Sosa was then composing. In 1612, however, Antonio de Sosa had been dead for twenty or more years, and Cervantes presumably decided not to oppose the claim of the Benedictine Abbot of Frómista, Fray Diego de Haedo, who had ascribed Sosa's work to his uncle, the former archbishop of Palermo and Inquisitor of the same name. As Camamis suggests, given the enormous reputation of the archbishop as a saintly and charitable man, and inasmuch as the nephew had assigned to him the paternity of the treatise, no one would have dared to accuse the probity and moral honesty of an illustrious prelate who had been known for his humane qualities (148).[58] Because the archbishop had died in 1608 and Cervantes remained silent on the subject, the true author of this splendid work was ignored for centuries.

And yet in England, a century later, the account of Cervantes's second escape attempt elicited a curious response from the historian John Morgan. The author of *History of Algiers* (London, 1731), which owes much to Haedo/Sosa's *Topographia*, Morgan seems fascinated by the passage in *Diálogo de los mártires* that describes Cervantes's second escape attempt, a section he translates with great care. When he arrives at the passage that reads *"del cautiverio y hazañas de Miguel de Cervantes se pudiera hacer una particular historia"* [of the captivity and feats of Miguel de Cervantes one could write a particular history], without recognizing this hero as the very author of *Don Quijote*—a best-seller in England since 1612, when Shelton's translation appeared—Morgan exclaims: "It is a Pity, methinks, that Haedo is here so succinct in what regards this enterprising captive" (566).

Sosa's account of Cervantes's second escape attempt, as well as his brief allusion to his four aborted escapes, implicitly emphasizes the disparity between the punishment deserved by the captive's offenses and the leniency shown by Hasan Pasha. One may surmise that the indomitable courage of the Spaniard and his extraordinary fortitude in the face of torture and death must have genuinely impressed the Venetian renegade Hasan. Sosa intimates something of the sort in his postscript to this Cervantine odyssey: *"Decía Hasán Baxá, rey de Argel, que como él tuviese guardado al estropeado español tenía seguros sus cristianos, bajeles y aun toda la ciudad. Tanto era lo que temía las trazas de Miguel de Cervantes"* [Hasan Pasha, king of Algiers, said that while the maimed Spaniard would be under his guard, his Christians, his vessels, and even the whole city were safe. This is how much he feared the schemes of Miguel de Cervantes] (*Mártires*, 181).

The Third Escape Attempt

Considering the price of his ransom, and the utter impossibility of obtaining such money, Cervantes, like his alter ego the Captive in *Don Quijote*, was bound to think of nothing but escape: *"[P]ensaba en Argel conseguir otros medios de alcanzar lo que buscaba, porque jamás me desamparó la esperanza de alcanzar la libertad"* [(I)n Algiers, I planned to seek other ways of attaining what I so much desired, because the hope of obtaining my freedom never deserted me] (*DQ* I, 40). Five months later, in March 1578, Cervantes endeavored to escape again. He states that, while in prison, weighed down with chains and irons as punishment for his aborted escape,

> envió a un moro a Orán secretamente, con carta al Sr. Marqués don Martín de Córdoba, general de Orán y de sus fuerzas, y a otras personas principales, sus amigos y conocidos de Orán, para que le enviasen algún espía o espías, y personas de fiar que con el dicho moro viniesen a Argel y le llevasen a él y a otros tres caballeros principales que el Rey en su baño tenía.

> [he secretly sent a Moor to Orán with a letter to the marquis, Don Martín de Córdoba, the Governor of Orán and its forces, and to other important people whom he counted among his friends and acquaintances in Orán, asking them to send one or more spies and trustworthy persons with the said Moor to Algiers and help him escape with three other important gentlemen who(m) the king was holding in his *baño*.]

> (*Información*, 54)

Don Martín de Córdoba, governor of Orán, would surely have been sympathetic to Cervantes's plea. A former captive himself, Don Martín had been captured in the battle of Mostaganem (1558) with thousands of Spanish soldiers—the disaster in which his father, the Count of Alcaudete, Governor of Orán, had lost his life. In 1559, Don Martín de Córdoba attempted to organize an uprising of Christian slaves in Algiers. He was betrayed, and many captives were put to death. His ransom cost the enormous sum of twenty-three thousand *escudos* (*Mártires*, 96–97). On this occasion, however, the governor of Orán did not hear from the prisoner Cervantes. The Moor who carried the letters was caught at the very doors of Orán by other Moors or spies who, finding the messages suspicious, seized him and brought him back to Hasan Pasha in Algiers. After examining the missives and seeing the name and signatures of Miguel de Cervantes, the *beylerbey* had the Moor impaled. Cervantes tells us that he died courageously, without revealing anything. As for himself, he summarily states that Hasan *"al dicho Miguel de Cervantes mandó dar dos mil palos"* [ordered the aforesaid Miguel de Cervantes to be given two thousand blows] (*Información*, 54–55).

Two thousand blows certainly implies death. The disobedient captive would be shackled hand and foot and given two thousand *bastinados* on the belly and soles of his feet, to kill him slowly. Alonso Aragonés, a witness, confirms that he was present when they impaled the Moor who carried the letter, and that Hasan Pasha, furious with Miguel de Cervantes, ordered him given two thousand strokes: *"y si no le dieron, fue porque hubo buenos terceros"* [and if they did not flog him, it was because there were powerful mediators] (*Información*, 66). Another witness, Diego Castellanos, an old friend of Cervantes, confirms that he was not beaten because *"muchos rogaron por él"* [many begged for him] (*Información*, 80). The cruel sentence was thus not carried out, and not a hand was raised against the captive. Cervantes is extremely discreet about this episode, both in his deposition and in his fiction. When speaking of "a Spanish soldier, a certain Saavedra by name," the Captive states only that although he "did things that dwelled in the memory of the people there for many years, and all to recover his liberty, Hasan never gave him a blow himself, nor ordered a blow to be given" (*DQ* I, 40).

Much has been conjectured in regard to this death sentence and why it was not executed. Some have speculated about a possible intervention by Dalí Mamí, by that point an admiral and averse to seeing the *beylerbey* sacrifice a valuable slave. More imaginative interpretations, following the love story of Zoraida and the Captive in *Don Quijote*, have hinted at a possible love affair between Cervantes and a Moorish woman who interceded with the pasha (Canavaggio, *Cervantes*, 87–88).[59] Canavaggio has offered the most plausible explanation for this episode, based on Cervantes's connection with one of the principal personages of Algiers, Agi Morato— Hājjī Murād or Hāyyī Murād—the famous Agi Morato of *La historia del cautivo* and other Cervantine works.

A Slavonic renegade from Ragusa, on the Dalmatian coast, Hājjī Murād was one of the richest men in Barbary. His prestigious status as a *hadji* (one who makes the pilgrimage to Mecca) was heightened by his influence with the Grand Turk, who employed him as a *chaouch*, or diplomatic envoy. His daughter, immortalized by Cervantes in *La historia del cautivo*, married aspirant to the Moroccan throne 'Abd al-Malik, exiled to Algiers by a palace conspiracy rigged by his brother. We shall learn more about this fascinating figure in chapter 2, in a discussion of various outstanding personages of Algiers. 'Abd al-Malik took over the throne of Morocco in 1576, only to be killed two years later during the triumphant battle of Alcazarquivir against King Sebastian of Portugal. After his death, his widow would marry none other than Hasan Veneciano in 1580 (Canavaggio, *Cervantes*, 88).

On two occasions, in March 1573 and August 1577, Hājjī Murād, acting as the Grand Turk's emissary in Algiers, made the first secret overtures to Spain, preludes to the Constantinople negotiations that would conclude in the great Hispano-Turkish truce of 1579–1580. The Spanish archives reveal the secret contacts made by Philip II through various intermediaries: the Gasparo Corso brothers, Valencian merchants and agents; Fray Rodrigo de Arce, a ransomer-monk known by Cervantes; the viceroy of Valencia, involved by Rodrigo in the second escape attempt of 1577; and finally, Don Martín de Córdoba (*Cervantes*, 88). In their engaging book on Cervantes, the Turkish-Algerian world, and the secret services in the time of Philip II, *Cervantes y la Berbería*, Emilio Sola and José F. de la Peña confirm that Don Martín de Cordoba had been involved the year before in secret transactions for the Spanish crown in Algiers. Under the cloak of negotiating the ransom of several captives, the governor of Orán sent an espionage agent to Algiers, Fray Miguel de Fresneda, who arrived on August 17, 1577.

Over the course of several days, Fresneda met with *beylerbey* Ramadān Pasha and with Hājjī Murād himself, who was always present in these meetings, after which Ramadān Pasha apparently sailed for Constantinople on August 22, 1577, taking Hājjī Murād with him. Hājjī Murād stated that he was horrified—*"se espantaba"*—to see that the king of Spain did not help his son-in-law 'Abd al-Malik against his nephew and opponent. As it turns out, 'Abd al-Malik had been lobbying at the Spanish court for support against the Turks. According to Hājjī Murād, the king's disregard for his son-in-law 'Abd al-Malik would have a bearing on the future actions of the sultan, for he (Hājjī Murād) was the Turk's alter ego. Hājjī Murād added that he was sailing to Constantinople to find a fleet with which to descend on Orán and Mers-el-Kebir, the North Africa towns controlled by the Spaniards, to destroy them. Nevertheless, Hājjī Murād sent a letter to Philip II requesting safe conduct to travel to Spain to negotiate directly with the

Spanish court in the name of his son-in-law. At the same time, he threatened the Spanish king with an uprising of the Moriscos of Valencia and
"all the others there are in Spain" who were ready to come to his son-in-
law's aid.

In all the meetings that Hājjī Murād had with Fresneda, however, he
never alluded to an entente between 'Abd al-Malik and Philip II against
the Turks, speaking, instead, of a general accord between the three powers. To maintain the ambiguity, he suggested that he was accompanying
Ramadān Pasha to Constantinople to prevent the departing *beylerbey* from
having a detrimental effect on his own (Hājjī Murād's) business in Constantinople, for Ramadān Pasha had been deposed because of his son-in-
law's request.[60] In July 1578, Hājjī Murād was again sent to Istanbul by
Hasan Pasha with a present for the sultan and the news of the Portuguese
invasion of Morocco. At the end of the summer, the French diplomatic
correspondence situated Hājjī Murād at the Ottoman court, organizing his
return to Algiers with the promise of coming back immediately to Istanbul
with fresh news (Sola and de la Peña, 119–20). Between intimidations and
ambiguous allusions, Hājjī Murād surfaced as the key figure of the Algerian political arena in the 1570s, a central personage in important political
negotiations with the Porte.

The second escape attempt of Cervantes, described earlier, and his interview with new *beylerbey* Hasan Veneciano, occurred on September 30,
1577, in the wake of these negotiations. This Cervantine episode cannot be
understood, as Sola and de la Peña persuasively argue, without taking into
account the hothouse ambience created by the "negotiating delirium" of
the Spanish spies in 1577 Algiers (*Cervantes y la Berbería*, 119–20). Writing
to the Spanish court from Algiers and Morocco in these months, the
Gasparo Corso brothers, merchants and agents for the Spanish crown, spoke
of conversations with newly arrived *beylerbey* Hasan Pasha and of the possibility of enticing him to the service of Spain, in exchange for money, lands,
and honors (SHIM, *England*, 1: 257–60). In this heated atmosphere of secret agents and spies, the cave episode probably contributed to Cervantes's
prestige among the captives and the Algerians. It is not improbable, says
Canavaggio, that Cervantes, "protected by his high-placed contacts, real
or imaginary, should have been summoned to the inner sanctum of the
chaouch in order to back up the official informants" (*Cervantes*, 88). Sola
and de la Peña also believe that Cervantes, regarded in Algiers as a personage with high contacts in Spain, would have become an "unofficial informer" to Hājjī Murād (236).

Let us remember that the letters of recommendation Cervantes car-
ried with him when he was captured would be read in different ways by
Christians versus Muslims. As Carroll Johnson contends, in the Spanish-
Imperial context, these letters meant "heroic soldier." In the Barbary world,

however, they possibly meant "spy of value" or "valuable merchandise" ("Coyote?" 15). Such interpretation may explain Cervantes's potential worth for the Algerians. Hasan Pasha's commentaries regarding the captive Miguel de Cervantes, as recounted by Sosa, may throw some light on this issue. The renegade ruler not only feared Cervantes's schemes and valor but also stated in public that for the security of his slaves, the corsairs, and Algiers itself, the captive had to be kept under tight and constant seclusion (*Mártires*, 181). At the same time, Cervantes's request to Don Martín de Córdoba to send some "spies" to Algiers, made in his letter of March 1578, suggests that the captive may have heard of the secret negotiations that took place the year before with Hājjī Murād and the departed Ramadān Pasha. The allusion to certain eminent acquaintances of Cervantes's in Orán and the importance of the plan that involved three other principal gentlemen, also imprisoned in the *beylerbey*'s *baño*, indicate that this was a carefully planned scheme aimed at the highest circles of influence in Orán. These data reinforce the likelihood that Cervantes and his friends—all elite captives—would have been informed of the secret negotiations that took place the year before in Algiers.

My research reinforces the conjectures advanced by Canavaggio and other critics regarding Cervantes's connections in Algiers. A report written by two members of the Order of Malta who went on a military reconnaissance mission of the coasts of Barbary in 1587 reveals that Hājjī Murād was in close contact with Fray Geronimo Caraffa, a Knight of St. John of an illustrious Neapolitan family who had been a captive in Algiers for many years. Caraffa claimed that Agimorat (Hājjī Murād), "who was the father-in-law of Maluc ('Abd al-Malik), formerly the king of Fez, now dead, [. . .] is the chief of the Moors and is loved and adored by all." Caraffa believed that it would be possible to reach an agreement with Hājjī Murād to help the Knights of Malta take Algiers, especially because he wished to liberate himself from the yoke of the Turks and had the support of the Moors. Hājjī Murād apparently spoke openly with Caraffa in many gatherings, repeating the same old story about Philip II and stating that "he was very amazed that the king of Spain, knowing his authority and the power he [Hājjī Murād] had in this reign, had never taken notice of him." The fact that Caraffa alludes to the death of 'Abd al-Malik, which occurred in 1578, suggests that his conversations with Hājjī Murād took place after that date, perhaps even while Cervantes was a captive in Algiers. These statements also intimate that Hājjī Murād talked freely with certain elite captives about politics and other undercover affairs.[61]

These anti-Turkish feelings created nationalist reactions against the Porte in Morocco and united the dispersed regional chiefs around their religious leaders.[62] In Algiers, the information provided by various spies and Christian slaves regarding Hājjī Murād's intimate feelings toward the

Turks suggests the existence of similar nationalist sentiments and the possibility that this skilled politician would have been the center of covert anti-
Turkish activities in the Turkish-Algerian regency, especially after the death
of his son-in-law 'Abd al-Malik in 1578. Two years later, as mentioned above,
Hājjī Murād's widowed daughter would marry *beylerbey* Hasan Veneciano,
thus sealing an alliance with Alūj Ali [Euch Alí], the powerful admiral of
the Turkish armada and Hasan Pasha's protector in Constantinople. Did
the feverish climate of spies and secret agents in 1577 and 1588 Algiers help
Cervantes, like Caraffa, to gain access to Hājjī Murād's ear, or to his inner
sanctum? This would explain the mediation efforts of *"buenos terceros"*
[good or powerful intermediaries] with Venetian renegade Hasan, which
apparently saved Cervantes from death on two occasions.

The Fourth Escape Attempt

In his last escape attempt, realized in September 1579, Cervantes persuaded
a Spanish renegade named Girón to buy an armed frigate through the mediation of a Valencian merchant who was in Algiers at the time. He describes this feat a year later:

> [Miguel de Cervantes] deseando servir a Dios y a su Majestad y hacer bien a
> cristianos, muy secretamente dio parte de este negocio a muchos caballeros,
> letrados, sacerdotes y cristianos que en este Argel estaban cautivos [. . .] con
> intención de hacerlos embarcar a todos y llevar a tierra de cristianos, que
> sería hasta número de sesenta cristianos, y toda gente la más florida de Argel.

> [Miguel de Cervantes, wishing to serve God and his Majesty and to do mercy
> to Christians, very secretly gave word of the venture to many gentlemen,
> jurists, priests, and (other) Christians who were then captives in this Algiers
> (. . .) with the intention of boarding them all, taking them to a Christian
> land; there were about sixty Christians (involved), the flower of those in
> Algiers.]

(Información, 56)

The plan was a variation of the ploy put into effect two years before, with
the help of his brother Rodrigo. This time, however, Miguel's plot was
more ambitious. Valencian merchant Onofre Exarque was to provide thirteen hundred doubloons for the purchase of an armed vessel with twelve
benches, a purchase that would be conducted by the Andalusian renegade
from Granada, who had changed his name to Abderramán when he apostatized. This was an ideal opportunity for Girón-Abderramán, who wished
to return to Spain and thus to the bosom of the church. In early October
1579, when everything was ready for the departure, the rebels were betrayed
by a second renegade of Florentine origin who went to see Hasan Pasha

and informed him of the plan. His disclosures were immediately confirmed by the real author of the treason, Spanish Dominican Dr. Juan Blanco de Paz. Born in Extremadura of Judeo-Morisco parents, it appears this Dominican acted out of resentment because he was not accepted as part of the fugitive group (Canavaggio, *Cervantes*, 93). Cervantes, who seemed to enjoy some freedom to walk around the city, went into hiding in a place provided by his friend Diego Castellano (*Información*, 56). Hasan Pasha issued an edict of death for anyone caught sheltering the runaway. In the meantime, Exarque, terrified that Hasan would use torture, that "Cervantes, as the guiltiest of all, would reveal who was in the plot, and that the said Onofre Exarque would lose his fortune, his freedom and perhaps his life," offered to ransom Cervantes out of his own money and to spirit him out of Algiers in the first boat departing for Spain.

With his usual courage, Cervantes refused this proposal. The scene is recounted by Cervantes himself in his deposition. Assuming full responsibility for the affair to save the Christian who hid him, he told his companions *"que no tuviesen miedo, porque él tomaría sobre sí todo el peso de aquel negocio, aunque tenía cierto de morir por ello"* [not to be afraid, because he would take the whole burden of this affair on his shoulders, even though he was sure that he would die for it] (*Información*, 56–57). He immediately presented himself before Hasan Pasha, who threatened to torture him *"con muchos tormentos, [para que] le descubriese la verdad de aquel caso y qué gente llevaba consigo"* [with many torments, so that he would reveal the truth of this affair, and the names of the people he was taking with him]. To intimidate him, Hasan made Cervantes believe he was going to be hanged: *"mandándole [. . .] poner un cordel a la garganta y atar las manos atrás, como que le querían ahorcar"* [ordering (. . .) to put a cord around his neck, and to tie his hands behind his back, as if they were going to hang him]. Refusing to betray his companions, Cervantes told the pasha that he was to blame for this affair, along with four other gentlemen who had just been liberated and who were to go in the vessel.

Even though Cervantes and other witnesses state that Hasan "was very outraged with him," the pasha, after threatening him with execution, granted him life again. This time Hasan Veneciano imprisoned Cervantes in his own palace, where there was a prison for reprobate Moors, putting him under heavy guard, in irons and chains, for five months (*Información*, 58). The oppressive conditions of this and other prisons for delinquents are described by Sosa, who claims that the prisoners were "all lying on the floor, and almost all, either with their feet fettered in wheel clamps, or with shackles and irons, and chains, under tight security" (*Topografía*, I: 208). Significantly, when Dalí Mamí returned to Algiers, Hasan Pasha bought his slave from him at the price fixed by the corsair, five hundred gold *escudos*.

Cervantes's account of his fourth escape attempt is, once more, as Canavaggio notes, especially laconic (*Cervantes*, 105). Many of the witnesses who testified later in the *Información de Argel* were involved in this plan, having been invited to leave on the ship: Alonso Aragonés (50 years old, from Córdoba), Diego Castellano (36, from Toledo), Rodrigo de Chaves (29, from Badajoz), Domingo Lopino (46, from Sicily), Fernando de Vega (40, from Toledo), Cristóbal de Villalón (45, from Valladolid), Luis de Pedrosa (37, from Osuna and resident in Marbella, and one of the organizers of the plot), Fray Feliciano Enríquez ("who gave some money for provisions"), and Antonio de Sosa (*"pues [Cervantes] me convidó a ser uno de los que en la fragata debía de ir"* [for Cervantes invited me to be one of those who would go in the frigate]) (*Información*, 148, 162).

Both Ensign Diego Castellano and Rodrigo Chaves affirm that corsair Morat Raez (*ra'ís*), a Spanish renegade from Murcia, pleaded for Cervantes's life. Castellano testifies that *"[Cervantes] se puso en las manos de un arráez muy grande amigo del rey, que se dice moro Atarráez [sic, Morat Arráez] Maltrapillo, renegado español, para que le entregase al rey porque le viniese menos daño"* [Cervantes put himself into the hands of a corsair, a great friend of the king who calls himself Moor Atarráez (Morat Arraez or *Ra'ís*) Maltrapillo ("Ragamuffin"), a Spanish renegade, so that he would hand him over to the king (*beylerbey*) in order that Cervantes would suffer less damage] (*Información*, 82). May we assume, like Canavaggio, an intervention by Ḥājjī Murād, who was about to become Hasan Pasha's father-in-law (*Cervantes*, 93)? As for Morat Raez Maltrapillo, he is surely the same character who reappears in *La historia del cautivo*, the Spanish renegade who translates Zoraida's letters "word by word." The Captive claims: *"en fin, yo me determiné de fiarme de un renegado, natural de Murcia, que se había dado por grande amigo mío, y puesto prendas entre los dos que le obligaban a guardar el secreto que le encargase"* (*DQ* I, 40) [in the end, I decided to confide in *a renegade from Murcia*, who professed to be a good friend of mine. We made pledges between us which bound him to keep the secret I had entrusted to him] (*Captive's Tale*, 85; emphasis mine).

Little is known of renegade Morat Raez Maltrapillo other than the various allusions to his name in Sosa's chronicles. In 1581, Maltrapillo was one of the principal corsairs of Algiers, owner of a small galley with twenty-two benches (*Topografía*, I: 89). Sosa calls Maltrapillo *"un gran traidor"* [a great traitor] for having been involved in the execution of a Greek resident of Cádiz named Niccolo—a slave burned to death in Algiers in 1574, in retaliation for the execution of an Algerian corsair in Cádiz (*Mártires*, 154). Morat Raez Maltrapillo participated in the 1577 capture of the galley *San Pablo* of the Order of Malta, in which Sosa was abducted. In this seizure, the corsair acquired as his share of the booty Knight of St. John

Antonio González de Torres, a Portuguese nobleman who became Maltrapillo's slave (*Topografía*, II: 86).

The real-life González de Torres is Sosa's interlocutor in *Diálogo de los
mártires de Argel*, where he offers some information on his master Maltrapillo. Various *chacales* [country Turks] recently arrived from Constantinople
and on their way to Fez gathered in his master's house, along with other
corsairs and oarsmen from Maltrapillo's galliot (light vessel). According
to González de Torres, the visitors asserted that in Turkey, Romania,
Anatolia, and Syria, *"todos hablan de Argel, como nosotros acá de las Indias
de Castilla y Portugal"* [they all talk of Algiers as we (the Spaniards) do
regarding the Indies of Castile and Portugal] (*Topografía*, II: 88). Comparing this anecdote with Sosa's accounts of corsair life in Algiers, we may
surmise that Maltrapillo's house was a gathering place for corsairs, renegades, and foreign merchants who passed through the city. As one of the
city's principal *ra'is*, his house was probably large enough to accommo-
date his own slaves, as well as the renegades who had become partners in
his thriving business. In any case, the data derived from both the *Información de Argel* and Sosa's dialogues suggest that renegade Morat Raez
Maltrapillo was well respected in Algerian circles—so influential, it seems,
that he might have changed the pasha's mind and thus saved Cervantes's
life in 1579.

As for the reputation of Algiers among the eastern Mediterranean ports
and cities, the visitors' assertions in the gathering at Maltrapillo's house
seem to be correct. González de Torres claims that the innumerable goods
and merchandise brought to Algiers *"han hecho y hacen a esta ciudad la
más rica de cuantas hay hoy en Levante y Poniente"* [have turned and turn
this city into the richest of those in the Near East and the West] (*Topografía*, II: 88). Through the words of González de Torres, Sosa tells us
that beyond the goods obtained during the corsair raids, the Jewish
and Moorish merchants of Algiers traded with Tripoli, Tunis, Bona, Con-
stantina, Tlemcen, Fez, Marrakesh, and other Maghribi cities, as
far away as Constantinople and England, while merchants brought their
merchandise from all over the Mediterranean, including Marseilles and
Valencia, Genoa, Naples, and Sicily (*Topografía*, I: 93–97).

The "Christians of Allah"

The mediation of Murcian corsair Morat Arraez Maltrapillo casts some light
on Cervantes's relations with the Christian renegades. Canavaggio remarks:
"the number of renegades who appear in Cervantes's work, the roles he
gives them, the carefully drawn image of them that he represents, all show
not only that he was motivated by an enlightened curiosity, but that he
was deeply moved by the thousands of children lost in the clash of two

civilizations" (*Cervantes*, 91). Numerous renegades had been seized as children, as Canavaggio suggests, at sea or on the Mediterranean islands and Spanish coasts. Called the "Christians of Allah" by Bartolomé and Lucile Benassar, these Mediterranean men opted for a more lucrative and often more successful life as corsairs, artisans, translators, or secretaries to the rulers in the Maghrib.[63]

Juan de Balcázar, a witness in the *Información de Argel* who was captured with Cervantes and also became a slave of Dalí Mamí, offers a glimpse of Cervantes's dealings with Spanish and Italian renegades. Balcázar reveals that Cervantes encouraged, comforted, and offered ingenious advice to five young renegades who belonged to some of the most famous Algerian corsairs, so that they would jump ship in Christian territory while sailing with their masters. Two of these boys belonged to the captain of the Algerian corsairs, Arnaut Mamí, known for his cruelty, while another two belonged to Dalí Mamí, Cervantes's and Balcázar's master. The scheme apparently worked, for Balcázar adds that *"si no fuera por la mucha industria y ánimo del dicho Miguel de Cervantes, los dichos muchachos se estuvieran todavía en Argel y fueran moros y prosiguieran en su mala inclinación y sucedieran en los oficios de sus amos"* [were it not for the great resourcefulness and encouragement of the said Miguel de Cervantes, the said boys would still be in Algiers and would still be Moors, and would continue in their bad inclination, and would succeed their masters in their trade] (*Información*, 105–06).

The anecdote reveals the sympathy existing between Christian slaves and renegades who, in spite of their apostasy, often kept their regional or national solidarities. On the other hand, Balcázar's account evinces that the "renegades" helped by Cervantes were adolescents (*muchachos*) who had probably been captured as boys. In their book on the "Christians of Allah," Bartolomé and Lucile Benassar discuss the many renegades who had been seized as children and forced to convert to Islam. Of 978 cases of renegades studied by the historians, half were under the age of fifteen when seized by Barbary corsairs, and a quarter were between fifteen and nineteen years old. The proportion is significant. Although these numbers are certainly incomplete, they illustrate the phenomenon of converting Christian children to Islam in early modern times. These levies seemed to respond, as the Benassars demonstrate, to a deliberate wish to incorporate Christian children, converted into Muslims, into a social system ready to receive them (320). In this way were constituted the cosmopolitan societies of the Maghribi corsair cities, especially of Algiers, a meeting point for all races and religions, where the autochthonous citizens shared power with the exogenous population. This Cervantine story regarding five young renegades exemplifies the point.

As Cervantes reveals in *El trato de Argel* and other works, the temptation to apostatize and become a Muslim was constant for the captives. Many slaves opted for apostasy when their hope of being ransomed collapsed and they faced the prospect of eternal slavery in Barbary. The incitations to convert to Islam were continual for such captives as artillerymen or gunners, and captains, pilots, or administrators, who were often incorporated into the Maghribi armies, corsair fleets, and urban economy or administration. Canavaggio conjectures: "There is no doubt that those Muslim authorities for whom he served as informant invited him [Cervantes] to join them, with the prospects of a brilliant career as a reward for his conversion to Islam" (*Cervantes*, 91). Daniel Eisenberg has questioned this issue in a provocative article entitled *"¿Por qué volvió Cervantes de Argel?"* ["Why Did Cervantes Return from Algiers?"]. Eisenberg surmises that Cervantes was often enticed by Spanish or Italian renegades, Turks, or Moors to obtain freedom and prestige through his adoption of Islam. Nevertheless, staying in Algiers as a renegade would have meant first, for Cervantes, making a living directly or indirectly from the commerce in human beings, a parasitic enterprise he despised, and second, abandoning his literary activities—his language, his poetry, his books—and the lively intellectual world of sixteenth-century Spain into which he plunged immediately after his return (Eisenberg, 249–50).

El trato de Argel stages an enlightening dialogue between an autobiographical character named Saavedra and a Spanish captive named Pedro, who has decided to apostatize and become a Turk. In a calm tone, marked by genuine understanding and even compassion, Saavedra persuades the doubting Pedro not to forsake his Christian faith: *"Un falso bien te muestra aquí aparente,/que es tener libertad, y, en renegando/se te irá el procurarla de la mente"* [A false good apparently appears before you,/which is to acquire liberty, and, upon apostatizing,/your mind will forget to obtain it] (*Trato*, IV, 2159–61). As discussed in chapter 3, centered on *El trato de Argel* and other Cervantine works, the controversy that brings these two characters together, as well as the inner conflict of the captive Saavedra—who is tempted to apostatize to gain freedom and a better life in Algiers—possibly speaks of an authentic inner debate of the future author, a wrenching debate later projected onto the stage.

Summary

In this historical voyage through the sixteenth-century Mediterranean, we have explored the Habsburg-Ottoman conflicts that led to the constitution of the Turkish-Algerian regency in the Maghrib and, later, to the consolidation of the city of Algiers as both the most celebrated and the most dreaded corsair center of the Mare Nostrum. The "Whip of the Christian World," as Algiers was called, threatened Christian Europe, especially the

Mediterranean coastline of Iberia, which was constantly raided by North African corsairs. The confrontations between Charles V and the Ottoman Sultan Süleymān and then between Philip II and Süleymān's successors at the Porte, fueled by the guerrilla warfare conducted by Barbary corsairs, culminated in the Battle of Lepanto, in which soldier Miguel de Cervantes fought heroically against the Turks. We have studied Cervantes's subsequent capture by Algerian privateers and his imprisonment in the sophisticated Maghribi city where he spent five years of his life. I have examined Cervantes's four escape attempts in which he narrowly escaped death side by side with archival documents and contemporary affidavits that elucidate these audacious ventures. Cervantes's escape attempts and the concomitant response of the Algerian authorities to his infractions have been situated in the context of the agitated political climate of the 1570s in Algiers, a political atmosphere often kindled by the presence of undercover Spanish agents who engaged in secret negotiations with Turks and Moors. This chapter also probed the relations of Cervantes with powerful renegades and key political figures of Algiers, such as influential Ottoman diplomat Hājjī Murād, who may have saved the captive's life twice. The recovery of Antonio de Sosa as the author of *Topographia, e historia general de Argel*, a seventeenth-century treatise attributed to Fray Diego de Haedo for centuries, is one of the highlights of this chapter. Dr. Sosa, as it turns out, is not only the best chronicler of Algiers at the time of Cervantes's captivity but also one of Cervantes's closest friends during their enslavement in Barbary. The next chapter recreates the atmosphere of Algiers in the second half of the 1570s, especially for the elite captives who were up for ransom, and studies the views of other Christian slaves and clerics who knew and befriended Cervantes during his Algerian imprisonment.

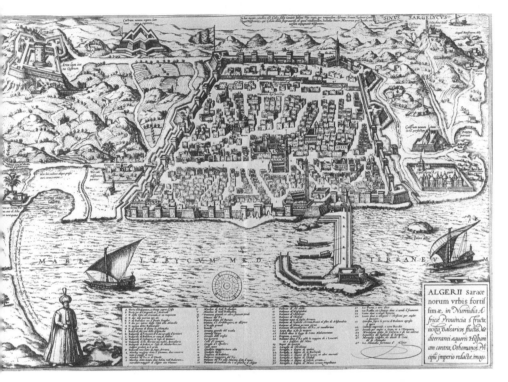

A Bird's-Eye View of Algiers. German engravers Georg Braun and Frans Hogenberg based this plan on an engraving by Antonio Salamanca (c. 1500-1562), a Roman engraver and publisher of maps who seems to have been inspired by Charles V's unsuccessful expedition in 1541. The text on the *left margin* describes the landing place and the route used by Charles V when he set out to besiege the city. The drawing shows the massive city walls, several detached forts and, in the city center, various public buildings and mosques, including the houses of the citizens, arranged in a rather schematic manner. Among the buildings depicted are the prison for Christian slaves, the Baño de la Bastarda, the Baño "of the lions and other animals" [the zoo], the principal palace of the king, and the palace of "Luchiali" [Alūj Ali Pasha]. The figure to the *left* represents Alūj Ali Pasha. The text in the *upper margin* refers to Duke Julian's daughter, La Cava, who is said to be buried beneath one of the hills. According to legend, Roderick, the Gothic king of Spain, ravished La Cava and, in revenge, Julian joined forces with the Moors, who conquered Spain.

SOURCE: Georg Braun and Fans Hogenberg, *Algerii Saracenorum vrbis fortissimae, in Numidia Africae Provinciae structae . . . imago* (1574). Reprinted by permission of Cornell University Map Collection, Olin Library.

The Assault of Charles V. In this fantastical view of Charles V's 1541 assault on Algiers, the Emperor's troops are shown on the *right* with cannons, when they actually landed on the opposite side. Algiers is represented as a medieval European city, surrounded by four forts, while the islands of Corsica and Sardinia and the boot of Italy appear to be very close to North Africa.

SOURCE: *Algeri: Assault of Charles V* (Bibliothèque Nationale, Paris). Legend: *Meso di Algeri. Bottom left*: A.S. Excud. 1541. The initials A. S. correspond to Antonio Salamanca, an Italian engraver. Reprinted from Gabriel Esquer, *Iconographie historique de l'Algérie depuis le XVIe siècle jusqu'à 1871* (Paris: Plon, 1929). Vol 1, Plate I, no. 14.

Algiers: The Siege of Charles V. Although the cartographer Münster knew only Germany, Switzerland, and Alsace from firsthand observation, he requested documentary material and views from foreign princes and cities. Judging from the inaccuracy of this map, he undoubtedly received outdated and incomplete information. The city in this engraving appears to be much smaller than it actually was in 1541. The Peñón of Algiers is labelled "Ivlia Cesarea Insula" even though Cherchell (Julio Caesarea) is situated on the coast, 96 kilometers southwest of Algiers. The Peñón, which appears to be detached from Algiers, had actually been joined to the city by a dam in 1529. The clamor of battle is represented by the cannon fire and armed soldiers *on the right* of the city walls and by the Imperial armada, *on the left*. Above "Giardini" are various enclosed gardens, and *to the left*, two hanged men.

SOURCE: *Algeri: Siege of Charles V* by Sebastian Münster, *Cosmographer oder Beschreibung aller Länder . . . ,* Basel, 1541 (Bibliothèque Nationale, Paris). Reprinted from Gabriel Esquer, *Iconographie historique de l'Algérie depuis le XVIe siècle jusqu'à 1871* (Paris: Plon, 1929). Vol 1, Plate VI, no. 17a.

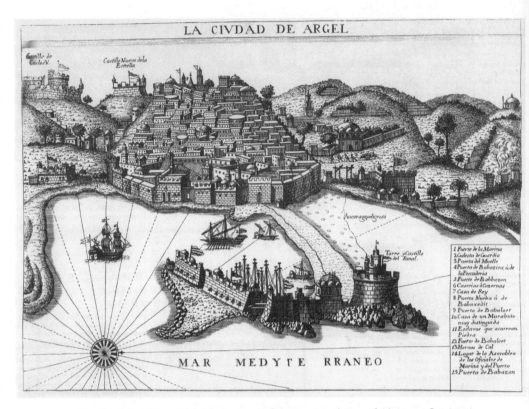

The Port and City of Algiers. A view of the port and city of Algiers reflecting its Islamic character, especially in the manner of the homes descending from the high ground to the heart of the city near the waterfront. The concise topographic key identifies a guarding galliot in the port (2); the fort of Babbazon [Bab Azoun] (5) and the gate of Bab Azoun (15) on the *left*; several Janissary barracks (6); and on the *right*, slaves carrying stone (11).

SOURCE: *La Ciudad de Argel* [The City of Algiers] (c. 1700) N.A. Reprinted by permission of Servicio de Publicaciones de la Agencia Española de Cooperación Internacional from *Planos y mapas hispánicos de Argelia: siglos XVI-XVIII / Plans et cartes hispaniques de l'Algérie, XVIe-XVIIe siècles,* ed. Mikel de Epalza and Juan Bautista Vilar, 2 vols. (Madrid: Instituto Hispano-Árabe de Cultura, 1988), I: 324, map 412.

Khair ad-Dīn Barbarossa. Born on the island of Mytilene, Greece, the brothers Arūj and Khair ad-Dīn Barbarossa were already famous Mediterranean pirates when the sheik of Algiers solicited Arūj's help to attack the Spaniards who were controlling the Peñón of Algiers, a fort constructed on an islet facing the city. Arūj assassinated the sheik, proclaimed himself sultan, and strengthened his power through a reign of terror. After his death in 1518, he was succeeded by his brother Khair ad-Dīn, the founder of the modern state of Algiers, who placed the city and its province under the mantle of the Ottoman Empire.

SOURCE: *Araideno [Khair ad-Dīn] Barbarossa.* Capriolo: *Ritratti di cento capitani ilustri* . . . (Rome, 1596, fol. 113, verso). Reprinted from Gabriel Esquer, *Iconographie historique de l'Algérie depuis le XVIe siècle jusqu'à 1871* (Paris: Plon, 1929), Vol I, Plate II, no. 4.

2

Writing Algiers:
Masters, Slaves, and Renegades

No hay en la tierra, conforme a mi parecer,
contento que se iguale a alcanzar la libertad perdida.[1]
—Cervantes, *Historia del cautivo* (*DQ* I, 39)

"DEL CAUTIVERIO Y HAZAÑAS de Miguel de Cervantes se pudiera hacer una particular historia" [On the captivity and heroic deeds of Miguel de Cervantes, one could write a particular history]. These are the words of Antonio de Sosa in his *Diálogo de los mártires de Argel* (180). Certainly, this history begs to be written. My study, which explores Cervantes's captivity and its effects on the ongoing process of creation that ends with his death, is an attempt to fill this gap. By examining Antonio de Sosa's enslavement in Barbary and the way he dealt with this ordeal by reading and writing continuously—an activity that involved ceaseless conversations with other captives, especially Cervantes—this chapter attempts to evoke the situation of elite (ransomable) Christian captives in Algiers in the 1570s, to conjure up, as it were, an entire past. Sosa's experience as the house slave of an important municipal officer of Algiers, Jewish renegade Mahamed, throws some light on the role of the renegades in the open frontier societies of the Maghrib, where fortunes were rapidly made in the strife over power.

This chapter also portrays some of the most colorful personages of Cervantes's Algiers, such as rulers Ramadān Pasha, Hasan Veneciano, and 'Abd al-Malik of Morocco, as well as Corsican merchants and secret agents Francisco and Andrea Gasparo Corso, all of whom Cervantes knew. Focusing on the question of culture and intellectual activities in the Ottoman Empire and the Maghrib, I aim to recreate the atmosphere that surrounded the captives interested in literary endeavors, such as Cervantes and Sosa, among others who composed poems, short pieces, or extensive works either in private prisons or in the *baños*. In addition, I examine Cervantes's ransom and liberation through the intervention of the Trinitarian order in 1580, together with the document known as *Información de Argel*—an inquest organized by Cervantes after his release from slavery.

Approaching this document from the perspectives of both literary history and trauma theory, I read the *Información de Argel* as a fundamental testimony that permits the survivor to keep living after his liberation.

Sosa and Cervantes: A "Particular History"

We know almost nothing of the emotional states suffered by the captive Cervantes in Algiers, of his intimate feelings as he faced defeat and imprisonment. In a letter written to Sicilian humanist and poet Antonio Veneziano on November 6, 1579, during his last imprisonment in Hasan Pasha's prison for Moors, Cervantes swears as a Christian, *"que son tantas las imaginaciones que me fatigan, que no me han dejado cumplir como quería estos versos que a v.m. envío"* [that *the many fancies wearying me* have prevented me from completing, as well as I would have wished, these verses I am sending to your Lordship] (Astrana Marín, III: 60; emphasis mine). Known as the father of Sicilian poetry, Antonio Veneziano was captured in April 1578, while en route to Spain from Palermo. His fame as a poet and scholar known for his translations of Latin epigrams into elegant Italian prose certainly attracted Cervantes. Accordingly, in spite of his heavy chains and of "the many fancies wearying" him, Cervantes contrived to write two glum *octavas* in response to Veneziano's long poem singing his love for "Celia," and to express the hope that they would be soon delivered from this land, *"de la cual Dios nos saque"* [May God pluck us from it!] (Astrana Marín, III: 60).[2] In October 1580, Sosa attested that for the past three years and eight months, he had maintained a close friendship and confidential conversations (*"conversación estrecha"*) with Cervantes (*Información*, 156). Throughout this time, Cervantes *"se ocupaba muchas veces en componer versos en alabanza de Nuestro Señor y de su bendita Madre [. . .] y otras cosas santas y devotas, algunas de las cuales comunicó particularmente conmigo y me las envió que las viese"* [often occupied himself in composing verses in praise of Our Lord and his blessed Mother (. . .) and other saintly and devout themes, some of which he discussed with me in private, and sent to me so that I would see them] (*Información*, 162–63). Other poems composed by Cervantes in Algiers as early as 1576, and dedicated to his companion of captivity, Italian jurist Bartholomeo Ruffino de Chiambery, confirm this facet of the writer, the lover of poetry. Years later, Cervantes would corroborate his penchant for poetry: *"Desde mis tiernos años amé/el arte dulce de la agradable poesía"* [From my earliest years I loved/the sweet art of amiable poetry] (*Viaje del Parnaso [Journey to Parnassus]*, I, 103).

Antonio de Sosa's life and work are so intertwined with those of Cervantes that it seems necessary to sketch a semblance of this fascinating figure who is not only one of Cervantes's closest friends in Algiers but also his first biographer. As we may recall, Sosa recounts the story of Cervantes's second escape attempt—the cave episode—in story 25 of *Diálogo de los mártires de Argel*. These data, discovered in 1752 by Fray Martín Sarmiento—who identifies the hero of this story with the author of *Don Quijote*—led Agustín Montiano y Luyardo to look for Cervantes's baptismal records in Alcalá de Henares.[3] Owing to Sosa's work, then, Cervantes's birthplace finally became known in eighteenth-century Spain. If Sosa's account unveiled an unknown episode of Cervantes's past, concomitantly, part of what we know about Antonio de Sosa emerges from the testimonies collected by Cervantes in 1580, in the *Información de Argel*.[4] Dr. Sosa appears in this document as the most authoritative witness among those who testify on Cervantes's behalf, a witness who closes this collection of testimonies with the moving statement on poetry and literature cited above. That this investigation was extremely important for Sosa is certain, for he overcame enormous difficulties to present his deposition. Claiming that he had read each and every one of the articles detailed in the inquiry, he declares that he was unable to render his affidavit in person "because of the continuous and tight confinement" in which his master kept him (*Información*, 155). Instead, on October 22, 1580, after the inquest had been formerly closed by Fray Juan Gil, Sosa managed to send an affidavit composed in his own hand. This forced Fray Juan Gil to reopen the investigation to append the new testimony, as can be deduced from the postscript in which he testifies that he recognizes Dr. Antonio de Sosa's handwriting and signatures, which he knows well (*Información*, 166).

An ecclesiastic related to the Order of St. John of Jerusalem of Malta, Dr. Antonio de Sosa was apparently also a doctor in canon law.[5] I am basing my presumptions on the juridical accent of Sosa's *Dialogues*, particularly in the passages concerned with the legal status of the slave, whom Sosa considers a "dead body"—that is, a juridically dead being—during the period of his captivity (*Topografía*, II: 19–20ff.). The title of *doctor*, awarded only to law or canon law graduates (in Salamanca, the equivalent title for theologians was *maestro* or *magister*), was a rare distinction in early modern Spain and Portugal. In strictly academic terms, the title of *doctor* was not a higher degree than that of the *licentia docendi*, because it did not require any further study, but rather a title of honor conferred on certain holders of the *licentia*. Yet only a small minority of *letrados* ever became doctors of law.[6] Dr. Sosa might have studied at the University of Salamanca, a Spanish institution favored by Portuguese students, or at that of Coimbra, Portugal, which also offered studies in canon law and law. A law degree, especially canon law, offered more possibilities of employment in the growing bureaucracy of a modern state, which explains the high number of registrations in the Faculty of Canon Law at Salamanca and the elevated number of Spanish and Portuguese students in this faculty.[7]

Sailing from Barcelona on his way to Valletta (Malta), Antonio de Sosa (or de Sousa) was captured in April 1577 with two hundred ninety other people aboard the galley *San Pablo* from the Order of Malta (*Topografía*, I: 370). Launched in the last days of March 1577 from Barcelona, this galley set sail for Valletta (Malta), separating itself from two other galleys of the Order of St. John that continued on their own toward Valletta. Some of the sailors who escaped in the moment of the corsair attack spoke of increasingly strong winds and rough seas that swept over the galley continuously, to the point that the crew had to throw the oars, the sails, and many firearms into the sea.[8] On April 1, 1577, the *San Pablo* was intercepted by a squadron of twelve Algerian galliots (small vessels)[9] commanded by Arnaut Mamí—the same corsair captain who had captured Cervantes—near the island of San Pedro, along Sardinia, and seized as a prize after a fierce battle, in which its captain, many knights, and crew members were killed. The surviving passengers, including Andreas de Sosa, listed as a brother of Antonio de Sosa, a good number of Knights of St. John, and others who were to become novitiate knights in Valletta, were taken as captives to Algiers.[10] The coincidences with the capture of Cervantes, whose ship was also swept away by a storm and then attacked by corsairs, are striking. In *El trato de Argel*, Cervantes's Moorish heroine Zahara describes the *mistral*, or strong northwest wind, that forced the *San Pablo* to take shelter on the island of San Pedro, where it was assaulted by Algerian corsairs, a story she heard from a Christian slave who lost there *"la dulce/y amada libertad"* [the sweet/and loved freedom] (*Trato*, II.1256–60). This unnamed Christian is none other than Antonio de Sosa, who returns to Cervantes's play through the words of an Algerian woman. The captive Silvia completes the information:

> La galera que dices, según creo,
> se llamaba *San Pablo*, y era nueva
> y de la sacra religión de Malta.
> Yo en ella me perdí. . . .

> [The galley of which you speak, I believe,
> was called the *San Pablo*, and it was new
> and of the sacred religion of Malta.
> I was captured on that galley. . . .]
>
> (*Trato*, II.1284–86)

While those captured on the galley were sold in the market of Algiers, the abducted vessel went to *beylerbey* Ramadān Pasha, as his share of the booty:

"todos los Bucos y cascos de navíos que se toman, tocan a los reyes de Argel"
[all the galleons and hulls of ships that are captured correspond to the kings
(*beys*) of Algiers"] (*Topografía*, 1: 370).

Antonio de Sosa and
Topographia, e historia general de Argel

Chapter 1 referred to Antonio de Sosa's monumental work, edited and published by Fray Diego de Haedo, who claimed to have received the draft
from his uncle, Archbishop Diego de Haedo (*Topografía*, 1: 10–11). We must
presume that after his release from captivity in 1581, Sosa visited Haedo
senior, who was then Inquisitor, in Palermo (Sicily) and left his manuscript
with him. It is likely that Sosa died in the following year or two, however,
and his work remained with the Haedos, uncle and nephew. Yet the book
took a long time to appear. Fray Diego de Haedo obtained permission to
publish it in October 1604, but more than one year went by before he
signed the dedication to his uncle on December 25, 1605 (*Topografía*, 9,
13). In this dedication, Haedo junior makes himself the coauthor of the
work allegedly composed by Haedo senior with information received from
various captives (10–11). Fray Diego de Haedo's role, then, is that of editor and publisher of his uncle's work. Seven more years would pass before
Topographia, e historia general de Argel would finally be published in 1612,
after the death of Archbishop Haedo in 1608. Thirty years thus elapsed
after Sosa entrusted his manuscript to the archbishop of Palermo (Camamis,
140–49). In a Cervantine manner, the "lost" manuscript of historian Antonio de Sosa eventually saw the light, fraudulently, under another man's
name.

Until now, most of what we knew about Sosa paradoxically came from
the three *Dialogues* now constituting volumes 2 and 3 of *Topografía e
historia general de Argel*, signed by Fray Diego de Haedo (1929 ed.). These
colloquies, entitled *Diálogo de la captividad*, *Diálogo de los mártires de
Argel*, and *Diálogo de los morabutos* [*Dialogue on Captivity, Dialogue of
the Martyrs of Algiers*, and *Dialogue of the Muslim Holy Men*], constitute a
categorical condemnation of Muslim culture and religion, in particular, of
the cruelties perpetrated by the Turks and renegades on the Christian captives. In this vein, the last, *Dialogue of the Muslim Holy Men*, is a theological discussion that emphasizes the "errors" of Islam compared to the
"excellences" of the Christian faith. Sosa is the protagonist of, and the common interlocutor in, these dialogues, where he appears under his own name,
"Antonio de Sosa." In *Diálogo de la captividad*—the longer and more complex from a philosophical perspective—Sosa tells his interlocutor, the Knight
of St. John Fray John Antonio González de Torres, that he has begun a

profound and serious study of captivity, based not only on various classical authors but also on "the memories of diverse cases" of Christian slavery and martyrdom in Barbary (*Topografía*, II: 118–19). The second colloquy, entitled *Diálogo de los mártires de Argel*, a continuation of the first, contains the most portentous of these registered cases, which Sosa was apparently "cleaning and correcting" while he was writing the first dialogue. Again, in a Cervantine fashion, the second colloquy incorporates the now corrected "papers," called *"Memorias de algunos martirios y otras crueles muertes [. . .] que algunos cristianos han recibido [. . .] en Argel"* [Memories of certain martyrdoms and other cruel deaths (. . .) that some Christians have suffered (. . .) in Algiers]. Although the short introduction to this work is a dialogue, the second part corresponds to the former *"memorias,"* read by Sosa's new interlocutor, Captain Jerónimo Ramírez, who, like Cervantes's Peralta in *El coloquio de los perros*, reads these papers as we read them (*Mártires*, 73; *Topografía*, III: 27).[11]

Haedo's/Sosa's work was very popular in seventeenth- and eighteenth-century France and England. His adherents praised the first part of *Topografía* "for the scrupulous exactness of the Spanish historian" (Rang, quoted by Monnereau, 365). Another Frenchman, Henri-Delmas de Grammont, acclaimed Haedo's/Sosa's "very clear and generally very accurate" account. The historian, says de Grammont, "rarely recounts an event of certain importance without invoking the authority of eye-witnesses" (*Histoire des rois d'Alger*, 15–16).[12] Sosa's three *Dialogues*, nevertheless, were considered tedious and full of fanatic religious views. English historian John Morgan, whose *History of Algiers* (1728) owes much to the *Topographia*, attacked these *Dialogues*: "excepting a few good Passages and Remarks, which I, occasionally, pick out, his three tedious Dialogues, in particular, concerning Captivity, Martyrs, and Morabboths, or Mahometan Santons, are silly enough, replete with nauseous Cant, and, in many Cases, insufferably partial" (Prologue, XXVII). Even so, Morgan recanted later, recognizing his debt to the Iberian author: "An author of whom I have made very good Use, and consequently must acknowledge my self very much his Debtor. In several parts of this History, I have delivered my real Sentiments concerning this very-often most impartial Spaniard" (*History*, 613).[13] Most of the European historians, then, focused primarily on the first part of *Topographia* and on the *Epítome de los reyes de Argel*, skipping the ensuing *Dialogues* with compelling information about the lives of Christian captives and renegades in sixteenth-century Algiers.[14] It is in these very personal *Dialogues*, bearing the mark of their protagonist Antonio de Sosa, that we find the most precious information on the character and captivity of this writer. As mentioned earlier, the attribution of these colloquies to Sosa is not new. As early as 1904, Cristóbal Pérez Pastor suggested that

Dr. Antonio de Sosa was the author of the notes that helped Diego de Haedo compose his *Topographia*.[15]

In various parts of his *Dialogues,* Sosa refers back to specific passages of *Topographia* and *Epítome de los reyes de Argel,* to the point that a critic has found marked correspondences and cross-references between these works.[16] In addition, Sosa plays with the problem of authorship, presenting a possible author for the whole work. In *Diálogo de la captividad,* while (Antonio de) Sosa and his interlocutor Fray Antonio (González de Torres) are discussing the horrendous cruelties inflicted on Christian slaves by the Algerians, the second Antonio suggests that *he* is the author of *Topographia e historia general de Argel:*

> Antonio [González de Torres]: 'Otra cosa hacen [los crueles habitantes de Argel] muy digna de notar *como dijimos más largamente en la Topografía.'*
>
> [Antonio (González de Torres): "The cruel inhabitants of Algiers do another thing, very important to note, *as we expressed at length in the Topografía."*]
>
> (II: 124; italics mine)

The passage goes on to describe the hatred felt by the Algerians, especially the renegades, toward the Christian priests, called *"papaces"* by the populace, *"contra los cuales más que contra todos los demás tienen terribilísimo odio y aborrecimiento increíble, y, por tanto, de muy mejor gana y más comúnmente los escogen y compran para quemar"* [for whom, more than for all the other slaves, they have a terrible hatred and incredible loathing and, therefore, with great gusto and more commonly they choose them and buy them to burn them] (*Topographia,* II: 124). The quoted text alludes to a section entitled "Descripción de Argel," included in the first part of *Topographia,* which explains that the death in Spain of a renegade Morisco, convicted by the law or by the Inquisition, was usually paid for in Algiers by the sacrifice of a Christian slave, preferably a priest or *papaz, "a los cuales infinitamente aborrecen y quieren mal"* [whom they infinitely abhor and detest] (*Topografía,* I: 175). The concordances between these texts not only speak to each other across Sosa's enormous treatise, linking the *Dialogues* with the "Descripción de Argel," but also confirm the existence of a single author for these works. The highlighted entry above also touches on the question of authorship, implied by the Spanish royal *we [plural mayestático]: "como* dijimos *más largamente en la* Topografía*"* [as *we expressed* at length in the *Topografía*]. This phrase may have several meanings, from the affirmation that the speaker, Antonio González de Torres, is the author of the whole work, to the playful innuendo implied by the plural *dijimos* (we said, we expressed), which could also suggest that both Antonios (de Sosa and González de Torres) are the joint authors of *Topographia, e historia general de Argel.*

Sosa's Master: Alcaide Mahamed

Sosa remained in Algiers for four and a half years, as the slave of Jewish "renegade" and city officer *Alcaide* Mahamed [Mohamed]. This renegade had converted from Judaism to Islam, then to Christianity, only to return to Islam again. His conversions recall those of the early modern Mediterranean men who lived astride the frontiers, obtaining their power from life on the edge. In regard to Mahamed's apostasies, Antonio González de Torres tells Sosa: *"He oído decir públicamente y platicar a muchos moros y turcos por todo ese Argel, que este alcaide Mahamet, el judío su patrón a ningún Dios reconoce, ni teme, ni adora; ni es moro o turco, ni judío, ni christiano"* [I have publicly heard and listened to many Moors and Turks say around this city of Algiers, that this Alcaide Mahamed, the Jew your master, does not recognize, nor fears nor adores any God; he is neither a Moor, nor a Jew, nor a Christian] (*Topografía*, II: 4). *Alcaide* Mahamed was in charge of the mint, and he apparently made counterfeit currency on the side: *"lo que todos dicen de su vida y costumbres más que gentílicas [es] [. . .] que no es [hace] otra cosa sino ocuparse días y noches en revolver moneda, contar moneda, pesar moneda, trafagar moneda, atesorar moneda, y hundir oro, plata, alquimia y hacer a ascondidas falsa moneda"* [what they all say regarding his more than gentile customs (is) (. . .) that he does nothing else but occupy his days and nights in rummaging through money, counting money, weighing money, bustling about money, amassing money, and melting gold, silver, practicing alchemy, and secretly making false money] (*Topografía*, II: 1–4, 85). As the passage suggests, Mahamed may have been also involved in usury. The Jews of Algiers indeed managed the mint, minting coins of gold, silver, or bronze. Sosa affirms that they often made counterfeit money by using alloys, false money that proliferated throughout Algiers and its provinces (*Topografía*, I: 111–12).

The *Alcaides* in Algiers were those who governed the lands and towns subject to Turkish rule, with their districts, although the title was kept by those who administered these districts for some time. Such a title was also given to anyone who held a public post in the city municipality, or in the house of the pasha. Bought or auctioned to the highest bidders, the position of *alcaide* included the very lucrative activity of tax farming attached to territorial jurisdictions, which explains why the public officials who assumed these functions usually became very rich (*Topografía*, I: 56–57). *Cayde* [Ca'id] Mahamed is listed among the twenty-three principal *alcaides* of Algiers living in 1581, thirteen of whom were renegades from all parts of the Mediterranean (*Topografía*, I: 58). Mahamed also owned a fifteen-bench corsair-galliot, which brought him additional revenues (*Topografía*, I: 90). The renegade used to recount with cynicism the story of his conversion to Christianity after he was captured by a Genoese corsair at the time of

Charles V's attack on Algiers (1541). Laughing sardonically, he would claim that he lived for fifteen years with such hypocrisy and dissimulation *"que le tenían por un santo"* [that they took him for a saint] (*Topografía*, II: 4).

The fact that the Jews were situated at the lowest point of the social echelon, even below the Christian slaves in Algiers and most cities of the Maghrib (*Topografía*, I: 111–14), may explain Mahamed's decision to convert to Islam. The mistreatment of Jews in Morocco and the Maghrib is described by a sixteenth-century traveler and writer from Granada, Luis del Mármol Carvajal: *"son los Iudíos en Affrica muy vituperados de los Moros y por doquiera que van les escupen en la cara y los aporrean, y nos les consienten traer çapatos, sino son algunos privados del rey, o de los alcaydes, todos los otros traen alpargatas de esparto"* [the Jews of Africa are extremely despised by the Moors and wherever they go they spit in their faces and beat them, and they don't permit them to wear shoes, except for some favorite or secretary of the king, or of the alcaides; all the others wear straw espadrilles].[17]

In the sixteenth and seventeenth centuries, the frontiers, although clearly demarcated, were fluid and permeable in every direction, especially so for those who had multiple identities, such as the Jews, the Moriscos, and the renegades from different points of the Mediterranean. At the time of Cervantes's and Sosa's captivity in Algiers, the Jews lived in two neighborhoods that contained around one hundred and fifty households, a figure that—at a conservative calculation of four to five people per household—gives us a population of approximately seven hundred and fifty Jews between 1577 and 1581. Some of them, according to Sosa, taught their children to write in Hebrew, as well as "in Morisco," which probably refers to Hispano-Jewish *aljamía*—writings composed in Spanish with Hebrew or Arabic characters (*Topografía*, I: 112). In effect, after the expulsion of 1492, many Hispanic Jews emigrated to the Maghrib, settling in Fez, Marrakesh, Orán, and Tetuán, among other North African cities (García Arenal and Wiegers, 38–44, 54–59). Two Jewish communities coexisted in these cities, each one keeping its language—Arabic or Spanish—its rituals and juridical traditions, and its synagogues. Numerous exiles brought with them their libraries and other precious objects. In Fez, whose Jews numbered about four thousand in the middle of the sixteenth century, the *meghorashim* [those "expelled" from Spain] were more numerous than the *toshabim* or *bəldiyin* [those from the country].[18] As Abraham Adrutiel stated in his complements to the *Safer Ha-Qabbalah* of *Rabad,* the sultan of Morocco, Mohammed Al-Shaykh Al-Watassi (1472–1505), had received the Jewish refugees with hospitality in his kingdom of Fez, "behaving kindly toward the people of Israel" (quoted by Zafrani, 216).

With his shifting loyalties, *Alcaide* Mahamed exemplifies the case of the Jewish or Christian renegades who found in the Maghrib a society in full expansion, where fortunes could be rapidly made and a man could accede to political or social positions unthinkable in Europe. Converting to another religion thus became a kind of "passport" for those whose circumstances forced them to live, literally, on the edge. Antonio González de Torres comments that *Alcaide* Mahamed inspired a common proverb in Algiers applied to astute and deceitful men: *"Malicioso y astuto como el alcayde Mahamet, el judío"* [Malicious and astute, like the alcaide Mahamet, the Jew] (*Topografía*, II: 5). These diatribes against Sosa's master, however, cagily spoken through his friend's mouth, are part of the work composed by Sosa himself.

Cayde [Kã'id] Mahamed's standing in Algiers is confirmed by the following anecdote, narrated by Sosa. After becoming *beylerbey* in 1577, Hasan Veneciano proceeded to govern aggressively with the exclusive aim of increasing his personal fortune. Elevating his percentage in the share of the corsair booty from five to seven percent, Hasan also augmented taxes enormously and seized most of the captives held for ransom from their masters. These acts would eventually lead to a rebellion of the janissaries, who requested the sultan to remove Hasan from office.[19] Renegade Mahamed was the only Algerian citizen to resist Hasan's arbitrary measures, adamantly refusing to give up his three Christian slaves—one of whom was Dr. Sosa. Although Hasan Pasha was unable to appropriate Mahamed's slaves, he retaliated in style. Mahamed's defiance *"les costó [a estos esclavos] cuatro años y medio del más terrible cautiverio que en todo Argel y en toda Berbería ha habido"* [cost these slaves four and a half years of the most terrible captivity there ever was in Algiers and in Barbary] (*Topografía*, I: 377). One can surmise that Hasan increased the price of the captives, forcing Mahamed to pay him a sizable quota of their ransom. At the same time, the public distrust felt for *Alcaide* Mahamed in Algiers discloses the social misgiving that paradoxically kept the renegades at bay. García-Arenal argues that in the Maghrib, the renegades constituted a caste with an important political and military role. In contrast, they stayed in a narrow social and political space that was their own, one particularly closed in regard to the rest of Muslim society. This place was defined in terms of client relations, or family relations with the master and the sovereign ("Conversions," 277).

As suggested above, Sosa's captivity in Mahamed's house apparently constituted the most terrible bondage. While the captive-narrator refuses to vituperate directly against his master, he makes Antonio González de Torres describe the horrors of this enslavement. Remarking that even thieves or conspirators against a king were not held in such conditions, González de Torres asks whether it is possible that a man whose only guilt is to have become the slave of a barbarian would be kept *"tan desnudo, tan hambriento, tan cargado de traviesas, atado a una piedra, encerrado tanto tiempo, solo, ascondido [sic] y soterrado en tan remoto frío, tan húmido y obscuro*

aposento; ¿hay crueldad o maldad como ésta?" [so naked, so hungry, charged
with fetters, chained to a stone, locked up for such a long time, alone,
hidden and interred in a remote, cold, humid, and obscure chamber. Can
there be cruelty or evil such as this?]. Sosa's spokesman then describes the
dark, humid hole in which the cleric was thrown three times, covered with
chains, barely coming out alive (*Topografía*, II: 3–4).

How captives were treated, in effect, depended on who their owners
were. Some private owners in Algiers kept their captives fettered in dungeons; others regarded their slaves as members of their households whose
living arrangements depended on their status in the house. Historian
Helen G. Friedman recounts that Don Miguel de Sosa (not related to
Antonio de Sosa), captured near Barcelona in 1586, spent fourteen years
as a slave of a Portuguese renegade named Morato, a corsair from
Tetuán. During his captivity, Sosa was kept in a small dungeon in his
master's house, in chains and fetters at all times, and was put to work
driving a flour mill that his master kept in his cell. He was not allowed
to speak with or to see other people, neither "Christian, Jew, nor Moor,"
and when he was finally ransomed by the Mercederians in 1609, he came
out "so weighed down with chains and misfortune and hardships that
all those present were moved" (quoted by Friedman, 71–72).[20] Similar
cases were seen in Algiers, such as that of a Corsican woman whose
master beat her continually and kept her for seven months in chains in
an underground dungeon, where she was forced to drive a mill night
and day (*Topografía*, III: 249–50). The sufferings of Christian captives,
especially their spiritual sorrows, are discussed in depth in chapter 3, dedicated to *El trato de Argel*.

Tacitly referring to Mahamed's mistreatment, Sosa declares that most
Jews treat their Christians well, except for those who have apostatized, "who
are worse than Moors and Turks." Many renegades, in effect, were cruel
to their slaves to prove that they were good Muslims. This would explain
the excessive brutality on the galleys, where most of the corsairs were renegades. In contrast, the Captive in *Don Quijote* tells of the famous renegade Uchalí (Alūj Ali), who had apostatized after being a galley slave for
fourteen years and had become admiral and later governor of Algiers:
*"moralmente fue hombre de bien, y trataba con mucha humanidad a sus
cautivos, que llegó a tener tres mil"* [morally he was a good man and he
treated his captives, sometimes as many as three thousand, with much hu-
manity]" (*DQ* I, 40). As for the Jews who owned Christian slaves, Sosa
claims that they usually did not mistreat them, because they feared that
their captives would complain to the *beylerbey* about being abused, in which
case the ruler would seize them. Now, if the Jew had converted to Islam,
the *beylerbey* could not appropriate his captives, which accounts for Hasan
Pasha's inability to carry off Mahamed's slaves (*Topografía*, I: 114). Yet in

spite of Sosa's chains and actual mistreatment in Mahamed's prison, his captivity in the large household of an important municipal officer of Algiers offered the Portuguese cleric a particularly rich vision of Algerian society at the end of the sixteenth century. The possibility of speaking to many renegades, including Mahamed's son-in-law Amud, a Kulughi, or offspring of renegades, who was one of Sosa's frequent interlocutors, allowed the cleric to elaborate a meticulous tableau of the social practices and events of the city. His statement *"cuánto pasa en Argel sé, y aun lo escribo todo, día por día"* [I know everything that occurs in Algiers, and I even take it down completely, day by day] (*Topografía*, III: 246, 253) is perhaps the most explicit testimony of Sosa's attentive collection of data for the composition of his texts.

The Maltese Connection

As previously mentioned, Antonio de Sosa was captured on the galley *San Pablo* from the Order of Malta with 290 people aboard, including various Knights of St. John, such as Fray Antonio González de Torres. Sosa's connection with the Order of Malta, to my knowledge, has not been mentioned until the present study. An entry from the Records of the Venerable Council of the Order of Malta, dated 9 July 1577, reveals that *"Antonius de Sosa et Andreas de Sosa, fratres, qui capti fuerunt cum triteme S. Paolo nuncupata et captivi sunt apud infideles, in gradum militum Prioratus Portugaliliae recepti sunt"* [Antonio and Andreas de Sosa, brothers, who were captured on the galley named San Pablo, and are captives among the infidels, have been received in the grade of knights by the Priory of Portugal] (*Liber conciliorum*, Archives 95, f. 4v.). In chapter 1 we discussed the Order of St. John of Jerusalem, a Christian military institution established in Malta in 1530 by Charles V, after the loss of Rhodes to the Ottomans. From this island the Christian knights sailed the entire western Mediterranean in pursuit of Muslim ships—Ottoman galleons or Algerian light vessels—that they captured and took back to Valletta.

The Order of St. John of Malta was divided into three classes: knights, chaplains, and sergeants of arms or serving brethren (religious men but not priests) who served the knights either at war or in the hospital. There were also seven tongues or "Langues" in the order, which, in order of precedence, were those of Provence, Auvergne, France, Spain, Italy, England, and Germany.[21] The entry into the Order of St. John as a novitiate knight was preceded by production of proofs of nobility, the examination of which gave rise to an inquest (Sire, 92). After this inquest, a nobleman was admitted into the Order of Malta as a "Knight of Majority," entering the novitiate at an age of between sixteen and twenty. After a twelve-month novitiate, the knights took simple vows, performed their Caravans (expeditions of at least six months on the order's ships), and could take solemn vows at the age of twenty-one. The average knight spent years in Malta serving on the numerous congregations that administered the order, and above all—if he could afford the expense involved—seeking the command of a galley or sailing ship, which was the most conclusive title of all (Sire, 83).[22]

The Latin entry cited above refers to the promotion of the Sosa brothers, following their capture on the *San Pablo*, to the dignities of the Order of St. John in the quality of knights ascribed to the Priory of Portugal. This means that the Sosa brothers were Portuguese, because to belong to any priory of the order, one had to have been born in that particular nation. Various entries in the *Liber conciliorum de la Cassière* between 1577 and 1581, while Sosa was a captive in Algiers, disclosed the deliberations of the general chapter (council) of the order in regard to Antonio and Andrea de Sosa's nobility, as well as that of knight Antonio González de Torres, *"penes infidelis detentorum"* [detained in the hands of infidels] (Mitzi, 782, 783, 796–97, 830).[23] This would suggest that Antonio de Sosa and his brother Andreas might have been on their way to Malta to become knights when they were captured.

There appears to be an error, however, in these data. Although Andreas de Sosa Coutinho was officially admitted as a Knight of St. John on August 21, 1580, after being liberated from captivity, his brother Emanuel de Sosa Coutinho, also captured on the *San Pablo*, was never received as a knight of Malta.[24] The Sosa Coutinho brothers, moreover, did not have another sibling named Antonio. The Antonio de Sosa of these documents thus seems to be Emanuel de Sosa Coutinho, later known as Fray Luis de Sousa, who became a famous Portuguese writer. In effect, Emanuel de Sosa Coutinho remained in prison for a year, after which he obtained permission from Hasan Pasha to travel to Spain, leaving his brother a hostage in Algiers until he collected the money for their ransom (Astrana Marín, III: 575–81). Cervantes mentions this specifically in *El trato de Argel*. He recalls that the Sosa brothers—who were confined with him in the *beylerbey*'s *baño*—ransomed themselves on their word of honor and kept their word like gentlemen by punctually paying their ransom to Hasan Pasha (*Trato*, IV.2362–65). The writer would later turn Manuel de Sosa Coutinho into a Portuguese character in *Persiles*, where he has him die of unrequited love.

As for Dr. Sosa's identity, there are two possibilities. A person called Frei Antonio de Sosa (or de Sousa) was admitted as a Knight of Saint John on December 22, 1540. Such a man might well have been Cervantes's friend and the author of the *Topographia*. His profession as a knight in 1540, when he would have been 21 to 24 years old, would make him 58 to 61 years old in 1577, which seems plausible given the respect with which Dr. Sosa was regarded by the Christian captives of Algiers. This conjecture, however, is problematic, for Dr. Sosa is never mentioned in any documents as a Knight of St. John; he is always referred to as "Dr. Sosa" by both Spanish friars and slaves—a title that refers to his status as a doctor in law. Sosa was also called *"papaz"* by Ahmed's son-in-law Amud, which alludes to Dr. Sosa's statute as an ecclesiastic. The consideration with which he was regarded by Spanish priests and ecclesiastics is revealed by Fray Juan Gil's words in the *Información de Argel*, in which he acknowledges receipt of Dr. Sosa's handwritten affidavit on behalf of Cervantes: *"Digo yo, fray Juan Gil, de la orden de la Santísima Trinidad y redentor de captivos por su Magestad en este Argel, que yo conosco al Dr. Antonio de Sosa, al presente captivo en este Argel, porque familiarmente le tracto y converso todo el tiempo que a [sic] que estoy en Argel; y que sé que es de tanta honra y de tal calidad, que en todo lo arriba dicho [Sosa] no diría sino la pura verdad, como quien es"* [I, Fray Juan Gil, from the Order of the Holy Trinity, ransomer of captives in this Algiers on behalf of His Majesty, state that I know Dr. Antonio de Sosa, presently a captive in Algiers, because I deal with him familiarly and converse with him all the time that I have been in Algiers; and that I know he is so honorable and of such qualities, that in what he has declared above he would say nothing but the pure truth, as the man he is] (*Información*, 166; Sliwa, 111).

Hence, until other documents are found in the archives of Malta on Sicily, we may surmise that Dr. Sosa might have been an ecclesiastic related to the Order of St. John of Malta.[25] Until then, we must rely on the rich information deriving from Sosa's *Dialogues*, from his testimony on behalf of Cervantes, consigned in the *Información de Argel*, and from a handful of other papers, such as a letter written in Latin in 1578 to Pope Gregory XIII and other leaders demanding the ransom of Mercederian monk Fray Jorge Olivar.[26] Sosa's *Dialogues*, in particular, demonstrate his enormous erudition, which covered the classics, from Plato to Pliny and Cicero, among others; the Holy Scriptures; and the fathers of the church, from St. Paul and St. Jerome to St. Augustine, to name only a few. Sosa knew Greek and Latin well and was adept in Hebrew, which he also read and wrote (*Topografía*, III: 196).

In regard to Sosa's liberation, an undiscovered petition directed to the Spanish court requesting the exchange of a corsair named Arnaut, imprisoned in Castilnovo (Naples), for Dr. Antonio de Sosa, a captive in Algiers, seems to have been made in 1580. Sola and de la Peña conjecture that Cervantes—who had been liberated in October of that year and had been in Madrid since December 1580—might have brought the request to the court. Nevertheless, the Order of St. John of Malta could also have intervened in this affair through Grand Master Jean l'Evesque de la Cassière, who was in close contact with the Spanish court, or through the viceroys of

Naples and Sicily.[27] In February 1581, the court wrote to the viceroy of Naples, Juan de Zúñiga, requesting him to investigate the matter of the exchange of Dr. Antonio de Sosa for corsair Arnaut and to advise them as to the convenience of accepting such a deal. Zúñiga responded to the king on June 9, 1581, with detailed information on Arnaut, a Genoese renegade who had been incarcerated in Tuscany for fifteen years. The corsair should not be released, alleged the viceroy, because of his experience as a seaman and connoisseur of the Italian coasts (Sola y de la Peña, 181–82).[28] Sosa's petition to the Spanish crown was thus denied. Nevertheless, he would be freed at the end of 1581. In effect, Dr. Sosa seems to have been ransomed after October 1581, when the information consigned in *Topographia* ceases to bear his characteristic mark—that is, his obsession "with accuracy and exactness" (Camamis, 89, 133–34; Sola, "Renacimiento," 32). The data given in the story of Hasan's retaliation against *Alcaide* Mahamed and his slaves confirm these dates, because Sosa claims that Mahamed's defiance cost these poor slaves four and half years of captivity, which coincides with the period elapsed between April 1577 and October 1581.

Various documents, in fact, place Antonio de Sosa in Madrid between December 1581 and February 1582. In the first notarized statement he appears as *"vecino de Madrid"* (a resident of Madrid), while in the third document, dated 3 February 1582, he simply seems to be in the city: *"estante en Madrid"* (Pérez Pastor, I: 235–37). During these months in the bustling city, he probably saw his friend Cervantes, who was back from his mysterious reconnaissance journey to Orán, realized in 1581 for Philip II's secret services. Several affidavits, subscribed in December 1581 and January and February 1582, show Dr. Sosa in the process of acknowledging a payment of one thousand three hundred twenty *reales* from María Ramírez, for the ransom of her daughter Mariana, a captive in Algiers, and obliging himself to help in this business over and above the sum received. María and Mariana Ramírez were related to Captain Jerónimo Ramírez from Alcalá de Henares, Sosa's interlocutor in *Diálogo de los mártires*. Captain Ramírez was among those captured in 1577 on the galley *San Pablo*, along with his widowed sister and niece (Pérez Pastor, I: 235–37). After February 1582, we lose track of Dr. Sosa, because he died probably at that point or soon after, and his monumental work, left in the hands of archbishop Haedo, appeared thirty years later under the name of Diego de Haedo.

Sosa's and Cervantes's Algiers

Beyond Sosa's close relation with Cervantes, my interest in captive Antonio de Sosa centers on the conditions of his captivity in Algiers and his insistence on reading and writing, regardless of the difficulties encountered. In spite of the differences regarding their situations as captives, there were points of contact between Sosa and Cervantes, such as the love for books and letters they shared and the multiple conversations they maintained on literary matters. Both Sosa and Cervantes were elite captives, held for exorbitant ransoms, the first, because he was probably a member of the Order of Malta, whose usually rich and belligerent members were the scourge of the Algerian corsairs; the second, because he was mistakenly identified as an important personage, close to Don Juan de Austria. Sosa, as we know, was the household slave of renegade Mahamed, who kept him chained in a room and sometimes hired him out to the municipality of Algiers for construction work. The cleric had two companions of captivity—another ecclesiastic and a Knight of St. John, both unnamed (*Topografía*, I: 377).

Cervantes, on the other hand, first owned by the corsair Dalí Mamí and then by Venetian renegade Hasan Pasha, seems to have had some periods of relative freedom between his incarcerations, when he was heavily fettered and covered with chains. A document subscribed on December 18, 1580, in Madrid, after Cervantes's release from slavery, reveals that during his captivity, Cervantes was forced to borrow more than two thousand *reales* from various Christian merchants who arrived in Algiers, "*para comer y otras cosas para pasar su cautiverio, porque el moro que le tenía cautivo no le daba de comer en todo el tiempo en que fue cautivo*" [to eat and for other things during his captivity, because the Moor who held him captive never fed him during the time in which he was a slave] (Pérez Pastor, I: 67; Sliwa, 114). Sixty years later, Emanuel d'Aranda, a Flemish captive in Algiers between 1640 and 1642, confirmed that his master Ali Pégelin did not feed him but that slaves were allowed to have three to four hours a day to make a living (*Relation*, 36).[29] D'Aranda also borrowed money from various merchants and repaid them with high interest, after his liberation (*Relation*, 39–40). Was Cervantes obliged to fend for himself, like other captives? Did he earn money in secretarial work, transcribing documents or writing letters for other captives? Astrana Marín believed that Cervantes may have served as a messenger or household servant for his master Dalí Mamí (II: 476–77). These questions remain open.

We learn both from Sosa's *Dialogues* and from the *Información de Argel* that despite the severe restrictions imposed by renegade Mahamed, certain visitors were permitted to call on Sosa in his cell. The names and identities of some of these callers, many of whom were Christian slaves who reported to Sosa about the daily happenings in Algiers, and the frequent displacements of these captives, including Cervantes, evoke a universe where communications appeared to be fluid, where conversations and encounters between the Muslim and Christian sides seemed quite free. The consequences of these interactions cannot be underestimated for Cervantes. This great fluidity of information and circulation of human beings is an essential element for understanding the early modern period and its actors in Algiers. Focusing on some of the men who participated in this complex North African frontier world, such as the frequent visitors who called on Sosa in his house-prison, may illuminate this issue: a series of unnamed galley slaves who recounted their sufferings to the chronicler with tears in their eyes (*Topografía*, II: 96); Knight of St. John Fray Antonio González de Torres, a slave of the renegade Maltrapillo and Sosa's interlocutor in *Diálogo de la captividad* (*Topografía*, II); Captain Jerónimo Ramírez, a slave of a Morisco renegade, and Sosa's converser in *Diálogo de los mártires;* an envoy of Mercederian monk Fray Jorge Olivar, who sent Sosa a chasuble and some church ornaments so that they would not be defiled after the cave affair involving Cervantes (*Información*, 159); Mahamed's son-in-law Amud, who is Sosa's interlocutor in *Diálogo de los morabutos* (*Topografía*, III: 193–273); captive *maestro* Cristóbal de Villalón, a frequent caller, who told Sosa the incredible story of the consecutive deaths of his master's eight children, all choked by demons (*Topografía*, III: 219)[30]; renegade Girón, known as El Dorador, who visited the clergyman at the time of Cervantes's second escape attempt, swearing before Sosa and his master Mahamed that he did not betray the fugitives (*Información*, 158); defrocked Dominican Juan Blanco de Paz, who attempted to pass before Sosa as an official of the Spanish Inquisition (*Información*, 164); a group of furious Christian captives who proposed to kill Blanco de Paz by stabbing him for his treason in the last escape attempt planned by Cervantes (*Información*, 160–61); Valencian merchant Onofre Exarque, who informed Sosa of his intention to ransom Cervantes and send him to Spain, after the failed escape of September 1579 (*Información*, 161–62); Fray Juan Gil, head of the Trinitarian rescue mission, who stated that he treated Sosa "with familiarity" and often communicated with him when he was in Algiers (*Información*, 166); and Cervantes himself, who visited Sosa and discussed poetry and other subjects with him, when they were not plotting escapes together (*Información*, 157, 160, 163).

Beyond these conversations, we must remember that Sosa shared his fate with two other Christian slaves, who surely lived in Mahamed's quarters. In his *Diálogo de los morabutos*, Sosa mentions various inhabitants of this large household that apparently also accommodated some of Mahamed's renegades. Besides an Italian (Roman) renegade named Jaffer, who was being taught to read and write in Arabic by a *Morabuto* or Muslim holy man, there were other houseguests: a French renegade called Mustafá, who died around 1579; a Greek renegade named Baluco Baxí Farat; an unnamed female captive from Corsica, whose cousin was also a slave in Algiers; an old Spanish slave called Pere Jordán, who was the porter of the compound; and an anonymous slave who was Sosa's companion (*Topografía*, III: 234, 243–49). To the diversity of this lively household we should add the Christian captives who continually visited Sosa. Even if these visits were stretched over a period of four years, we may surmise that they were representative of the life of elite Christian captives in Algiers at the end of the sixteenth century. Sosa's multiple encounters with men of every social class and provenance, from the lowliest Christian galley slave to knight Fray Antonio González de Torres and Trinitarian monk Fray Juan Gil, among others, give an impression of the meetings between Christian slaves, as well as between captives and renegades, Turks and Jews in Algiers.

Sosa attests not only to his close friendship with Cervantes but also to their familiar conversations during their captivity in Algiers: *"todo el tiempo que a [sic] que estoy captivo en Argel, que son tres años y ocho meses, lo conozco [a Cervantes] y he tratado y comunicado muy a menudo y familiarmente [con él]"* [all the time that I have been a captive in Algiers, which is three years and eight months, I have known him (Cervantes) and have very often dealt with him and communicated with him in a familiar way] (*Información*, 156). On at least two occasions, Cervantes invited Sosa to participate in an escape. Let us recall Cervantes's second escape attempt of 1577—the cave episode—recounted by Sosa in *Diálogo de los mártires de Argel*, a plan frequently discussed by both men: *"Yo fuí uno de los que con el dicho Miguel de Cervantes comunicó muchas veces y en mucho secreto el dicho negocio; y que para el mismo negocio fui muchas vezes convidado y exhortado, y no se hizo cosa en el tal negocio que particularmente no se me diese dello parte"* [I was one of those who often communicated in heavy secrecy with Miguel de Cervantes about the said business, and for this business I was invited several times and exhorted to come, and nothing was done in this business that I was not particularly informed of]. Sosa even claims that while the fugitives were hiding in the cave, Cervantes would visit him to let him know what was happening, *"importunándome muchas veces que yo también me encerrase con los demás en la dicha cueba; y el día que se fue él [a] encerrar en ella se uino despedir de mí"* [begging me many times to hide with the others in the said cave; and the day he went into hiding in it he came to say good-bye to me] (*Información*, 157).

The cleric's testimony also points to Cervantes's amazing mobility in Algiers, one that allowed him to visit other captives, renegades, and foreign merchants, when he was not fettered in the *baño* for attempting to escape. Granted, some of these outings occurred in his master's absence, such as the comings and goings connected with the episode of the cave, between April and September 1577, when Dalí Mamí was at sea engaging in privateering (*Topografía*, 1: 85–86). The relative freedom of Cervantes in the streets of Algiers is especially emphasized by Sosa's account of the conspiracy of September 1579, in which the cleric played a relevant role. Sosa was not only one of those who was to go in the sixty-bench frigate *"porque el dicho Miguel de Cervantes comunicó muchas vezes el negocio con-*

migo, dándome relación de lo que hacía y ordenaba [. . .] y me convidó a ser uno de los que en dicha fragata habían de ir" [because the said Miguel de Cervantes often shared the affair with me, informing me of what he was doing and ordering (. . .) and he invited me to be among those who were to go in the said frigate]. He was also one of the masterminds of the escape: *"Y así, no se trató cosa alguna sobre este negocio [la evasión] que él [Cervantes] y los dichos mercaderes no tratasen y consultasen conmigo, y tomasen mi parecer y consejo sobre ello"* [And, thus, nothing was discussed regarding this business (the escape) that he (Cervantes) and the merchants did not discuss and consult with me, asking for my opinion and advice on it] (*Información*, 160). If these claims underline the deep friendship and affinities that linked Antonio de Sosa and Miguel de Cervantes, they also reveal the profound respect felt by Christian captives for the ecclesiastic, a central figure among the enslaved community of Algiers. As I have shown in these pages, slaves and renegades from all social strata and conditions visited Antonio de Sosa continually and consulted him on crucial questions often involving issues of life and death.

"Arms and Letters" in Algiers

More than one critic has suggested that Cervantes began drafting his play *El trato de Argel*, which ends with a prayer to the Virgin Mary recited by a chorus of captives, in Algiers, or that he composed some of the poems scattered throughout *La Galatea* while in captivity, two possibilities that cannot be overlooked. Sosa's constant references to his own life as a Barbary slave may pry open some further perspectives on the intellectual endeavors of the captive Cervantes. Even though he was chained to a rock in Mahamed's house-prison, Sosa had books on hand and regularly took advantage of his solitary confinement to read pious and serious works (*Mártires*, 1–4; *Topografía*, III: 1, 13-16). Particularly revealing are the opening lines of *Diálogo de los mártires*, in which captain Jerónimo Ramírez greets Sosa with this question: *"De manera que ¿siempre que acá vengo le he de hallar ocupado en los libros?"* [So, every time I come, must I find you occupied with books?]. Sosa's answer confirms that he spent much time reading: *"en una soledad como ésta y en un encerramiento tan apartado de toda plática y conversación en que este bárbaro de mi patrón me tiene, ¿qué major ocupación que leer libros santos y buenos?"* [In a solitude such as this, and in an imprisonment so closed off from every talk and conversation in which this barbarian, my master, keeps me, what better occupation is there than reading saintly and good books?] (*Mártires*, 55; *Topografía*, III: 1). The book Sosa is then reading tells the life of St. Paulino, bishop of Nola, a friend of St. Augustine. Fourth-century St. Paulino spent all his fortune rescuing captives and, finally, offered himself in exchange for a young slave, kept by Vandal king Genseric in Carthage (*Mártires*, 65; *Topografía*, III: 15–19). Through his dialogue with Captain Ramírez, Sosa constantly alludes to St. Augustine and St. Gregory and to numerous Greek and Roman authors whose works he probably cites by heart. In another revealing passage of *Diálogo de los morabutos*, Sosa shows his friend, renegade Amud, a copy of Joan León's *Descripción del África*, a book he is studying, loaned to him by a Muslim from Granada brought up in Fez (*Topografía*, III: 201).

In spite of his imprisonment, moreover, Sosa took time to study Algerian society and to interview many renegades about Maghribi history. In no other way could he have written the minute descriptions of Algerian life and customs consigned in *Topographia* or the history of the Turkish-Algerian rulers recounted in *Epítome de los reyes de Argel*. We know that since the first day of his arrival in Algiers, Sosa wrote continuously, reporting, among other things, how many captives entered the city, and how they came (*Topografía*, III: 253). In *Diálogo de los morabutos*, renegade Amud expresses his admiration for Sosa's prodigious memory concerning the remedies prescribed by a Muslim holy man to cure his daughter, who was possessed by evil spirits. He asks Sosa: *"¿Más cómo tienes esas cosas en la memoria? Es cierto que estudias en ellas todos los días y noches"* [But, how do you keep these things in your memory? It is true that you study them every day and night] (*Topografía*, III: 213). The meticulous Sosa, in effect, recalled each and every part of the medicines prescribed by the *marabout*, which involved a red rooster, cooked in a certain way, and then placed with its head, feathers, and entrails in a special pot next to the river. The passage gives Sosa the opportunity to denounce Algerian medicine, which he deems to be nothing but fraud. These anecdotes illuminate a complex cultural network in Algiers. The existence of this cultural network is confirmed by Sosa's frequent allusions to the time he spent reading and writing, as well as conversing about literary matters with other slaves, especially Cervantes, and by his references to the abundant ethnographic data he collected during his captivity. Such issues open many questions in regard to Cervantes's life and intellectual activities in Algiers.

The introduction to Sosa's *Diálogo de los mártires* is, accordingly, a hymn to the book, an exaltation of the classic and Christian traditions to which Sosa is tributary. The discussion on books that opens this work not only echoes the praise of books made by Don Quijote but also suggests that madness can be caused by reading gentile books. As an allegory of reading, Sosa recounts the story of the sacking of Pavia, Lombardy, by the general of Francis I's armies, Monsieur de Lautrech (1527). After a terrible assault, the French soldiers took the city of Pavia, killing everyone at hand. Some Gascon soldiers entered by force the house of a Neapolitan druggist and drank all the sweet medicines and electuaries they found in his house: *"y a poco perdieron unos el juicio, otros el sentido, otros enfermaron terriblemente"* [and soon some lost their sanity, others their senses, others got terribly sick] (*Mártires*, 59). The message is clear: Like the sweet medicines drunk by the soldiers, pagan or questionable books could cause madness and even death. Sosa's style, however, cannot be more radically opposed to that of Cervantes, for the cleric generally seasons his arguments with an unbearable list of quotations from *"toda la caterva de filósofos"* [the whole herd of philosophers], as Cervantes would later say in his prologue to *Don Quijote*. Yet Sosa's literary connections with Cervantes cannot be overlooked.

For Sosa, as for Cervantes, *"es impossible que de todo libro [. . .] no se saque algún fruto y provecho"* [it is impossible that from any book (. . .) one may not obtain some fruit and benefit] (*Mártires*, 57). Granted, this is a Renaissance topic, one particularly exploited by Golden Age Spanish writers. Books are especially gifted teachers: *"si el que trata con ellos antes era bueno, hácese con ellos mejor; el prudente, muy más sabio; el discreto, muy más entendido"* [if he who deals with them was good before, he becomes even better; if prudent, even wiser; if discreet, much more learned and proficient] (*Mártires*, 59; *Topografía*, III: 5). Many of Sosa's phrases, in effect, evoke popular Cervantine formulations, such as the idea of fiction as a garden that nurtures the spirit. In Sosa's words, *"aquellos [libros] que enseñan y nos muestran el bien vivir en cualquier modo, forma, estilo, y artificio que sea, todos y cada uno de ellos [. . .] no son menos que unos lindos y ricos jardines; en los cuales el juicio, paseándose y discurriendo con atención, va cogiendo lindas y suavísimas flores"* [those books which teach and show us how to live in whatever way, form, style, and artful device, each and every one of them are nothing less than beautiful and rich gardens; where judgment, walking around and passing with attentions, goes about collecting beautiful and very gentle flowers] (*Mártires*, 59). This text evidently recalls the prologue to the *Novelas ejemplares*, where Cervantes proposes through an allegory that fiction offers the human psyche a much needed spiritual break: *"horas hay de recreación donde el afligido espíritu descanse. Para este efeto se plantan las alamedas, se buscan las fuentes, [. . .] y se cultivan, con curiosidad, los jardines"* [there is time for recreation, when the tormented spirit can rest. That is why poplar groves are planted, springs are made into fountains, (. . .) and gardens created in wonderful design].[31]

Sosa is never more eloquent in his praise of books and reading than in the following passage of *Diálogo de los mártires*: *"la lectura es donde la memoria se renueva, el juicio se despierta, la voluntad se inflama y todo el hombre toma aliento y recibe fuerzas animosas para proseguir el bien y pasar más adelante"* [reading is where memory is renewed, judgment awakened, the will is inflamed and the whole of man catches his breath and receives strength to do good and to move forward] (*Mártires*, 57). Beyond his penchant for classical citations, Sosa's prose is the clear Castilian of the Golden Age, written in a personal tone. His views on wisdom are expressed in the famous adage: "*tres cosas hacen a un hombre sabio, prudente y discreto: o tratar con los que son tales, o peregrinar muchas tierras, o leer muchos libros de filósofos*" [three things make a man wise, prudent, and discreet: to deal with men who have those qualities, or to travel through many lands, or to read many philosophy books]. Cervantes would later write in *Persiles*: "*el ver mucho y el leer mucho aviva el ingenio de los hombres*" [seeing much and reading much arouses the wit of men] (II, 6: 187).

While books were probably scarce in Algiers, in spite of the numerous volumes captured from Christian ships and galleons, many Spanish and Italian captives were men of letters, as was presumably the Morisco educated in Fez who read Leo Africanus. Sosa confirms these facts: "*Hartos buenos ingenios y aun doctísimos en todas buenas artes y ciencias tenemos cautivos hoy en día en Argel, y que cautivan cada día los corsarios desta tierra*" [We have many good minds, and even very cultured minds, in all the arts and sciences today, as captives in Algiers, and whom the corsairs of this land capture each day] (*Topografía*, II: 80). Attesting to the presence of a large crowd of learned captives—ecclesiastics, religious men, priests, lawyers and jurists, doctors, teachers, and preachers of various languages and nations— Sosa counted a total of sixty-two cultured Christian slaves in 1579 Algiers: "*¡Cosa jamás vista en Berbería!*" [Something never seen in Barbary!] (*Mártires*, 71; *Topografía*, III: 24). On the contrary, the chronicler laments the utter lack of refined intellects among the upstart Algerian society, fashioned by renegade corsairs from all over the world, Turks, and Moors: "*Tratamos con gente muy diferente, muy agreste y bestial, que ni saben qué cosa sea culto y ornamento de ingenio, ni de otra cosa hacen caso, sino de la crápula y lujuria, y de vivir como animales del campo*" [We deal with very different people, very savage and bestial people who don't know what are culture and ornaments of the intellect, and are only interested in licentiousness and lechery, and living like farm animals] (*Topografía*, II: 81).

Such a view, of course, was that of many early modern Europeans who represented Turks and Moors as the embodiment of lust and barbaric ignorance. This point may be linked to one more aspect of Western stereotyping, the presentation of Saracens, Moors, and Turks as incarnations of evil. The stereotype of the devilish Moor or cruel Turk was often employed by the Europeans to demonstrate the iniquities of Islam and to portray Muslims as agents of Satan.[32] A typical example is that of priest Pierre Dan, a captive in Algiers in the 1630s, whose *History of Algiers* abounds in curious stories of cannibalism—devoured cadavers—horrendous tortures, and indescribable horrors. Its title speaks for itself: *Histoire de la Barbarie, et de ses corsaires. Des royavmes, et des villes d'Alger, de Tvnis, de Salé, & de Tripoly [. . .] Ov il est traitté de levr govvernement, de leurs moeurs, de leur cruautez, de leur brigandage, de leurs sortilèges [. . .]* [History of Barbary and of its corsairs. Of the kingdoms, and the cities of Algiers, Tunis, Sale, & Tripoli [. . .] Which discusses their government, their customs, their cruelty, their brigandage, their spells . . .].[33] Certain Europeans, however, saw Islam in a different light. As confirmed by Cervantes's fictions, it was difficult for learned Europeans who had lived in close contact with the Muslims to demonize Islam in such a crude way. The case of Antonio de Sosa is a special one. If it is true that his captivity was one of the worst seen in Algiers, Sosa was also a fanatically religious man, determined to prove the evils of Islam and the tortures perpetrated by the Algerians on their slaves. In spite of this, his *Epítome de los reyes de Argel*, which presents the history of the rulers of Algiers since its foundation to the last years of the sixteenth century, is a balanced work of investigation that shows a careful and impartial historian at work.

As for the existence of Muslim intellectuals in sixteenth-century Algiers, not many learned men appear in Cervantes's fictions or in Sosa's descriptions of this freewheeling society, distinguished by its cultural crossbreeding and its hybrid lingua franca, which was a mixture of all Mediterranean languages. An exception in this case was *beylerbey* Ramadān Pasha, the owner of Rodrigo Cervantes, who ruled Algiers between 1574 and 1577. Described by Sosa as a just, honorable, peaceful, and generous man who had an orderly family life, this ruler was extremely dedicated to his books: *"Hombre de buen gobierno [. . .], y muy aficionado a la licción [lectura] de libros arabescos y turquescos y de su ley. En los cuales, de continuo, ocupaba el tiempo que los negocios le vacaba"* [A man of good government (. . .), very fond of reading Arabic and Turkish books, and books of his law [religion], in which he continuously occupied the time that his affairs left him free]. His physical description completes this portrait: "Ramadān Pasha was a man of fifty-five years, [. . .] dark-skinned, well bearded and with black hair, with a round face, and with both eyes a little cross-eyed" (*Topografía*, I: 374). This ruler governed for three years with such equity and justice that no one complained: *"En este tiempo estuvo Argel en la mayor tranquilidad y sosiego que nunca"* [In this time Algiers had the greatest tranquility and peace ever experienced] (*Topografía*, I: 370).

Hasan Pasha was also described as a cultured man, although neither Cervantes nor Sosa mentions this. We have already encountered this personage in relation to Cervantes's last three escape attempts. Hasan's career is another example of meteoric success in the Turkish-Maghribi corsair society. Hasan Veneciano, whose Christian name was Andreta, was captured as a young man in a Slavonic vessel where he was assistant to the ship's scribe (*Topografía*, I: 374). Taken to Tripoli, he became the slave of a galley soldier who made him apostatize. After his master died, he came to be the property of corsair Dragut, and at the latter's death in the siege of Malta (1565), he passed on to the famous corsair 'Alūj Ali, called Euchalí or Uchalí by the Spaniards. Thriving under 'Alūj Ali's patronage, Hasan was soon promoted to tax collector, official accountant, and bursar during 'Alūj Ali's Algerian government (1568–1571). Sosa attributes these rapid advancements to Hasan's qualities: *"siempre fue astuto, entremetido, audace [audaz], atrevido y desenvuelto"* [he was always astute, a meddler, audacious, daring, and savvy]. These traits were enhanced by *"otras bellaquerías de turcos"* [other wickednesses of the Turks], which made him *"muy querido de Ochalí"* [well loved by 'Alūj Ali], a phrase that alludes to Hasan's reputation for sexual diversity. When 'Alūj Ali was made *kapudan pasha* of the Ottoman fleet, Hasan followed him to Istanbul (*Topografía*, 1: 374–75).

In June 1577, Hasan Veneciano returned to Algiers as the new *beylerbey* appointed by the Ottoman Sultan. His arrival was received with optimism by the principal Spanish agents in the city. In a letter to Philip II written in October 1577, a Valencian merchant and informer to the king, Francisco Gasparo Corso, calls Hasan *"muy grande amigo mío y de Andrea mi hermano"* [a very good friend of mine and of my brother Andrea]. He adds that Hasan *"es un hombre muy leído y sabe muy bien escribir y contar en nuestra lengua, que es la más principal cosa que pueda tener, ansí para reconocerse el error grande en que está, como para poderle tratar en cartas y avisos secretos"* [is a very well-read man and he knows very well how to write and count in our language, which is the best possible thing that one could have, not only to recognize the errors into which he has fallen, but also so that we can deal with him through secret letters and warnings]. In his conversations with Gasparo Corso, Hasan presumably claimed that he "did not believe in the religion of Mohammed," being "more of a Christian than a Moor," and that he hoped to return soon to his country (SIHM, England 1, 1: 258; Oliver Asín, 285–86).

The five Gasparo Corso brothers were important Corsican merchants who ran an agency that coordinated diplomatic activities between the northern Mediterranean states and the Muslim countries. Their headquarters were in Valencia, a meeting point for diplomats and couriers across the Mediterranean. The agency engaged in the translation of dispatches for various courts and in negotiations over commercial transactions between Europe and the Islamic world. While Francisco resided in Valencia, Andrea, the most famous of the brothers, managed the Algerian office, where he became the intimate adviser of exiled aspirant to the Moroccan throne 'Abd al-Malik, whom we briefly encountered in chapter 1. After 'Abd al-Malik acceded to the throne in 1576, Andrea followed him to Marrakesh and became the sultan's agent with the Spanish and Portuguese governments. The rest of the three Gasparo Corso brothers settled, respectively, in Algiers, Marseilles, and Barcelona, points from which they managed the family affairs (García-Arenal, "Textos," 168–69; Sola y de la Peña, 110; Yahya, 47).[34]

As for Hasan Pasha, his mother tongue was Tuscan, which explains why he communicated so well with Francisco and Andrea Gasparo Corso, the last of whom was well known by Cervantes. Could we infer that in his encounters with Cervantes, Hasan also used the Tuscan language, which Cervantes knew from his travels and sojourns in Italy? If Hasan's "letters" perhaps encompassed only the realm of official correspondence with various heads of governments, he performed quite well in this area, as attested to by a courteous letter written in April 1579 to Henri III of France, in which Hasan firmly deplores not being able to accept the new consul sent to replace Captain Maurice Saurou, French consul in Algiers, *"la chose répugnant à l'esprit des marchands, du peuple, et de tous"* [the thing being repugnant to the spirit of the merchants, of the people, and of all] (*Correspondance des Deys*, 1–2). The question of Hasan's cruelty to captives is discussed in other chapters of this book. This approximation to the renegade ruler focuses instead on aspects of his culture and his relation with influential Turks and Europeans. Be that as it may, Cervantes paints two very different pictures of the Venetian renegade who saved his life three times: The first portrait appears in *Don Quijote*, where the Captive calls him *"homicida de todo género humano"* [murderer of the entire human race] (I, 40), a view that corresponds to that painted by Sosa and most of the early modern Christian chroniclers.[35] The second depiction, inserted in *Los baños de Argel*, is a more tempered perception of Hasan Pasha, here represented as an indulgent man capable of administering justice and of ordering that no harm be done to Tristán, a comic character accused by a Jew: *"No le hagan mal a este cristiano"* [No harm should be done to this Christian] (*Baños*, III.2536).

'Abd al-Malik of Morocco

Another Algerian personage known for his culture and sophistication was the famous 'Abd al-Malik of Morocco (1541–1579)—called Muley Maluco by the Spaniards. 'Abd al-Malik was exiled to Constantinople and Algiers during the reign of his brother, Sultan 'Abd Allah al-Galib bi-llah (1557–1574), who was inclined to dispose of his siblings. Around 1574, 'Abd al-Malik married the daughter of powerful Ottoman official Hājjī Murād in Algiers—she was the historical beauty who inspired the characters of Zoraida and Zahara in Cervantes's *La historia del cautivo* and *Los baños de Argel*.[36] Fray Luis Nieto, an eyewitness in the battle of Alcazarquivir, or Battle of the Three Kings, in which Don Sebastian of Portugal, 'Abd-al Malik of Morocco, and his nephew Abu 'Abd Allah Muhammad lost their lives, affirms that 'Abd al-Malik *"hablaba nuestro español muy claro, y lo escribía; sabía también la lengua italiana muy escogidamente, y la lengua turquesca la hablaba mejor que ninguna, dejado su lenguaje natural, que era arábigo, en el cual era muy singular poeta"* [spoke Spanish very clearly, and he also wrote in the same language; he also knew the Italian language admirably well, and spoke the Turkish language better than any other, besides his natural language which was Arabic, in which he excelled as a poet] (*Guerras*, 454).[37] Cervantes probably met this famous member of the Sā'di dynasty during his first months of captivity in Algiers, when 'Abd-al Malik was recruiting troops for his invasion of Morocco.[38] Can we suppose, like one of Cervantes's biographers, that on learning about the captive's gift for writing or reciting poetry, 'Abd al-Malik invited him to his palace (Navarro Ledesma, 92–93)? In any case, Cervantes presents a very positive image of this personage in his play *Los baños de Argel*, through captive Osorio:

> Muley Maluco [. . .]
> El que pretende ser rey
> de Fez, moro muy famoso
> y en su secta y mala ley
> es versado y muy curioso.
> Sabe la lengua turquesca,
> la española y la tudesca,
> italiana y francesa,
> duerme en alto, come en mesa
> sentado a la cristianesca.
> Sobretodo es gran soldado,
> liberal, sabio, compuesto,
> de mil gracias adornado.

> [Muley Maluco ('Abd al-Malik) (. . .)
> He who aspires to be King
> of Fez, a very famous Moor,
> well versed and conscientious
> in his doctrine and perverse law.
> He knows the Turkish language,
> the Spanish and the German,
> the Italian, and the French (languages).
> He sleeps on a bed (on high) and he eats at a table,
> seated in Christian style.
> Above all, he is a great soldier,
> liberal, wise, composed,
> adorned by a thousand graces.]
>
> (*Baños*, III.2595–2607)

This image of 'Abd al-Malik alludes to 1575 or 1576, during Cervantes's first years of captivity in Algiers, when the pretender to the Sā'di throne was still living in the city and enlisting adepts for his invasion of Morocco and

Fez (*"el que pretende ser rey/de Fez"*). The vivid description of the future sultan suggests that Cervantes might have met this famous personage in Algiers. His portrait of 'Abd al-Malik agrees with that of Fray Luis Nieto: "a very ingenious and very wise man, discreet in everything" (*Guerras*, 454).[39] As implied by Cervantes, the European customs of 'Abd al-Malik must have seemed bizarre to the Turkish and Moorish population of Algiers, who generally slept on animal skins or mattresses laid down on the ground and ate at very low tables, without chairs. In 1577, the English ambassador to Marrakesh, Edmund Hogan, alluded to the sultan's love for European music, which made him bring English musicians to Morocco (Oliver Asín, 258–59). Fray Luis Nieto confirms that 'Abd al-Malik "knew how to strum various instruments and to dance very gracefully" (*Guerras*, 455).

At ease in various cultures, 'Abd al-Malik took care to enhance his image for the Europeans, as revealed by his relations with Elizabeth I of England, Henry III of France, and Philip II of Spain, among other rulers. A panegyric celebrating 'Abd al-Malik's accession to the throne in July 1576 was published in Valencia through the mediation of Viceroy Vespaciano Gonzaga Colonna and of Andrea Gasparo Corso, in November of the same year.[40] The text, composed in Spanish by a Dominican who was in the service of the sultan, shows that 'Abd al-Malik was lobbying for favor at the Spanish court. Certainly, 'Abd al-Malik's captivating personality and his skillful diplomatic maneuvers with European states and churches seem to have impressed most European observers. His subjects, however, tended to see him as an Islamic revisionist, and his Ottoman patrons—from whom he was trying to free himself—viewed him as one who engaged in *jihād* (holy war) activity (Yahya, 72–73).

The rulers described above serve to illustrate the charisma radiating from certain cultured personages in Algiers at the time of Cervantes's captivity. The question of books and letters in this multiethnic city is a complex one, especially so because of the lack of reliable information on the subject. As it turns out, if we compare the literary and intellectual atmosphere of the most important Maghribi cities, particularly Algiers, in the sixteenth century, with the intellectual ambiance and love of books existent in the Ottoman Empire, we have to concede that Constantinople was the foremost of the Ottoman capital cities. These questions, especially relevant from the standpoint of Cervantes's experiences in Barbary, are explored in the following section.

Books and Manuscripts in the Ottoman Empire

According to Sosa, in sixteenth-century Algiers, a city mainly engaged in corsair and merchant activities, learning was probably limited to the primary schools where children learned the Koran by heart. Many of the famous Algerian ra'īs, in effect, came from humble origins, generally from peasant or fishermen stock around the Mediterranean. In contrast, several of the Turkish admirals attached to the Porte were known for their scientific achievements and literary endeavors. Such were Pīrī Re'īs and Sīdī'Alī Re'īs, two of the commanders of the squadrons with which Süleymān conquered many cities on the coasts of Arabia, Persia, and the northwest of India. Pīrī Re'īs was the author of a dazzling world map depicting the new continent of America, based on one made by Columbus and on various Portuguese charts, as well as of two exceptional geographical treatises, one on the Aegean and the other on the Mediterranean. Sīdī 'Alī Re'īs was a poet as well as a sailor, and besides his productions in verse, he composed a description of his travel overland to Constantinople from Guzerat [Gudjarāt], where his fleet had been damaged. He was the author of several mathematical and nautical treatises and of a valuable work entitled *Muhīt*, on the navigation of the Indian Ocean, which he drew from the best Arabian and Persian authorities of his time.[41] Ottoman literature flourished in the time of Süleymān the Magnificent (1520–1566), an enlightened and educated man who was also a brilliant poet. Although only a small minority of the Ottoman population could read, nearly all composed poetry and participated in public contests reciting their compositions. The greatest of the Ottoman lyric poets, Mahmmūd 'Abd al-Bākī the Immortal, sang during the reign of Süleymān, as did nine other famous poets who vied with 'Abd al-Bākī for the favor of the sultan. One hundred and fifty fine poets adorned this literary reign at Constantinople. Three hundred more illuminated the distant provinces of the empire. There were excellent historians, such as Minister of Foreign Affairs Ferīdūm Beg and Persian Lari, who wrote various histories of Ottoman campaigns and compiled a collection of state papers containing eight hundred forty documents from the eleven Ottoman sultans to Selim II (1566–1574).[42]

Early modern Constantinople, moreover, revealed a bookish culture and a prosperous book trade that, in spite of the absence of printing, involved collectors of richly illuminated manuscripts. Many of these books were held in the religious libraries attached to the great mosques or the imperial libraries founded by the sultans and their entourage. In 1534, *kapudan pasha* Khair ad-Dīn Barbarossa, whom we studied in chapter 1, became the founder of a private library at the service of readers, to which he bequeathed twenty books (Bilici, 49). Private collectors either belonged to the military class—at the top of the social hierarchy—or were members of the judiciary (Uluç, 86).[43] Passing through Istanbul between 1589 and 1590, Moroccan ambassador Abû-l-Hasan 'Alîb Muhamad al-Tamghrûtî affirmed: "There are enormous quantities of books in Constantinople. Libraries and markets overflow with them. Books from every country in the world arrive in the city. We took with us a great number of them full of interest" (quoted by Hitzel, 20). The coffeehouses, or *kahvehane*, that opened in Istanbul in 1555 with immediate success showed this Ottoman penchant for bookish culture. Describing these coffeehouses, which numbered fifty at the end of Süleymān's reign (1529–1566), historian Ibrâhîm Peçevi noted: "Certain men of the learned class [. . .] used to get together in groups of twenty or thirty in each of the *kahvehane*. Some read books and elegant treatises, others played backgammon and chess. Others brought their barely-finished poems and engaged in discussions regarding art (quoted by Hitzel, 31).[44] The existence and circulation of exceptional books, and the evocation of the places where public reading was encouraged in Istanbul, attest to the strong activity associated with literary endeavors in Ottoman society during the second half of the sixteenth century.

In the Maghrib, the sixteenth century brought about internal wars among aggressive rulers. The most important cities, such as Fez, Marrakesh, Tlemcen, Algiers, and Tunis, constituted themselves into independent territories, while the countryside was in the hands of Berber and Arab tribes who often attacked travelers. As discussed in chapter 1, the turn of the century also delivered the first batch of Spanish and Portuguese conquerors into the region. These incursions created the circumstances that enabled the Ottoman Turks, posing as the defenders of Islamic lands against the invasive banners of Christianity, to establish a foothold on the Maghribi coast and to impose themselves as the rulers of the Hafsid and Zayyanid states. In Morocco, the Portuguese threat led to the access to power of the Sharifian dynasty, that of the Sā'dis. The intervention of Muslim and Christian corsairs who allied themselves with the two great powers that dominated the Mediterranean aggravated the anarchy that reigned in these territories. As a result, intellectual life in the region suffered enormously. The sclerosis of intellectual activities revealed itself through the general abandonment of the profane sciences, while, in the religious ones, the rigid stand of the *marabouts* (holy men) and their followers reflected the spirit of intolerance that swept over the region at the end of the fifteenth century, one that lasted until the eighteenth century with the wars of Muslim and Christian privateers (Abun-Nasr, 142–43).

Despite his diatribes against the Algerians and the inhabitants of Barbary, Sosa recognized the famous schooling in the human sciences in Islam and the work of philosophers, doctors, and astrologers in Muslim Spain, such as Avicenna [Ibn Sīnā], Averroes [Ibn Rushd], Rasis (historian Ahmad ar-Razi, the Moor), and Avempace (philosopher Ibn-Baja), among others. Sosa's allusions to these Andalusian scholars and philosophers, joined to his biased commentaries on Algerian culture, paradoxically point to the continuum that connected al-Andalus with the Maghrib for centuries, affirming the cultural solidarity and continuous exchanges between the two Mediterranean shores. With every retreat of Islam in Spain, the Maghrib collected a good number of Andalusian intellectuals. The fall of Granada in 1492 accented this spiritual and historical participation, one ironically highlighted by the book that Sosa was reading in 1579, *Della descrizione dell'Africa* (1550), composed by Leo Africanus (*Topografía*, III: 201–04).

Leo Africanus's work appeared among the collection of travel accounts published by Giovanni Ramusio, entitled *Delle navigationi e viaggi* [*Of Navigation and Voyages*] (1554). Leo's *Africa* was an instant best-seller, soon translated into French and Latin, among other European languages. Juan León el Africano—Leo Africanus, as he was called by Pope Leo X after his conversion to Christianity—was born in Granada between 1489 and 1495, with the name of al-Hasan b. Muhammad al Wazzān al-Fāsī (the man of Fez), also known as al-Gharnāthī (the Grenadine). Following the Conquest of Granada, his family emigrated to Fez, then the seat of Arabic learning. At the time, there was an abundance of Arabic scholars in Fez who studied not only the best writers in their own language but also translations of the Greek and Roman authors. Leo studied Arabic letters in one of the two schools of the city described in his work, besides Koranic theology and grammar, rhetoric, poetics, law, philosophy, and history. His constant allusions to recondite Arabic writers, and also to the Latin classics, make his English translator John Pory claim in 1600 that Leo "was not meanely but extraordinarily learned" (*Geographical Historie*, 5).[45] Around 1510, Leo joined the entourage of Sultan Muhammad al-Burtughali (1505–1524), the ruler of Fez. Many of Leo's wanderings across the Maghrib, and through Constantinople, Egypt, Arabia, Babylonia, and parts of Persia, were conducted while carrying out diplomatic missions on behalf of the sultan. Returning to Morocco by sea, he was captured by Sicilian corsairs and presented to Pope Leo X, Giovanni de' Medici, who had him catechized and later baptized. During his stay in Italy, Leo taught Arabic at Bologna and wrote other scholarly works. His firsthand geographical and ethnographic descriptions of the lands visited at the beginning of the sixteenth century turned him into one of the most cited geographers of the early modern period (Épaulard, *Description de l'Afrique* v–ix; *Encyclopedia of Islam* [*EI-2*], II: 723–25).

The depiction of Leo's travels in the Maghrib provides a cultural panorama of the region for the first part of the sixteenth century. His description of the great city of Fez is among the most enchanting pieces of his work. Endowed with running water that flowed abundantly through the city, Fez was also graced by two- and three-story houses, many public baths with running hot and cold water, hospitals, and hotels, as well as more than seven hundred mosques and oratories. In the imposing mosque of al-Karawiyyīn, one of the most highly regarded centers of Muslim religious learning, renowned professors taught Islamic law to the people from dawn to sunset (*Description de l'Afrique*, I: 182–85). There were eleven theological colleges in Leo's time, some with one hundred boarding rooms for students, such as the exquisite Medersa Bou Anania, constructed by Marīnid Sultan Abu 'Inan between 1350 and 1357.[46] Leo Africanus laments that the permanent wars that ravaged the Maghrib in the first quarter of the century depleted the colleges, greatly limiting the students' stipends, so that intellectual life had declined since he had left North Africa, not only in Fez, but in all the cities of the Maghrib (*Description*, I: 186–87).

At the turn of the sixteenth century, there were approximately thirty bookstores in Fez, among the multiple stores surrounding the great mosque (*Africa*, I: 192). In regard to Marrakesh, Leo Africanus deplores that the two hundred shops of sale-books that once existed around the Mosque of Kutubīya [mosque of the libraries] disappeared with the civil wars, so that "at this time, there is not a single book-seller in the whole city to be found" (*Africa*, I: 102). Although the Almohads built schools and libraries and brought from Spain the most illustrious scholars, philosophers, and physicians to Marrakesh, such as Ibn Rushd (Averroes), who died in Fez in 1198, these great traditions did not survive the dynasty. In the beginning of the sixteenth century, the library of the Almohad palace was used as a poultry house, and the madras built by the Marīnids was in ruins (*EI-2*).

Famous Flemish grammarian Nicholas Clénard [Clenardus], who sojourned in Fez for a year in 1541, learning Arabic and attempting to buy books, recounts that even though there were so many men of letters, he saw no bookstores in the city, only bookstalls installed on Fridays by the Great Mosque. There, each week, after the prayer, there was an auction sale of books and ancient manuscripts. This merchandise was intensely sought, and all tried to auction it at the greatest prices. As for the Christians and the Jews, Clénard claims that they could not enter this place unless they wanted to be stoned to death, so scrupulously "jealous are the Muslims over their manuscripts vis-à-vis those who do not practice the religion of Mohammed."[47] Clénard's commentary explains the harsh beating suffered by Antonio de Sosa some twenty-five years later in Algiers, when he attempted to handle a beautiful book that turned out to be the Koran, an anecdote we shall discuss shortly.[48]

And yet, despite the civil wars that ravaged Morocco in the sixteenth century, books continued to be dearly appreciated by its rulers, as the theft of the sultan of Morocco's library reveals. In 1612, owing to the triumphs of his opponent, religious leader Ibn Abi Mahalli, Sultan Muley Zidan had to leave Safi, taking refuge in Sus, in the south of Morocco. He rented the ship of Provençal captain and French consul Jean Phillipe de Castelane and asked Castelane to transport his belongings to Santa-Cruz do Cabo de Gué, Agadir, where the sultan would meet him with his entourage. Castelane instead sailed for France with the treasures. En route to France, the ship was attacked and captured by Don Pedro de Lara, a Spaniard, who took the booty to Spain. The greatest part of this booty was the private library of the sultan, which contained about four thousand books and exquisite manuscripts collected by his father. In 1614, the books were deposited in El Escorial, where they remain even today, constituting one of the most important Arabic funds of Europe.[49] This anecdote closes our literary excursion through Constantinople and parts of Morocco, a detour that enlightens the complex cultural situation of the Maghrib during the sixteenth century. The intellectual decline of the region discussed by Leo Africanus and other authors explains the possible shortage of books and of Muslim intellectuals in Cervantes's and Sosa's Algiers.

A Handsomely Bound Book, Carried by a Black Slave

The above lines point to some of the problems presumably encountered by Christian captives in Barbary. Most of the books found in the region were probably Islamic religious treatises, which were barred from the Christians. These books were written in Arabic, a language that most Christians did not know how to read. Very few Christian slaves, in fact, took it on themselves to learn Turkish or Arabic. One exception involved Jean Parisot de la Valette, the famous Knight of St. John who became the grand master of the Order of Malta in the 1560s (1557–1568). During his earlier captivity in Barbary, La Valette learned Arabic and Turkish, languages that, according to Brantôme, he spoke fluently (*Oeuvres*, VI: 248).[50] Another involved Father Jerónimo Gracián de la Madre de Dios, Santa Teresa's confessor, who relates that during his captivity in Tunis, he became friends with a Spanish renegade who began to teach him to read and write in Turkish, a language the renegade knew well (*Tratado de la redención*, 67).

These cases, however, seem to be rare. It was the renegade, in fact, known for his knowledge of various languages and cultures, who generally crossed geographical and religious boundaries, serving as translator, secretary, or agent for various Maghribi or European rulers. Such was the case with Samuel Palache, a Jewish adventurer who moved back and forth from Morocco to Spain serving different masters, finally crowning his career in Amsterdam around 1610 as an agent of the sultan of Morocco (García Arenal and Wiegers, 169). We may recall from Cervantes's *La historia del cautivo* that protagonist Ruy Pérez de Viedma is forced to appeal to a renegade from Murcia, familiar with Arabic, to read the letters sent by the Moorish Zoraida and to write back to her in Arabic.[51] At the same time, while only a handful of Christian captives and renegades were able to read and write in Arabic or Turkish, European books, written in Spanish, Italian, French, or Latin, were probably scarce in Algiers. It is fair to surmise that some of the educated Christian slaves attempted to obtain those hard-to-find books, either by buying them from the corsairs or, like Antonio de Sosa, by borrowing them from other educated Christians or Muslims. The obsession with books in Algiers is suggested by the anecdote involving Sosa, mentioned above. During his first days as a slave, dejected and disconsolate, he happened to glimpse, on the other side of the street, a handsomely bound book, carried by a black slave, who belonged to learned *beylerbey* Ramadān Pasha. Thinking that it was one of the volumes captured on the galley *San Pablo*, where he was abducted, Sosa ran across the street, excitedly calling to the slave, and attempted to examine the book, which happened to be the Koran, an audacity for which he was harshly beaten and insulted (*Topografía*, III: 263). The Algerians apparently believed that letting a Christian slave touch the Koran even with a finger was a grave sin, claims Sosa, and that reading before him, so that he could hear what the sacred text said, was even a worse crime. How can a Christian who does not know Arabic, asks Sosa, understand the things consigned in that book (*Topografía*, III: 236)?

In spite of these difficulties, Sosa was able to obtain books, as well as ink, pen, and paper in sufficient quantities to consign the monumental historical and ethnological information contained in *Topographia, e historia general de Argel*, including his *Dialogues* on captivity. Another friend of Cervantes's, jurist Bartholomeo Ruffino de Chiambery, contrived to write, while imprisoned in the *beylerbey*'s *baño*, a bulky history of the fall of La Goleta and Tunis, dedicated to Duke of Savoy Filiberto Emanuele, a work begun in 1575 and kept in hiding until he sent it to the duke in February 1577. The poor captive hoped to find a favorable climate for his liberation with his work (Astrana Marín, II: 527). A doctor in both law and canon law, Ruffino de Chiambery was captured in the attack on the forts of La Goleta and Tunis by the Turks in September 1574. If his position as an auditor of the Italian armies at Tunis and La Goleta spared him from becoming a galley slave, he was nevertheless kept in the *beylerbey*'s *baño* and obliged to do hard labor in the defensive ditches of Algiers.[52] Cervantes wrote the laudatory poems for the work composed by his companion of captivity.

These encounters with books, pen, and paper open new questions in relation to the quotidian experiences of captive Cervantes. Was he, like his friend Sosa, able to write and obtain books, or like Sosa and Ruffino de Chiambery, capable of acquiring ink, pen, and paper for his compositions? Dr. Sosa's revelations about the literary compositions of Cervantes, which they shared and discussed over the course of three years and eight months, and the mention of other Cervantine writings suggest that he was. We might assume that in spite of the difficulties involved, a captive who, among other feats, was able to smuggle a letter out of the *beylerbey*'s *baño* or to compose various poems and letters while heavily chained in prison—a writer who would later say *"soy aficionado a leer aunque sean los papeles rotos de las calles"* [I am fond of reading even the scraps of papers from the street] (*DQ* I, 9)—would have found ample possibilities to solve a "minor problem" such as this in a cosmopolitan city like Algiers.

A Man of Great Valor and Constancy

Sosa's close friendship with Cervantes, as well as his social and religious acquaintances in Algiers, induces us to explore another dimension of Cervantes's life, namely, his relation to other captives. The *Información de Argel*, with its twelve witnesses of every social class, metier, and education, offers a wide portrait, drawn from different angles, of Cervantes's character and social relations. The presentation of an *Información*, or notarized affidavit, was a common procedure for Christians who returned from slavery in Barbary. When a Spanish captive in Algiers or any other Muslim city was ransomed, he would write an *Información* on his life and habits during his captivity, not only on his personal services, but also as a proper justification vis-à-vis the civil authorities and the Inquisition of having sustained his Catholic faith and not having renounced it among the infidels. Let us recall that the men who lived in Muslim territories as captives became immediately suspect to the Spanish authorities who were not able to accept the freedom of thought tolerated in the Maghrib (Sola and de la Peña, 204). The *Información*, then, was a "passport" that would allow the repatriation and social reintegration of the freed captive. Often drawn in Algiers proper, like Cervantes's affidavit, other *Informaciones* would be formalized before a notary on returning to Spain. Such were the legal statements signed by Alonso de Contreras and his father, Juan de Contreras, who stayed in Algiers as a hostage for Don Martín de Córdoba (1572); by Jerónimo de Aguiar, who signed a *Relación* in Bizerta, where he was a captive (1574); by Sebastián de Santiago, a captive in Algiers (1575); by Captain Miguel de Mutillón, who served for fifty-three years in Tlemcen, Mostagán, Orán, and other Spanish enclaves (1588); and by Luis Díaz, a captive for fourteen years in Algiers and Constantinople, who escaped with another four hundred Christian slaves during an uprising (1590).[53] Cervantes's *Información de Argel* is thus in line with the procedures commonly carried out by Christian captives after being released from captivity.[54]

On the other hand, the *Información de Argel* is much more than this. It includes a copious collection of testimonies assembled by Cervantes as a defense against the slander campaign launched by Dr. Juan Blanco de Paz, the defrocked Dominican who betrayed the group involved in Cervantes's last escape attempt to Hasan Veneciano.[55] I discussed in chapter I the sabotage of Cervantes's fourth escape attempt by renegade Blanco de Paz. It is believed that this defrocked Dominican betrayed the group of fugitives out of resentment because he was not invited, or accepted, as part of the escapees (Canavaggio, *Cervantes*, 93). Hence, Blanco de Paz sent a Florentine renegade named Juan to inform Hasan Pasha about the plot. After the treason, Blanco de Paz apparently disseminated vicious rumors in relation to Cervantes and intimated that he was elaborating a report on these and other matters for the Spanish Inquisition, which he claimed to represent in Algiers. As mentioned before, Blanco de Paz visited Antonio de Sosa in his cell, passing himself off as an officer of the Inquisition, but he was not able to provide proofs of his investiture when Sosa required them (*Información*, 160–61).

The motive for the defamation of Cervantes and others seems to have sprung from Blanco de Paz's irascible character and his fear of retaliation on the part of the organizer of the plot, Miguel de Cervantes. In any case, there is a unanimous consensus in the testimonies that constitute the *Información de Argel* regarding Blanco de Paz. Two captives who had befriended him before the treason, Rodrigo de Chaves from Badajoz and Domingo Lopino from Sardinia, draw an image of a choleric and violent individual who once slapped the face of two other clerics and even kicked them in anger (*Información*, 62, 125–26). A vengeful and resentful man, Blanco de Paz appeared to be also a cheat—various witnesses speak of bribes offered to concoct malicious reports—and a liar who shamelessly accused captive Dr. Domingo Becerra of double-crossing the Christians before Hasan Pasha (*Información*, 88–90). As a renegade, Blanco de Paz had much to gain from this betrayal, which could have earned him the favor of the Algerian ruler. Nevertheless, Alonso Aragonés claims that the reward received by Blanco de Paz for his treason was one gold *escudo* and a pot of grease (*Información*, 69).

The twelve witnesses of the *Información de Argel* clearly present a Manichean view of the two antagonists: while Blanco de Paz emerges in these depositions as an evil figure, capable of treachery and other villainies, Miguel de Cervantes appears as a spirited and generous captive, always ready to help his comrades. We must remember, however, that most of the men who testified in this inquiry were involved in the escape attempt organized by Cervantes. The betrayal, then, could have had grave consequences for them, including the death sentence. Some of these captives even talked of stabbing and killing Blanco de Paz (*"matarle y darle de puñaladas"*) as a revenge for his perfidy, but they were dissuaded from this by Dr. Sosa (*Información*, 161). Their resentment and anger against this Judas is thus understandable. As Dr. Sosa clearly states, *"el dicho juan blanco tenía por enemigos a todos los que entraban en este negocio y heran [sic] dél participantes"* [the said Juan Blanco had made enemies of all those who engaged in this business and were participants in it] (*Información*, 161).

Concomitantly, if there was a general consensus among these men in relation to Blanco de Paz, there also was a rare agreement that transcended simple friendship and concerted obligations regarding captive Miguel de Cervantes. Ensign Diego Castellano from Toledo, who had known the maimed soldier for ten years, even before they had arrived in Algiers, affirmed that *"[Cervantes] ha vivido con mucha limpieza y honestidad de su persona y que no ha visto en él ningún vicio que engendre escándalo a su persona y costumbres"* [Cervantes has lived in a clean and honest way and that he (Castellano) has not seen any vice that breeds scandal either on his person (Cervantes's) or his customs] (*Información*, 81). Some of the witnesses obviously asserted that Cervantes was a good Christian who confessed and received Communion when the Christians were accustomed to do so, who always defended the Catholic faith, and who comforted and encouraged many slaves so that they would not become renegades (*Información*, 70–71). I do not doubt Cervantes's religious beliefs, which were probably sincere. Leaving aside the issue of Cervantes's religiosity—reiterated opinions that various critics see as obligatory in the context of a group who feared the power of the Inquisition—I would like to focus, instead, on the human dimensions of such testimonies.

Hernando de Vega, fifty-eight years old, a slave of Dalí Mamí, and a captive for much longer than Cervantes, declares that the former soldier *"fue tenido en mucha reputación y corona [. . .] respecto de haber sido hombre de mucho ánimo y constancia"* [was greatly esteemed and held in high respect (. . .) in regard to having been a man of great valor and constancy]. Vega adds that

por ser el dicho Miguel de Cervantes persona natural y lustrosa, demás de ser muy discreto y de buenas propiedades y costumbres, todos se holgaban y huelgan tratar y comunicar con él admitiéndole por amigo [. . .], así los muy reverendos padres Fray Jorge de Olivar, [. . .] como [. . .] Fray Juan Gil [. . .] como los demás cristianos, así caballeros capitanes, religiosos, soldados.

[Because the said Miguel de Cervantes is such an ingenious and enlightened person, besides being very discreet, and of good qualities and customs, all were and are happy to deal and communicate with him, receiving him as a friend (. . .), such as the very reverend priests Fray Jorge de Olivar (. . .) and Fray Juan Gil (. . .), as well as the rest of the Christians, gentlemen, captains, religious men, and soldiers.]

(*Información*, 98–99)

A sensitive witness who paints the view of the popular slave sectors of Algiers, Hernando de Vega speaks of other commoners, like him, who befriended Cervantes: *"gentes de la comunidad, que lo quieren y aman y desean por ser, de su cosecha, amigable y noble y llano con todo el mundo"* [people of the community who like and love him and want to be with him, because he is genuinely friendly, noble, and unassuming with everyone] (*Información*, 99). Juan de Balcázar, from Málaga, claims that Cervantes's valor in aiding various renegades to escape *"merece premio y galardón"* [merits a prize and the public's esteem], an anecdote discussed in chapter 1. Balcázar concludes that *"caballeros, letrados, y sacerdotes huelgan de tratar con el susodicho Cervantes"* [gentlemen, jurists, and priests are happy to deal with the said Cervantes]" (*Información*, 106). Fernando de la Vega, from Toledo (no relation to Hernando), states that Cervantes *"es de buen trato y conversación"* [has a very pleasant manner and conversation] (*Información*, 123). Another witness insists on the captive's continuous associations with educated men: *"Le he visto tratar y conversar con los más principales cristianos de esta esclavitud, sacerdotes, magistrados, religiosos, caballeros, y capitanes y otros criados de su majestad, con mucha familiaridad"* [I have seen him deal and converse with the principal Christians here enslaved, priests, jurists, religious men, gentlemen, captains, and other servants of his Majesty, with great familiarity] (*Información*, 70).

Luis de Pedrosa, a thirty-seven-year-old resident of Marbella, is an enthusiastic devotee of Cervantes: "*En todo Argel, [aunque] [. . .] haya otros caballeros tan buenos como él, [. . .] en extremos tiene especial gracia en todo, porque es tan discreto y avisado que pocos hay que le lleguen"* [In all of Algiers, although (. . .) there are other gentlemen as good as him, (. . .) he has such extreme grace in everything, because he is so discreet and well informed, that there are few who match him]. Pedrosa is especially impressed by Cervantes's relations with "*caballeros, letrados, comendadores y capitanes religiosos"* [gentlemen, jurists, commanders, and knights of the religious orders]. He confirms that Fray Juan Gil, head of the Trinitarian rescue mission, then in Algiers, not only liked to converse with Miguel de Cervantes but often invited him to his table; for instance, on October 14, 1580: "*este testigo ha sabido que hoy, en este dicho día, le convidó a comer"* [this witness has learnt that today, on this very same day, he (the priest) invited him to dinner] (*Información*, 142). The emphasis of the witness ("today, on this very same day") suggests how amazed he was by this invitation.

"A Particularly Fine, Noble, and Virtuous Person"

The issue of Cervantes's dinner with Fray Juan Gil was also underlined by another witness, recently arrived and already ransomed Diego de Benavides, a twenty-eight-year-old from Baeza. Benavides had come from Constantinople with the successor of Hasan Veneciano, Jaffer Pasha, a Hungarian eunuch and courtier, privileged by the support of the Turkish sultan. Having just arrived in August 1580, Benavides could testify only about Cervantes as a person, because he did not know the facts of his captivity. He claims that on reaching Algiers, he negotiated his ransom and proceeded to rescue himself. As soon as he was a free man, he asked other Christians for the names of the gentlemen with whom he could communicate:

> Y le respondieron que principalmente estaba uno muy cabal, noble y virtuoso, y era de muy buena condición y amigo de otros caballeros, lo cual se dijo por el dicho Miguel de Cervantes. Y así este testigo lo buscó y procuró [. . .]. Luego [. . .] Miguel de Cervantes, usando de sus buenos términos, se le ofreció con su posada, ropa y dineros que le sirviese; y así, lo llevó consigo y lo tiene en su compañía, donde comen de presente juntos y están en un aposento donde le hace mucha merced. En lo cual este testigo halló padre y madre, por ser nuevo en la tierra, hasta que Dios sea servido que haya navíos para irse a España ambos dos, él y dicho Miguel de Cervantes que también está rescatado y franco.

> [And they answered him that there was a particularly fine, noble, and virtuous person, of good character, and a friend of other gentlemen—which was said in reference to the said Miguel de Cervantes. And thus, this witness looked for him and found him (. . .). Then (. . .) Miguel de Cervantes, making use of his good manners, offered his help and his lodgings, clothes and money to help him; and thus, Cervantes took him with him and kept him in his company, where they presently eat together, and they are in a lodging where Cervantes is very kind to him. Accordingly, this witness found a father and a mother, because he was new to the land, until God wills that there would be ships leaving for Spain, for both of them, himself and the said Miguel de Cervantes, who is also ransomed and free.]

> (*Información*, 133–35)

Cervantes, of course, was a free man at the time of the inquiry conducted on his behalf, as Benavides maintains in his affidavit. This enabled Cervantes to help Benavides with clothes and moneys and to offer him his hospitality. As Sola and de la Peña suggest (253), it is impossible to visualize a more touching story of friendship and solidarity between two captives than the one recounted by Diego de Benavides.[56]

The most moving declaration regarding Cervantes, however, comes from the popular strata of Christian slaves in Algiers, from Sardinian captain Domingo Lopino, forty-six years old, who had known Cervantes for four years, ever since Lopino arrived from Constantinople as a captive. Captain Lopino alleges that he was a "participant in the business" of the escape by boat planned for fall 1579, *"de lo cual, por no venir a la obra, perdió su libertad, que la esperaba y tenía por momentos por cierta"* [due to which,

because the escape had failed, he had lost his freedom, which he had expected and envisioned for moments as certain] (*Información*, 110). If it
often seems that Lopino is struggling with words, barely confirming what
is asked of him, in a crude language made of set phrases, the situation
changes when questions of honor and appreciation of his own worth are
asked. Then, the rough captain from Sardinia, who has been a captive for
years in both Constantinople and Algiers, breaks into an incredible mono-
logue bursting with dramatic force, which deserves to be cited at length:

> Este testigo, por ser persona de calidad y que ha servido a su magestad treinta
> años [. . .] en [. . .] su real servicio, como ha sido de capitán y de pesquisidor
> en el reino de Cerdeña, que son ocasiones honrosas y calificadas, por donde
> este testigo debe ser inclinado a tener mucha reputación en frecuentar y
> comunicar con los semejantes. Y, así, [. . .] dese[a]va y procuraba de allegarse
> y juntarse con el dicho Miguel de Cervantes, respecto de que, de ordinario
> [. . .] lo [. . .] veía tratar con caballeros, capitanes, comendadores y letrados
> y religiosos y otros criados de su magestad. Porque [. . .] veía este testigo
> que de todos éstos [. . .] [Cervantes] era querido, amado, reputado, y esti-
> mado. Y cuando veía tan notoriamente, a este testigo le daba cierta especie
> de envidia en ver que cuán bien procedía y sabía proceder el dicho Miguel
> de Cervantes [. . .]. Porque cierto, [. . .] [Cervantes] ha tratado muy virtuosa
> e hidalgamente; y no solamente todos los que he dicho, [. . .] mas [a] los
> padres redentores que han venido a hacer rescate, como fue el padre Fray
> Jorge de Olivar, y el muy reverendo padre Fray Juan Gil de la Corona de
> Castilla. Los cuales le han admitido, ansí en conversación como en haberlo
> sentado a su mesa, de lo cual tomaban contento. Y visto por este testigo,
> holgaba de tener por amigo al dicho Miguel de Cervantes y alcanzar de su
> buen trato y conversación, porques [sic] cierto de quererlo y amarlo, por
> merecerlo.

> [This witness, because he is a man of quality who has served his majesty for
> thirty years (. . .), in royal offices, such as being a captain and investigator in
> the kingdom of Sardinia, which are honorable and qualified occupations, be-
> cause of which this witness must be a person inclined to have a high reputa-
> tion in frequenting and communicating with his fellow men. And thus, (. . .)
> he wished and tried to approach and affiliate himself with the said Miguel de
> Cervantes, because, ordinarily, (. . .) he saw him deal with gentlemen, cap-
> tains, governors, jurists, and religious men, as well as with other servants of
> his majesty. Because (. . .) this witness could see that Cervantes was liked,
> loved, respected, and esteemed by all. And when this witness saw this so
> clearly, he felt a certain envy to see how well the said Miguel de Cervantes
> behaved and knew how to behave (. . .). For certainly, (. . .) [Cervantes] has
> treated these men in a very virtuous and gentlemanly way; and not only those
> I have alluded to (. . .), but the fathers who have come to negotiate ran-
> soms, such as was Fray Jorge de Olivar, and the very reverend Fray Juan Gil,
> from the Crown of Castile, who have admitted him, not only to their con-
> versation but also to their table, from which they received pleasure. And all
> of this seen by this witness, he enjoyed having Miguel de Cervantes as a friend

and winning his very pleasant manner and conversation, for it is certain that
he is liked and loved, because he deserves it.]

(*Información*, 112–13)

This eloquent testimony evokes the image of the speaker as a brave, some-
what rustic man who gave an inordinate importance to his public image.
Probably because of his humble origins on the island of Sardinia, Captain
Lopino seemed fascinated by the world of influential men, to which he
would have liked to accede. His rapture with hierarchies surfaces in the
overblown presentation of himself as a captain with a distinguished career
at the king's service, and in his naive confession regarding the envy he felt
for Cervantes's success among elite captives and priests in Algiers.

More important, Lopino's testimony illustrates Cervantes's civility and
innate graciousness, which allowed him to deal with men of every social
station, from the ransomer priests who invited him for dinner to illustrious captives, such as aristocrat Knight of St. John Fray Antonio de Toledo—who assisted the Cervantes brothers in the second escape attempt—
to learned scholars and poets, such as Dr. Sosa and Antonio Veneziano,
down to the popular strata of Christian galley slaves and renegades from
different Mediterranean countries. As many testimonies reveal, these dis-
parate groups of men accorded their respect, friendship, and even their
love to the captive Cervantes. The fact that these witnesses rendered their
testimony at Cervantes's request by no means invalidates their declarations.
Reading these affidavits in a discerning way, as I have attempted to do in
these pages, opens the legal documents of the *Información de Argel* to the
nuances and revelations offered by each witness. In effect, the eclectic,
multicultural visions of the twelve witnesses who testify in this inquest illuminate distinct facets of Cervantes's character, presenting a kaleidoscopic
portrait of the captive. Above all, the different perspectives lead us to infer
that Cervantes's conversation and tactfulness captivated men of all social
classes and conditions. Could we not say that this conversation reflected
the qualities and style of the captive Cervantes, the same qualities reflected
in Cervantes's novels? "The style shows the man" (*stylus virum arguit*),
says a Roman adage, reiterated in the well-known French dictum: *"Le style
est l'homme même"* [Style is man himself]. The style that emerges in these
testimonies on behalf of the former captive Cervantes speaks of a clear intelligence, a special ingenuity and determination, a natural kindness, a
critical conscience, and a comprehension of human frailties, among other
qualities. Certainly, the picture that arises from the *Información de Argel*
emphasizes, on the one side, Cervantes's courage, the unwavering resolution and boundless energy that drove him to undertake extreme ventures—
such as the four escape attempts in which he barely escaped death—and,
on the other, his generosity and consideration for his fellow captives, his
genuine tact and politeness, and, finally, his love for poetry and literature.

This love for poetry and literature surfaces in Cervantes's associations with poets, scholars, and men of letters in Algiers, such as Dr. Sosa and other friends from the *baño*.

The Ransom of Miguel de Cervantes

Up to now, I have focused principally on the Algerian world in which Cervantes lived for five years, leaving aside the bureaucratic universe of Madrid with its public officials, to whom the Cervantes family appealed continuously between 1575 and 1580 to free their loved ones. Astrana Marín and Canavaggio, among others, have painted the ceaseless efforts of surgeon Rodrigo de Cervantes and his wife Leonor de Cortinas to rescue their sons, selling their belongings and attempting to obtain subsidies from the Council of Castile and the King's Council, all in vain. Cervantes's mother, passing herself off as a widow, then applied for a loan to the Council of the Crusade. On December 15, 1576, she received a conditional loan of sixty ducats for the ransom of her sons Miguel and Rodrigo (Astrana Marín, II: 519–21; Pérez Pastor, II: 33–37; Sliwa, 45–48). We have discussed Rodrigo's rescue in 1577 and Miguel's intervention in this affair through his request to the Mercederian monks to ransom his brother first. Rodrigo left Algiers on August 24, 1577, with a contingent of one hundred six rescued captives (Canavaggio, *Cervantes*, 86; Pérez Pastor, II: 41–46). In March 1578, Rodrigo senior presented to the Council of Castile a new appeal for a subsidy, supported by a deposition in which various witnesses testified to Miguel's military services, his heroism in the Battle of Lepanto, and his captivity in Algiers (*Información*, 23–42; Sliwa, 49–55). Apparently this had no effect. A year later, Cervantes's mother requested the Council of the Crusade for a postponement of her payment of thirty ducats assigned to the ransom of her son Miguel, and for an additional subsidy of five hundred ducats,

> por ser yo pobre y no poderse allegar el dicho dinero hasta agora que la Trinidad envía a rescatar captivos y ha de llevar este rescate [. . .] y si V.S. no me hace esta limosna será causa para que el dicho mi hijo no se rescate porque ninguna posibilidad tengo por haber vendido cuantos bienes tengo para rescatar a Rodrigo Cervantes, mi hijo, que juntamente fue captivo con el dicho Miguel de Cervantes.

> [because I am poor and the money has not been found until now that the Trinitarians are sending (friars) to rescue captives and they need to take this ransom with them (. . .). And if Your Worship does not do me this charity it will be the reason that my said son will not be rescued, because I have no possibilities, having sold all my worldly goods to ransom Rodrigo de Cervantes, my son, who was captured with the said Miguel de Cervantes.]

> (Pérez Pastor, II: 72)

As this eloquent appeal discloses, it is Cervantes's mother, Leonor de Cortinas, who emerges as the heroine of these ventures. In the testimonies granted between 1575 and 1580—the period of captivity of her sons Miguel and Rodrigo—Leonor appeared ten times before different public notaries, six times ignoring her husband, and four times passing herself off as a widow. Beseeching bureaucrats, resuscitating her husband when needed, she demonstrated great ingenuity and zeal in her endeavors, as suggested by her request to the Council of War for permission to export to Algiers eight thousand ducats' worth of merchandise from Valencia. In November 1578, she received a license from the king for only two thousand ducats of exports, *"para el rescate del dicho Miguel de Cervantes"* [for the ransom of the said Miguel de Cervantes] (Sliwa, 57). Despite her contacts with the Valencian authorities and with merchant Hernando de Torres in Valencia, she probably failed to find the guarantor needed for this enterprise.[57]

In July 1579, Leonor de Cortinas, passing herself off as a widow again, handed to Fray Juan Gil, attorney general of the Order of the Holy Trinity, the sum of two hundred fifty ducats for the ransom of her son Miguel, *"que es de edad de 33 años, manco de la mano izquierda y barbirrubio"* [who is thirty-three years of age, crippled in his left hand, and who has a blond beard] (Sliwa, 63). Miguel's sister Andrea de Cervantes contributed fifty ducats toward her brother's ransom (Sliwa, 64–65), which brought the sum received by the Trinitarians to three hundred ducats. It was all that Leonor de Cortinas herself and her family were able to collect in these years despite strenuous efforts. The Order of the Holy Trinity worked for the ransom of captives with charity moneys as well as with private and public funds. Accordingly, on August 31, 1579, Philip II ordered the treasurer of the Crusade to give Fray Juan Gil one hundred ninety thousand *maravedises,* "which he should spend and distribute in rescuing Christian captives from these kingdoms who were made captives at the service of His Majesty." Four days later, the money was delivered to the friar (Pérez Pastor, II: 383). In truth, Cervantes should have been able to obtain part of this money for his rescue, because he was from Castile and had been captured "in the service of His Majesty." On May 29, 1580, the Trinitarians arrived in Algiers with these and other moneys and orders from the Royal Council to ransom select Spanish captives. Seven thousand Christians were out at sea with their masters, the Algerian corsairs. Others had become renegades or had died. Hasan Pasha, who had been deposed by the Ottoman sultan in favor of a new ruler, was preparing for his return to Constantinople (*Topografía,* I: 372, 377–79).

During the months of June and July 1580, the Trinitarians succeeded in ransoming one hundred eight Christian slaves, who returned to Spain in August (Astrana Marín, III: 67). In the next couple of months, Fray Juan

Gil managed to ransom seven principal captives from Hasan, among them, Diego de Benavides, whose testimony we read earlier—the notarized deed of his ransom was signed by Cervantes (Astrana Marín, III: 85). And yet, in spite of his "infinite appeals and requests," Fray Juan Gil was unable to negotiate Cervantes's ransom (*Información*, 59). Hasan claimed that because he had the pick of the lot, he would not give away any of these gentlemen for less than five hundred *escudos* in Spanish gold (quoted by Astrana Marín, III: 73).[58] On September 19, 1580, Hasan was about to sail for Constantinople with four galleons brimming with slaves and renegades, and seven more of the Ottoman fleet. Among the Turkish galleys was the *San Pablo*, captured from the Order of Malta, which would carry Ramadān Pasha—who was accompanying Hasan to the Porte (*Topografía*, I: 373–74, 388; Astrana Marín, III: 85–86). Miguel de Cervantes was on one of these galleys, *"con dos cadenas y unos grillos"* [with two iron chains and shackles] (*Información*, 69). Fray Juan Gil decided to add funds destined for captives who had not appeared to the two hundred eighty *escudos* still at his disposal from the money sent by the Cervantes family. In exchange for Jerónimo de Palafox, whose price had been set at one thousand gold *escudos*, Fray Juan Gil offered five hundred *escudos* for Miguel de Cervantes. Hasan accepted, but on the condition that the five hundred *escudos* be paid in Spanish gold. While the galleys prepared to set sail, the monk ran to buy the Spanish gold from the merchants, returning just in time to free Cervantes. That very same day, Hasan sailed for Constantinople (*Información*, 69, 162; Astrana Marín, III: 87).

Sosa states that if Fray Juan Gil had not rescued Cervantes on that same day, perhaps the captive would have never been released: *"y nunca tuviera libertad"* [and he would never have obtained his freedom] (*Información*, 162). Certainly, in the case of the Spanish captives, to be transferred to Constantinople or other cities of the Ottoman Empire supposed a perpetual imprisonment. The Redemptionist Orders did not apply in the eastern Mediterranean, where missions of peninsular or Italian merchants that often helped to ransom Christian slaves were not frequent, either, so these captives would probably never see their families again (García Arenal and de Bunes, *Los españoles*, 226).[59] García Arenal and de Bunes calculate that the median time of captivity of a ransomable Spanish slave in the Maghrib was between four and seven years (226). Cervantes would later claim in *Persiles* that *"[la Fortuna] no es otra cosa sino un firme disponer del cielo"* [Fortune is nothing less than Heaven's unwavering plan] (IV.14, 474).[60]

The moment of liberation is an especially complex one for any captive. His or her feelings of joy are usually numbed by the shock and incredulity of being alive and free again. Stunned by their ordeal, freed prisoners are often unable to feel any happiness at the overwhelming news of their liberation. Many days and perhaps weeks will pass before the former captive realizes he or she is really alive and finally free. A clinical psychologist who treats victims of kidnapping in present-day Colombia illustrates the point: Although we may believe that a kidnapping or a period of captivity ends when the person comes home—a return celebrated by a family reunion, perhaps a party, or a special dinner, and much happiness—"in reality, the mind of the person who was kidnaped continues being kidnaped for a long period of time."[61] These are some of the traumatic effects of captivity, subsequently discussed in relation to Cervantes. Years later, through his spokesman Ruy Pérez de Viedma, Cervantes evokes the taste of freedom: "*No hay en la tierra, conforme a mi parecer, contento que se iguale a alcanzar la libertad perdida*" [To my mind, there is no happiness on earth to compare with recovering lost liberty]" (*DQ* I, 39).

Back in Algiers, Fray Juan Gil drew the deed of ransom, in the customary manner:

En la çiudad de Argel, a diez e/nueve dias de el mes de Septiembre [de 1580]/ en presencia de mí el dicho notario,/el muy reverendo fray/Juan Gil, redentor susodicho, rescató/a Miguel de Zeruantes, natu/ral de Alcalá de Henares, de e/dad de 31 años [sic], hijo/de Rodrigo de Çervantes e/de doña Leonor de Cortinas,/vesino de la villa de Madrid, mediano/de cuerpo, bien barbado, estrope/ado de el braço y mano izquierda, captivo en la galera del *Sol*,/yendo de Nápoles a España[. . . .] Perdióse a veinte seis/de Septiembre del año de mill/y quinientos e setenta y çinco. Estaba en/poder de Açán bajá, rey. Costó/su rescate quinientos escudos de oro/en oro. No lo quería dar su pa/trón, si no le daban escudos de oro/en oro de España, porque si no, le/llevaba a Costantinolla [sic][. . . .] Fué ayudado con la limosna de Francisco de Caramanchel, [. . .] con çincuenta doblas. E de/la limosna general de la orden fue ayu/dado con otras çincuenta. Las demás/restantes, a cumplimiento de las mil/e treçientas y cuarenta, hiço o/bligación de pagallas a la dicha Orden,/por ser maravedís para otros cap/tivos, que dieron deudos en España/para su rescate, e por no estar/a el presente en este Argel no se han res/catado. [. . .] En fee de lo cual lo firma/ron con sus nombres, testigos: Alonso Berdugo e/Francisco de Aguilar, Miguel de Molina, Rodrigo de Frías, xpianos. Frai Juan Gil,/Pasó ante mí, Pedro de Rivera, notario/apostólico.

[In the city of Algiers, on the nineteenth day of September (of 1580), in my presence, as the said notary, the very reverend Fray Juan Gil, the said Redemptionist, ransomed Miguel de Cervantes, a native of Alcalá de Henares, 31 years old (sic), son of Rodrigo de Cervantes and doña Leonor de Cortinas, residents in the city of Madrid, medium bodied, well bearded, crippled in his left arm and hand, captured in the galley *Sol*, sailing from Naples to Spain (. . .). He was lost on 26 September 1575. He was in the hands of Hasan Pasha, king. His ransom cost 500 gold escudos in gold. His master did not want to free him, if he was not paid with gold escudos, in Spanish gold, otherwise, he would have taken him to Constantinople (. . .). He (Cervantes) was helped by the charity of Francisco de Caramanchel (. . .) with fifty doblas. And from the general charity of the Order he was helped with another fifty. As for the rest, in complying with the one thousand three hundred and forty doblas, he signed an obligation to pay them to the said Order, because these are maravedís destined for other captives, whose families in Spain gave the money for their rescue, and because they are not presently in Algiers, they have not been rescued (. . .). Testifying to which, they signed as witnesses: Alonso Berdugo and Francisco de Aguilar, Miguel de Molina, Rodrigo de Frías, Christians. Fray Juan Gil. I witnessed the following, Pedro de Rivera, Apostolic Notary]

(Libro de la Redempçion fol. 157 v–58 v;
quoted by Astrana Marín, III: 89–91).[62]

Canavaggio calculates that the five hundred gold *escudos* paid for Cervantes's liberation would have been equivalent, in 1989 moneys, to U.S. $17,000 (*Cervantes*, 315–16). This amount would be approximately U.S. $24,500 for the year 2001.[63]

Three weeks later, on October 10, 1580, Miguel de Cervantes asked Fray Juan Gil, in representation of the king of Spain in Algiers, to open an inquest regarding his captivity, life, and habits, to be presented, if needed, to the Royal Council so that it would grant him favor. As we have seen, this was a customary procedure for captives returning from Barbary. In the presence of Trinitarian monk Fray Juan Gil and of Pedro de Rivera, apostolic notary in Algiers, twelve witnesses, including our friends Dr. Sosa and Diego de Benavides, will ratify and expand the statements submitted by former captive Cervantes. The reader is already familiar with this inquest, known as *Información de Argel*, which is cited at length in this chapter. As Canavaggio suggests, before leaving Algiers, Cervantes "intends to settle his accounts" (*Cervantes*, 95). Not only does he have to explain to the authorities the five years spent in Algiers as a captive, but he also has to face the slander campaign mounted by Dr. Blanco de Paz, who had spread vicious rumors about him in the city. We do not know the content of these allegations, which Carmelite Feliciano Enríquez described as *"cosas viciosas y feas"* [vicious and ugly things] (*Información*, 150). Was Cervantes accused of shady dealings with Hājjī Murād, or of immoral relations with Hasan Pasha, known for his homosexuality? Whatever the imputations, we sense the danger coming from the slanderous Blanco de Paz, who stated he would be willing "to damage the reputation of anyone who would try to hurt him, even if it were his own father" (*Información*, 116).

Insinuations regarding Cervantes's alleged homosexuality have recently been raised by certain critics. Among the reasons adduced for this supposition are Cervantes's two encounters with Hasan Pasha, in 1577 and 1579, and the inexplicable way in which the captive's life was twice spared. In regard to this question, Canavaggio has argued that it is difficult to prove the homosexuality of someone who did not leave a single piece of writing on his intimate life, especially when direct testimonies are scarce ("*¿Un arte nuevo?*" 46–47). I fully agree with this consideration. Cervantes, as we have seen, was exceedingly discreet about his private life, even in his fiction. We have no personal letters or texts that mention confidential questions, such as his feelings for his wife Catalina de Salazar, or his reactions to the misfortunes and wayward ways of his daughter Isabel de Saavedra. As shown in this study, Cervantes's close friendship with Antonio de Sosa—his interlocutor, literary critic, and frequent advisor during his captivity—was especially important for the future writer. And yet, we find no direct allusions to Antonio de Sosa in Cervantes's fiction, where numerous historical and literary characters appear. Instead, the two Sosa Coutinho brothers who were captured with Antonio de Sosa on the galley *San Pablo* are mentioned in *El trato de Argel* with other knights of Malta (IV.2365), while Manuel de Sosa Coutinho reappears as a character in *Persiles*. Speaking of the great blanks in Cervantes's life, Blas Matamoro proposes that the Cervantine enigma should be viewed in Baroque terms: "The people of this period were masked, fugitive people, addicted to fiction and to disguise. The masterpiece of these maneuvers is the character of Don Quijote, whose ancestry we ignore, as well as his reliable surname, and we cannot even say for sure if he was crazy or sane" (49).

To examine the question of Cervantes's presumed homosexuality, let us focus briefly on the sixteenth-century Muslim world, rabidly criticized by the Europeans. Sosa's dialogues, as well as other early modern works on captivity in Barbary, illustrate how the frontier universe of the Maghrib was demonized by the ransomer friars and ecclesiastics who denounced the dangers threatening young Christian slaves, males and females alike. Christian slaves and renegades, in effect, encountered in Barbary a permissiveness in sexual matters on the part of Muslim society that clearly opened new horizons for them (Benassar and Benassar, 478). In the first place, marriage was not a sacrament that lasted for life. A man could have several wives, but he could also repudiate a wife, according to Islamic law. In the second place, while Christian ethics condemned the sins of the flesh, Muslim law invited the believer to satisfy his or her sexual instincts. "Your wives are as fields for you: go then, into your fields whence you please," recommends the Koran (Sura 2: 223). If many renegades took advantage of the newly found sexual freedom, unthinkable in Christian Europe, some even converted to Islam because of its views on sexual practices. A renegade tried in absentia by the Inquisition in 1648, *Alcaide* Morat, alias Miquell Coll from Majorca, who lived in Algiers in the 1630s, had four wives: a Moorish woman, a Turkish woman who was the widow of his former master, and two more wives. A thriving functionary of the corsair city, he had taken full advantage of the Koranic injunction (Benassar and Benassar, 432–33, 475).

In addition, while in the Europe of the Counter-Reformation "fornication" constituted a mortal sin, in the Muslim world, sexual freedom was ample and included, among the accessible pleasures, those offered by boys (Benassar and Benassar, 478).[64] This was the infamy that public opinion in Europe attributed to the Muslims, an opinion supported by the accounts of the religious men and ambassadors who traveled to Barbary. Cervantes himself both described and condemned these sexual practices in his fiction, especially in *El trato de Argel*. Numerous young captives, generally adolescents, were regularly enticed or forced by their masters, Turks and renegades alike, to engage in passive sexual practices. Many youths accepted these conditions, which offered them advantageous compensations. The open sexuality of Algiers makes Portuguese cleric Antonio de Sosa claim at the end of the 1570s: *"cuando considero aquello que el apóstol San Juan escribió en sus revelaciones, que vio una bestia con siete cabezas y con diez cuernos y todos ellos coronados con unas coronas, se me representa Mahoma y su ley, y que veo a esta bestia en Argel, adorada públicamente, con los siete vicios mortales o capitales"* [When I consider what the Apostle John wrote in his Revelations, that he saw a beast with seven heads and with ten horns, and all of them crowned with crowns, I imagine Mohamed and his law, and I see this beast publicly adored in Algiers, with the seven mortal or capital sins] (*Topografía*, I: 165–66). For his part, French priest Pierre Dan alleged in the 1630s that the city was the reincarnation of the Babylon of the Apocalypse: "Babylon the Great, mother of the prostitutes and of the abominations of the earth" (quoted by Benassar and Benassar, 478). In this demonizing atmosphere, it is easy to see how Algiers, the land of sexual liberation, would be seen as the domain of Satan by European ecclesiastics.

Emilio Sola and José F. de la Peña have addressed the issue of Cervantes's alleged homosexuality in a chapter of their book *Cervantes y la Berbería* (218–75). As discussed beforehand, in the accessible frontier world of the Maghrib where fortunes were rapidly made, the acquisition of wealth was often associated with convenient accommodations from a moral, religious, or political standpoint. Sola and de la Peña link the open sexual (bisexual) practices of the renegade corsairs to questions of power in the Maghrib. The treatment of personal property in Algiers, where private goods could be inherited by renegades or end up in the public treasury if there were no heirs, and the cultural miscegenation of a society constituted by men and women from all over the world, gave rise to corresponding structures of power (219–21). Antonio de Sosa recounts that many corsairs had *"garzones"* [*bardashes*, or boy-lovers] whom they dressed lavishly and brought on their expeditions (*Topografía*, I: 60–72). In the celebrations that took place after a successful corsair raid, *"acostumbran los arraeces y leventes vestir muy ricamente a sus garzones—que son sus mujeres barbadas— y presumir y contender de quien más número de garzones tiene, más hermosos y más bien vestidos"* [the corsair captains and the ship-soldiers are in the habit of dressing their lads—who are their bearded women—very lavishly and to show them off and compete over who has a greater number of lads, more beautiful and better dressed] (*Topografía*, I: 88–89). These relations between renegade corsairs and their slaves are touched on by Cervantes, who refers to Alūj Ali and Hasan Veneciano: *"le cautivó el Uchalí, y le quiso tanto que fue uno de los más regalados garzones suyos y [. . .] el más cruel renegado que jamás se ha visto"* [Uchalí captured him (Hasan), and was so fond of him that he became one of the man's pampered favorites and (. . .) one of the cruelest renegades I ever saw] (*DQ* I, 40).

Hasan, as we know, became a very powerful man, with thousands of slaves, like his master Alūj Ali. Sosa portrays Hasan in 1580 as a married man with two children—a boy who died young, and a girl, three years old (*Topografía*, I: 388). Like the famous Khair ad-Dīn Barbarossa, whom chronicler Fray Prudencio de Sandoval called *"lujurioso en dos maneras"* [lustful in two manners],[65] Hasan was apparently bisexual, like many other renegades in Barbary. Accordingly, the power relations between renegade corsairs and their slaves were bound to change when the captive became a man, and a *ra'ís* or *levente* [ship-soldier], thanks to the favors of his master. With this change of status and the acquisition of new power, as Sola and de la Peña argue, it is probable that the *bardaxa* or *bardash*—that is, the catamite or passive agent in the sexual relation—became a *bujarrón*— the active partner or sodomite—in another relationship, if he wished. At the same time, he would be promoted from being a corsair's favorite to corsair, or to ship-soldier and master of other *"garzones."* The condition of being the *bardash* in the relation with a corsair master, then, was probably transient, like other ordeals the slave had to endure while he was in captivity. In Sola and de la Peña's interpretation, this seems more like a question of power than one of sex (*Cervantes y la Berbería*, 227).

The accusations against Cervantes by Dr. Juan Blanco de Paz have to be read in the context of the European vision of Algiers as a "land of scandal," the new Babylon envisioned by numerous Spanish and French ecclesiastics. At the same time, such incrimination cannot be understood outside of the complex relations of power existing in Algiers between the renegade corsairs and their converted slaves. Regarding the eroticization of Cervantes's two dramatic encounters with Hasan Veneciano, the first one in October 1577, when he was beaten, and the second in 1579, after his last escape attempt, Sola and de la Peña advance that the maimed Spaniard—haggard, poorly fed, and badly dressed—would have presented a sad sight not conducive to a love story with ruler Hasan Veneciano (*Cervan-*

tes y la Berbería, 261). *"El estropeado Cervantes"* [the maimed Cervantes]—as Sosa calls him in his account of the second escape attempt—with his hands tied and a rope around his neck, probably offered a painful image leading more to rejection than to sexual attraction, even for a lover of *"garzones"* and *bardashes* like Hasan Veneciano. At the time of these encounters, moreover, Cervantes was not a boy or adolescent anymore, an age group preferred by the Turks and renegades who favored these sexual practices.

Sola and de la Peña prefer to focus on the encounter between two men of fundamentally different backgrounds, in radically different situations, the one extremely powerful, the other a slave, both of approximately the same age, Hasan being thirty-four years old and Cervantes, thirty-two years old, at their second meeting. The historians explored the admiration the renegade Hasan might have felt for the maimed Spanish captive distinguished by his courage and solidarity for other slaves. Something of the sort surfaces, indeed, in Sosa's earlier account of Hasan's commentaries on the occasion of Cervantes's second escape attempt. In addition, if Cervantes ever participated in the discreet negotiations suggested by Canavaggio, this would have increased his status in the eyes of the Algerians. Finally, there was the central economic motif, which explains Hasan's "mercy." Most of the fugitive slaves who were tortured or drastically punished for their infractions were commoners, not elite captives who would bring a high ransom (Sola and de la Peña, *Cervantes y la Berbería*, 262).

Historians Sola and de la Peña trace the evolution of an unfounded conjecture, from the reading of sexual ambiguity and phantasmatic images in Cervantes's fiction by Françoise Zmantar to the "incertitudes of desire" in the totality of Cervantes's work by Louis Combet, transformed first into "sexual diversity" and then into simple "homosexuality," at least in thought by Rosa Rossi.[66] Sola and de la Peña demonstrate that this presumption is not founded on archival evidence or testimonies, nor on Cervantine scholarship, nor even on any studies that examine life in sixteenth-century Algiers (*Cervantes y la Berbería*, 258–59). If the sexual practices of a certain society should definitely be studied—as these historians have done in their suggestive book—these practices, they argue, should not be turned into the central basis of a propaganda that reiterates the early modern visions of Barbary circulated by Spanish clerics and Inquisitors. Dismissing the suggestions of homosexual practices between captive Cervantes and Hasan Veneciano, the critics observe: "lately, just as in the nineteenth century the Cervantine scholars tried very hard to look for Neapolitan or Barbary girlfriends for Cervantes, today it seems that it has become fashionable to find him boyfriends" (*Cervantes y la Berbería*, 227).

I close this discussion with the most authoritative witness on Cervantes's captivity, Antonio de Sosa, perhaps the most adamant critic of deviant sexual practices in sixteenth-century Algiers. Dr. Sosa states in his testimony: *"En tres años y ocho meses que a [sic] que conozco al dicho Miguel de Cervantes no he notado o visto en él ni vicio ni cosa de escándalo; y si tal fuera, yo tampoco no le tratara ny comunicara, siendo cosa muy notoria que es de mi condición y trato no conversar sino con hombres y personas de virtud y bondad"* [In the three years and eight months that I have known the said Miguel de Cervantes, I have not noted nor seen any vice or scandalous behavior in him; and if it were so, I would not deal with him or communicate with him either, my condition and relations being well known, which do not allow me to converse except with men and persons of virtue and goodness] (*Información*, 163). Coming from the most severe critic of sexual diversity among the Turks, this declaration on behalf of Cervantes constitutes a categorical statement. No more needs to be said on the subject.

Información de Argel: An Act of Witnessing

In the last pages we have experienced the testimonial impact of the *Información de Argel*, as well as the immeasurable richness of the testimonies consigned by Cervantes and his companions of every social class and education (*Información*, 153–66). For this inquiry instituted at his request, Cervantes composed twenty-five statements or questions that constitute the longest extant text written by him in Algiers concerning his military career and his captivity in Barbary. More important than these statements, however, are the emotions aroused and the wounds perpetrated in Cervantes by the experience of captivity, traumatic effects not necessarily seen at first glance in this early testimony to his ordeal. Cervantes's fictions speak of the desperation felt by those men or women torn away from their families, abandoned to their fate in "well-guarded Algiers," a city completely surrounded by the sea and the desert, where escape was virtually impossible. Attempting to escape four times by means of dangerous plots in which he barely eluded death, imprisoned over and over again in the *beylerbey*'s *baño*, heavily fettered, often clamped in irons and chained, threatened with terrible tortures and even a mock execution, living every day as if tomorrow would never come, Cervantes endured one of the most difficult ordeals that a human being can suffer. From an Existentialist perspective, Ciriaco Morón Arroyo has proposed that to be a captive *"es vivir con toda la plenitud la experiencia de que no debes contar jamás con el próximo instante"* [is to live to the full the experience that one can never count on the next moment].[67]

The experience of captivity ruptures the continuity of life or, if you will, the experience of continuity one had, what Cervantes himself refers to as the "broken thread." If returning to "life" poses the problem of suturing the psychic tear caused by the catastrophic event, it also raises the question of how to keep on living after the encounter with death. I would suggest that beyond the formalities prescribed for those who returned from Barbary, the long *Información* written by Cervantes served to reestablish a continuity with the past, *"anudando este roto hilo"* [tying this broken thread], as the writer would later say in his prologue to *Persiles,* written on his deathbed. From this angle, the inquest on the part of the freed captive went far beyond the efforts to ensure a future position with the crown after his return to Spain, and it went far beyond the attempts to clear his name from the slander campaign mounted against him by renegade Juan Blanco de Paz. This first testimony of Cervantes after his deliverance permitted the survivor to continue the process of survival after liberation.

Massive trauma, however, precludes its registration; the observing and recording mechanisms of the human mind are, so to speak, destroyed, out of function, as Dori Laub suggests ("Bearing Witness," 57). In spite of the overwhelming reality of the traumatic experience, the victim's narrative—the very process of bearing witness to massive trauma—begins with someone who testifies to an absence, to an event that has not been registered, that has been knocked out, as it were, of the psyche. While historical evidence of the catastrophic event that constitutes the trauma may abound, the trauma—as a known event and not simply as an overwhelming shock—has not been truly witnessed yet, not been really apprehended by the mind of the victim. The emergence of the narrative that is being listened to—and heard—is, accordingly, the process and the place wherein the apprehension, the knowing of the event is initiated. In this metaphorical delivery, psychoanalyst Dori Laub explains, the listener is "a party to the creation of knowledge *de novo.* The testimony to the trauma thus includes its hearer, who is, so to speak, the blank screen on which the event comes to be inscribed for the first time." By extension, claims Laub, the listener to trauma comes to be a participant and a co-owner of the traumatic event: through his or her very listening, he or she comes to partake of the experience of trauma ("Bearing Witness," 57).

Rereading the *Información de Argel* from the perspective of trauma studies makes one view the extended statement composed by Cervantes after his liberation as a significant testimony to the trauma of captivity. In his first prose composition, a narrative complete with sections or "chapters," Cervantes bears witness for the first time to the trauma he experienced during his five years of slavery in Algiers. The listeners to and readers of these statements—Fray Juan Gil and the twelve witnesses called by Cervantes—not only literally shared Cervantes's traumatic experience; they also partook anew of the event through their listening to Cervantes's testimony and their corroboration of it in their own declarations. It is through the listening to the former captive's statements, read out loud, and through the confirmation or expansion of Cervantes's affidavit, that both a subjective and a historical truth emerged. "It is the encounter and the coming together between the survivor and the listener which makes possible something like a repossession of the act of witnessing" states Laub. "This joint responsibility is the source of the reemerging truth" ("Bearing Witness," 85). In this encounter between the survivor, Cervantes, and the listener, Fray Juan Gil, and between Cervantes and each and every witness who responded to the inquiry, a historical truth was reconstituted: "The testimony constitutes, in this way, a conceptual breakthrough, as well as a historical event in its own right, a historical recovery." If there were no witnesses—testimonies—this fundamental truth would not exist. Concomitantly, the loss of the capacity to be a witness to oneself is, according to Laub, "the true meaning of annihilation, for when one's history is abolished, one's identity ceases to exist as well" (Laub, 82, 85).

The imperative to give testimony, to attest to one's own experience, cannot be effected during captivity. In catastrophic situations, the human mind cannot really understand what is occurring: The dimensions and consequences of the event transcend our ability to apprehend, to imagine, and to transmit. Likewise, as suggested above, it is possible to infer that during his captivity, Cervantes did not have the possibility of assimilating the traumatic event, of integrating it into his psyche. Testimony was the way in which Cervantes—the survivor, the witness—initiated the construction of a narrative, the reconstruction of his own history. I believe that this first act of attesting to his traumatic experience allowed Cervantes to reclaim his own history and to break out of his emotional imprisonment to start a new life in Spain.

Soon afterward in Madrid, on December 18, 1580, Cervantes personally opened a second *Información*, in which he testified again to his captivity and ransom and acknowledged his financial debt to the Trinitarian order that rescued him. His witnesses were two former captives who shared his fate in Algiers, Rodrigo de Chaves from Badajoz and Francisco de Aguilar from Aguilar, Portugal (Pérez Pastor, I: 65–68; Sliwa, 113–15). While Chaves, who had been imprisoned with Cervantes in Algiers, had already testified for him in the *Información de Argel*—we read his declarations regarding Blanco de Paz—Aguilar signed Cervantes's deed of ransom in Algiers and might also have returned to Spain with Chaves and Cervantes. We may surmise that this new affidavit and the declarations of his two witnesses again helped the former captive Cervantes to apprehend the traumatic event and to give it a historical dimension. Through these testimonies, and by and through his very talking and writing, Cervantes was not only composing another narrative of the event but also breaking out of Algiers. Such inquiries, however, are official documents, composed in the terse style of a notarized legal statement. The most eloquent declarations on Cervantes's captivity, indeed, are the literary testimonies embedded in his work, starting with *La Galatea* and *El trato de Argel,* a document of fundamental importance from the perspective of personal and collective testimony. These important questions regarding literary testimonies are discussed in the next chapter.

How the Chriſtian Slaues are beaten at Algiers.

Christian Slave Beaten in Algiers. One of the punishments meted out to Christian slaves by the Algerians consisted of beating the victims on the soles of their feet.

SOURCE: *How the Christian Slaves Are Beaten in Algiers,* from a drawing in Emanuel d'Aranda, *The History of Algiers and Its Slavery: With Many Remarkable Particularities of Africk . . .* (London: John Starkey, 1666). Reprinted by permission of the Division of Rare and Manuscript Collections, Carl A. Kroch Library, Cornell University. Call number: Rare DT 284 A66 1666

French Christian Slave in Algiers. The legend reads: "This slave is a very erudite and learned French gentleman, who endured cruel sufferings during fifteen years under three different masters until he was finally sold to another, more reasonable, master who employed him in spinning and weaving cotton cloth from which they made shirts and clothes. He was captured at the Djerba Islands in 1670 and ransomed in 1685."

SOURCE: *Esclave Chrestien François à Alger* [French Christian slave in Algiers]. Engraving by Leroux et Jolla (Bibliothèque Nationale, Paris). Reprinted from Gabriel Esquer, *Iconographie historique de l'Algérie depuis le XVIe siècle jusqu'à 1871* (Paris: Plon, 1929), Vol I, Plate XV, no. 39.

Algerian Corsair Captain. The German engraver Wolffgang travelled to England with his younger brother. On his return trip to Germany, he was captured by Algerian corsairs, taken to Algiers as a slave, and later ransomed by his father. He apparently painted while in captivity. He later published a series of engravings on Algerian life both in black and white and in color. This corsair captain flaunts a moustache, as well as the wide-pleated breeches and Turkish slippers used in Algiers. He is armed with a Damascene knife and a scimitar. The *Ra'is*, captains of Algerian corsair vessels, formed a powerful corporation (Taifa) which often opposed the *beylerbeys* of Algiers.

SOURCE: Andreas Matthäus Wolffgang: *A Ra'is: Algerian Corsair Captain.* Aug. Vind. sculp. (Bibliothèque Nationale, Paris). Reprinted from Gabriel Esquer, *Iconographie historique de l'Algérie depuis le XVIe siècle jusqu'à 1871* (Paris: Plon, 1929), Vol I, Plate XII, no. 33.

An Admiral of the Algerian Fleet. This admiral of the corsair fleet is dressed with the short-sleeved woolen doublet which permitted the hand- and arm-washing required by Islamic tradition and with the white pleated breeches made of canvas worn by Algerian Turks. He wears the *cuzaca*, an elaborately woven silk ribbon that held the ornate Damascene knife carried by most Algerians, and a scimitar.

SOURCE: Andreas Matthäus Wolffgang: *Algerian Ra'is.* The legend reads: *Admiral of the Algerian Fleet.* Auguste Vindel sculp. (Bibliothèque Nationale, Paris). Reprinted from Gabriel Esquer, *Iconographie historique de l'Algérie depuis le XVIe siècle jusqu'à 1871* (Paris: Plon, 1929), Vol I, Plate XII, no. 73.

A Jew from Algiers. Matching Sosa's description of the Algerian Jews, this character wears a white shirt covered by a black cassock that descends to the knees and slippers with heels. The Jews in Algiers were not allowed to wear shoes, only slippers. The black headdress falls like a half-sleeve from the back of the head and identifies the subject as a member of the French, Italian, or Majorcan castes.

SOURCE: Andreas Matthäus Wolffgang: *A Jew from Algiers.* Auguste Vindel sculp. (Bibliothèque Nationale, Paris, Est. Of. 2, 6). Reprinted from Gabriel Esquer, *Iconographie historique de l'Algérie depuis le XVIe siècle jusqu'à 1871* (Paris: Plon, 1929), Vol 1, Plate XXIX, no. 77.

3

Staging Captivity:
El trato de Argel

Para borrar o mitigar la saña
de lo real, buscaba lo soñado.[1]
— Jorge Luis Borges, *"Un soldado de Urbina"*

AS WE SAW IN CHAPTER 2, the *Información de Argel* can be read in ways that transcend the social and legal dimensions of its twelve affidavits. This deposition may be viewed as a fundamental testimony that permits the survivor to continue living after his liberation. Testimony thus constitutes a historical event in itself, one that signals the beginning of a historical recovery that has a therapeutic effect for the survivor. Starting from this early testimony composed in Algiers, Cervantes proceeds to the creation of increasingly complex narratives emerging from his North African imprisonment, thus opening up through his art the possibility of speaking of the limit-experience of human bondage.

This chapter explores the relation between drama and history and between speech and survival in Cervantes's *El trato de Argel [Life in Algiers]*, a play that bears witness to the sufferings of the Christian captives in Algiers. My reading is often filtered through *Los baños de Argel [The Dungeons of Algiers]*, a subsequent drama by Cervantes that reworks most of the themes found in *El trato*. I study these plays side by side with the testimony of other captives across the centuries, such as Antonio de Sosa in sixteenth-century Algiers and Primo Levi in twentieth-century Auschwitz. Sosa's life as a captive in early modern Algiers and Levi's survival in the Lager, as well as their writing of it afterward, may shed some light on Cervantes's Algerian experiences. By examining the ways in which issues of biography and history are reinscribed and fundamentally reelaborated by Cervantes's dramas, I propose to study the complex links between poetry and testimony, trauma and creation in the Spanish writer.

"As a Child, I Was Fond of Plays"

Cervantes's dramatic vocation and enduring devotion to the theater are demonstrated throughout his life.[2] He would be, in effect, the first to stage in sixteenth-century Spain the ordeals of Barbary captives, among other innovations that make him a pioneer of Spanish drama. Speaking of Cervantes's indisputable penchant for the theater, Alberto Sánchez argues that *"el cultivo del teatro fue su* ocupación *activa en algunas temporadas y su* preocupación *constante durante toda su vida"* [the cultivation of the theater was his active *occupation* in some seasons and his constant *preoccupation* during his whole life].[3] Evidence of this natural calling can be found throughout Cervantes's fictions. In *Don Quijote*, *El licenciado Vidriera* [*The Glass Graduate*], *Persiles*, the prologue to his *Ocho comedias*, and in his play *Pedro de Urdemalas*, among other works, Cervantes develops a thorough critique of the Spanish theater of his time, one that spans from the foundation of this drama to the qualities a good actor should have.[4]

Cervantes certainly discovered a new way of connecting life and literature, dissimulating himself behind masks and delegating his powers to supposed narrators, such as Cide Hamete Benengeli. Even so, Cervantes does not always remain behind the scenes. In the famous episode where Don Quijote encounters the company of players, directed by Angulo el Malo—an itinerant company that travels from town to town staging the allegorical religious play *Las Cortes de la Muerte [The Parliament of Death]*—we may discover a clear reference to the thoughts and feelings of the author, expressed through the words of Don Quijote.[5] Clearly, Don Quijote's words do not always coincide with those of Cervantes, but in this case their significance is illuminating: *"Desde muchacho fui* aficionado a la carátula *y en mi mocedad se me iban los ojos tras la farándula"* [As a child I was *fond of plays* and in my youth, I was a keen lover of the actor's art] (*DQ* II, 11; emphasis mine). That this youth represents Cervantes himself is corroborated by a symmetrical passage, composed years later by the author (Sánchez, 15). The passage comes from *Adjunta del Parnaso [Postscript to Parnassus]*, an attached appendix in prose to *Viaje del Parnaso [Journey to Parnassus]* (1614), which is, in turn, a festive mythological poem full of autobiographical references.[6] In the scene mentioned above from *Adjunta al Parnaso*, false poet Pancracio de Roncesvalles asks the already famous novelist: *"Y vuestra merced, señor Cervantes, ¿ha sido* aficionado a la carátula? *¿Ha compuesto alguna comedia?"* [And Your Grace, Mr. Cervantes, have you been *fond of plays*? Have you composed any comedies? (emphasis mine)]. The writer answers:

Sí, [. . .] muchas; y a no ser mías, me parecieran dignas de alabanza, como lo fueron *Los tratos de Argel*, *La Numancia*, *La gran Turquesca*, *La Batalla Naval*, *La Jerusalém*, *La Amaranta o la del Mayo*, *El bosque amoroso*, *La Única*, y *La bizarra Arsinda*, y otras muchas de que no me acuerdo.

[Yes, (. . .) many; and if they were not mine, I would deem them worthy of praise, as were *Life in Algiers*, *Numancia*, *The Great Turkish Sultana*, *The*

Battle of Lepanto, The Jerusalem, Amaranta or The May One, The Enamored Woods, The Unique One, and *The Dashing Arsinda,* and many others that I don't remember.]

(*Adjunta*, 182–83)[7]

If the significance of the parallel passages certainly speaks for itself, the list of dramatic works composed by Cervantes and staged in former times confirms his commitment to the theater in the early phases of his career. New winds were blowing, however, in the summer of 1614, when Cervantes was writing these lines, and the old novelist, who had never abandoned the theater, was forced to concede with a trace of melancholy that *"las comedias tienen sus sazones y tiempos, como los cantares"* [comedies have their seasons and times, like songs] (*Adjunta*, 183). Admitting the temporal condition of plays, whose success depends on changing social trends, this phrase also reveals Cervantes's sadness at his ultimate rejection by a public indoctrinated by Lope de Vega's *Comedia.* In addition, the dialogue with fictional character Pancracio de Roncesvalles gave the writer the opportunity to announce the imminent publication of his yet unrepresented plays: *"seis [comedias] tengo con otros seis entremeses"* [six comedies I have with another six interludes] (*Adjunta*, 183). These *Comedias* appeared with various other plays and interludes in the autumn of 1615, six months before his death, with the title of *Ocho comedias y ocho entremeses nunca representados [Eight Comedies and Eight Interludes never Represented].*

Cervantes's revolutionary decision to publish his unstaged plays, articulated in his "Prologue to the Reader," deserves to be cited at length:

Algunos años ha que volví yo a mi antigua ociosidad, y, pensando que aún duraban los siglos donde corrían mis alabanzas, volví a componer algunas comedias; pero no hallé pájaros en los nidos de antaño; quiero decir que no hallé autor que me las pidiese, puesto que sabían que las tenía; y así, las arrinconé en un cofre, y las consagré y condené al perpetuo silencio. En esta sazón me dijo un librero que él me las comprara, si un autor de título no le hubiera dicho que de mi prosa se podía esperar mucho, pero que del verso, nada [. . .]. Tornó a pasar mis ojos por mis comedias, y por algunos entremeses que con ellas estaban arrinconados, y vi no ser tan malas ni tan malos que no merecieses salir de las tinieblas del ingenio de aquel autor [. . .]. Aburríme y vendíselas al librero, que las ha puesto en la estampa.

[Some years ago I returned to my old idleness (to my writing) and, thinking of the centuries where praise for my work still flowed, I composed again some plays, but I found out that time does not stand still; I mean, that I did not find stage managers who asked for my plays, although they knew I had them; and thus, I dumped them in a trunk and I consecrated them and condemned them to oblivion. At this time, a bookseller told me that he would buy them from me if it were not that a famous impresario had not told him that you could expect much from my prose but nothing from my verse (. . .). I examined my plays again, and also some of my interludes which were dumped together with them, and I saw that they were not so bad that they did not deserve to come out of the darkness of that stage manager's understanding (. . .). I got bored and I sold them to that bookseller, who has published them.]

(Prologue, *Ocho comedias [OC]*, 14: 15)

As Sevilla Arroyo and Rey Hazas observe, the unusual publication of these plays at a time when playwrights did not collect and publish their works until years after they had been staged acknowledges a protest on the part of Cervantes against the commercial system of the Spanish theater and its stereotyped dramatic codes, a system headed by Lope de Vega (*OC*, 2: iii). This collection of plays not only confirms Cervantes's enduring passion for the theater but also reveals his confidence in the unquestionable quality of his dramatic production.

A Pioneer of Spanish Drama

The play *El trato de Argel* is perhaps the first work conceived by Cervantes after his liberation from captivity and return to Spain. While Geoffrey Stagg claims that this drama was written in 1577, during Cervantes's captivity in North Africa, Franco Meregalli situates its writing in 1580, the year of the author's return to Spain.[8] Cervantes probably did not write this play while in captivity, but it is possible that some of the poetry included in it was created in Algiers. We discussed in chapter 2 the extant sonnets composed by Cervantes in 1577 and 1579 and dedicated to captives Bartolomé Ruffino de Chiambery and Antonio Veneziano, evidence that Cervantes wrote poetry during his confinement. Antonio de Sosa corroborates that Cervantes *"se ocupaba muchas veces de componer versos en alabaza de Nuestro Señor y de su bendita Madre y [. . .] otras cosas santas y devotas, algunas de las cuales comunicó particularmente conmigo, y me las envió que las viese"* [occupied himself many times in composing verses in praise of Our Lord and his Blessed Mother, and (. . .) other saintly and devout themes, some of which he discussed with me in private and sent to me so that I would see them] (*Información*, 163).

Following his homecoming in November 1580, Cervantes dedicated himself for months to various extraliterary activities, such as the legal endeavors to prove his services to the crown and attest to his ransom and release from captivity; his trip to Portugal and ensuing mission to Orán, undertaken for Philip II between May and June 1581 (Astrana Marín, III: 142–43; Sliwa, 120–22; Canavaggio, *Cervantes*, 98–103). During this year in Portugal, he also planned his first projected trip to the Indies, around December 1581.[9] Back in Madrid, on February 17, 1582, Cervantes wrote a letter to "the illustrious Lord Antonio de Eraso, member of the Council of Indies, at Lisbon," in which he thanked him for his support and advised him of his bad luck: *"El oficio que pedia no se provee por su Magestad y ansi es forçoso que aguarde a la caravela de auiso [de las Indias] por ver si tray alguno de alguna vacante que todas las que aca avia estan ya proveydas"* [The post I applied for is not being filled by His Majesty; so I am forced to wait for the dispatch vessel (from the Indies), to see whether it brings news of some vacancy, because all those posts that were vacant are already filled] (Sliwa, 124–25; Canavaggio, *Cervantes*, 102). In spite of Eraso's backing, Cervantes had not been able to find a post in the Indies, and he had not managed to obtain a position in Madrid, either. Cervantes also told Eraso in this letter that he was devoting himself to the writing of his novel *La Galatea*.

In addition to his displacements and requests, for Cervantes the year 1582 coincided with intense literary activity. He resumed his relations with a circle of poets that included his old friend from Italy, Pedro Laynez; Gabriel López Maldonado, who was putting together a *Cancionero [Collection of Poems]*; Luis Gálvez de Montalvo, who would compose the bucolic novel *El pastor de Fílida [Fílida's Shepherd]* (1582), praised in *Don Quijote*; Juan Rufo, who was about to publish his epic *La Austriada* (1583); and Pedro Padilla, who had just edited a *Thesoro de varias poesías [Collection of Poems]* (1580). At the end of 1582, Cervantes composed the preliminary sonnet that graced Rufo's epic and collaborated on Padilla's *Romancero* (Astrana Marín, III: 133, 218). Starting from 1583, most of the books published by these poets would be adorned by a sonnet written by Cervantes. These activities, as Canavaggio suggests, situate the composition of *El trato de Argel* between 1581 and 1583, when Cervantes probably discovered the theater of Juan de la Cueva, and while he was writing *La Galatea*, whose language recalls that of *El trato*.[10] For a whole year, moreover, from October 28, 1580, to November 30, 1581, the theaters in Madrid were closed as a sign of mourning for the death of Ana, wife of Philip II (Astrana Marín, II: 293–97).

The composition of *El trato de Argel* thus coincided with the rise of a true industry of the spectacle that spurred the construction of new *Corrales* in Madrid, such as *El Corral de la Cruz*, opened in 1579, and *El Corral del Príncipe*, inaugurated in 1583 (Astrana Marín, III: 301).[11] In the prologue to his *Ocho comedias*, Cervantes refers to that early period of escalating theatrical activity in Spain: *"Se vieron [entonces] en los teatros de Madrid representar* Los tratos de Argel, *que yo compuse;* La destruición de Numancia *y* La batalla naval*"* [We saw then staged in the theaters of Madrid, *Life in Algiers*, which I composed, *The Destruction of Numancia*, and *The Battle of Lepanto*].[12] Although the last work has been lost, we may reasonably assume that the extant ones, *El trato de Argel* and *La Numancia*, were part of the twenty or thirty plays that were apparently performed and discreetly praised by the public of the *Corrales*: "*que todas ellas [mis comedias] se recitaron sin que se les ofreciese ofrenda de pepinos ni de otra cosa arrojadiza; corrieron su carrera sin silbos, gritas, ni barahúndas*" [for all of my plays were represented without their being offered offerings of cucumbers and other throwing weapons; they ran their course without whistling, yelling, or pandemonium] (*OC*, 14: 12). Certainly, a fervent enthusiasm for the theater bloomed in Spain during these years. Between 1582 and 1587, thirty theatrical managers worked in Madrid, staging plays that were generally performed for two to three days or, if very popular, for eight to ten days (Astrana Marín, III: 314–17). That *Los tratos de Argel* was one of Cervantes's initial works is indicated by the fact that the writer always mentions it first: In the earlier passage cited from *Adjunta al Parnaso*, Cervantes lists ten comedies, headed by *Los tratos*. Likewise, dramatist Agustín de Rojas mentions *Los tratos* among other early plays in his novel *El viaje entretenido [The Entertaining Journey]* (1603).[13]

The play *El trato de Argel*, also known as *Los tratos de Argel*, consequently inaugurated Cervantes's career as a playwright.[14] The author initiated his new profession by returning to the very site of his captivity, the city of Algiers, "*gomia y tarasca de todas las riberas del mar Mediterráneo, puerto universal de corsarios, y amparo y refugio de ladrones*" [the most insatiable glutton of all the Mediterranean shores, a universal haven for pirates and a shelter and refuge for thieves], as he would call the capital of privateering in *Persiles* (III: 10, 334).[15] Still fresh in Cervantes's mind, the sufferings of the captive were reenacted for the first time on the Spanish stage, in poetry that functioned as a denunciation of, and a collective testimony of, the ordeals of human bondage. George Camamis has vindicated the great originality of *El trato*, which gave the Spanish public "the first realist staging of the lives of captives." These innovations, reworked years later in *La historia del cautivo*, would make this tale "the first modern novel on the subject of captivity" (Camamis, 53).

This turns Cervantes into a pioneer of Spanish drama, as Sevilla Arroyo and Rey Hazas have recently substantiated: "*[Cervantes] inauguró, así, una suerte de minigénero teatral, las comedias de cautiverio, berberiscas o turquescas, que él mismo perfeccionó y enriqueció*" [Cervantes thus inaugurated a sort of mini-theatrical genre, the plays on captivity, Barbaresque or Turkish, that he himself improved and enriched] (*OC*, 2: xi). Even Lope de Vega imitated Cervantes's drama in *Los cautivos de Argel [The Captives of Algiers]*, a play composed around 1599, the year of Philip III's wedding.[16] Cervantes's ensuing captivity plays, *Los baños de Argel*, *El gallardo español [The Gallant Spaniard]*, and *La gran sultana [The Great Sultana]*, published thirty years later in his *Ocho comedias*, thus "opened new spatial, temporal, structural and semantic paths" for Spanish theater (Sevilla Arroyo and Rey Hazas, *OC*, 2: xi).

The fundamental assessment of Cervantes's dramatic production achieved its turning point with Joaquín Casalduero, whose classic work *Sentido y forma del teatro de Cervantes [Meaning and Form of Cervantes's Theater]* (1966) opened new critical horizons. Casalduero, in effect, noted the dramatic force of Cervantes's theater, "its passion, its gaiety, its wit and inventiveness, its moving action, its jokes, and the art of its composition," qualities that make the reader or spectator "surrender to it without reserve, in a total way" (26). Bruce Wardropper also claimed that "Cervantes was as experimental in his time as Brecht, Ionesco, or Arrabal in ours. That these playwrights would have been received with greater understanding is due to the fact that literary tradition weighs less on our own period of transition than on that of Cervantes" ("Comedias," 158). Finally, in his admirable study of Cervantes's dramatic production, entitled *Cervantès dramaturge: un théâtre à naître [Cervantes Dramatist: A Theater to Be Born]* (1977), Jean Canavaggio proposes that Cervantes's drama reveals "an extreme diversity that discloses at the same time a profound unity. The richness of the autobiographical, historical, literary, and folkloric elements that this theater brings into play impregnates his fiction." For Canavaggio, the theater of Cervantes, discredited for centuries and even considered stillborn by some, is *"un théâtre à naître,"* a theater now ready for rich new readings and interpretations (448–50).

Such commendations are confirmed by the extraordinary success of various *Comedias* by Cervantes, recently staged in Spain and other countries. While *Los baños de Argel* was adapted in 1980 by playwright Francisco Nieva and staged with enormous acclaim in Madrid, *La gran sultana* was performed for the first time in 1992 by Spain's Compañía Nacional de Teatro Clásico. Directed by Adolfo Marsillac, with textual adaptations by Alberto de Cuenca, and a luxurious set design by Carlos Cytrynowski, the play was inaugurated in Seville in 1992, and continuously presented to great acclaim in Madrid, Barcelona, Almagro, and other cities, as well as in London and Mexico City, until 1994.[17] Cervantes's modernity was praised by director Marsillac: *"Esta obra nos fascina [. . .] por lo extraordinario del mundo que presenta, por el irónico romance amoroso de la pasión desbordada y enloquecida, [. . .] por el perfume de una civilización sensual y miniaturista y, sobre todo, porque este texto—este hermosísimo y refrescante texto—es un canto arrebatado a la tolerancia"* [This play fascinates us (. . .) because of the extraordinary world it represents, because of the ironic amorous romance with its overflowing and mad passion, (. . .) because of the perfume of a sensual and miniaturist civilization and, above all, because this text—this very beautiful and refreshing text—is an impassioned song to tolerance].[18]

Staging Sixteenth-Century Plays

The lavish twentieth-century staging of Cervantes's plays, with the glowing applause of their postmodern public, lead us to question the ways in which these *Comedias* were staged and produced in the author's time. A synthesis of early modern Spanish dramatic practices may shed some light on these issues. How plays were staged in Spanish theaters at the end of the sixteenth century is a much-debated question. Once a play was sold to a play manager, he was free to stage it according to the needs of his company or the conditions of the scenarios in use. The facilities found in a *Corral* in Madrid or in a theater in Seville would not be the same, for instance, as those of a public plaza or town, a convent, a private home, or a palace. In some dramatic spaces, the staging would use adornments, windows, and balconies; in others, it would be limited to verbal decor, just as we are nowadays in the radio broadcasting of a drama. Canavaggio, in fact, affirms that even after Lope de Vega and his generation, people would go "to *hear* and not to *see* a play" (*Cervantes*, 176–77). The common Golden Age usage *"oír la comedia"* [to listen to, to see a play] might have contributed to this confusion. The verb *oír* [to hear] and its derivative forms had various meanings in early modern Spain, one of which referred to seeing, as illustrated in the famous adventure of the lions in *Don Quijote*, Part II, which we shall discuss later. While he gets ready to face an enormous lion from Orán, which he is attempting to set free from his cage, Don Quijote tells the Knight of the Green Coat, Don Diego de Miranda: *"Si vuestra merced no quiere ser oyente desta que a su parecer ha de ser tragedia, pique su tordilla, y póngase en salvo"* [if your grace has no desire to be a spectator (a hearer) of what, according to your view, is bound to be a tragedy, just spur that mare of yours and ride to safety] (*DQ* II, 14).

In the prologue to his *Ocho comedias y ocho entremeses*, Cervantes alludes to a certain Navarro from Toledo, a set designer who was a successor of Lope de Rueda: *"[Navarro] levantó algún tanto más el adorno de las comedias [. . .] [e] inventó tramoyas, nubes, truenos, y relámpagos, desafíos y batallas; pero esto no llegó al sublime punto en que está ahora"* [Navarro developed somehow more the adornment (set design) of the plays (. . .) (and) he invented stage machinery, clouds, thunder, and lightning, duels and battles; but this did not attain the sublime level we have now] (*OC*, 14: 12). These words, written in 1615, indicate that Spanish theaters at the turn of the century relied on set designs and scenography for the staging of plays. Recent studies on early modern Spanish staging, such as those of José María Ruano de la Haza, among others, stress the visual dimension of the *Comedia*. Ruano de la Haza indicates that techniques of representation in the Spanish theater were simple yet extremely flexible, like those of the modern experimental theater, in which certain objects give the public a clear idea of where the action is evolving.[19] On the other hand, Theresa Kirshner's analysis of an early play by Lope de Vega, *Los hechos de Garcilaso de la Vega y el moro Tarfe [The Deeds of Garcilaso de la Vega and Tarfe the Moor]* (1579–1583)—a play staged in the same period as Cervantes's *El trato de Argel*—shows that Lope used basic elements of staging, such as a big canvas depicting the city of Santa Fe with its towers all illuminated with candles and lanterns, while the stage directions call for sounds of trumpets and bells in the background. The critic goes on to demonstrate the importance of scenography, albeit rudimentary, in twelve plays by Lope staged between 1579 and 1606.[20] Granted, this elemental staging of the 1580s and 1590s cannot be compared with the scenery and set designs adopted by the *Comedia* in the 1630s, which resulted in the spectacular outdoor representations at the Buen Retiro. Even so, Kirshner's studies, among others, show that at the time of Cervantes's first incursions in the theater, there was already a vivid preoccupation with and a distinct development of staging in the Spanish theater, as Cervantes claims.

As for the staging of *El trato de Argel*, we may assume that it was elemental, in spite of the astonishing innovation introduced by the appearance of a lion on the stage, as we shall see shortly, and by that of the demon invoked by Moorish servant Fátima. The action of this play evolves in the most imprecise decor, barely suggested by certain allusions. The sparsity of stage directions, however, does not indicate an absence of scenography. Poets in early modern Spain were usually frugal in their annotations because they knew that the staging of a particular scene depended on the resources that stage managers would have at their disposition (Ruano de la Haza, 28–29).[21] The complex staging of *La Numancia*, among other early Cervantine plays that offer both elaborate staging and stage directions, illustrates Cervantes's interest in these issues. *La Numancia* (c. 1583), as J.E. Varey has demonstrated, calls for the presence of city walls and a tower, as well as of special dramatic effects, such as the rising of a demon from the underworld (the trapdoor) among various pyrotechnic flares and fireworks (*"El teatro,"* 213).

Using as an emblem *El retablo de las maravillas [The Tableau of Marvels]* by Cervantes, where the words engender a fictional visualization, and where all the things shown have a mere verbal presence, Ignacio Arellano suggests that *"todo escenario del Siglo de Oro es un retablo de maravillas que se ofrecen, con la esencial ayuda de la palabra, al enajenado espectador para su instrucción y emocionado deleite"* [every scenario in the Golden Age is a tableau of marvels offered, with the essential help of the word, to the deluded spectator beside himself or herself for his or her instruction and excited delight] (202). Arellanos's remarks, which emphasize the place of words—especially poetry—in the *Comedia*, are especially fitted to address the dramatic verses and tableaus of *El trato de Argel*. They also invoke the powerful poetry of *El trato*, testifying for the first time in Spain to the sufferings of the Christian captives in Barbary.

"Live Painting of the Sufferings of Captivity"

The plays *El trato de Argel* and *Los baños de Argel* occupy a central place in Cervantine dramatic production. Both works are tragicomedies, closer to the tragic conception of drama than the other plays of the author. Both evoke the profoundly traumatic experience of Cervantes's captivity. As Antonio Rey Hazas argues, these dramas by Cervantes *"son el resultado literario de una experiencia vital insoslayable, imposible de olvidar, que había marcado para siempre su biografía y su quehacer literario"* [are the literary result of an inescapable vital experience, impossible to forget, that had marked forever Cervantes's biography and his literary work].[22] Through his spokesman Aurelio, Cervantes characterizes *El trato* as *"trasunto de la vida de Argel"* [a reflection of life in Algiers], an image that has been adopted by the critics who have studied the autobiographical dimension of this play. Defined by Cotarello Valledor as *"relación o pintura viva de los sufrimientos del cautiverio"* [an account or live painting of the sufferings of captivity] (188), the drama has also been called *"relación viva, doliente y trágica de las torturas del cautiverio de Argel"* [a vivid, painful, and tragic account of the tortures of captivity in Algiers] (Astrana Marín, III: 32), or *"presencia viva de una memoria dolorida"* [living presence of a painful memory] (Zamora Vicente, 247).[23]

Such statements, however, beg the question of how traumatic experience is worked into a literary play. In this sense, the definition that inadvertently touches on the perplexing essence of trauma is that of Alonso Zamora Vicente: *"presencia viva de una memoria dolorida."* Such a phrase invokes the uncanny nature of trauma, which returns relentlessly to haunt the survivor. In addition, as modern historiography has confirmed, *El trato* contains abundant descriptions of life in Algiers, including a number of authentic historical personages—corsairs, captives, and ransomer friars—who intervene in the action. The detailed precision with which the ordeals of the Christian slaves in Barbary are evoked—the corsair raids, the auctions of human beings in the slave market of Algiers, the torments and tortures, sufferings and tribulations endured by Christian captives, their love affairs, apostasies, successful or failed escapes, and ransoms—points to a vast tableau of life in the Maghrib, whose veracity has been generally underlined by critics. The vision that emerges in *El trato*, moreover, coincides with the testimonies of Cervantes's companions in the *Información de Argel* (1580) and, especially, with the historical and ethnographic information contained in *Topographia, e historia natural de Argel* (1612), composed by Antonio de Sosa. Yet the truth and apparent verisimilitude of the play raise the question of representation in relation to trauma: specifically, what type of representation is generated by trauma? This is the question that I will attempt to answer in this chapter. Canavaggio has shown the profound complexities of *El trato de Argel* and *Los baños de Argel*, two dramas that describe specific Algerian realities while playing with an intricate system of literary and historical references (*Cervantès dramaturge*, 64–70). As it turns out, such games of concealment and revelation in Cervantes may also be related to the workings of trauma.

One may ask why Cervantes felt compelled to launch his dramatic career with a play that specifically enacted his own sufferings as a captive on the stage. Is it not that the theater is the best embodiment of that "other scene," the unconscious? As André Green reminds us, of the three great awe-inspiring works of literature that Freud analyzes in terms of their relations with parricide—*King Oedipus, Hamlet,* and *The Brothers Karamazov*—two are plays.[24] Freudian theory, in fact, owes more to drama than to any other form of art because of the affinity between the theater and the dream. The theater is not only that "other scene": "It is also a stage whose edge materially represents the break, the line of separation, the frontier at which conjunction and disjunction can carry out their tasks between auditorium and stage in the service of representation" (Green, 1).

If the texture of dramatic representation is not the same as that of the dream, it would be tempting to compare it with fantasy, a type of "theater" in which a narrator describes an action occurring in a certain place, where he does not take part directly; he is present, yet detached. In the dream, on the other hand, "we find the same equality, *de jure*, if not *de facto*, that reigns between the various protagonists sharing the space of the stage" (Green, 2). Broadly speaking, then, it would be more appropriate to state that the theater may be situated between dream and fantasy. This position of drama between dream and fantasy leads me to question its relation to Cervantes's traumatic experiences. As it turns out, the choice of the theater as a medium in which to display the sufferings of the Christian captives is a crucial one, as my reading of Cervantes's play through the lens of trauma studies will show.

Let us now briefly recall the plot of *El trato de Argel*. The play presents different vignettes of the torments and complex experiences of the Christian slaves in Algiers. Among those who have been captured by the Algerian corsairs are two young lovers, both Spaniards; a Sardinian family, composed of a mother, a father, and three children, one still nursing; a Spanish soldier called Saavedra; and other slaves of different ages and social conditions. In the first act, slave Aurelio laments his afflictions, while his mistress Zahara attempts to seduce him in vain. Other captives appear, such as Saavedra, who exhorts Philip II to chase the pirates from Algiers; Leonardo, who has become the lover of his Moorish mistress; and Sebastián, who recounts the martyrdom of a Valencian priest burned at the stake in the North African city.

In the second act, Spanish renegade Ysuf confesses his passion for a newly arrived Spanish slave, named Silvia, to Aurelio. Now, Silvia happens to be Aurelio's beloved, captured in a raid on the coasts of Spain, where Aurelio was also seized. Another scene shows the slave market of Algiers, where a Spanish family is torn apart and its members sold to the highest bidders. All this intrigue is complicated by a double love story: the thwarted tale of the Christian captives, Silvia and Aurelio, who are subjected to the passions of their masters, Ysuf and Zahara. The rest of the play dramatizes the tortures of Aurelio battling the temptations of Zahara's amorous advances; the escape attempts of two slaves, one of whom is miraculously saved, as we shall see; and the imminent liberation of Aurelio and Silvia, finally freed by the "king" of Algiers, Hasan Pasha. In the closing scene, a chorus of slaves prays to the Virgin Mary and praises the arrival of a ship bringing ransomer monks with money to rescue various captives. The ending, however, is not a happy one. While Aurelio and Silvia will be liberated, other captives stay behind, like the unnamed slave who states: *"No tengo bien, ni le espero/ni siento en mi tierra quien/me pueda hacer algún bien"* [I have no worldly goods, nor do I expect to have any/nor do I feel that there is someone back home/who could do me any favor] (*Trato*, IV.2482–84).

From the very outset, then, *El trato de Argel* plunges both the audience and the reader into the city of Algiers, represented in its title as an actual dungeon: *Comedia llamada* trato de Argel, *hecha por Miguel de Cervantes questuvo* [sic] *cautivo en él siete años [A play entitled* Life in Algiers, *composed by Miguel de Cervantes who was a captive in this city for seven years].*[25] Because the titles of plays were usually displayed at the door of the *Corrales*, on posters written by hand or outlined with red ochre on the wall, it may be surmised that the palpitating subject of Cervantes's drama would have attracted a large public. This public started milling around the doors of the *Corrales* before noon, reading the posters announcing the works that were to be staged. There was a sense of great anticipation and, generally, a full house when a *"comedia nueva"* was advertised (Ruano de la Haza, *La puesta*, 38).[26] The Spanish public, in effect, was very fond of plays: With the exception of Ash Wednesday and Holy Week, plays were staged almost every day of the year in Madrid, and *autos* or allegorical religious plays were continuously performed during the festivities of Corpus Christi (Astrana Marín, III: 293–94).

El trato de Argel refers to the captives' lives in Algiers: the word *trato* means "way of life." Yet this term also applies to a commercial deal, specifically, to the negotiation itself; in this case, to the appalling commerce in human beings, bought and sold as slaves in Algiers. Cervantes alluded twice in his play to this *trato*, called *"trato mísero intratable"* [miserable, untreatable treatment/*dealings*], and *"trato feo"* [ugly *dealings*] (I.15; IV.2535; emphasis mine). This is the central activity of Algiers, the corsair capital par excellence in the early modern Mediterranean. Even today, in Spanish, the term *trato* refers to commerce in animals, and *tratante*, to the person who engages in this business. The economic stakes behind this inhuman *trato* are confirmed by ruler Hasan Pasha in the last scene of the play: *"De pérdida y ganancia es este juego"* [This is a game of loss and gain] (IV.2382).

The slight exaggeration represented by the mention of seven years of slavery, instead of the actual five suffered by the author, can be read as a deliberate sleight of hand. In theory, Islamic legislation stated that a captive could not be retained for more than seven years, but, as Sosa and other travelers told us, the Turks did not heed this rule (*Topografía*, III: 238).[27] The allusion to the seven years of captivity, however, would have evoked the religious symbolism attached to the number seven, so compelling in the Old and New Testaments—such as the seven years of good harvests and famine prophesied by Joseph to the Pharaoh (Genesis 41:1–36) and the seventy years of captivity predicted by Jeremiah to the people of Judah (2 Chronicles 36:22–23).

As it turns out, the seven years of captivity in Cervantes's title also allude to the seventh circle of Dante's *Inferno*, where all forms of violence are punished. The import ascribed to the number seven is replayed by the *Siete partidas* of Alfonso el Sabio. The prologue to this treatise includes a *Septenario* [Septenary] that explains the biblical and doctrinal symbolism of the number seven, among which are listed the most important planets, heavens, days of the week, parts of the earth, and arts. The list is followed by a description of the seven parts in which this treatise is divided (*Siete partidas*, 14–15).[28] These chains of associations, invoked by the mention of the seven years of captivity in the title of Cervantes's *Comedia*, would have contributed to the vivid interest of the public in this drama. Surely, among this public, there were former captives or relatives of actual captives in Barbary. The long title of Cervantes's drama, with its reference to the experience of the author (*Comedia llamada* trato de Argel, *hecha por Miguel de Cervantes questuvo* [sic] *cautivo en él siete años),* probably evoked the solidarity of the people attending the play, and even an identification with the Spaniard who had been imprisoned in Barbary for seven long years. The prolonged nature of his suffering, enhanced by the belief that the number seven was the symbol of pain, stresses the visions of purgatory and hell on earth projected by Cervantes's play, starting with its first lines.

"Smithies of the Devil"

As *El trato de Argel* opens, captive Aurelio appears alone on the stage. He is chained. The absolute insularity and desolation of the slaves' lives in Algiers are evoked by Aurelio's lamentations, which compare the impossible sufferings of the captive with both a purgatory and a hell on earth:

> ¡Triste y miserable estado!
> ¡Triste esclavitud amarga,
> donde es la pena tan larga
> cuán corto el bien y abreviado!
> ¡Oh purgatorio en la vida,
> infierno puesto en el mundo,
> mal que no tiene segundo,
> estrecho do no hay salida!
>
> [Sad and miserable state!
> Sad and bitter enslavement!
> Where the sorrow is as long
> as the good is short and abbreviated!
> Oh Purgatory in life,
> Hell placed in this world,
> evil that has no equal,
> strait that has no exit!]
>
> (*Trato*, I.1–9)

The *redondillas* in this soliloquy emphasize the beginning of each verse. The first one, *"Triste y miserable estado!,"* introduces us into the lament, whose coherent development maintains the intensity of the passion. Aurelio's outcry vividly laments the indescribable reality of life in Algiers for the Christian slaves. Truly, there seems to be no way out of the limit-experiences evoked by the captive. Aurelio's allusion to a purgatory and hell on earth recalls the seven years of captivity mentioned in the title of the play, which, in turn, summon contemporary images of purgatory, with its seven tiers or mountains. As Henry Sullivan has argued in his reading of *Don Quijote* II, as an allegory of purgatory, the possibility of a "Purgatory in life" was zealously promoted by the Counter-Reformation in the period in which Cervantes was writing his great novel.[29] Since the sixteenth century, moreover, an intense elaboration of the Catholic doctrines on purgatory was cultivated by the Jesuits in Spain and Portugal and all over Europe. There are important treatises or statements on the subject by Cardinal Robert Bellarmine, S.J. (1588), P. Jerónimo Martínez de Ripalda, S.J. (1591), Manuel de Sá, S.J. (1599), Francisco Suárez, S.J. (1603), and French Jesuit Guillaume Baile, among others (Sullivan, 79).

Aurelios's lament indeed proceeds by allusions to the seventh circle of hell portrayed in Dante's *Divina Commedia*. In his compelling analysis of *El trato*, Stanislav Zimic has advanced the premise that the scenes represented in the four acts of Cervantes's play correspond to the four spheres of Dante's *Inferno*: Incontinence, Violence, Ordinary Fraud, and Treacherous Fraud, with their respective circles.[30] The dramatic scenes of *El trato de Argel* certainly invoke in part "the abysmal verticality of an *Inferno*" symbolically represented by a city completely surrounded by the desert and the sea, an inferno also recalled by the eternal sufferings and punishments of the captives (Zimic, 41). In addition, Aurelio's verses reveal the inadequacy of language to express catastrophic events and its incapacity to articulate the unspeakable. The verses *"purgatorio en la vida"* and *"infierno puesto en el mundo"* conjure not only the torments described in Dante's *Inferno* but also other, even more horrifying tortures, for the condemned men of Algiers do not suffer on account of their sins, evildoings, or weaknesses. Their sorrow arises from tragic accidents in their lives, determined by an incomprehensible destiny: *"dura, inicua, inexorable estrella"* [hard, wicked, inexorable fate] (*Trato*, 1.339).

Almost four centuries later, Primo Levi would invoke Dante's *Inferno*, this time in response to the horror of the Lager, where thousands of men, women, and children were dying of cyanide poisoning and then being reduced to ashes. His novelistic memoir of Auschwitz *Si questo è un uomo [If this Is a Man]*, written shortly after his return home in 1946, presents *l'univers concentrationnaire* movingly yet convincingly.[31] At the outset of chapter 2, Levi, prisoner 174517, realizes that he must be in hell: "Today, in our times, hell must be like this [. . .]. It is not possible to sink lower than this [. . .]. Nothing belongs to us anymore" (*If this Is a Man*, 33). Sometime in 1944, young Italian Jew Primo Levi recited Canto XXVI of *The Inferno* to a young French Jew, Jean Samuel, as they walked through Auschwitz. This scene is the turning point of Levi's memoirs of survival, whose title *If this Is a Man* responds to Dante's verses:

> Consider where you came from: You are Greeks!
> You were not born to live like mindless brutes
> but to follow paths of excellence and knowledge.
>
> (*Inf.*; *If this Is a Man*, 119)

In the nightmare of the Lager, the lines "Consider where you came from," learned by heart in school, acquire an apocalyptic dimension, hitting the prisoner Levi "like the blast of a trumpet, like the voice of God!" (119). Dante's verses "Consider where you come from [. . .]/You were not born to live like mindless brutes" signal the absolute reality of evil and dehumanization—of both the perpetrator and the victim. These lines proclaim the uniqueness of the human race and the possibility of salvation offered by culture, all the more in the inferno of Auschwitz. Even so, if Dante's poetry is muted by the Final Solution, Levi's reinterpretation of "The Song of Ulysses" from Dante's *Inferno* offers a reply to the indescribable horrors of the Holocaust.

The *Inferno* summoned by Cervantes in *El trato de Argel* is the medieval hell of the *Divina Commedia*, centered on concentric circles of violence, torture, and death, where the hope of salvation is nonexistent for the common slave. Zimic suggests that all forms of violence contained in the seventh circle of Dante's *Inferno* are represented in detail in the scenes of captivity in Algiers: tyranny, homicide, suicide, blasphemy, sodomy, and usury (45).[32] The individual afflictions, both physical and spiritual, evoked by the character Aurelio— *"necesidad increíble, muerte palpable, trato mísero, pena del cuerpo y del alma"* [Incredible need, palpable death, miserable dealings, sorrow of the body and soul] (*Trato*, I.13–16)—have also been described by a writer we have already met, Antonio de Sosa. In his *Diálogo de los mártires de Argel*, authored by a character with his own name, Sosa portrays the tortures imposed on the Christian slaves by their Algerian masters. His climactic description of these ordeals, which turn Algiers into an image of hell, is worth citing again. The whole city, affirms Sosa, including its plazas, houses, streets, countryside, its marina, and its ships, can be compared to *"unas herrerías propias y naturales del demonio"* [some natural and proper smithies of the devil], where one continuously "hears nothing but beatings, torments, and cries" from the tortures invented to kill Christians (*Topografía*, II: 125). These images of hell, which so poignantly recall Dante's *Inferno*, lead us to the descriptions and denunciations of these torments provided by both Cervantes and Sosa.

"How Come these Dogs Don't Die?"

We are already familiar with parts of Antonio de Sosa's life as a prisoner in Algiers. A fuller account of his enslavement is presented throughout his work by the narrator himself or through his spokesmen. The cleric claims that for four years he has been locked in a dungeon, covered with chains, and shackled to a stone (*Topografía*, III: 213); that he has been forced to haul rocks and sand and to mix lime, while chained, without being fed until the evening (*Topografía*, III: 176); that he has gone hungry, when sick, for his master withheld his ration of bread from him, thinking he was going to die (*Topografía*, II: 103). Even while he is writing these words, Sosa and his friend Antonio González de Torres see five or six squalid Portuguese slaves, almost naked and shivering with fever, who have been lying in the cold for weeks at the doorway of their master's house. Passing by, their owner cynically asks: *"Cómo, ¿no acaban de morir esos perros? ¿Aún*

viven?" [What! How come these dogs don't die? Are they still alive?]
(*Topografía*, II: 104–05). Sosa's narrative emphasizes another aspect of this
hell, namely, the torment of seeing other captives being tortured to death
or beaten as they lay sick, while being impotent to help them. The horror
of the Algerian machinery prevented the captives from experiencing what
Angel Loureiro has called, in his reading of Jorge Semprún's memoirs, a
"fraternity in death," in Semprún's poignant words: *"être avec l'autre dans
la mort qui s'avançait"* [to be with one another as death advanced against
us].[33] The torturing visions of Algiers make Sosa allude to his imprisonment as a great favor from God, which spares him from witnessing so many
cruelties (*Topografía*, II: 84).

In his later play *Los baños de Argel*, composed between 1589 and 1590,
Cervantes confronts his public with a visual image of these tortures. The
stage directions note: *"Sale un cautivo cristiano, que viene huyendo del
Guardián, que viene tras él dándoles palos"* [A Christian captive comes out
running away from the guard, who comes after him beating him] (*Baños*,
I.35). The scene portrays the tortures inflicted on a feeble and bloodstained
slave, discovered in hiding by a guard. As he beats him, the guard shouts:
"¡Oh chefere! ¿Desta suerte/siempre os habéis de esconder?" [Oh infidel (dog)!
In this way/must you always be hiding?] (*Baños*, I.280–84). The captive
pleads that he has been sick with a raging fever that half-crazed him during the past two days. Even so, the guard just beats him more as he shouts:
"¡Perro, camina!" [Walk, dog!] (*Baños*, I.291). Watching the scene, another
captive, Vivanco, comments:

> ¿No es un notable desatino
> que está un cautivo vecino
> a la muerte y no le creen?
> Y cuando muerto le ven,
> Dicen: "¡Gualá [¡Por Alá!], que el mezquino
> Estaba malo, sin duda!"
>
> [Is it not a notable absurdity
> That a neighbor and captive would be
> at the point of death and they don't believe him?
> And when they see him dead,
> They say: "By Allah! The poor man
> was, in effect, sick!"]
>
> (*Baños*, I.297–302).

Vivanco's words stress the impassivity and indifference of the Algerian slave
owners, who remained unmoved by the sight of their sick or dying slaves.
This dramatic scene echoes a similar passage in Sosa's *Diálogo de la captividad*, where Sosa and his interlocutor González de Torres discuss the practices of Algerians. Using the lingua franca of Algiers, González de Torres

portrays a scenario in which the ailing slaves, *"todos descoloridos y des-figurados de la enfermedad y de dolores"* [all pale and disfigured from ill-ness and pain], are beaten by the slave drivers to make them work:

[a estos cristianos] los llevan delante de sí y por detrás los van aguijando a palos y aun con aguijones de hierro y puntas de palo, picando más que a bestias. Y como el pobre cristiano, lastimado del aguijón es forzado a moverse [. . .], vanle detrás diciendo: "así, así, ahora estar bueno, mira cane como hacer malato," y así con grandes risas y palos y aguijones, lo llevan medio muerto a la viña o jardín, y a palos le hacen luego echar mano del azadón y cavar hasta la noche.

[They make these Christians walk in front of their masters who, from the back, goad them with sticks and even with iron goads and points of wood, pricking them more than beasts. And as the poor Christian, no matter how sick he is, goaded and hurt by the pricking, is forced to move on (. . .), they tell him from the back: "so, so, now you good, look dog how to make sick" (sic); and thus, with great laughter, and beatings, and goading they take him half-dead to the vineyard or to the farm, and with beatings they then force him to take the mattock and to dig until night.]

(*Topografía*, II: 105)

Not all slaves were subject to such torture. Those captives who had special skills, such as artisans, master craftsmen, carpenters, or boat builders, were generally well treated. Besides being well fed, they were paid with money or gifts of cloth and silk when a vessel was completed (*Topografía*, I: 80–81). Sosa tells of a Catalan slave, known as Maestro Pedro, who had been a captive for many years and had become a master of the galleys. He had his own house in Algiers, which contained a small chapel where mass was regularly officiated with a considerable attendance of Christian slaves, es-pecially females, because neither Arabs nor Turks frequented this oratory. His privileged position, however, did not deter Pedro and six other mas-ters of galleys from seizing a boat and fleeing to Valencia in 1582 (*Topografía*, I: 196–97).

Many captives managed businesses, especially the taverns set in the *baños*, which were frequented by other slaves after a day of hard labor, and by the Muslims themselves, in spite of the Islamic ban on the con-sumption of alcoholic beverages. These tavernkeepers paid a percentage of their profit to their masters and to the state. French priest Pierre Dan, a slave in Barbary in the 1630s, claimed that Christian captives kept the nu-merous taverns and cabarets of Algiers, where bread, wine, and meats of all kinds were sold. According to Father Dan, Turks and renegades alike haunted these taverns (*Histoire de la Barbarie*, 99). Sosa, in fact, claims that he never saw as many drunkards in Seville, Lisbon, or Cádiz as in Algiers: *"No irá ninguno en cualquier tiempo por una calle que no tope destos*

borrachos, y muchos dellos alcaydes muy principales, Arraeces y hombre ricos"
[No one can go through the streets at any time without meeting some of
these drunkards, and many of them are very principal city officials, corsair
captains and rich men] (*Topografía*, I: 178). Emanuel d'Aranda, a Flemish
captive in Algiers in the 1640s, provides a curious finale to these lines: He
recounts that by paying for a bottle of wine, one would be served food
without cost (*Captifs*, 39).

Wealthy captives who could afford to bribe the guardians of the *baños*
were often able to buy special privileges. This is illustrated by Cervantes in
Los baños de Argel. In the play, the guardian *bají* (chief guardian of the
baño) calls the captives out to work:

Guardián:	¡Hola; al trabajo, cristianos!
	No quede ninguno dentro;
	así enfermos como sanos,
	[. . .]
	Que trabajen todos, quiero
	Ya [pa]paz ya caballero
	¡Ea, canalla soez!
	[. . .]
Esclavo:	[. . .] ¿Donde irán los caballeros?
Guardián:	Déjalos hasta mañana,
	Que serán los primeros.
Esclavo:	¿Y si pagan?
Guardián:	Cosa es llana
	Que hay sosiego do hay dineros.
[Guardian:	Hey! To work, Christians!
	No one remains inside;
	sick or healthy.
	(. . .)
	I want everyone to work,
	Even priests, even noblemen.
	Hey, you rotten swine!
	(. . .)
Slave:	(. . .) Where will the noblemen go?
Guardian:	Leave them for tomorrow
	Then, they will be the first.
Slave:	And if they pay?
Guardian:	It is clear that where there is money
	There is rest.]

(*Baños*, I.227–56)

The passage stresses the compulsory nature of work in the *baños*, where
numerous captives, including the sick slaves and the priests *(papaces)*, were
sent out to do hard labor in the quarries, along the roads of the regency,

on state farms, or in the city arsenal and shipyard. In addition, slaves were often rented out by their masters to the municipality of Algiers, or to the *ra'is*, to serve as oarsmen in privateering expeditions; the owner of the galliot would pay the slave owner twelve gold *escudos* per trip for each slave-head hired (*Topografía*, I: 82).

The fate of elite captives, however, would differ according to their influence and ability to bribe prison guards. Such captives could be held prisoner for many years, if their ransom did not materialize. We discussed in chapter 1 the initial bargains that fixed the ransom prices of new captives. This price would be determined according to the economic stakes anticipated by their owner. In *La historia del cautivo*, the Captive asserts that many gentlemen were sent out of the *baños* to do hard labor to make them write to their families requesting the money for their ransom. In the active prisoners' brokerage of Algiers, where a small investment would later bring a huge profit, many prisoners, like Cervantes himself, changed owners several times before they were ransomed. Images of the ugly *tratos* that regulated the sale and distribution of Christian captives in Barbary proliferate in Cervantes's fictions. They also raise questions in regard to the language used to depict this absolute reality.

The Lingua Franca of Barbary

The use of the lingua franca of Barbary by both Cervantes and Sosa invokes some questions in regard to language and trauma. Both Cervantes and Sosa suggest that language is overcome by the reality of evil in Algiers. As noted above, Aurelio's laments regarding the sufferings of Christian captives in Barbary reveal the inadequacy of language to describe the inferno of the *baños*. Silence may be the best response to the unendurable: *"Cállese aquí este tormento,/que, según me es enemigo,/no llegará cuanto digo/a un punto de lo que siento"* [Be silent here, my torment,/which, since it is my enemy/what I say will not approximate/what I feel] (1. vs. 21–24). Speaking of the cruelties perpetrated against the galley slaves, brutally beaten by the corsairs, their arms and backs broken, their ears and noses cut off, among other horrible tortures used to force them to row faster, Sosa states: *"No basta lengua humana para decirlo, ni pluma para declararlo"* [There is no human language which could express this, nor pen that could declare it] (*Topografía*, I: 860).

Four centuries later, Theodor Adorno launched his criticism against the literature of the Holocaust with his famous statement that poetry after the Holocaust would be a barbaric act.[34] Much of the current debate on the Holocaust has focused on the inadequacy of language to convey horror, a horror beyond the compass of human imagination. Primo Levi had no illusions about the shortcomings of language. The centrality of the linguistic issue stands out in his book on Auschwitz: "Language lacks words to express this offense, the demolition of a man" (*If this Is a Man*, 32). The incapacity of language to express these events is emphasized by Levi:

> Just as our hunger is not that feeling of missing a meal, so our way of being cold has need of a new word. We say 'hunger,' we say 'tiredness,' 'fear,' 'pain,' we say 'winter,' and they are different things. They are free words, created and used by free men who live in comfort and suffering in their homes. If the Lagers had lasted longer, a new harsh language would have been born.
> (*If this Is a Man*, 129).

Levi's words evoke the harsh language of Algiers, the lingua franca spoken in the early modern city described by many captives as hell itself. Quantitative surveys drawn by various historians reinforce the impression of a continuing North African offensive against Spain's coasts that spanned the sixteenth to the eighteenth centuries (Friedman; Benassar and Benassar). The North African inferno, in fact, lasted well into the eighteenth century, longer than the Nazi concentration camps, in spite of the efforts of the Europeans to destroy this fortified city-prison. My comparison of sixteenth-century Algiers with the modern Lager may seem shocking to some readers. Cervantes's and Sosa's descriptions of captivity in Algiers, among others, nevertheless allow me to draw certain analogies between these two *univers concentrationnaires*, separated from each other both temporally and geographically. Certainly, if the Algerians did not resort to the Final Solution as an institutionalized rule to exterminate their "captives of war," the extent of the tortures and dreadful deaths perpetrated on these captives was appalling. These prisoners, moreover, were not prisoners of war in the traditional sense but rather men, women, and children who lived and worked on the Spanish coasts (Friedman, 31).

I am also aware that the number of slaves imprisoned in Algiers cannot be compared to the staggering numbers of prisoners and victims of the Nazi concentration camps. Sosa reminds us that the Christian slave population of Algiers reached twenty-five thousand in the last decades of the sixteenth century, a century considered as the peak for acquisition of captives in the city. Yet, the proportion of this slave population to the total inhabitants of Algiers—calculated in the 1570s at approximately one hundred twenty-five thousand—is mind-boggling: The Christian slaves constituted between twenty and twenty-five percent of the population of Algiers. From the perspective of Spanish demography, this massive number of slaves would have been equivalent to two percent of the population of Andalucía, calculated at about one million two hundred thousand people at the end of the sixteenth century. On the other hand, between 1520 and 1660, in a period of one hundred forty years, six hundred thousand captives were bought and sold in the Algerian slave market (Wolf, 151). These numbers amount to about ten percent of the total population of the Crown of Castile, calculated as about six million people in the sixteenth and early seventeenth centuries.[35] To these computations we should add the voluminous number of slaves kept in the fetid underground dungeons of Tunis and Tripoli, among other neighboring ports. The proportion of the number of slaves kept in North Africa to the population of various Spanish provinces across the sixteenth and seventeenth centuries thus permits me to make these odious comparisons between early modern Algiers and the modern concentration camps. In addition, I would suggest that the horror of Algerian captivity, with its denigration of human life, carried over into language, as we saw in the sample of the lingua franca offered earlier. This leads me to explore the new semantic reality created in the *baños*.

In *Don Quijote*, the Captive defines the lingua franca as *"lengua que en toda Berbería, y aun en Constantinopla, se halla entre cautivos y moros, que ni es morisca, ni castellana, ni de otra nación alguna, sino una mezcla de todas las lenguas, con lo cual todos nos entendemos"* [a language employed all across Barbary, and even in Constantinople, which is neither Moorish, nor Spanish, nor any other language for that matter, but a jumble of all languages, with which we all communicate]. The Captive later speaks of *"la bastarda lengua"* [the bastard language] that was used in Barbary (*DQ* I, 41).[36] This lingua franca was indeed a mixture of various languages, for the most part Italian and Spanish, with some sprinklings of Portuguese (*Topografía*, I: 115–16). Such confusion of words was increased by the bad pronunciation and even worse grammar of the Turks and Moors, who did not know how to conjugate Spanish or Italian verbs or change their tenses. As Sosa tells us, this pidgin language constituted *"el hablar franco de Argel, casi una jerigonza o, a lo menos, un hablar de negro boçal traído a España de nuevo"* [the common parlance of Algiers, almost a gibberish, or, at the least, the lingo of a black man, recently brought to Spain, who does not know any language other than his own] (*Topografía*, I: 116).

The analogy between the lingua franca of Barbary and the devalued Negro speech or *"habla guinea"* [Guinea speech] used by early modern Spanish and Portuguese writers to represent black discourse is intriguing. Such speech constituted not a vehicle of communication but a sign of difference and inferiority.[37] Accordingly, if the black body symbolized slavery in sixteenth-century Europe, it also connoted inferiority on the scale of humanity. By comparing the speech of the Algerians with that of black slaves in Spain, Sosa suggests that like the blacks, the inhabitants of Algiers were morally inferior. Even though the official language of the regency was Osmanli Turkish, itself a fusion of Arabic, Persian, and Turkish words, the influx of slaves from all over the world made everyone in Algiers—Turks,

Arabs, women, and children alike—use the lingua franca, which, in turn, forced the Christians to employ this jargon (*Topografía*, I: 116).

Let us recall Sosa's earlier representation of the lingua franca of Barbary, expressed through González de Torres: *"así, así, ahora estar bueno, mira cane como hacer malato"* [so, so, now you good, look dog how to make sick] (sic). The phrase accompanied the punishments inflicted on various sick slaves, as they were beaten and goaded with sharp sticks. In Act III of *El trato de Argel*, the stage directions order two Moorish boys to appear flaunting a jingle in lingua franca to two Christian slaves: *"Joan, o Juan, non rescatar, non fugir. Don Juan no venir; acá morir, perro acá morir; don Juan no venir, acá morir"* [Joan, or John, no rescue, no escape. Don Juan not come, here die, dog here die; Don Juan not come, here die] (sic) (65). The jingle, which refers to the death of Don Juan de Austria, who died prematurely on October 1, 1578, clearly announces that there is no hope for the captives, no hope of ransom nor hope of escape from Algiers, where they will finally die. This early manifestation of Cervantes's interest in dialects and jargons focuses on the hybrid frontier world inhabited by Muslims and Christians, a fringe world that would remain one of Cervantes's obsessions throughout the years. A variation of this jingle in lingua franca reappears in *Los baños de Argel*, where various Moorish children harass two Christian slaves by repeating the barbarous chant: *"¡Rapaz cristiano,/non rescatar, non fugir;/Don Juan no venir;/acá morir, perros, acá morir!"* [Christian lad,/no rescue, no escape;/Don Juan not come,/here (you) die, dogs, here die!] (sic) (II.1217–21). Reiterating the death of Don Juan de Austria, the cruel chant made in distorted Spanish informs the captives once more that they will die, like dogs, in Algiers. The repetition of this phrase in lingua franca in two Cervantine plays separated by various years is significant. It appears in Cervantes's texts as a leitmotif that inexorably returns.

These examples of the lingua franca of Algiers transcend what Leo Spitzer called "linguistic perspectivism" to reveal a sinister underside. Both Cervantes's and Sosa's texts stress the lurid contexts in which the lingua franca was exploited. The new semantic reality created in or around the dungeons of Algiers suggests that the suppression of linguistic laws and material had as a consequence the erosion of entire categories of thoughts and emotions. In effect, the Turkish words used by Cervantes in his captivity plays seem to be almost always related to violence, as displayed by the shouts the guardian *bají* or the pasha himself addresses to various Christian slaves, as we shall see in this chapter.[38] To this confusion of languages, with its gruesome connotations, we could apply the words of Primo Levi regarding the Lager: "one is surrounded by a perpetual Babel, in which everyone shouts orders and threats in languages never heard before" (*If this Is a Man*, 44). In sixteenth-century Algiers, the Tower of Babel returned as a symbol of the destruction of humankind and the concomitant destruction of language. Primo Levi would later address the issue of language as a politicized phenomenon in *I sommersi e i salvati [The Drowned and the Saved]*.[39] Speaking about the German used in the Lager, Levi claims that he realized much later that the Lager's German was a language apart: "it was a variant, particularly barbarized, of what a German Jewish philologist, Klemperer, had called *Lingua Tertii Imperii*, the language of the Third Reich [. . .]; it is an obvious observation that where violence is inflicted on man it is also inflicted on language" (*Drowned*, 97).

A passage from Antonio de Sosa's *Diálogo de los morabutos* closes this section on the connotations of the lingua franca of Barbary. Sosa's interlocutor, renegade Amud, opens the dialogue about the Muslim holy men with a discourse in lingua franca: *"Como estás Papaz? [. . .]. Dio grande no pigliar fantesia. Mundo cosi cosi. Si estar scripto in testa, andar, andar. Sino acá morir"* [How are you, Father? (. . .). God great, no grab fantasy. World cosi cosi. If it is written on head, you go, you go. If not, to die here] (sic) (*Topografía*, III: 193). Constructed from Spanish and Italian verbs in the infinitive mixed with assorted nouns from both languages, these mutilated phrases emphasize Amud's vision of the world, particularly his Islamic determinism, which sees destiny *(mekteb)* as a fate already "written."

Various Koranic verses allude to the inexorability of what has been written by the "Pen of Destiny," as it is called in the Islamic world. As Luce López-Baralt has suggested in an illuminating article, that primordial Pen, associated with the Sacred Script of the Creator and his Supreme Intellect, writes on the "Well-Preserved Tablet" *(lawh al-mafūz)*, also of Koranic lineage.[40] This inexorability of destiny written on the Well-Preserved Tablet is expressed in a word: *maktūb*, which means "it is written." Such is the phrase that stands out in Amud's remark. In his pidgin discourse, the renegade is simply telling Dr. Sosa that he should not fantasize about his liberation: If God has decreed it—ergo, it would be written by the Pen of Destiny on his head—he will be freed; otherwise, he will die as a prisoner in Algiers. Even though Amud's attitude toward Dr. Sosa is not cruel, what surfaces in this passage is the ineluctable nature of death as a concrete fate for the Barbary captives, a fate especially accentuated by this demonstration of the lingua franca. These examples of the lingua franca of Algiers, with its mixture of unconjugated verbs snatched from different languages, and its truncated phrases emphasizing torture, violence, and death, illustrate the manner in which language was also distorted and exploited in early modern Algiers, a city that relied for its subsistence on the commerce in human beings.

"Nothing More Than a Dead Body"

The physical sufferings of the captive, however, cannot be compared to his or her spiritual affliction, as Sosa's words demonstrate: *"aquella profunda, terrible, y continua desolación que en todos sus trabajos le acompaña, la cual [. . .] es uno de los mayores [. . .] tormentos que un hombre de carne puede sentir"* [that profound, terrible, and continuous desolation that accompanies him in all his travails, which (. . .) is one of the greatest (. . .) torments a man of flesh and blood can endure] (*Topografía*, II: 159). The desperation felt by many captives is also illustrated by Santa Teresa's confessor, Fray Jerónimo Gracián de la Madre de Dios, a captive in Tunis between 1593 and 1595, who recalls his first days as a slave aboard a corsair frigate:

> El bizcocho se había acabado, el agua era muy hedionda, el calor y hedor de aquel lugar, grande, y así la turbación, la hambre, la sed, el calor, la estrechura y las quejas y gemidos de los cautivos, todo daba pena [. . .]. Era necesario que el Padre acudiera a consolar a sus compañeros, que perdían la paciencia, a confesar algunos heridos que estaban a la muerte, consolar y acudir a otros que le pedían pan y agua llorando, que parecían como si él tuviera allí una gran despensa, o que fuera su padre o madre, y no cautivo como ellos; a reprimir a algunos que blasfemaban por verse esclavos, reprender a otros que concedían ya con los turcos en tratos nefandos, principalmente algunos mozos desbarbados [. . .]; animar a otros que estaban ya tentados y trataban ya renegar la fe.

> [We had run out of biscuits, the water was very fetid, the heat and the smell of that place, great, and thus, the confusion, the thirst, the heat, the narrow confinement and the complaints and moans of the captives, everything caused grief (. . .). It was necessary for the priest to come to console his companions, who would lose their patience, to take the confessions of some injured men, who were about to die, to comfort and come to the aid of others who asked for bread and water, crying, so that it seemed as if he had a great dispensary there, or as if he were their father or mother, and not a captive like them; to control some of them who cursed God at seeing themselves turned into slaves, to reproach others who already agreed to engage in the nefarious sin with the Turks, especially some beardless young men (. . .); to encourage others who were already tempted and tried to renounce their faith.]
> (*Escritos de Santa Teresa*, II: 457)[41]

Father Gracián's vivid description of his first days of captivity in a Tunisian galliot, in the midst of horrendous heat and the fetid conditions of the crammed vessel, speaks for itself. While some captives cried and moaned, others waited for the imminent death of those injured in the corsair attack, and still others reacted according to the range of human responses associated with such a catastrophe. If the behavior of the priest in these lurid conditions is exemplary, his candid depiction of the shock and desperation felt by the sailors and passengers of the captured galley discloses the most common reactions of the men and women subjected to this terrible experience. More important, what surfaces distinctly in this passage is the desperation felt by the captives, which led some to curse God, others to renounce their faith, and still others to accept the sexual advances of the corsairs, perhaps to save themselves.

Both the character Aurelio in *El trato* and Sosa in his *Dialogues* insist on the feelings of isolation and absolute destitution that invaded the captives in this hell where death was confronted daily. For Aurelio, captivity represents the sum of all misery on earth, a locus of unending woes, nearly impossible to portray: *"¡Cifra de cuanto dolor/se reparte en los dolores,/daño que entre los mayores/se ha de tener por mayor!"* [A portion of every grief/ distributed among the sorrows,/evil that among the greatest,/has to be viewed as the greater] (I.9–12). This is an encounter with death, in other words, life as death, or death invading life, especially the life of the spirit: *"¡Necesidad increíble,/muerte creíble y palpable,/trato mísero intratable,/mal visible e invisible!"* [Incredible need,/palpable and credible death,/untreatable misery of treatment,/visible and invisible evil!] (I.10–16). The death evoked in these verses is not that of the Other but a personal, palpable death, experienced in advance by the captive—hence the incapacity of words to express one's own death and the host of significant adjectives that pile up, addressing the impossibility of believing that this horror is real *(increíble, creíble, palpable, visible, invisible)*. Sándor Ferenczi, the great clinician of limit-experiences, states that for human beings, traumatic pain is the experience nearest to death ("Reflexions," 139–47). With traumatic pain, a piece of oneself is irretrievably lost, as Cervantes seems to suggest through his character Aurelio. Indeed, Aurelio later states that the poor captive who finds himself among the Algerian rabble, subject to certain damage, can ask God for his freedom or *"contarse viviendo ya por muerto"* [can count himself already dead while living] (II. 1352–55).

Sosa echoes Aurelio's words when he states that the legal status of the slave is that of a "dead body." In various passages of his *Dialogues*, Dr. Sosa affirms that during the period of his captivity, the slave was a "juridically dead" entity: *"Pues la honra, el título y el ser que el derecho da a un esclavo es que le llamó y declaró por no más que un cuerpo muerto o sin ser, mas antes es el mismo nada y como si no fuera en el mundo"* [For the honor (moral dignity), title, and (juridical) existence that the law assigns to the slave consists in calling him and declaring him nothing more than a dead body, or an entity without being; even more, he is nothing itself and as if he did not exist in the world] (*Topografía*, II: 119). This experience is a common one even today, especially for victims of kidnapping and other terrorist actions. During my own captivity at the hands of Marxist guerrillas in Colombia in the 1980s, confined to a windowless cell, I felt like a dead body cut off from all other living beings who were outside. This encounter with death made me understand extinction as "not being there while life goes on." Separated by hundreds of years, slaves in sixteenth-century Algiers and captives of fascist governments and terrorist organizations in modern and postmodern times suffer the brutal experience of being suddenly dispossessed of everything that had given a meaning to their life. Sosa found a metaphor for this appalling experience: *"con mucha razón llamó la escritura divina a la esclavitud, escoba que de una mano y en un momento todo barre, sin dejar cosa o bien alguno"* [with reason, the Sacred Scriptures called slavery a broom that with one hand, and in a moment, sweeps away everything, without leaving a worldly thing or a single good] (*Topografía*, II: 20). What this broom sweeps away, as Sosa suggests, is the capacity to project—to create projects—that structures life itself.

The idea of the captive as a dead being also appears in the works of Cervantes and other Golden Age writers. In *El trato*, as discussed above, Aurelio claims that the man who loses his freedom *"puede [. . .] contarse, viviendo, ya por muerto"* [can (. . .) count himself as already dead while living] (II.1355). As Camamis has advanced, the author who most insists on this definition is Calderón (102). His drama *El príncipe constante [The Persevering Prince]* refers to a historical event, the captivity of Prince Fernando of Portugal and his death in Fez in 1443. Fernando, the youngest son of King Juan of Portugal, took part with his father and two brothers in the conquest of Ceuta (Africa) in 1415. Years later, Enrique (the Navigator) and his brother Fernando organized a military expedition to Tangier that suffered a brutal defeat. Fernando and other nobles were left as hostages in Fez, where he died. In Calderón's play, Prince Don Fernando compares his enslavement to death:

> Morir es perder el ser.
> Yo lo perdí en una guerra
> Morí, luego ya no es cuerda
> Hazaña, que por un muerto
> Hoy tantos vivos perezcan.
>
> [To die is to lose one's life (one's being).
> I lost it in a war:
> I lost my being, thus I died.
> I died, therefore it is not a sane
> Venture that, for a dead man
> So many living men would now die.]
>
> (II.1371–76)[42]

Sosa takes this confrontation with death even further, to the complete shattering of prior beliefs or forms, which brings the soul to the edge of the precipice. He evokes the pernicious malady of the soul that persuades the captive that he or she has no hope, that there is no mercy in God, no pity, no compassion, not even goodness, and that, in fact, God is not the same as He once was (*Topografía*, II: 162). In this limit-experience of despair that leads the Christian to doubt even the existence of God, *"se vuelve la desventurada alma loca, desatinada, sin juicio y tan trastornada, que [. . .] al último se despeña, y viva se arroja en el infierno"* [the unfortunate soul becomes crazy, foolish, out of its right mind, and so disturbed, that (. . .) finally, it falls over a precipice, and it hurls itself alive into hell] (*Topografía*, II: 162).

Not only do Sosa's words capture the depths of dejection of the abandoned Christian slave but they also obliquely allude to suicide, committed by many captives. In texts composed by prisoners or slaves who rowed during part of their captivity, one finds frequent mentions of suicide. Antonio González de Torres recounts the grief felt at the sight of the galley slaves, working until they dropped dead from rowing or other torments, some falling dead over their oars; some, over their benches. Still others, *"desesperados [. . .] se ahorcan con alguna soga que atan al banco, de la cual echandose a la mar quedan colgando, como hicieran ahora dos, uno [. . .] que era de nación napolitano, y otro español en la de jaffer arráez, renegado ginovés"* [being desperate, (. . .) hang themselves with some rope that they tie to the bench, from which, by throwing themselves into the sea, they remain hanging, like two men just did, one (. . .) who was of Neapolitan origin, and the other, Spanish, in the galliot of Jaffer *ra'is*, the Genoese renegade] (*Topografía*, II: 95). Such suicides were understandable, given that galley slaves often became delirious from lack of sleep or died of thirst or exhaustion (*Topografía*, II: 95–97; Friedman, 66–67).

If the ideology or religious considerations of sixteenth-century Spain did not encourage the explicit mention of suicide, as above, it is often implied by the suicidal escape attempts enacted by various Christian slaves and depicted in *El trato*. In this drama, a captive decides to flee overland from Algiers, but a companion warns him of the grave dangers implied: *"¡Dificultosa empresa, cierto, emprendes!"* [A difficult venture you embark on!] (III.1543). Captive Per Álvarez answers imperturbably: *"¿Pues qué quieres que haga, dime, hermano?"* [So what do you want me to do? Tell me, brother!] His friend insists:

> ¿Caminarás de noche?
> [. . .]
> Por montañas, por riscos, por honduras?
> Te atreves a pasar, en las tinieblas
> de la cerrada noche, sin camino
> ni senda que te guíe adonde quieres?
> ¡Oh libertad y cuánto eres amada!

[Will you walk at night?
(. . .)
Through mountains, through crags, and wilderness?
Do you dare to walk in the pitch dark
Of the bleak night, without a road
nor a path that guides you where you want to go?
Oh freedom! How much you are loved!]

(III.1590–94)

The implications are clear: The endeavor is suicidal. For captive Per Álvarez, in the hands of a master who asks for an enormous ransom, abandoned by all, his parents dead and his brother a miser who has robbed him of his inheritance, there is no other hope of recuperating his freedom: *"Y la insufrible vida que padezco,/de hambre, desnudez, cansancio y frío,/determino morir antes huyendo,/que vivir una vida tan mezquina"* [And the insufferable life I endure,/of hunger, nakedness, exhaustion, and cold,/I think it is better to die by fleeing/than to live such a miserable life] (III.1557–60). Zimic has rightly observed that Per Álvarez's decision to flee represents one of the tragic alternatives to his dilemma—*"morir huyendo"* [to die flee-ing] (47). The other is to die in captivity.

The insistent presence of death in these scenes pressures me to broach the problematic issue of trauma as a death already experienced. The term *experience*—from the Latin *experiri*—should be strictly understood here as the crossing of a danger.[43] In catastrophic experience, we could stretch this meaning further to include the "crossing of death." Concentration camp survivor and writer Jorge Semprún testifies to this "crossing." In his po-etic memoir *L'écriture ou la vie [Literature or Life],* he claims that after his liberation, he had a sudden intuition, a revelation "not of having es-caped death, but, instead, *of having been traversed by death; of having lived it, in some way*" (24; emphasis mine). Marked by "the death imprint," the survivor is one who remains alive after this bodily or psychic intrusion of death. The problem is how to approach truth in trauma, when the truth is that of this encounter with death, an unspeakable experience. Again, it is Semprún who sheds light on this issue. Referring to the possibility of re-counting the experience of the Lager, he states: *"ne parviendrons a cette substance (d'un récit possible), à cette densité transparente que ceux qui sauront faire de leur témoignage un object artistique, un espace de création"* [only those who will know how to turn their testimony into an artistic object, a space of creation, will attain that substance (of a possible narra-tive), that transparent density] (*L'écriture ou la vie,* 23). Cervantes prefig-ures these modern writers on trauma by showing us that the only way to touch trauma is through figuration. His literary testimonies reveal that only the artifice of a masterful narrative is capable of transmitting, albeit par-tially, the truth of testimony.

Cervantes's Doubles

This difficulty in describing absolute horror, of uttering the truth of cata-strophic events has been addressed by numerous creators, literary critics, psychoanalysts, and historians.[44] Freud himself felt obliged to take a de-tour via literature to illustrate how the experience of trauma repeats itself inexorably through the unwitting acts of the survivor, and against his own will. The story of Tancred and Clorinda, from Tasso's epic poem *Geru-salemme liberata* (1580–1581), allows Freud to explain traumatic repetition, even while suggesting that trauma is a voice that bears witness to an un-known truth, the truth that Tancred himself cannot fully know. In other words, just as Clorinda's voice, in Tasso's poem, unexpectedly cries out from a tree the second time she is unwittingly wounded by Tancred, trauma is a wound that cries out to a reality that is not always available to the victim. As Cathy Caruth brilliantly puts it, "if Freud returns to literature to describe traumatic experience, it is because literature, like psychoanaly-sis, is interested in the complex relation between knowing and not know-ing. And it is, indeed at the specific point at which knowing and not know-ing intersect that the language of literature and the psychoanalytic theory of traumatic experience precisely meet" (*Unclaimed Experience*, 3).

The impossibility of telling, then, is also inhabited by the radical oth-erness of the traumatic experience, the fact that trauma is not fully regis-tered as it occurs. Trauma consequently often returns in disjointed frag-ments in the memory of the survivor, fragments sometimes too intense and tumultuous to express in utterances or in writing, as my discussion of Cervantes's play will demonstrate. Such fragmentation also occurs in the psyche. Freud acknowledged the more severe forms of splitting rather late in his career.[45] Melanie Klein, however, encountered very early on in her work with children the factualness of the splitting of the ego. She showed that it was centrally involved in the earliest defensive maneuvers of the ego.[46] These primitive defense mechanisms underlie neurotic (normal) defenses. In the case of the survivor of a catastrophic experience, splitting, or creat-ing doubles who are put in charge of the experience, permits the subject to approach what he or she cannot experience or relive directly. This dou-bling in the service of survival is clearly observed in the play *El trato de Argel*.

As discussed in chapter 1, Per Álvarez's escape reenacts Cervantes's first escape attempt, effected four or five months after his capture, in January or February 1576. Trying to reach the nearest Spanish fortress in Orán, the captive planned to walk some four hundred kilometers across the wilder-ness. We alluded earlier to the Berber tribes who hunted fugitives for booty; to the wild animals, such as lions, hyenas, and cheetahs, that often attacked the travelers; and to the shortage of food and water that made such escape a nightmare. Fugitive Per Álvarez evokes the tribulations that induce him to return to his jailers in Algiers. In the wilderness, distraught by "the continuous howling of wild animals" (IV.1951–52) and half-crazed by hunger and thirst—"*he perdido el tino*" [I have lost my mind] (IV.1968)—the runaway thinks only of death or of returning to captivity: "*ya espero de esta afrenta/salir con entregarme/a quien de nuevo quiera cautivarme*" [I hope to escape from this ordeal/By surrendering to anyone who may want to recapture me] (IV.1962–67).

Even though Per Álvarez is miraculously saved in the play, another fugitive in *El trato* is caught and clubbed to death as the pasha watches and orders more and more beatings "*¡Oh yuraja caur! [jefe cristiano]. Dadle seiscientos/palos en las espaldas muy bien dados,/y luego le daréis otros quinientos/en la barriga y en los pies cansados*" [Oh *juraha caur*! (Christian chief!) Give him six hundred/bastinados on the back very well executed/and then you will give him another five hundred/on the stomach and on his tired feet] (IV.2346–54). Despite these threats, the doomed Christian dares to question the law that punishes escapees with such rigor: "*¿Tan sin razón ni ley tantos tormentos/tienes para el que huye aparejados?*" [So many torments have you prepared, without reason nor law, for a man who escapes?] Hasan Pasha responds with fury, ordering his guards to intensify the tortures: "*¡Cito cituf breguedi! ¡A callar judío rápidamente! ¡Atalde,/Abrilde, desollalde y aun matalde [sic]¡*" [Shut up quickly, you Jew! Tie him up!/ Open him up, tear him to shreds, and even kill him!] (IV.2346–53). The Turkish insult *(cito cituf breguedi)* that brands the Christian as a Jew confirms the place of the Jews at the lowest echelon of Algerian society, even below the Christian slaves, as seen in chapter 2.

In an enlightening article that studies the autobiographical aspects of *El trato*, the late Françoise Zmantar argued that this drama stages two antagonistic worlds: that of Muslim Algiers and that of Spanish Christianity in the city. In the same way, the play is structurally organized through the representation of inverted and complementary couples who often mirror each other in a distorted glass. Life in Algiers is similarly situated in a double scene: in the secrecy of the home and in the street. Aurelio represents the figure of the captive confined to a private home. Saavedra, his double and complement, belongs to the street. Each of them has an inverted double in the play, embodied by another character (Zmantar, "Saavedra" 192–93). One of the couples depicted in *El trato* is constituted by Per Álvarez, the slave who succeeds in escaping to Orán, and by the anonymous Spaniard who fails in the same enterprise. Seized at the end, this man is taken before Hasan Pasha, who punishes him by torture and death, as we saw above.

Per Álvarez carries an old Spanish name, equivalent to *Pedro*, a name that abounds in the *Cantar de Mio Cid* and that is rounded off by an equally ancient patronymic, *Álvarez*. The second captive, however, remains unnamed. Despite his anonymity, Cervantes gave this slave an inverted identity, a medieval and historical identity, in the persona of Per Álvarez, the only character in the play who has a patronymic and who carries within the identity of the other. As Zmantar suggests, this anonymous captive evokes the image of Cervantes, who failed in his four escape attempts and who appeared two times, manacled and chained, before Hasan Pasha, the ruler who spared his life ("Saavedra," 193). This doubling speaks to trauma —specifically, to its construction of a new reality consisting of two conflicting tableaus between which there are no connections. It also alludes to the difficulties, on the part of the writer, of recalling and reliving the traumatic experience.

Regarding Cervantes's first escape attempt, witness Diego Castellano stated that Cervantes and a group of six Christian slaves fled from Algiers, guided by a Moor who was to take them to Orán. After walking for several days, the Moor deserted them, so it was necessary for Cervantes "to turn back to Algiers, to the same prison where he was before" (*Información*, 75).[47] Pardoned by his first master Dalí Mamí, Cervantes was nevertheless mistreated and kept in severe confinement, with more fetters and chains (*Información*, 50). If Cervantes was spared, probably because of the gains Dalí Mamí hoped to obtain through his ransom, most slaves who attempted to escape from Algiers endured torture and sometimes death. Alluding to analogous infractions during the rule of Hasan Veneciano (1577–80), Sosa claims that in only two and a half years, between September 15, 1577, and February 14, 1580, the pasha cut off the ears of nineteen Christian captives of different nationalities, some of whom had tried to escape overland toward Orán, for attempting to flee from Algiers (*Topografía*, II: 113–14). In addition, a Genovese slave was shot to death with arrows for endeavoring to take over a galliot sent by Hasan Pasha to Bona to collect wheat (ii: 113). The Algerian ruler, however, was not the only one to engage in such practices. Corsair Arnaut Mamí, famous for his cruelty, had his house and ships full of mutilated Christian slaves whose ears and noses had been cut off for not rowing as fast as he liked (*Topografía*, II: 115). Between 1577 and 1579, another corsair captain, Turk Cadí Raez [Caid Ra'īs], a former governor of Bizerta, cut off the ears of five of his captives who tried to flee. These examples suffice. The list of tortures imposed on Christian captives, especially for attempting to escape, is interminable, and Sosa recounts these atrocities in detail.[48]

Lest we think that these punishments were a specialty of the Algerians, let us remember that the period under consideration here was not a humane age overall. The use of physical force to increase productivity of slaves and forced laborers, enhanced by the exercise of extreme cruelty to punish them for their offenses, was common to many European nations as well. In Spain, for instance, as Mateo Alemán reported, the conditions at the

royal quicksilver mines in Almadén, in the 1590s, were appalling. The prisoners or slaves who toiled in the mine, many of whom were Muslim captives or Moriscos, were frequently whipped, even when they were ill, if
they could not comply with the work quotas. Other slave-miners suffered
from mercury poisoning, which often led to insanity or death.[49] Slaves in
sixteenth- and seventeenth-century Valencia, including North African captives, did not fare better. They were ill fed, ill dressed, and often poorly
housed, while some were beaten to make them work harder (Friedman,
75).[50] As for the brutal mutilations described above, they seem to have been
customary in the early modern period. In his account of Columbus's second voyage to the Indies (1493), Miguel de Cuneo described the penalty
imposed on certain men who secretly engaged in gold bartering with the
Indians: *"a unos se les cortaron las orejas y a otros la nariz, que daba pena
verlos"* [some had their ears cut off, and some their noses, which was sad
to see].[51] Such penalty was still in use in 1648 when the French decreed
that criminals who had been sentenced to death were to have their noses
and ears cut off instead and be condemned to the galleys. The procedure
caused the rowers to have such difficulty breathing that they could not be
employed at the oars for long periods (Friedman, 74).[52] These illustrations
of early modern punishments and treatments of slaves take us back to the
absolute reality of Algiers evoked by Cervantes in his play.

The Miraculous Lion

The question of how to represent the truth of trauma is elicited by various
scenes from *El trato de Argel*. As discussed earlier, perhaps the only way of
expressing unspeakable truths is through figuration, as Cervantes, among
other survivors, shows in his work. In *El trato*, the writer uses figuration
to describe an unbearable reality—specifically, in the scene where exhausted
and half-crazed fugitive Per Álvarez is saved from death by a miraculous
lion. Let us focus, then, on the scene that presents Per Álvarez at the point
of dying from fatigue and thirst in the desert. The captive now offers a
desperate prayer to the Virgin Mary, perhaps one of the poems Cervantes
composed in Algiers:

> ¡Virgen bendita y bella,
> mediadora del linaje humano
> sed Vos aquí la estrella
> que en este mar insano
> mi pobre barca guíe
> y de tantos peligros me desvíe!
> ¡Virgen de Montserrate,
> [. . .]

enviadme rescate,
sacadme de este duelo.

[Blessed and beautiful Virgin,
comforter of the human race,
be thou here the star
that in this insane sea
guides my poor boat
and protects me from so many dangers!
Virgin of Montserrat,
(. . .)
send me a ransom,
take me out of this sorrow.]

(IV.1974–91)

The autobiographical dimension of these lines is evident. From an aesthetic perspective, however, these awful shattered lines cannot compare with the other poetic compositions that grace *El trato de Argel*. Putting himself in the hands of the Virgin, the fugitive lies down to sleep in the brush. As he sleeps, a lion comes out and tamely stretches out next to him. The calm is broken by the arrival of another runaway slave who also hides in the brush. He is discovered by a Moorish boy who shouts: *"¡Nizara!, ¡Nizara!"* [A Christian! A Christian!] (IV.85). At his cries, other Moors appear and seize the captive, beating him as they exit the stage. These outcries awaken Per Álvarez, who finds the lion resting next to him. Horrified, he asks himself whether this fierce beast will proceed to devour him, thus ending his woes, but then reckons that *"tanta mansedumbre/no se ve ansí fácilmente/en animal tan valiente"* [such tameness/is not easily seen/in such a brave animal] (IV.2032–34). This lion may have been sent by heaven to guide him to Orán: *"sin duda es divina cosa"* [certainly, this is a Godsend] (IV.2042). Similar cases have been seen: *"otro león ha llevado/a la Goleta a un cautivo/que le halló en un monte esquivo/huido y descaminado"* [another lion has taken/a captive to La Goleta/for he found the fugitive in the brush/running away and lost] (IV.2048–51).

Various anecdotes regarding lions and slaves are discussed by Luis del Mármol Carvajal, a former captive in Fez and traveler in the Maghrib, in his *Descripción de África* (1573), a work Cervantes might have read. Legends about a captive who meets a lion in the desert and remains unperturbed proliferated among the North African slave population. Possibly inspired by the fable recounted by Seneca of the benevolent lion who saved the life of the slave Androcles, these stories claimed that if a captive walked calmly and courageously, he would not be attacked. The beast would wait for a favorable occasion, often following him to the nearest city. As Mármol notes with irony, many then concluded that the lion guided the fugitive through the wilderness.[53]

Lions were very popular in Golden Age Spain. They appeared among other animals, such as horses, bears, tigers, and even hydras, in early Spanish literature and on the stage. The lions in literature were unusually friendly, probably because of their symbolism as the king of beasts, a natural lord and master associated with evangelists, in particular with St. Mark. More important, the medieval lion was an archetype of Christian morality—in other words, a symbol of Christ. Identified with the hero of the chivalric-heroic tradition, the lion often accompanied a knight, as suggested by Chrétien de Troyes's work, *Chevalier au lion [The Knight and the Lion]*. The first romance of chivalry in Spanish, *El caballero Cifar [The Knight Cifar]* (c. 1350) presents a lioness that carries a child in her jaws, and a later chivalric novel, *Palmerín de Inglaterra [Palmerín of England]* (1547), a book lavishly praised by the priest in *Don Quijote*, features a savage who hunts with two lions on a leash.

As far as I know, the first lion to appear on the Spanish stage was introduced by Cervantes in *El trato de Argel*. After that marvelous scene, Spanish theater, led by Lope de Vega, went on to present lions and other animals, especially horses, in the *Corrales*. Lions emerged in various *Comedias* by Lope, such as *El hijo de Reduán [The Son of Reduán]* and *El cardenal de Belén [The Cardinal from Bethlehem]*, to cite only two of these plays. Calderón put a lion on the stage in *El mayor encanto amor [The Greatest Enchantment Love]*, a feat repeated in *La aurora de Copacabana [The Dawn of Copacabana]*, where a lion and a tiger materialize in South America, in spite of the geographical faux pas.[54] How these works were staged, then, has intrigued many critics, from Menéndez Pidal to novelist Thornton Wilder, among others who questioned whether live animals went onstage in the Spanish Golden Age theater. As Ruano de la Haza has demonstrated, live horses regularly made a spirited entrance in the *Corrales*, although they were generally not brought onto the stage. The suggestion made by Wilder that theatrical manager Baltasar de Pinedo was probably in possession of a lion, perhaps a "poor aged and edentate beast" or even a lion skin that appeared in three plays by Lope de Vega between 1599 and 1606, thus seems to be misguided. Ruano de la Haza has shown that lions in early modern plays were generally represented by comedians covered with lion skins.[55]

The amazing presence of a lion in Cervantes's first dramatic production underlines the playwright's innovations. This feat, in turn, recalls the return of the lion in *Don Quijote*, Part II, this time as a travesty of the fantastic scene depicted in *El trato*. Thirty years later, in effect, the old lion from Orán makes a reappearance on the plains of La Mancha, encountering, instead of a runaway slave, a crazy, middle-aged knight, Don Quijote. The reenactment of the earlier scene allows Cervantes to satirize chivalric romance while making fun of his former plots and creations. In this hilarious episode, Don Quijote, on foot and with sword and shield in hand, attempts to let the formidable beast out of his cage to stage a fight with it. After Don Quijote opens the cage door, the enormous African lion looks at him fiercely, stretches and yawns very slowly, and finally sticks out a tongue almost a foot and a half long. Then, to the knight's dismay, *"el generoso león, más comedido que arrogante [. . .], volvió las espaldas y enseñó sus traseras partes a Don Quijote, y con gran flema y remanso se volvió a echar en la jaula"* [the noble lion, more civil than haughty (. . .), turned its back on and showed its hindquarters to Don Quijote, and slowly and calmly stretched out on the floor of the cage] (*DQ* II, 17).[56] After this farcical adventure, Don Quijote will be called *"El caballero de los leones"* [The Knight of the Lions].

The lion scene from *Don Quijote* may shed some light on *Los tratos de Argel*. Certainly, the spectators of Cervantes's play would have associated the scene of the tame lion with the biblical story of Daniel, thrown into the lions' pit. As a symbol of mortal danger, lions play an important part in the Bible. They mete out divine punishment, ravaging transgressors and recalcitrants (1 Kings 13:24–28, 20:36; 2 Kings 17:24–26; Jeremiah 50:17). Only exceptional men can vanquish a lion, like the divinely inspired Samson and David. The lions of the Daniel tradition, however, are a different breed. They are the only ferocious beasts that are turned into docile animals in biblical narrative. Such images evoke Isaiah's visionary lion that in a future age shall "eat straw like the ox" (Isaiah 11:6–9, 65:25). Daniel's lions consequently announce an era of universal peace that will bring the restitution of Israel's fortunes and its victories over its historical enemies (Isaiah 11:11–16).[57] As it turns out, these allusions speak to Cervantes's play.

That a fierce lion appears before a captive who bears a medieval Spanish name, *Per Álvarez*, is not fortuitous. Both his name and the presence of the beast would have reminded the audience of the adventure where the sleeping Cid meets a lion that has escaped from its cage. While the hero's sons-in-law hide in terror, the Cid gets up and faces the lion, which humbly kneels down and puts its jaws on the ground (III.2278–2300). The essential gist of the episode, reiterated in chronicles and romances, was part of a corpus of traditions that later reappeared in the *Cantar de Mio Cid*. More important, the lion in medieval times was supposed to sleep with its eyes open, as St. Isidore of Seville reiterates: *"cum dormierint, vigilant oculi."* Hence, the figure of the lion was associated with vision and with constant vigilance, an idea related to the image of the Christian who should remain always alert against the enemy. In the episode of the sleeping Cid, the lion incarnates the moral values of the hero, in this case, the Cid Campeador, who, in the end, is the true lion.[58] These intertextual connections turn Per Álvarez into a new Cid, a devout Spanish captive who is an exemplary representative of the moral values embodied by the Cid.

Cervantes's hero—a defeated Christian slave—triumphs in a spiritual way because of his human failure, his captivity. Rewarded by the Virgin to whom he prayed for his ransom, Per Álvarez illustrates the belief that only faith will lead to freedom. These images of salvation through faith associate the scene of the lion in Cervantes's play with the biblical story of Daniel, who emerged unscathed from the lion's den. They are also meant to foreshadow, through Cervantes's Christian hero, the triumph of Christianity over Islam.

Given the pivotal function of the lion scene in Cervantes's *El trato de Argel*, and the central place this scene occupies in this chapter, we may ask ourselves whether this episode is more than a fabulous adventure arbitrarily included by the poet to give variety to his drama. In other words, why did Cervantes resort to allegory to evoke his own aborted escape through the desert? Allegory, as we have known since the time of Quintilian, is the alienation of words from meaning: "Allegory [. . .] presents either one thing in words and another in meaning, or even something quite opposed."[59] That is the definition offered by rhetoricians though the Middle Ages and the Renaissance. In the simplest terms, Angus Fletcher maintains, "allegory says one thing and means another."[60] A good allegory, to use Edwin Honig's words, "beguiles the reader with a continuous interplay between subject and sense in the storytelling, and the narrative" (5). The scene of the lion in Cervantes's play in fact pressures the reader to find other meanings for the miraculous apparition of the beast in the midst of a dramatic getaway. This scene not only points to the two opposed messages of allegory but also signals to allegory as escapist figuration. This episode thus offers an escape from the autobiographical scenario reenacted by almost-deranged and half-dead Per Álvarez, an evasion that can also be read as a fantastical wish fulfillment. The other as savior (the Virgin, the lion) opens a space where one would be able to heal, as it were, all the wounds imposed by the traumatic experience.

Like dreams and fantasies, allegory generally arises in periods of loss, as Stephen J. Greenblatt corroborates, "periods in which the powerful theological, political, or familial authority is threatened with effacement" (*Allegory*, ix). This effacement of all familiar parameters of authority is clearly evident in the melodramatic scene that conjures up Cervantes's first escape from Algiers. Moreover, as Mieke Bal puts it in her *Reading Rembrandt*, "allegory is a mode of reading that takes the represented event out of its own history to put it in a different one."[61] This is precisely what Cervantes does with the story of Per Álvarez. What the writer reveals in this reenactment of an autobiographical event is the impossibility of representing the truth of trauma. Rewriting the scene in an allegorical manner, putting it into a different story, inventing doubles, like the fugitive Per Alvarez and the nameless slave who split the burden of reliving the traumatic event, and providing a "happy ending" to an otherwise ghastly tale offers an escape from the ordeal of reliving the traumatic experience. But precisely, this would be the privilege of the writer, as Freud suggests in his article "Creative Writers and Day-Dreaming": to lift the tragic, to display a world untouched by the inexorable destiny encountered at the time of the traumatic experience.[62] My initial question regarding Cervantes and allegory may now be answered with another question: "Why is it," writes Paul de Man of allegory, "that the furthest reaching truths about ourselves and the world have to be stated in such a lopsided, referentially indirect mode?" (2). In Cervantes, "the furthest reaching truths" about himself, the truths that have to do with trauma, have to be stated metaphorically, in this case, through an extended metaphor.

Trauma and Creation

The episode of the lion thus points to the associations between trauma and creation in Cervantes. As it turns out, the reenactment of the traumatic experience generally produces an outburst of fantasy in Cervantes. In the deus ex machina placed in *El trato*, we can see how this junction of trauma and creation operates. The recollection and literal representation of Cervantes's first escape attempt in Algiers seems to thrust the witness—the writer Cervantes—further and further into the vortex of trauma, as the former captive *relives* his ordeal, evoking his anguish at being lost in the desert, prey to the wild beasts; inhabiting again his hunger, exhaustion, and physical terror; and, finally, his wish to die. The scene ends in the desperate prayer recited to the Virgin—the atrocious poem cited above. Recalling the traumatic event—telling it—might become brutally traumatizing, in effect, if the price of speaking is *reliving* the catastrophic experience. Poets and writers who have broken their silence may have indeed paid with their life for that transgression. (Paul Celan, Jean Améry, Primo Levi, and Bruno Bettelheim all committed suicide.) In Cervantes, as the poet touches the painful core of trauma, a fantastical vision appears in the image of the lion sent by the Virgin to lead Per Álvarez to safety.

In trauma, the abyss into which anxiety has propelled us turns into the space where the fantasy of omnipotence is erected—this is the space of fantasy, of oneiric constructions, and, as Freud has shown us, of creation. Anxiety, in fact, seems to open the way for symbolization. In his fine analysis of anxiety, J.B. Pontalis states: *"J'ai de l'angoisse, je suis douleur. L'angoisse peut encore se dire, se monnayer en formations de symptômes, se moduler en représentations et fantasmes, ou se décharger dans l'agir [. . .]. La douleur, elle, n'est qu'à soit. L'angoisse reste communicable, appel indirect à l'autre"* [I *have* anxiety, I *am* pain. Anxiety can still be expressed, it can be minted into symptom formations, modulated into representations and fantasies, or discharged in acting out [. . .]. Pain, indeed, only refers to itself. Anxiety can be communicated, as an indirect appeal to the other].[63] Certainly, the disjointed, almost fragmented prayer to the Virgin in *El trato de Argel* constitutes an extreme appeal to the other, the M(other), represented in the play by the most exalted and idealized woman of Christendom, Mary. In the context of captivity, this appeal to the nurturing M(other) points to trauma as a disruption of the link between the self and empathic other, a link first established by the expectation of mutual responsiveness in the mother–child bond. As Dori Laub and Nanette Auerhahn have illustrated in an insightful article, the essential experience of trauma is an "unraveling of the relationship between self and nurturing other, the very fabric of psychic life."[64] There is in trauma, then, a metaphoric absence of a mother, namely, the absence of a mothering function that would mediate needs and prevent a catastrophic event. The prayer to the Virgin in Cervantes both confirms and attempts to correct this lack.

Our previous discussion of the symbolism attached to the lion in medieval and Renaissance literature opens the way for another view of Cervantes's glorified brute in *El trato*. In this quasi-oneiric scene, the lion, a symbol of Africa, is "tamed" by the Virgin—by Christianity. This emasculated beast evokes an equally defeated father figure at the service of the primeval mother. In a curious text written at the end of his life, Sándor Ferenczi illuminates the concept of splitting of the ego, adumbrated earlier in this chapter. Ferenczi shows that, following trauma, a very particular form of intellect can be developed as one of the permanent by-products of survival: The splitting of the ego produces a disconnection between a feeling part of the psyche, brutally destroyed, and another part that knows it all yet does not feel anything.[65] In this narcissistic splitting of the ego, a separation occurs in the very same personage that was until then capable of feeling and another he or she who knows. Here, the Freudian distinction between affect and representation is radicalized, because the affective part is shattered and the subject is amputated of a part of himself or herself. The other part, separated from all affect, emotionally detached, becomes a sort of pure knowledge that views the scene from above. In this brusque transition from an object relation, which has become impossible, to a narcissistic relation, explains Ferenczi, *"l'homme abandonné des dieux échappe totalement à la réalité et se crée un autre monde dans lequel, délivré de la pesanteur terrestre, il peut atteindre tout ce qu'il veut"* [the man abandoned by the gods totally escapes reality and creates another world for himself, in which, delivered from terrestrial burdens, he can attain everything he wishes] ("Fragments," 287–89). Abandoned by the gods, former captive Cervantes escaped reality by creating another world for himself in which he is saved. Almost childlike in its simplicity, the fantasy of salvation through the lion announces a recurrent pattern in Cervantes: The reenactment of the traumatic event usually generates a burst of fantasy in his fictions.

In a study of the "burning-child dream," analyzed by Freud in the *Interpretation of Dreams*, Lacan points to the connections between trauma and fantasy. "The place of the real," states Lacan, "which stretches from the trauma to the fantasy—in so far as the fantasy is never anything more than the screen which conceals something quite primary, something determinant in the function of repetition—this is what we must now examine" (*Four Fundamental*, 60). Lacan went on to say that the Real has to be sought beyond the dream—or the fantasy—in what the dream has enveloped, "hidden from us behind the lack of representation of which there is only one representative" (60). *El trato* is the first Cervantine work to reveal the painful intrusion of the traumatic event proper concealed behind the impossibility of representation, even while disclosing the clear connections between trauma and fantasy in Cervantes himself.

The oneiric scene of Per Álvarez's salvation is not the only one to signal such a paradigm in this drama. Let us consider, for instance, Aurelio's first soliloquy on captivity, examined earlier, which summons the painful memories of former slave Cervantes, memories that generate the interdependent motifs of captivity and love in the play.[66] In the moment of Aurelio's greatest despair—*"bañado en lloros"* [bathed in tears]—the image of Love (Silvia) appears as delivery: *"mi cuerpo está entre moros,/mi alma en poder de Amor"* [my body is in the hands of Moors,/my soul in the power of Love] (1.27–28). The scene now brusquely shifts from the depiction of Aurelio's literal bondage ("my body is in the hands of Moors") to the metaphorical image of the chains of love ("my soul [is] in the power of Love"), thus pointing to the symbolic associations that function as an avenue of escape.

Another scene in the play poignantly illustrates this Cervantine pattern: the passage in which the Moorish woman Zahara recounts the storm that wrecked the galley *San Pablo*, from the Order of Malta, and the ensuing attack of the corsairs in which Antonio de Sosa was captured in 1577. At the most critical point of Zahara's soliloquy, when she relates the death of the ship's captain and of two passengers and mentions the slaves captured by the Turks, Cervantes's spokeswoman escapes into another reality:

> El robo, las riquezas, *los cativos*
> que los turcos hallaron en el seno
> de la triste galera me ha contado
> un cristiano que allí perdió la dulce
> y amada libertad, para quitarla
> a quien quiere rendirse a su rendido.
> Este cristiano, Silvia, este cristiano;

> *este cristiano* es, Silvia, quien me tiene
> *fuera del ser* que a moras es debido,
> *fuera de* mi contento y alegría,
> *fuera de* todo gusto, y *estoy fuera,*
> que es lo peor, *de todo mi sentido.*

> [The story of the looting, the riches, the *captives*
> that the Turks found in the bosom
> of the sad galley has been told to me
> by a Christian who lost there the sweet
> and beloved freedom, to take it away,
> in turn, from she who wants to surrender to her slave.
> That Christian, Silvia, that Christian;
> *that Christian* is, Silvia, he who has me
> *beside myself* and the boundaries heeded by Moorish women,
> *beside* my joy and happiness,
> *beside* any pleasure, and I am,
> that is the worst—*beside all my senses.*]
>
>   (II, 1256–67; emphasis mine)

This soliloquy points to a doubly autobiographical scenario in Cervantes: the story of Sosa's capture, which speaks to their lives as slaves in Algiers and to their close friendship during four years, and the scene of Cervantes's own capture, a year and a half before, revivified by the story of the *San Pablo*'s seizure. Both sides of the story that intertwines Sosa's and Cervantes's lives are reenacted by Zahara's tale. In addition, her soliloquy is marked by insistent and vehement repetitions, such as the iteration of the term *cristiano*: "*un* cristiano *que allí perdió la dulce y amada libertad*" [a *Christian* who lost there the sweet and beloved freedom] and "*este cristiano*" [this Christian], a term feverishly reiterated in Zahara's verses. Clearly, the phrase "*este cristiano*" refers not only to Antonio de Sosa, who recounted this ordeal to Cervantes, but also to Cervantes himself, the writer who evokes the loss of his own freedom through his spokeswoman, Zahara.

In the same way, the repetition of the syntagmas "*fuera de*" [outside of, or beside]—"*fuera del ser*" [beside myself], "*fuera de mi contento*" [beside my joy], "*fuera de todo gusto*" [beside any pleasure], "*estoy fuera* [. . .] *de todo mi sentido*" [I am (. . .) beside all my senses]—reveals that the process of testimony is a ceaseless struggle that often puts the witness to the test—in Cervantes's own words, "beside himself or herself." Accordingly, there is in the center of trauma a danger, a nightmare, a fragility that defies all healing. In these fictional processes of witnessing, erratic and continuous, conscious or unconscious, what ultimately matters is not the simple establishment of the fact but the experience itself of *living through* testimony, of giving testimony. Cervantes's strategies of evasion—the turning away from the nightmare of reality to invent an imaginary world removed from the atrocious world of captivity in Algiers—present testimony, even fictional or artistic testimony, as a crisis that connects narrative to history.

Apostasy: "To Give the Soul to Satan"

El trato portrays other effects of captivity—in Saavedra's precise terms, "cómo se echa a perder aquí un cristiano,/y más, mientras más va, va [em]peorando" [how a Christian here is spoiled,/and more, the more he stays, the worse he becomes] (IV.2126–28). Through their enslavement in Algiers, the poor Christian captives who believed that God would protect them from their enemies suffered a profound spiritual shock and asked themselves questions for which there seemed to be no answers. Desperation increased as more and more years passed in the baño, without hope of delivery, and if ransom did not materialize, the captive began to think of the only possibility left: apostasy. Sosa recapitulates the despairing thoughts of the Christian deserted by all: "Este mesmo desdeño, este desamparo, este olvido de Dios [. . .] [es lo] que más cuotidianamente siente y experimenta un desdichado cautivo en todo su cautiverio" [this same scorn, this neglect, this abandonment from God (. . .) [is that] which a wretched captive feels and experiences the most daily during his whole captivity] (Topografía, II: 163). Not a moment of repose exists in this torment that fills the days, weeks, months, or years of captivity for many slaves in Algiers or Constantinople. Such sufferings can be compared to those of Job, who cries to God in vain: "Llamo señor con clamores, ¿no me oís? Aposta me pongo delante de vuestros ojos, ¿no me queréis?" [I call you with clamors, Lord, don't you hear me? I deliberately put myself in front of your eyes, don't you love me?] (Topografía, II: 163). Dispossessed of God—"para solo el mal afortunado cautivo parece que no hay Dios" [for only the unfortunate captive there seems to be no God] (Topografía, II: 164)—the solution was, for many, to convert to Islam.

Sosa's earlier allusions to the desperation that led the captive to fall over a precipice and throw himself into hell also referred, then, to the multiple apostasies of Christian slaves, who ended by embracing Islam to obtain freedom from their chains. Cervantes, moreover, defines renegar [to apostatize] in El trato as "[dar] el ánima a Satanás" [to give the soul to Satan] (III.1810–11). We may recall that in the 1570s, more than half of the inhabitants of Algiers were "Turks by profession"—that is, renegades. Most of these renegades, born and brought up in the Christian faith, had apostatized of their own free will. The number of these renegades apparently exceeded that of all the Moors, Turks, and Jews of Algiers (Topografía, I: 52).

As Cervantes reveals in *Los tratos de Argel* and other works, the temptation to apostatize and become a Muslim was a constant for the captives. The character Saavedra illustrates this claim: *"Cautivo he visto yo que da de mano/a todo aquello que su ley le obliga,/y vive a veces vida de pagano"* [Many a captive have I seen who pays lip service/to everything that his faith obliges him to keep/and he lives sometimes the life of a pagan] (IV.2129–31). The various tableaus in the play that allude to the temptation to become a Turk to gain a good life in Barbary possibly speak of an authentic inner debate in the future author, a crucial drama later projected onto the stage. I alluded in chapter 1 to the question posed by Eisenberg: "Why did Cervantes return from Algiers?" Like Canavaggio and Sola, the critic assumes that Cervantes was invited to convert to Islam with the enticement of freedom and of acceding to the circles of power in the city (249–50). This is certainly conceivable, as suggested by Cervantes's associations with important political figures of Algiers. Becoming a renegade, however, would have meant, for Cervantes, accommodating himself to the commerce in human beings that he despised and forsaking his writing, his poetry, and his books, intellectual activities that he kept alive in spite of all difficulties during his captivity.[67]

In this respect, *El trato* presents an enlightening dialogue between the autobiographical character named Saavedra and a Spanish captive significantly called Pedro, who has decided to become a Turk, adopting the name of Mamí.

Saavedra: ¿Renegar quieres?

Pedro: Sí quiero, mas entiende de qué hechura.

Saavedra: Reniega tú del modo que quisieres,
                que ello es muy gran maldad y horrible culpa,
                y correspondes mal a ser quien eres.

Pedro: Bien sé que la conciencia ya me culpa,
                pero tanto el salir de aquí deseo,
                que esta razón diré por mi disculpa.

                Ni niego a Cristo, ni en Mahoma creo:
                con la voz y el vestido seré moro,
                por alcanzar el bien que no poseo.

                Si voy en corso, séme yo de coro,
                que, en tocando la tierra de cristianos
                me huiré, y aun no vacío de tesoro.

[Saavedra: Do you want to apostatize?

Pedro: Yes, I do, but only in a certain way.

Saavedra: Apostatize in any way you want
            since this is a great evil and a terrible sin,
            and this does not befit your character.

Pedro: My conscience already blames me,
            but I wish to leave this place so badly,
            that this is the reason I shall give in my defense.

            I don't deny Christ, nor do I believe in Mohammed;
            with my voice and my clothes I will be a Moor,
            in order to obtain the good I don't possess now.

            If I go on a privateering expedition, I know by heart
            that, upon touching the land of Christians,
            I will escape, and, indeed, not without treasures.]
                                        (*Trato* IV. 2142-55)

In a calm tone, marked by profound empathy and understanding, Saavedra persuades the doubting Pedro not to forsake his Christian faith: *"Un falso bien te muestra aquí aparente,/que es tener libertad, y, en renegando/se te irá el procurarla de la mente"* [A false good apparently looms before you,/ which is to acquire liberty, and, upon apostatizing,/your mind will forget to obtain it] (IV.2159–61).

Another scene in the play, from Act III, dramatically emphasizes the powerful forces of need and opportunity in relation to the religious and moral conflicts of the Christian slaves. Two allegorical figures, Necesidad [Need] and Ocasión [Occasion], stage a debate with captive Aurelio. Cervantes tells us in his prologue to *Ocho comedias* that these figures represent *"las imaginaciones y los pensamientos escondidos del alma"* [the hidden imaginations and thoughts of the soul] (*OC*, 9: xii). Their essential function, as Edward C. Riley argued, is to externalize the conflict going on in the hero's mind.[68] They remain invisible to Aurelio, and ostensibly to all but the audience, thus implying that the dramatic battle, represented by external means, is actually internal (Riley, 624).

Debilitated by these combats, Aurelio wavers between his desire for sensual Zahara and his love for virginal Silvia. The climax of the scene occurs when Aurelio practically surrenders to Zahara's seduction: *"Sígueme, Aurelio, agora que se ofrece/la* ocasión *de no estar Yzuf en casa"* [Follow me, Aurelio, now that the *occasion* presents itself, for Ysuf is not home]. As the Occasion incarnates itself in the circumstance that Zahara's husband, Ysuf, is not home, Aurelio accepts Zahara's invitation: *"Sí seguiré señora; que ya es tiempo/de obedecerte, pues soy tu esclavo"* [Yes, I shall come, Madam; for it is time to obey you, since I am your slave] (IV.1764–67). This poignant allusion to the word *esclavo*, here invoked in both its literal and figurative meanings, moves the utterance to another scenario, at once "other" and close, a scenario that summons the realm of desire. Through the metaphoric use of the term *esclavo*, Aurelio is clearly emphasizing the nature of the chains that bind him to Zahara. With these verses, as Casalduero remarks, sensuality takes possession of the scenario (245). But while Zahara awaits the slave in her bedroom, and Necesidad and Ocasión applaud Aurelio's imminent rendition (*";Ya se rinde!"* [He has surrendered!]), the captive asks himself:

> Aurelio, ¿dónde vas? ¿Para dó mueves
> el vagaroso paso? ¿Quién te guía?
> ¿Con tan poco temor de Dios te atreves
> a contentar tu loca fantasía?
> [. . .]
> ¿Tan presto has ofrecido y dado al viento
> las justas, amorosas fantasías,
> y ocupas la memoria de otras vanas,
> inhonestas, infames y livianas?
> ¡Vaya lejos de mí el intento vano!
> ¡Afuera, pensamiento malnacido!

> [Aurelio, where are you going? Where are you aiming
> your wandering steps? Who guides you?
> With so little fear of God do you dare
> to please your delirious fantasy?
> (. . .)
> So swiftly have you offered and forgotten
> the just, amorous fantasies,
> and occupied your mind in other vain,
> dishonest, infamous, and light fancies?
> Go away from me, vain intention!
> Out, contemptible thought!]

(III.1775–79, 1787–92)

This self-questioning betrays the exact nature of the combat that splits Aurelio in two. His attraction for Zahara arises as a transgression against both his faith and his love for Silvia. Such transgression extends to the Muslim prohibition against love between a Moorish woman and a Christian slave, as he recognizes: *"al cristiano no es lícito dé gusto/en cosas de amor a mora alguna"* [it is not licit for a Christian/to please a Moorish woman in matters of love] (II.1275–76). Sosa recounts that the adultery of a Moorish woman with a Christian was punished by burning the man alive or forcing him to apostatize without remission. Such laws, however, were not always heeded by the Algerians. In his report on the city of Algiers, composed in the early seventeenth century, Fray Melchor de Zúñiga relates that Moorish women often entered the *baños* disguised as captives, or at night, climbing over the ramparts, obviously aided by bribes distributed to the prison guards.[69]

Many apostasies occurred in extremis, when a Christian was found laying with a Moorish or Turkish woman. The culprit was then given the option of converting to Islam and marrying the woman, or being impaled (Benassar and Benassar, 384). As Bartolomé and Lucile Benassar inform us, adultery between Christian men and Muslim women was frequent. A Greek slave from Patmos, named Juan, seduced a married woman in seventeenth-century Algiers, only to be caught in bed with her by the husband. In the fight that ensued, the lover killed the husband. The "Turkish" owner of the slave had his captive circumcised, after which he made him marry the woman (Benassar and Benassar, 384). Sosa confirms that the first time an adulteress was caught with a Christian, she would be publicly whipped and exposed throughout the land, and the second time, she would be thrown into the sea with a rock tied to her neck (*Topografía*, I: 166). Despite these punishments, the significant number of conversions to Islam accepted in urgency by captives to save themselves from death after engaging in sexual relations with Moorish women and being discovered by husbands, fathers, or brothers speaks to a certain freedom in the interior of the houses where these women lived. Let us also note the autonomy that Moorish women apparently had: After being widowed, many women chose to marry their slaves (Benassar and Benassar, 477).

This discussion on the amorous relations between Moorish women and their Christian slaves takes us back to Aurelio and his enamored owner Zahara in Cervantes's play. Aurelio's dilemma of choosing between sensuous Zahara and chaste Silvia is associated with the conflict between the Muslim and the Christian religions and ways of life. Aurelio's surrender to Zahara and his change of status would thus signify his abandonment of Christianity. The sensual dimension of Zahara's Muslim world, then, is tightly connected to the lure of apostasy, as demonstrated by my review of its relation to the sexual transgressions of the captives. These dangers and concomitant temptations of Islam give a novel dimension to the scene of the lion in *El trato*. The lion, as we may recall, stood as a symbol of vigilance, the constant vigilance recommended to the Christian, who should remain always on guard against the enemy. Rereading the scene of the lion from the perspective of that describing sensual temptation in Algiers imparts to it a rich new meaning.

Sosa indeed corroborates in one of his diatribes against the renegades, quoted in chapter 1, that apostatizing meant not only gaining freedom and a comfortable life as a renegade but also acceding to the sensual pleasures available in the open societies of the Maghrib.[70] In chapter 2 we examined the sensual dimension of this world, which revealed its seductions to a great number of Christians and renegades. While many took advantage of the newly found sexual freedom inconceivable in Europe, others converted to Islam to enjoy the open sexual practices of Algiers or other Muslim centers. The integration into the new society through marriage, moreover, usually represented a good deal for the captive, who obtained his freedom from slavery and, in many cases, additional financial rewards. Such rewards frequently included access to the social status of the father-in law, who was also often a renegade (Benassar and Benassar, 472). Moorish servant Fátima makes these connections, as she tries to induce Aurelio to accept the love of her mistress: *"libertad se te promete;/los hierros se te quitarán,/y después te vestirán"* [we promise you freedom;/your fetters will be removed,/and then, we shall clothe you] (1.189–91).

With his wounds still bleeding, Cervantes attempted to demonstrate the degenerating effects of a long captivity on human beings who were constantly tempted to renounce their faith and collaborate with the enemy. Aurelio's final triumph over his spiritual conflict—*"¡Cristiano soy, y [he] de vivir cristiano!"* [I am a Christian! And I must live like a Christian!] (III.1795)—consequently underlines the victory of Christian fortitude in this drama. Yet Aurelio's poignant rejection of Islam and its lures precisely evokes the attractions of this universe, as well as the ordeals of the slaves who endured a long captivity in Barbary. This captivity was haunted not only by constant punishments and death threats but also by temptations of escape into another world, at once desired and rejected, as Cervantes keenly demonstrates. Aurelio's words speak to the wounds left by such "crossings."

A Collective Testimony

The torments and continuous sufferings of the captives, including death, dramatized in various scenes of *El trato*, turn this drama into a collective tragedy. Yet this is not a tragedy in the traditional—that is, classical—sense. Franco Meregalli, among others, has defended the unity of this play against the rigid nineteenth-century neoclassic criticism that severely chastised its dramatic form and, especially, its "lack of unity": *"¿Qué mayor unidad que la comunidad de cautivos, cada uno de los cuales [. . .] contribuye a caracterizar su destino individual, pero con una voz que forma parte de un coro: y es el coro el protagonista y la diversidad es una manifestación de la unidad?"* [What greater unity than the community of captives, each of whom (. . .) contributes to characterize an individual destiny, but with a voice that is part of a chorus: (where) the chorus is the protagonist, and diversity is a manifestation of unity?] (Meregalli, 403). Other critics have focused on the unity of the play as revealing a technique similar to that used in *La Numancia*, the protagonist of which is a group connected by a common destiny, a catastrophe that embraces all.[71] This turns *El trato de Argel* into a tragedy in the present, post-Holocaust sense.

El trato is not only the first dramatic testimony of Cervantes regarding his traumatic experience: It is also a collective testimony of captivity, voiced through the writer's poetry and the voices and performances of an amazing number of actors.[72] In chapter 2, I discussed the testimonial process as similar in nature to the psychoanalytical process itself, in that it is yet another medium that provides a listener to trauma, another medium, as Dori Laub describes it, of reexternalization—and thus historicization—of the event ("Bearing Witness," 70). Referring to the historical testimonies recorded by the Video Archive for Holocaust Testimonies at Yale, Laub—a Holocaust survivor himself—argues that in spite of the irreconcilable differences between these two perspectives, the process that is set in motion by psychoanalytical practice and by the testimony is "essentially the same," both in the narrator and in the analyst or interviewer as a listener ("Bearing Witness," 70). Bearing witness to trauma, moreover, is a process that encompasses the listener: "For the testimonial process to take place, there needs to be a bonding, the intimate and total presence of an *other*—in the position of one who hears. Testimonies are not monologues; they cannot take place in solitude. The witnesses are talking to somebody: to somebody they have been waiting for, for a long time" ("Bearing Witness," 70–71).

The theater, of course, makes possible this encounter between the witness and the listener. In her work *Lire le théâtre*, Anne Ubersfeld reminds us that theatrical "communication" is not a passive process; it also indicates a social practice.[73] More than any other activity, the theater demands work on the part of the spectator, a complete inscription, both voluntary and involuntary, in the dramatic process. Two elements vie with each other in the spectator's activity: on the one hand, reflection, and on the other, passionate contagion, the trance, the dance, everything coming from the body of the actor that elicits emotions in the body and psyche of the spectator. The spectator of the theatrical ceremony is thus prompted by the signs (the signals) to suffer emotions that, without necessarily being the same emotions represented, enter into a determined relation with them (Ubersfeld, I: 41–42). Bertolt Brecht underlines the fundamental law of the theater that turns the spectator into a participant, a decisive *actor* who has no need to intervene in any *happening* (*"Petit Organon"* §77; quoted by Uberfeld, I: 34).

In addition, as I mentioned earlier, we may infer that among the public watching the staging of *El trato de Argel*, there were former captives and relatives of other men and women enslaved in Barbary, spectators who would have profoundly empathized with the moving testimony presented by Cervantes's play. The problem of captives in North Africa was a phenomenon that deeply pervaded all of Iberian society and influenced the

Spanish outlook on life. Let us remember that the total number of captives in Algiers at the end of the sixteenth century was approximately equivalent to ten percent of the population of the Crown of Castile at the time, an extraordinary fact that touched almost every Spaniard. From the massive campaigns led by the ransomer monks to raise funds for the rescue of captives, to the processions held when these ransomed men and women returned home, to the chains and shackles hung in churches and public buildings to signify liberation, the cruel reality of captivity in Barbary was ever present for the Spaniards. Not only did Cervantes's drama enact for the first time on the Spanish stage the sufferings of the captives, but also its staging made possible an encounter between the survivor and the listener (the spectator), so that an individual and a collective testimony could take place.

If the theater produces an awakening of fantasies, it also elicits an awakening of conscience, the one being accompanied by the other, as Brecht claims, in the association of pleasure and reflection. In this reenactment of the event in the presence of a witness, the spectator, like the analyst or the interviewer, takes on the responsibility for bearing witness. Through the medium of the theater, Cervantes's traumatic story is finally told, transmitted, heard. Laub emphasizes that "it is the encounter and the coming together between the survivor and the witness" that makes possible something like "the repossessing of the act of witnessing. This joint responsibility is the source of the reemerging truth" ("Bearing Witness," 85). Speaking of Claude Lanzman's film *Shoah*, Nelly Furman writes that this film is so effective because it "forces us first of all to hear, to listen," therefore challenging our notions of facts and "our understanding of history."[74] Something similar must have occurred with Cervantes's play, the first Spanish drama that confronted the viewer with the daunting reality of captivity in Barbary.

As a testimony of captivity, *El trato* illustrates the workings of trauma: Its episodic, disconnected scenes that threaten to become too intense duplicate the way trauma returns to the memory of the survivor. Like the flashbacks or traumatic scenes that recur continuously, reliving each time the reality of the past, the traumatic reenactment conveys, to use Caruth's words, "both *the truth of an event*, and *the truth of its incomprehensibility*" (*Explorations*, 153). *El trato* reflects both the breakdown of understanding and the difficult reenactments of the traumatic event(s). The text of this drama is fragmented, shattered to the infinite, among the vertiginous scenes that follow one another and the various destinies presented to the spectator. As Zmantar shrewdly notes in her article on Saavedra and *El trato de Argel*, even the autobiographical dimension of the play is fragmented to the core, dramatized through the assorted characters who depict different

facets or experiences of the captive Cervantes ("Saavedra," 35). This, in
effect, is nothing new to the theater, especially if one regards the stage as
a closed area where the elements of the divided self confront each other.
Paul Claudel affirmed, in relation to his drama *L'Échange [The Exchange]*,
that the four characters were four parts of his self, and Victor Hugo thus
describes the decomposition of his *"moi"* (his self) in one of his plays: *"Mon
moi se décompose en Olympio: la lyre, Herman: l'amour, Maglia: le rire,
Hierro: le combat"* [My self is decomposed in Olympio: the lyre, Herman:
love, Maglia: laughter, Hierro: combat] (quoted by Ubersfeld, 1:26). The
splitting of the ego, however, becomes overdetermined when the play reenacts a history of collective trauma.

Critics have observed that Aurelio and Saavedra in *El trato de Argel*
represent two parts of Cervantes. The reality of the splitting revealed by
Aurelio-Saavedra certainly imposes itself as a poetic autobiographical figuration. Yet the idealized notion put forth by Casalduero (238), which envi-
sions Aurelio as the poetic core of Cervantes and Saavedra as the historic
and religious sentiment in the writer, has to be transcended. I propose,
instead, that beyond the splitting of Aurelio-Saavedra, Cervantes's traumatic experience is also rewritten and restaged by the thirty-eight characters who incarnate the ordeal of Algerian captivity. Many characters, in fact,
including the captive Saavedra—the writer's alter ego, who reappears in
La historia del cautivo and *El gallardo español*—represent Cervantes's fragmented subjectivity. As previously suggested, Per Álvarez and the unnamed
slave who tries to escape to Orán in vain both dramatize Cervantes's own
escape attempt and reiterate the testimony offered by the former captive
Cervantes in the *Información de Argel*. In the dramatic reconstruction of
the catastrophic event, the *I* of the narrative discourse is everywhere, assumed by all the characters. *El trato* thus depicts a collection of fragmented
images, inverted figures redoubled in the mirrors of the play, ungraspable
memories of life in Algiers. The different testimonies and perspectives enacted in *El trato*—from the discussion of various characters who debate
whether to convert to Islam to gain freedom, to Aurelio's conflict between
his attraction for Zahara and his love for Silvia, to the burning at the stake
of a Valencian priest in Algiers, to the story of the slaves who attempt a
suicidal escape through the desert—imply a fragmentation of testimony
and of voice. These fragmented scenes and discourses, almost unconnected
in their sequences, enter into a dialogue between the individual and the
collective, between the spectator and the characters, rendering in this way
a collective testimony of captivity in Algiers.

"Cuando llegué cautivo" [When I Arrived as a Slave]

This chapter concludes by way of Saavedra, the character that bears the significant name finally adopted by Cervantes—Miguel de Cervantes Saavedra—perhaps as a dramatic testimony of his Algerian experience, or a scar of his encounter with trauma. Cervantes officially adopted the surname *Saavedra* in 1586 and 1587, in documents related to his marriage to Catalina de Salazar (Sliwa, 143–46).[75] The addition of the surname *Saavedra* to Cervantes's name and signature and the implications of this action in regard to the writer's traumatic experience are explored in chapter 4 on *La historia del cautivo*. For the moment, let us recall that extreme trauma creates a second self. Robert Jay Lifton posits that "in extreme involvement, as in extreme trauma, one's sense of self is radically altered. And there is a traumatized self that is created." Lifton insists that this is not a totally new self, that it is what one brought into the trauma as affected significantly and painfully, confusedly, by trauma: "It's a form of doubling of the traumatized person. And in doubling [. . .], there have to be elements that are at odds in the two selves, including ethical contradictions."[76] The process of splitting, in effect, maintains the two attitudes (or selves) simultaneously with no dialectical relationship established. This doubling not only illuminates the relation between Aurelio and Saavedra in *El trato*, including their intimate differences, but also sheds light on the other refracted couples of this drama.

Saavedra, in fact, appears all over this play, popping in and out of scenes, striving heroically to convince other captives to keep their faith in spite of threats and seductions. His obsessive preaching elicits captive Leonardo's wry comment: *"Amigo Saavedra, si te ar[r]eas/de ser predicador, ésta no es tierra/do alcanzarás el fructo que deseas"* [Saavedra, friend: if you strive to be a preacher, this is no land where you might reach your desired goal] (1.366–68)

Representing the epic model of the captive who sustains his faith and patriotism even in the face of death, Saavedra possibly points to an image of the self created in captivity in the service of survival, perhaps even to those aspects of Cervantes's ideal ego, possessed of everything that is of value that helped him to endure his captivity. This image, projected onto the Spanish stage, embodies the values of Philip II's Spain. It is Saavedra who recites some of the most beautiful verses in *El trato de Argel*, verses that epitomize the testimony of Cervantes:

> Cuando llegué cautivo y vi esta tierra
> tan nombrada en el mundo, que en su seno
> tantos piratas cubre, acoge y cierra,
> no pude al llanto detener el freno

que a pesar mío, sin saber lo que era
me vi el marchito rostro de agua lleno.

[When I arrived as a captive, and saw this land,
ill famed in all the world, whose bosom conceals,
protects, embraces such a throng of pirates,
I could not keep from weeping,
so that, in spite of myself, without knowing what it was
I saw my gaunt face bathed in water.]

(I.396–403)

The poem dramatizes the experience of the unsuspecting captive suddenly confronted with the horror of his or her enslavement. The eloquence of the *tercetos* brings before the spectator and the reader the face of the captive as he encounters the shores of Algiers. Certainly, the power of evocation lies in the words, in the poetry itself, rather than in the declamation and movements of the actors charged with incarnating the text. The poem thus reaches the spectator, the listener, over the historical and geographical abyss from which the lyric originates, and across the violence and traumatic images that traverse the stage.

More important, however, is the poem's evocation of the splitting of the self produced by trauma. Saavedra's verses invoke the image of an inverted Narcissus, whose self-estrangement does not let him face the traumatic pain felt by his body *"que a pesar mío, sin saber lo que era/me vi el marchito rostro de agua lleno"* [so that in spite of myself, without knowing what it was/I saw my gaunt face bathed in water]. Indeed, the body of Saavedra, separated from his self, aches and cries on its own. His tears seem to surge from another being. Ferenczi's version of traumatic splitting may illuminate this Cervantine passage. In his clinical notes, Ferenczi states, referring to a clinical case: "This story can be interpreted in two ways: on the one hand, it reveals the passive resistance that the patient opposes against the aggressions of an exterior world; on the other, it represents the splitting of the person into a sensible part, brutally destroyed, and into another, which knows all, but does not feel anything" ("Reflexions," 106). Saavedra's verses indeed seem to be saying: "I don't suffer; at most, a part of my body cries." This passage speaks to the very paradoxical indirectness of psychic trauma, namely, to the circumstance that the possibility of traumatic knowledge can arise only within the very act of its denial.

As I said earlier, the powerful poetry of Cervantes testifying to his traumatic experience in *El trato de Argel* must have moved many spectators who identified with the ordeal of the Barbary captives. Addressing Philip II, Saavedra recounts the story of Charles V's historic defeat in Algiers: *"Esas cosas, volviendo en mi memoria,/las lágrimas trajeron a los ojos"* [Those

things, returning to my memory,/brought tears to my eyes] (1.409–10).
Those lines are an homage to Garcilaso de la Vega, the great poet whom
Cervantes admired above all.[77] Saavedra's tears flow twice in this poem:
first, when the captive arrives in Algiers, and later, when the memories of
Charles V's tragic loss return, revealing the inexorability of the captive's
destiny and the impossibility of salvation in this invincible prison-city, completely surrounded by the desert and the sea.

Saavedra's verses summon the terrible tempest that destroyed Charles's
Imperial armada in 1541, where about one hundred fifty ships were lost,
along with twelve thousand men who drowned or were massacred by the
Berber tribes as they came ashore unarmed. In a heavily idealized reading
of Saavedra's tears, Casalduero states: *"Son las primeras lágrimas vertidas
por la historia de España. Saavedra no llora por él, llora por la historia de
España"* [These are the first tears shed for the history of Spain. Saavedra
does not cry for himself, he cries for the history of Spain] (225). I would
suggest, instead, that Saavedra cries both for himself and for Spain. These
are not only the first tears shed for the politics of Philip II around 1580,
politics that permitted the existence of Algiers, a city viewed by Cervantes
as an immense dungeon filled with Christians. These tears speak, above
all, to an identification of Cervantes/Saavedra with the image of vanquished
Charles V and, concomitantly, with a perception of a shattered Spain. Images of devastation pervade Saavedra's words: Only a catastrophe such as
Charles V's defeat can compare to the cataclysm experienced by the captive.

Saavedra's (or Cervantes's) tears testify to the incommensurability of
the traumatic occurrence, whose overwhelming impact puts the limits of
the witness and of the witnessing to the test. Although Saavedra ultimately
disappears from the stage, his verses and tears resonate through the songs
and tears of the captives who pray to the Virgin, asking for deliverance:
*"¡Vuelve, Virgen Santísima María,/tus ojos que dan luz y gloria al cielo,/a
los tristes que lloran noche y día/y riegan con sus lágrimas el suelo!"* [Turn
your eyes, Saintly Virgin Mary,/which give light and glory to heaven,/to
the sad ones who cry night and day, and who water the ground with their
tears] (IV.2548–2601). These tears that insistently return to the text mark
the collective testimony of the captives even while they water the ground
of Algiers.

If *El trato de Argel* testifies to the impossibility of bearing witness to
trauma, it also enacts the liberation of the testimony through the medium
of drama and poetry. As a chorus of testimonies and performances, this
play, *"trasunto de Argel"* [reflection of Algiers] inaugurates both Cervantes's
dramatic production and his literary testimonies, in poetry that reveals the
links between trauma and creation in the writer. The last words in *El trato*

are left to Aurelio, the hero who has encountered death and who now speaks to the audience in the name of the author, the survivor: *"Si ha estado mal sacado este trasunto/de la vida de Argel y trato feo,/pues es bueno el deseo que ha tenido,/en nombre del autor perdón les pido"* [If this reflection of life in Algiers and its ugly dealings has been badly represented, since the intentions of the author were good, I ask forgiveness in his name] (IV.2534–37). If Saavedra's connections with Cervantes are well established, Aurelio closes the play as that other self of the author who can bring back to his people a knowledge of death and, therefore, a knowledge of life, a profound new knowledge that both questions and invokes our human comprehension.

Torture of the Hook. The Flemish author Olfert Dapper (1639-1689) published a series of books on Africa. This drawing depicts the "Torture of the Hook" in Barbary: the victim would be hung from the scaffold by two chains attached to hooks driven through a hand and foot.

SOURCE: *Tortures in Algiers*, from Olfert Dapper, *Eigentliche beschreibung der insulen in Africa . . .* (Amsterdam, 1671), 167. Reprinted by permission of the Division of Rare and Manuscript Collections, Karl A. Kroch Library, Cornell University Library. Call number: Rare Dt7 D21 ++

The Gate of Bab Azoun. The drawing represents a busy view of the famous Gate of Bab Azoun in Algiers, with loaded camels entering the city. *Above right:* the topographic letter key identifies the houses of the people living below the ramparts (D), and the hooks used for torture attached to both sides of the gate on the city walls (B). *Right:* a victim hangs from one of the hooks.

SOURCE: *The Gate of Bab Azoun* in Algiers from Olfert Dapper, *Eigentliche beschreibung der insulen in Africa* . . . (Amsterdam, 1671), 241. Reprinted by permission of the Division of Rare and Manuscript Collections, Karl A. Kroch Library, Cornell University Library. Call number: Rare Dt7 D21 ++

An Algerian Holy Priest. Bonnart (1642-1711), a French painter and engraver, published 135 costume plates. The legend to this engraving reads:
"Muslim Holy Priest: This Mohammedan Marabout / appears formi-
dably dressed in his Law / and with more zeal for the Koran / than a
Christian has for his Gospels." Revered by Turks and Moors alike, the
marabouts were in charge of the mosques in Algiers. Some taught in
the Koranic schools, while others were hermits. Their dress, depicted
here as a very wide shirt and a coat which descends to the feet, varied
according to Turkish or Moorish fashion.

SOURCE: Henri Bonnart: *Marabout of Algiers* [Muslim Holy Man]
(Bibliothèque Nationale, Paris). Reprinted from Gabriel Esquer, *Icono-
graphie historique de l'Algérie depuis le XVIe siècle jusqu'à 1871* (Paris:
Plon, 1929), Vol I, Plate XXIX, no. 78.

Turkish Soldier from Algiers. The legend reads: "This Turk whose mien is so proud / Is a true corsair of Algiers / Who, in order to fill his game-bag / Does not fear trouble nor danger." The Turkish militia of Algiers (*Odjack*) was recruited primarily from among the Turks of Asia Minor. The *Odjack* had a political role in Algiers, often influencing the naming or removal of the *beylerbeys*. This janissary wears the traditional dress of Algerian Turks, with a collarless vest, a cassock with short sleeves, and buttoned false sleeves made of taffeta or silk which could be removed for the ritual washing of hands and arms before the prayer. He dons a white turban and the yellow, orange, or red leather walking-boots (*borceguíes*) worn during the winter in Algiers.

SOURCE: Henri Bonnart: *A Turkish Soldier from Algiers* (Bibliothèque Nationale, Paris). Reprinted from Gabriel Esquer, *Iconographie historique de l'Algérie depuis le XVIe siècle jusqu'à 1871* (Paris: Plon, 1929), Vol I, XXVII, no. 75.

4

An Erotics of Creation:
La historia del cautivo

De todos los sucesos sustanciales que en este suceso
me acontecieron, ninguno se me ha ido de la memoria,
ni aún se me irá en tanto que tuviere vida.[1]
—Cervantes, *La historia del cautivo* (*DQ* I, 40)

THIS IS PERHAPS THE PLACE to rethink the mysterious links that associate the dungeon—the prison—with literary invention in Spain's major writer. Let us recall that in his prologue to *Don Quijote*, the author affirms that this book was engendered *"en una cárcel, donde toda incomodidad tiene su asiento"* [in a prison, where every misery is lodged] (*DQ* I: 50). Ignoring his Algerian imprisonment and the recurrent images of captivity in Cervantes, critics have often interpreted this phrase as a symbolic declaration.[2] Years after his return from Algiers, during his Andalusian wanderings, Cervantes suffered a brief confinement in Castro del Río in 1592 and was again imprisoned in the Royal Prison in Seville in 1597 because a merchant who disappeared after going bankrupt took with him moneys Cervantes had deposited with him. Put in irons, thanks to an iniquitous judge, as Canavaggio remarks (*Cervantes*, 172–76), the former captive must have relived his long incarceration twenty years before in the *baños* of Algiers. Like the *baños* of Hasan Pasha, the Royal Prison in Seville was turned into a source of inspiration by Cervantes. His close encounters with the underworld of Seville allowed him to create the authentic pimps, bullies, beggars, madmen, and delinquents that people his novels.

As for the claim that the "prison where every misery is lodged" was a metaphorical prison for Cervantes, it would be strange to think, as Emilio Orozco Díaz has affirmed, that the writer who was twice incarcerated in both Castro del Río and Seville—precisely in the enormous Royal Prison of Seville, where he spent seven months between 1597 and 1598—would be alluding, when referring to the place where he conceived his novel, to the world as prison, as if he were a mystic writer. Should we not acknowledge, like many critics, asked Orozco Díaz, the influence in Cervantes's fiction of that heterogenous world of incomparable material and moral misery, the violent and picaresque world of the prison of Seville, where the writer

may have met so many strange characters and heard so many stories? (121).
Can we not suppose that Cervantes, like Antonio de Sosa and Fray Luis
de León, could have used that forced idleness—"obligado ocio," as Fray
Luis de León called his prison years—to think and write? Recall that Cervantes composed poems and letters while confined to the *baños* of Algiers.
More important, even if we decide that *Don Quijote* was engendered in a
metaphorical prison, the effects of captivity on Cervantes cannot be denied, as this study shows.

The marks of the prison reappear in Cervantes's last novel, *Persiles*, a
narrative that literally emerges from a dungeon: *"Voces daba el bárbaro
Corsicurbo a la estrecha boca de una mazmorra"* [At the top of his voice
Corsicurbo the barbarian was shouting into the narrow mouth of a deep
dungeon] are the first words of this narrative.[3] Even more crucially, the
hero of Cervantes's posthumous novel rises from this dungeon where the
barbarians keep their slaves, and the whole of *Persiles* originates in this sub-
terranean prison, which recalls those of Tunis and other Barbary slave centers (*Persiles*, 51–52/17). Among other fictions, the novellas *El amante liberal [The Liberal Lover]* and *La española inglesa [The English Spanish Girl]*
obsessively return to the motif of human bondage. Starting with the ab-
duction of the protagonists, both novels depict corsair attacks in the Mediterranean and the Atlantic, as well as historical names and personages that
belong to Cervantes's Algerian experiences. As a paradoxical mixture of
history and fiction, these novellas advance across the frontier where life
and creation encounter each other. To use John J. Allen's felicitous phrase,
Cervantes makes literature by basing himself on his own life; Don Quijote
creates a life based on literature.[4] Such alliance between life and work, between traumatic knowledge and literary creation, pressures me to examine
the limit between autobiography and fiction in Cervantes, especially in his
most famous autobiographical piece, *La historia del cautivo [The Captive's
Tale]*, interpolated in *Don Quijote*, Part I. Using an overdetermined term
whose ramifications will become clear below, I propose to call this weaving of trauma and fiction an "erotics" of creation.

Staging Signatures

In *Otobiographies* (1984), Jacques Derrida asks what is at stake when an
author puts his or her name to a piece of writing. To put one's name on
the line (with everything a name involves and that cannot be totaled in a
self), to "stage signatures," to create an immense biographical rubric out
of all one has written is "a matter of life and death."[5] Indeed, the name,
which should be distinguished from the bearer, always refers to death
(*Otobiographies*, 7). Derrida returns to the subject in various places, specifically in his moving adieu to the acclaimed literary critic and essayist

Roland Barthes: "The proper name [...] alone and by itself says death, all deaths in one. It says death even while the bearer of it is still living. While so many codes and rites work to take away this privilege, because it is so terrifying, the proper name alone and by itself forcefully declares the unique disappearance of the unique [...]. Death inscribes itself right in the name" ("The Deaths of Roland Bathes," 34). In his readable account of, and intertextual dialogue with, Jacques Derrida, Geoffrey Bennington explains the interplay between the proper name and death: "My proper name out-lives me. After my death, it will be possible to name me and to speak of me. Like every sign, including the 'I,' the proper name involves the neces-sary possibility of functioning in my absence, of detaching itself from its bearer: [. . .] one must take this absence to a certain absolute, which we call death."[6] Bennington concludes: "even while I am alive, my name marks my death." The name, the signature, is already the name of its bearer, "the name of the dead person, the anticipated memory of a departure" (148).

   The second chapter of Derrida's *Otobiographies* addresses the *dynamis* of the borderline between the work and the life of German philosopher Nietzsche, especially in his *Ecce Homo*. Such a mobile and powerful fron-tier—thus the reference to a dynamics—is neither a thin dividing line nor an invisible or indivisible trace found in the space of the philosophemes, on the one hand, and the life of an author identifiable with a name, on the other. This divisible limit, rather, cuts across two "bodies," the corpus (the work) and the body of the subject, according to laws that we barely begin to discern (*Otobiographies*, 5–6). The intertextual crossings between the corpus and the author's life are illustrated by Derrida's brilliant dis-cussion of Freud's *Beyond the Pleasure Principle*, entitled "Coming into One's Own," a text that draws on numerous episodes from the life (of Freud) to interpret, expound, and illuminate the work (of Freud).[7] But it does so, as Christopher Norris has demonstrated, by way of deconstructing those categories, declining to acknowledge any distinction between them, on the one hand, "life" and "work," and on the other, the various activi-ties of theory, speculation, and biographical suppositions advanced both by Freud and his followers.[8] In the end, Derrida argues, we cannot draw a line between the theories presented in Freud's text and the complex of "autobiographical" motives that went into its writing ("Coming into One's Own," 15).

   Like his reading of Nietzsche, cited earlier, Derrida's texts on Freud suggest that the fact that an author inscribes certain details of his own life history in a self-professed "scientific text" is no reason to conclude that the document in question is "without truth-value, without value as sci-ence or as philosophy" (141). Instead, its value may lie specifically in its power to break off this illusive opposition and inaugurate a reading atten-tive to the various points of exchange in a text, to the weaving of life and work. Speaking of *Beyond the Pleasure Principle*, Derrida affirms: "This text is autobiographical, but in a completely different way from what was believed before [. . .] a domain opens up in which the 'inscription' of a subject in his text is also a necessary condition for the pertinence and performance of the text, for its worth beyond what is called subjectivity" (135). Derrida's discussion of these encounters sheds light on my reading of the intertextual crossings between life and work in Cervantes.

This chapter studies the frontier that traverses Cervantes's bodies (the corpus and the body of the man Cervantes). I examine in these pages a space that we can call autobiographical, or rather *otobiographical*, to give a slight twist to the term and to move it, at the same time, along the lines intimated by Derrida. My study of the paradoxical borderline between the life and the work of Cervantes—an unclear line that is also divided, dislocated, so to speak—will necessarily include, then, a new analysis of the proper name and of the signature in Cervantes. Because the question of the proper name is necessarily connected with death, as we have seen, this study explores the encounter with death that marks Cervantes's name and signature *Saavedra*. The challenge is enormous for, as we know, Cervantes advanced behind a plurality of masks, names, and pseudonyms with which the author produced a constant yield of protection that obscured his marks in the text. The fact that Cervantes's creations are so profoundly intertwined with his life makes me approach this topic in a similar fashion, through a complex interweaving of life and literature. Readers will have to follow me, then, as I meander from life to creation in Cervantes and vice versa in this chapter.

As for the notion of the *otobiographical*, stressed by Derrida's reading of the "third ear" in Nietzsche's *Ecce Homo*, my own experience as a captive, a hostage of Colombian guerrillas between December 1982 and July 1983, urges me to read and listen to Cervantes with another ear, perhaps even with the psychoanalytic "third ear" proposed by Theodore Reik in a well-known statement. Having suffered the ordeal of captivity that strips the victim of his or her humanity and brands the survivor with the imprint of death, I read and listen to Cervantes with the understanding of one who knows that creative writing may be the best way to express feelings that are almost inexpressible, to accept what is at the limits of the bearable.

La historia del cautivo, interpolated in *Don Quijote*, Part I, offers an ideal venue for the study of the border between life and work in Cervantes. This tale not only provides a clear résumé of Cervantes's military career in the Mediterranean, followed by an extraordinary depiction of captivity in Barbary; it also unveils one of the most beautiful fictions of Cervantes's work, the story of Algerian convert Zoraida. Introduced by the famous "Discourse on Arms and Letters" delivered by Don Quijote at the inn (I, 37–38), the Captive's tale holds an ambiguous relation with the stories that frame it, to the point that this tale functions both as a link and a borderline between the episodes that precede it and those that follow it in *Don Quijote*. Even more, Don Quijote's famous speech on "Arms and Letters" and the dramatic story recounted by captive Captain Ruy Pérez de Viedma are connected in more than one way. Don Quijote's discourse is suggestively interrupted by the sudden arrival at Juan Palomeque's inn of a strange couple: a man recently released from captivity in Barbary and a mysterious veiled woman named Zoraida. Furthermore, the matter of Don Quijote's discourse is not at all immaterial to *The Captive's Tale* but provides the ideological framework for the lives that the Captain and his brother the Oidor [Judge] will dramatize with irony in the text.[9] In the same way, from the moment the Captive appears at the inn, the theme of captivity haunts the text: Very soon, Don Quijote himself will be literally kidnapped, turned into a prisoner, and taken to his hometown in a cage (*DQ* I, 46). Don Quijote's "Discourse on Arms and Letters" and Captain Pérez de Viedma's tale thus point to the mobile and mysterious frontier that traverses the corpus and *el cuerpo* in Cervantes.

At the borderline between history and legend, *La historia del cautivo* interrogates us from the double register of autobiography and fiction. The tale is dated by a particular phrase and point in time that permit us to situate the Captive's narration in 1589: *"Este hará veinte y dos años que salí de la casa de mi padre"* [This will be the twenty-second year since I left my father's house] (I, 39). Because Ruy Pérez de Viedma left Spain with the Duke of Alba, who assumed the reign of government of Flanders in September 1567—and because he witnessed the execution of the Counts of Egmont and of Horn, on June 5, 1568—we must conclude that the present telling of this tale takes place between 1589 and 1590. Given Cervantes's custom to indicate the date of composition in his fiction, critics have supposed that *La historia del cautivo* was written in 1589 and later included in *Don Quijote* (Allen, "Autobiografía," 151).[10] Particularly suggestive, in this sense, is the hypothesis advanced by Luis Andrés Murillo, who proposes that *La historia del cautivo* was redacted as an autonomous tale in the years 1589–1590 and later included in *Don Quijote*. The tale recounted by Captain Ruy Pérez de Viedma would thus be a prolegomenon to the novel, an *Ur-Quijote*, as Murillo indicated.[11] Its correspondences with the novel will be addressed in my analysis below.

To date is to sign, as Derrida reminds us, and to date from a particular site or location is also to identify the place of the signature (*Otobiographies*, 11). Various dates or signatures punctuate *La historia del cautivo*, mapping critical points in the Captive's autobiographical narrative. The first date identifies La Mancha, specifically Juan Palomeque's inn, as the originating place of the signature. After a beginning colored by folkloric motifs, *La historia del cautivo* moves to the Mediterranean, only to return, once more, to the *baños* of Algiers. It is in the recreation of Cervantes's Algerian captivity that a significant signature appears, this time as the mark of Cervantes's own name: *"Un soldado español, llamado tal de Saavedra"* [A Spanish soldier called something de Saavedra] (1, 40). Cervantes thus emerges as a phantasmatic apparition in the mise en scène of his own enslavement. As suggested in chapter 3, *Saavedra* was not Cervantes's last name, nor one that his direct ancestors bore. The writer assumed this surname after his return from Barbary.

A distant relative, Gonzalo Cervantes Saavedra, surely influenced Cervantes in his choice of a new appellation. Known as a poet and writer, Gonzalo was forced to flee his native Córdoba in 1568 after a bloody duel, a story curiously similar to that of the young Cervantes, who might have had analogous reasons for his escape from Madrid in 1569 (Astrana Marín, I: 23–25). Gonzalo embarked in Don Juan de Austria's galleys and perhaps even fought in the Battle of Lepanto. In *La Galatea* (1585), Cervantes lists the name *Gonzalo de Cervantes Saavedra* among those Cordovan poets praised in the *"Canto de Calíope"* ["Song of Calliope"].[12] Ruined after a dissipated soldierly life, Gonzalo sailed for the Indies in 1594, with a destination of Peru, but he perished in a shipwreck near the port of Havana (Astrana Marín, I: 26–27). Whether he used Gonzalo as a role model or not, Cervantes was certainly fascinated by the surname *Saavedra*, which punctuates his life and his fiction.

The surname *Saavedra* appears for the first time in Cervantes's play *El trato de Argel.* Saavedra, as we may recall, is the name of the loyal captive who functions as a spokesman for the author in this drama. Emerging next to the historical Hasan Pasha, among countless authentic and fictional personages, Saavedra epitomizes the ordeal of captivity, as shown by the eloquent verses analyzed in chapter 3: *"Cuando llegué cautivo y vi esta tierra/ tan nombrada en el mundo, que en su seno/tantos piratas cubre, acoge y cierra,/no pude al llanto detener el freno"* [When I arrived as a captive, and saw this land,/ill-famed in all the world, whose bosom conceals,/protects, embraces such a throng of pirates,/I could not keep from weeping] (*Trato*, 1.396–493). If Saavedra incarnates the values of Philip II's Spain, he also clearly stands for captive Miguel de Cervantes, perhaps even embodying the psychological attributes that allowed him to endure his captivity. Cervantes would give this name again to the hero of *El gallardo español [The Gallant Spaniard]*, a historical play probably written between 1597 and 1606, around the period in which the writer was composing his great novel. This play dramatizes the capture of Orán from the Spaniards in 1563 by the historical Hasan Pasha, the son of Barbarossa (c. 1517–1570)—a homonym of Venetian renegade Hasan Pasha.

After his repatriation, Cervantes traveled to Orán in 1581 as a special envoy for Philip II (Sliwa, 120–21). There he met with the governor, Don

Martín de Córdoba, as well as with the *caïd* of the neighboring port of Mostaganem, who wished to collaborate with the Spaniards.[13] Undoubtedly, the former captive must have recounted his long captivity to Don Martín de Córdoba, including his efforts to smuggle a letter out of the *baño* in 1578, addressed to Don Martín himself. Don Martín, as we might recall, was familiar with these *baños*. As a young man, he had been a captive in Algiers. In turn, he might have told the future writer the story of the Spanish resistance to the siege of Orán, which would be evoked years later by Cervantes's play *El gallardo español*. Don Martín de Córdoba had been, in fact, the hero of this legendary opposition against the Turks.

Passages, Margins, Frontiers

Beyond the threads that intertwined their separate captivities, however, Cervantes might have had other points of contact with Don Martín de Córdoba. The governor was a man of the frontier—in this case, the oppressive frontier constituted by the Spanish presidio of Orán, which stood like an island amidst the North African enemy territories. Since the turn of the century, Orán had become Spain's new frontier in the crusade against Islam. It was not fortuitous that a *relación* published in Seville in 1554, recounting a combat or rivalry competition between Christians and Moors, would explicitly state that Christian knights had to fight continuously "en Orán porque es frontera" [in Orán because it is the frontier].[14] The term *frontera*, as defined by Covarrubias, refers to *"la raya y término que parte dos reinos, por estar el uno frontero del otro"* [the line and boundary that cuts (separates) two kingdoms, one being in front of the other]. In the same way, the adjective *fronterizo* [bordering] was used to qualify the soldiers who served on the frontiers. The opposition and contiguity suggested by these definitions were replayed by life in the North African presidios, where Spanish soldiers both established relations with and fought against their Berber and Moorish neighbors. Like his father and brother before him, Don Martín de Córdoba was a *"soldado fronterizo."* This aligns him with the hero of Cervantes's play *El gallardo español*.

Don Fernando de Saavedra, the protagonist of *El gallardo español*, is a frontier man who fluctuates between the Spanish presidio of Orán and the Moorish *aduar* [camp] where beautiful Arlaxa lives. Like a typical frontier captain, Don Fernando de Saavedra responds to the challenge of noble Moor Alimuzel and crosses over to the enemy camp, where he becomes a voluntary captive and fraternizes with his adversary. Nevertheless, in the midst of the Turkish-Berber attack on Orán, the hero suddenly turns against the Moors and heroically defends the threatened Christian bastion. His ambiguous status as both a disguised Moor and a Christian hero is emphasized by a question posed in Orán: *"¿Que sea moro, Don Fernando?"*

[Is it possible that Don Fernando is now a Moor?], a question answered in the affirmative: *"Así lo van pregonando / los niños por la ciudad"* [Such is the news spread by children through the city] (*Gallardo*, II.1280–83).[15]

As Don Fernando's behavior suggests, defecting to the other side was quite common in the North African presidios, where Spanish soldiers suffered incredible hardships.[16] Modeled on historical Don Fernando de Cárcamo, who courageously defended the fortress of Mers-el-Kebir during the 1563 siege of Orán, Don Fernando de Saavedra is also conspicuously reminiscent both in name and exploits of the valiant captive of the "Río-verde" ballads that close the first part of Ginés Pérez de Hita's *Guerras civiles de Granada*. The "Ballad of Sayavedra" refers to Juan de Sayavedra, a historical personage captured by the Moors of Granada in 1448.[17] That this hero was also a frontier man who moved in the fringe permeable to the culture of the antagonist is significant. As María Soledad Carrasco Urgoiti has argued, the truce was the most frequent condition of the medieval Spanish frontier, where communications often took place, including commercial exchanges, official visits of dignitaries, and clandestine incursions. During these intrusions, men from either side attempted to go unnoticed by using the dress, the gestures, and perhaps the language of the neighboring state (*"El gallardo,"* 2).

An important consideration surfaces now in the face of the multiple resonances that Cervantes manages to evoke through the names of his characters. The family that exemplified the culture of the frontier during various centuries in medieval Spain was neither the Mendoza, the Fajardo, nor the Narváez families. It was the *Saavedra* family. Originating in Galicia, the Saavedra settled in Seville around 1351 and by the fifteenth century had turned into one of the most influential lineages of the city, known for their defense of and their forays across the frontier with the kingdom of Granada. Marked by their intense attraction for this boundary, the Saavedra made their fortune literally living on the edge, to the point that the frontier became the thread of their life. To be a Saavedra, as Cervantes certainly intuited, was to be, from birth, part of a destiny that was at once tragic and glorious, a destiny on the borderland often sealed by death.[18]

The historic hero of the medieval ballad "Juan de Saavedra" was, in fact, a member of the famous Saavedra (or Sayavedra) family from Seville. He was defeated and captured by the Moors near Marbella, in an expedition in which most of his men were killed. Taken to Granada as a captive, he was held hostage for an enormous ransom. This forced him to leave two of his daughters as hostages while he strived to obtain the money for their rescue from the king and the city council of Seville (Sánchez Saus, 168). The similarities with the capture and captivity of Cervantes are striking. Like the inhabitants of the sixteenth-century culturally mixed Maghrebi borders, the legendary Sayavedra was presumably tempted to apostatize and cross over to the enemy side, where he would have been received with honors as a "new Muslim." In a version of the "Romance de Sayavedra," the king of Granada attempts to win Sayavedra over with offers of worldly goods: *"Calles, calles, Sayavedra,—cese tu melancolía;/tórnate moro si quieres —y verás qué te daría:/darte he villas y castillos—y joyas de gran valía"* [Quiet, quiet, Saavedra,—end your melancholy;/turn into a Moor, if you want—and see what I would give you:/I will give you towns and castles— and jewels of great value] ("Sayavedra," vv. 26–28). Sayavedra's heroism in this ballad consists in keeping his Christian faith in spite of these entice-ments. The *Romancero* immortalizes Sayavedra by killing him as he con-fronts a squadron of Moors alone.

The reappearance of the name *Saavedra* in Cervantes's play *El gallardo español,* a play that emphasizes the dramatic call of the frontier in relation to its hero, suggests that *Saavedra* is an incarnation of limit. As we have seen, *Saavedra* evokes the cultural and geographical frontiers between the Christian and the Muslim worlds. These frontiers not only refer to the boundaries and barriers between geopolitical units, countries, nations, or communities, but also to those between cultural domains or "territories," philosophical or religious traditions, linguistic idioms, and languages in general. The question of the frontier and of the subjects who lived on the borderland, betwixt and between, as it were, recalls the period of margin-ality or "liminality" described by anthropologist Victor Turner in his study of rites of passage.[19] Turner has defined this liminality as an interstructural situation that constitutes transitions between states, *state* being defined here as "a relatively fixed or stable condition" that includes legal status, profes-sion, rank, or degree, but also as the mental or emotional condition in which an individual or group may be found at a particular time. Many rites of passage tend to have well-developed liminal periods. This "state of tran-sition" is a process that involves a transformation (Turner, 95).

The state of captivity, as well as the situation of the soldiers who in-habited the borderline between two cultures, transformed these individu-als into transitional beings or "liminal personae," whose status recalls the liminality intrinsic to most rites of passage. Like the liminal persona in the rite of passage, who is "at once no longer classified and not yet classified" (Turner, 96), both the captives and the *soldados fronterizos* in North Af-rica had been detached from a point in a fixed social structure to enter an ambiguous liminal period or zone. As Turner has claimed, the liminal per-sona is neither living nor dead from one aspect, and both living and dead from another, a definition that echoes Cervantes's and Antonio de Sosa's description of the captive as a "dead being." In addition, the liminal be-ings have nothing: no status, no property, insignia, secular clothing, rank, kinship position, and so on. Similar to the captives, the liminal persona is characterized by his or her utter deprivation.

These connections highlight the importance of liminality and, concomitantly, of frontier and borderline states in Cervantes's works. His relations with Algerian renegades, from poor slaves to powerful personages, and the significant role these renegades play in his fictions have been discussed in earlier chapters of this study. Cervantes's fascination and preoccupation with those who lived in the in-between, partaking of various cultures, remains constant throughout his work. Other Cervantine characters, such as Zoraida, the female protagonist of *La historia del cautivo*, move in this fringe world open to various cultures. The frontier is a relevant historical and structural motif in *El amante liberal* and *La española inglesa*, among other fictions that focus on the crisscrossing of geographical and cultural boundaries, including different languages. Could we not associate this fixation with the frontier with the condition of Don Quijote, who incarnates the borderline between madness and sanity, moving from one to the other at the flick of a switch, astonishing friend and foe alike?

As this discussion intimates, I propose that Cervantes's captivity placed him for several years in the liminal situation of the captive, the renegade, the *soldado fronterizo*, or the liminal persona who is neither this nor that and yet is both at the same time. This would explain his identification with borderline character Aurelio in *El trato de Argel* and his simultaneous rejection of this position through Aurelio's (and Cervantes's) double Saavedra. From this perspective, we could view Cervantes's captivity, including its traumatic effects, as a rite of passage, a type of transitional passage across the Spanish and Mediterranean frontiers that allowed him to grow into another persona. The frontier thus holds a privileged and symbolic place in Cervantes's complex network of symbols, as confirmed by the characteristics of those who bear the name *Saavedra* in his fictions. *Saavedra* also alludes to another frontier in Cervantes, namely, to the line that crosses the corpus and the body of the writer and, more specifically, to the significant surname he adopted after his return from Barbary.[20]

Assuming Paternities

The earliest documents signed with Cervantes's two names—*Cervantes Saavedra*—appear several years after his repatriation. The writer began adding the surname *Saavedra* to his patronymic in 1586 and 1587, in official documents related to his marriage to Catalina de Salazar.[21] Accordingly, on August 9, 1586, in the town of Esquivias, Miguel de Cervantes *Saavedra* signed a deed acknowledging the receipt of the dowry assigned to his wife, Catalina de Palacios Salazar, in which he lists the assets received from his mother-in-law and promises to manage Catalina's property adequately. On the same day, his mother-in-law Catalina de Palacios appointed Miguel de Cervantes *Saavedra* as the "absolute administrator" of all her worldly possessions (Sliwa, 142–43). Eight months later in Toledo, on April 28, 1587, Miguel de Cervantes *Saavedra* designates his wife Catalina Palacios Salazar as having power of attorney with full authority to conduct any business in his name and to represent him legally (Sliwa, 143–44). Not having been able to obtain a position in Castile, Cervantes is leaving for Andalucía, where he would work for approximately ten years as the new commissary officer for the supply of Philip II's galleys. In most of the letters and documents signed in Seville and other Andalusian towns after 1587, his name appeared as Miguel de Cervantes *Saavedra*.

The addition of a second surname, a name that did not correspond to his immediate family, was certainly significant in a man who was about to turn forty, a writer who had recently married a woman almost twenty years his junior—his marriage was celebrated on December 12, 1584. The import of this action must be definitely signaled, even while observing that altering one's name or adopting a surname that did not belong to one's father did not constitute an exceedingly bizarre deed in sixteenth-century Spain. Criminals often changed or dropped their last names, in the same way that the *Conversos* processed by the Inquisition—whose names were appended to the *sanbenitos* fixed to the church walls—were obliged to adopt new appellations. The general custom that allowed an individual to adopt a different surname from that of his father is often highlighted by the novels and *Comedias* of the Golden Age. As if emphasizing these practices, seventeenth-century author and playwright Vélez de Guevara (1579–1644), a personal friend of Cervantes, also changed his original name, Luis Vélez de Santander, to Luis Vélez de Guevara, the name by which he is still known.[22]

The transmission of patronymics in the Castilian nobility or lesser nobility indeed followed complicated and even unpredictable courses, even beyond the seventeenth century. For this reason, to propose that Cervantes should have used his mother's surname, *Cortinas*, after his patronymic is a crass error perpetuated by various critics (Combet, 553; Zmantar, 186). In general, the patronymic was reserved for the primogeniture and the first sons, while the rest of the offspring received various surnames from the lineage, such as those of the mother and certain close relatives. In Cervantes's own family, his sister Magdalena would assume the surname *Pimentel de Sotomayor* instead of the patronymic Cervantes bestowed on her and on her siblings.[23] And Cervantes's mother, Leonor de Cortinas, adopted her mother's patronymic, which, in turn, followed that of her father Diego Sánchez de Cortinas (Astrana Marín, II: 144–47).

To illustrate the complexities of naming in early modern Spain, let us consider the case of nobleman Nicolás de Ovando, Andrea de Cervantes's lover. The first-born Nicolás received the illustrious patronymic of his mother, María de Ovando, rather than that of his father, Luis Carrillo. The mother's surname, *Ovando*, was more prestigious.[24] The rest of the children received different last names, taken from various branches of the family: some became Carrillo, others Ovando, while the third son was named Bernal Francés de Zúñiga, in honor of a great-grandfather (Astrana Marín II: 44–45). Another striking example is provided by the name of architect Juan de Herrera: his parents were Don Pedro Gutiérrez de Maliaño and María Gutiérrez de la Vega, and his grandfather was Ruy Gutiérrez de Maliaño de Herrera (Ángel de los Ríos, 60). I will examine this topic in greater depth in the section that studies the uses and meanings of the surname (*apellido*) in medieval and early modern Spain (see "Saavedra: A Cry of War"). Notice, however, that these practices regarding the bestowal of surnames among the Spanish gentry do not explain Cervantes's use of the name *Saavedra* in his life and fictions.

Saavedra was also the patronymic given by Cervantes to his natural daughter Isabel, a name she would bear exclusively until 1608, when her father's full names would be conferred to her in the letter of dowry that announced her forthcoming marriage: *"Isabel de Cervantes y Saavedra, [. . .] hija legítima de Miguel de Cervantes Saavedra"* [legitimate daughter of Miguel de Cervantes Saavedra].[25] Let us note in passing that the writing and staging of *El trato de Argel* (c. 1581–1583) anticipates Isabel's birth— around 1584. Cervantes married Catalina de Salazar in December of that year. The quinquennium between 1581 and 1586 was thus crucial for the writer. It marked his return to Spain after his official mission to Orán in 1581; his reinsertion into Spanish society after an absence of twelve years, five of which were spent in prison in Algiers; the writing and staging of his plays *El trato de Argel* and *La Numancia,* among other dramatic works; and the publication of his first novel, *La Galatea* (1585).

Three critical events punctuated the intense literary activity of this period: the birth of his natural daughter, Isabel, which he probably kept secret; his marriage to Catalina de Salazar, the young woman from Esquivias mentioned above; and the death of his father, Rodrigo de Cervantes, in 1585. The death of the father, as Freud claims, is "the most important event, the most poignant loss, of a man's life."[26] For Freud, as we know, the death of the father led to an intense work of mourning, a trip to the underworld in the manner of Aeneas that gave rise to the idea of carrying out a self-analysis and writing a book on dreams.[27] In an enlightening article on death and the midlife crisis, Elliot Jaques has shown that at about the age of forty, an enormous crisis is produced by the brusque realization that there is not much time to live, a crisis accentuated by the death of the parents, which habitually occurs around this point. This moment of truth, if the subject is able to surmount it, produces considerable changes in regard to life attitudes in both ordinary individuals and artists. In certain gifted individuals, such a turning point results in a liberation of possibilities, permitting the man or woman who was merely creative to become a creator finally, and that person who was already a genius to change inspiration, methods of work, and even genres of production. To create, as Didier Anzieu argues, is always to kill someone in an imaginary or symbolic way. This process is facilitated if someone has just died because one can kill that person with the least feelings of guilt.[28]

We do not know whether mourning set in motion a process of intense psychical work in Cervantes or perhaps even a new awareness that had a liberating effect on his creation. The name *Saavedra*, however, appeared in this agitated phase of his life. For these reasons, we may speculate that beyond the complex symbolic network that the surname *Saavedra* invokes, its adoption by Cervantes was linked to both the death of his father and the birth of new illusions. The name *Saavedra* surfaced, in fact, amidst an explosion of creativity in the writer, in a fertile period of literary and dramatic productions—such as the series of plays staged in the initial phases of his career and the publication of *La Galatea* (1585). More specifically, *Saavedra* emerged in the context of two inaugural enterprises: it is the name of the hero in Cervantes's first play and also the surname bestowed on his first child, Isabel. As the late Françoise Zmantar proposed in a brilliant article, Cervantes apparently assumed his paternity on two consecutive occasions. In the second patronymic designation, Saavedra incarnates not the hero of *El trato de Argel* but the father who assumes a new issue: Isabel is the only daughter who can be attributed to Cervantes ("Saavedra," 187). To sum up, the first notarial documents bearing Cervantes's two family names, Cervantes *Saavedra*, surface in 1586, approximately a year after his father's death and in the context of his marriage to Catalina de Salazar. The new name, associated with creation, seems to be a defense against death, an affirmation of life, and a link to immortality.

This affirmation of life around biological continuity, a quest that asserts a mode of symbolic immortality, is often seen in survivors of catastrophic events. More important, the survivor's overall task involves that of a formulation, or "reformulation," of the meaning of life. As Robert Jay Lifton maintains, this task consists of "evolving new inner forms that include the traumatic event, which in turn requires that one find meaning or significance in it so that the rest of one's life need not be devoid of meaning and significance" (*Broken Connection*, 176). In any case, the struggle for resurgent modes of symbolic immortality is crucial to the survivor, as shown by Cervantes's response to this tremendous challenge in the literary testimonies that speak to his Algerian experience and in his creation of great works of art.

Three years later, in *La historia del cautivo*, Cervantes would assume the name of *Saavedra*, no longer as a camouflaged identity that vindicates the heroism of the Christian captives but as a second identity that speaks of his traumatic experience in Algiers. Saavedra in this tale is the name of the Christian slave whose valorous deeds and resistance to Hasan Pasha elicit the admiration of the protagonist, Ruy Pérez de Viedma, an alter ego of Cervantes. Even so, just as he starts alluding to the heroic feats of the soldier called *"tal de Saavedra,"* the Captive recedes from this scenario: *"y si no fuera porque el tiempo no da lugar, yo dijera ahora algo de lo que este soldado hizo, que fuera parte para entretenernos y admiraros harto major que el cuento de mi historia"* [And if it weren't that we haven't the time, I'd stop and tell you some of the things this soldier did, which would amuse and astonish you far more than my own tale] (*DQ* I, 40). His brief mention of a certain Saavedra, alias Miguel de Cervantes, shows both a desire to reveal and a need to conceal. These lines are about remembering and not remembering, about looking and not looking back; in this sense, they show the marks of trauma. In the same way, the Captive's phrase discloses a radical dissociation between the author and his character. Hence, the onomastics reference in the mouth of the Captive opens an abyss between the two characters, performing a radical split between the Captive Ruy Pérez de Viedma and the phantasmatic Saavedra, whose name reveals the presence of Cervantes in the reenactment of his captivity.

To recapitulate: Beyond the splitting of the subject suggested by the doubling evinced by these lines, the name *Saavedra* signals the threshold between life and death through its connections with trauma and with the death of Cervantes's father. Yet *Saavedra* also invokes the limit between the Christian and the Muslim worlds, between the heterogeneous universe of the "Christians of Allah" and the ambiguous space of those who returned to Spain "tainted" by a long captivity in Barbary. This is the liminal or in-between zone defined by Mary Douglas as the site of the unclean, the "polluted."[29] As literal *revenants*, brought back to life, the Barbary slaves were regarded by other Spaniards as "tainted" or "polluting." It was not fortuitous, then, that *Saavedra* would designate a frontier man both in the history of the wars with Granada, where the legendary Saavedra stood out, and in Cervantes's play *El gallardo español*. As discussed earlier, the hero of this drama, Don Fernando de Saavedra, oscillates between various names and identities, even wearing a turban and Moorish dress to impede the capture of Moorish Arlaxa by the Christians. Later, speaking to a character who believes him to be a Moor, he alludes to Don Fernando de Saavedra as *"su otro yo"* [his other self] (v. 2581).

"Su otro yo" [His Other Self]

In *El trato de Argel*, the character named Saavedra implicitly reveals the same kind of straying across the Christian and Muslim borders. Chapter 3

focused on the two faces of this hero: Saavedra is the heroic Christian soldier who upholds his faith to the end, yet at the same time, he is the inverted double of captive Aurelio, who almost succumbs to the enticements
of Islam. The same kind of doubling is suggested by *La historia del cautivo*:
Ruy Pérez de Viedma and Saavedra represent two sides of former captive
Miguel de Cervantes Saavedra. This splitting of the subject in extreme
trauma is not accidental, as we have seen: "Doubling is an active psychological process, a means of *adaptation to extremity*," writes Lifton.[30] In
Cervantes's case, this adaptation to extremity is constantly rewriting itself
as the writer creates images that relive the catastrophic experience, including
its excruciating truths, which are revived by the self that is being recreated.

At the heart of the traumatic syndrome is the diminished capacity to
feel, or psychic numbing. In *The Broken Connection* (1980), Lifton suggests that the survivor undergoes a reversible symbolic form of death to
avoid a permanent physical or psychic death (173). The psychic numbing
that occurs in response to the most acute kinds of trauma is characterized
by particularly profound forms of splitting so that separate, contradictory
selves seem to coexist in the subject. To be sure, the dissociative disintegration in the sense of the coming apart of crucial components of the self
is partial and, to a large extent, temporary—a process in the service of pre-
venting more total and lasting disintegration (*Broken Connection*, 175).
Moreover, as Sándor Ferenczi illustrates, the splitting of the ego in trauma
measures, as it were, the extent of the damage, at the same time that it
indicates the part of the self that the subject can withstand, permitting access to perception of only what can be endured ("*Refléxions*," 144–45).

Let us focus now on the surname *Saavedra* and the way Cervantes puts
his name on the line by simultaneously staging signatures and fictions that
originate on the border where life and work encounter each other. On May
21, 1590, Cervantes addressed a *Memorial* to Philip II requesting a post in
the Indies. This petition seems to have been redacted approximately in the
same period as *La historia del cautivo*, for it bears a profound resemblance
to this narrative. In this document,

> Miguel de çervantes sahauedra dice que ha seruido a V.M. muchos años en
> las jornadas de mar y tierra que se han ofrescido *de veinte y dos años a esta
> parte*, particularmente en la Batalla Naval, donde le dieron muchas heridas,
> de las quales perdio vna mano de vn arcabuçaco—y el año siguiente fue a
> Nauarivo y despues a la campaña de Tunez y a la goleta; y viniendo a esta
> corte con cartas del señor Don Joan y del Duque de Çeça para que V.M. le
> hiçiese merced, fue cautivo en la galera del Sol él y vn hermano suyo, que
> tambien ha seruido a V.M. en las mismas jornadas, y fueron llevados a argel,
> Donde gastaron todo el patrimonio que tenian en Rescatarse y toda la hazi-
> enda de sus padres.
>
> (Sliwa, 225–26)

[Miguel de Cervantes Saavedra says he has served Your Majesty many years on the campaigns on land and sea *in the course of twenty-two years to this date*, particularly in the Battle of Lepanto, where he received many wounds, and lost (the use of) a hand from an harquebus shot—and the next year (1572) he went to Navarino and then to the campaign of Tunis and to la Goleta; and coming back to this court with letters from Don Juan of Austria and the Duke of Sessa so that Your Majesty would grant him favor, he was captured in the galley *Sol*, he and a brother of his who has also served your Majesty in the same campaigns, and they were taken to Algiers, where they spent all the patrimony they had and all the worldly goods of their parents in rescuing themselves].

Cervantes's claim that he had served His Majesty *"en las jornadas de mar y tierra que se han ofrescido* de veinte y dos años para acá"* [on the campaigns on land and sea *in the course of twenty-two years to this date*] clearly echoes the Captive's phrase: *"hace veinte y dos años que salí de la casa de mi padre"* [*this will be the twenty-second year* since I left my father's house] (I, 39). Time, indeed, has not passed for the former captive. When listing his services to the crown and delineating his soldierly career in the Mediterranean, especially his captivity, he becomes the captive who counts time by going back to the period of his first poems in Madrid (1567), before he left for Italy and joined Philip II's Mediterranean armies. This may explain the similarities between Cervantes's literary creation and his petition to the crown. Cervantes in fact endorses his name twice in this *Memorial*: at the outset, where he formulates his appeal to the king under his new name, and in his closing signature, *Miguel de Cervantes Saavedra*.

The parallels between this document and *La historia del cautivo* are striking. The *Memorial* seems to be an outline, or a pretext of the tale told by the captive Captain, one also signed by the name *Saavedra*. In the course of several months, then, Cervantes put his name on the line twice. In regard to the signature *Miguel de Cervantes Saavedra*, which Cervantes had been staging for various years, I propose that during the time elapsed since his liberation, the writer had begun to recover from trauma and its sequelae, joining the name *Saavedra* to his own surname *Cervantes*, thus soldering the shattered selves that appear as separate entities in his fictions. His move recalls the adoption of a new name by Cervantes's contemporary, Inca Garcilaso de la Vega, a man Cervantes probably met during his Andalusian excursions.[31] In a series of name changes occurring over various years, Inca Garcilaso dropped his baptismal name, *Gómez Suárez de Figueroa*, and adopted that of his father, *Garcilaso de la Vega*. He later added the name of his mother's kin, *Inca*, so that, in the end, he would become the assertive Inca Garcilaso de la Vega of *Comentarios reales de los Incas*. Max Hernández has adumbrated the complex web of substitutions and restitutions that compelled Garcilaso to assume his origins, taking on a name and patronymic chosen by himself.[32] Cervantes's assumption of the name *Saavedra* is, in like manner, inscribed in a horizon of memories, expectations, and desires. It is under the name Miguel de Cervantes Saavedra that, fifteen years later, the author of *Don Quijote* will achieve success and then enduring fame.

Saavedra: A Cry of War

Before wrapping up this theme, however, I would like to underpin my arguments with some reference points regarding the constitution of names and patronymics in early modern Spain, a discussion that will shed light on the question of Cervantes's signature. At the end of the ninth century in Spain and other European countries, a proper name was not enough to distinguish individuals from one another. Patronymics appeared during this period, under the form of an adjective ending in *ius*, or of the genitive of the father's name, a custom probably derived from Jewish or Muslim cultures: Fernánd*ez*, the son of Fernando; Sánch*ez*, the son of Sancho; Rodrígu*ez*, the son of Rodrigo; and so on. By the thirteenth century, these denominations had become increasingly common, and, therefore, a nickname or sobriquet was appended to the patronymic as an additional name that evoked a moral or physical quality or defect, a geographical origin, or a trade. In aristocratic families, this nickname was often replaced by the *apellido* [surname] that originated in the name of the *solar* [ancestral home] owned by the chief of the family.

The true aristocratic *solar* was an extensive piece of land, a type of *latifundium* peopled with vassals who cultivated the land, in the most prominent part of which stood a fort or mansion inhabited by the lord (de los Ríos, 47–49).[33] In his interlude *El retablo de las maravillas [The Tableau of Marvels]*, Cervantes humorously refers to the nonexistent *solar* of a poor musician, through the slogan that defined true gentry in Spain: "*hidalgo de solar conocido*" [a gentleman with a known ancestral home].[34] Such ancestral homes, in effect, gave their *apellidos* to their possessors through surnames that were proudly claimed by their descendants. The gentry in medieval and early modern Spain carried their baptismal name, followed by a patronymic and by the name of the *solar* or ancestral home *(apellido)*, a denomination somehow similar to the Roman *tria nomina nobiliarum*. These three designations are clearly detected in the aristocratic name of Pedro Téllez de Girón, duke of Osuna: Pedro is his individual name; Téllez, his patronymic; and Girón, his *apellido* or surname, a true nickname that functioned like the Latin *cognomen* (an individual sobriquet). The term *apellido*, which today designates every family name in Spain and Latin America, thus has an aristocratic and, as we shall see, warlike origin.

For Covarrubias, *apellido* comes from the Latin *appello*—to speak or talk to, to apostrophize, to invoke. The *apellido* was the war cry or sign of mutual recognition for the Christians during the period of the *Reconquista*. Such a cry would serve to summon the warriors, to give others courage in combat, to recognize comrades-in-arms, to ask for help, and to sing of victory. The *apellido* could be the name of a saint (Santiago!) or that of a master. At the same time, each lord or master distinguished himself by the surname that referred to his ancestral home and lineage, one that he himself and his clansmen would invoke. These kinship structures, constructed around the *apellido*, are evoked by the character Mauricio in Cervantes's novel *Persiles*, when referring to his own name: *"Tuvo principio mi linaje, tan antiguo, bien como aquel que es de los Mauricios, que en decir este apellido le encarezco todo lo que puedo"* [My ancestry had a beginning just as ancient as that of the Mauricios, a surname synonymous with the highest praise] (*Persiles* I, 12: 111/62).

Cervantes also alludes to the verb *apellidar* in the sense of giving a war cry, specifically in the dramatic scene of *El amante liberal* that describes the assault of a Turkish vessel by various captives who take arms against their jailers and cut their the throats *"apellidando Libertad, libertad"* [crying Liberty, Liberty].[35] Significantly, in this scenario of captivity, the cry "Liberty!" becomes the war cry or *apellido* of the captives. The last meaning of the term is that stressed by Covarrubias in his *Tesoro*: "Apellidar, *aclamar tomando la voz del rey, como: 'Aquí el rey, o Viva el rey'; y entre las parcialidades, declarándose a voces por una de ellas [. . .]. Y así los del apellido se juntan y llegan a su parcialidad. Y de aquí los nombres de las casas principales se llamaban apellidos, porque los demás se allegaban a ellos, y unos eran Oñez y otros Gamboa"* [*To summon* (to call by the surname/to give a war cry), to acclaim taking the voice of the king, as: 'In the name of the king, or long live the king!'; and, between the clans, sometimes declaring themselves for one of them (. . .). And thus, those brought together by the same surname join each other and their clan. And derived from this custom, the names of the principal dynasties are called *apellidos* (surnames) because other warriors would gather together with them, and some were Oñez and others Gamboa]. As this definition reveals, *apellido* referred to the host brought together by the same surname.

Besides an aristocratic lineage that alluded to a geographical place, the *apellido* more often than not recalled a notoriously recognized deed. In other words, the *apellido* also functioned as a literal surname, or sobriquet. Such was the case of the surname *Machuca* [Clubber], bestowed on the legendary Diego Pérez de Vargas for clubbing down various Moors with a thick bough torn from an oak tree, a story recounted by Don Quijote in the episode of the windmills (*DQ* I, 8), which is deliciously illustrated by Gustave Doré.[36] From then on, as Don Quijote tells Sancho, Vargas and his descendants bore the name *Vargas y Machuca*.[37] A similar legend surrounds the surname *de la Vega*, used by poet Garcilaso de la Vega and his ancestors. This surname presumably originated in an exploit realized by a certain Gonzalo Ruiz de la Vega, famous for killing a Moor who had challenged the Christians by hanging from the tail of his horse the inscription *"Ave María."* The legendary tale was reincorporated into the cycle of ballads emanating from the siege of Granada by the Catholic monarchs, a collection included in Ginés Pérez de Hita's *Guerras civiles de Granada*. The *Romancero* revived both the mythical triumph over the defiant Moor and the story of the surname that perhaps proceeded from it: *"Garcilaso de la Vega/desde allí se ha intitulado,/porque en la Vega hiziera/campo con aquel pagano* [Garcilaso de la Vega/he has been called that from then on/ because in the Vega (the meadows)/he fought in a duel with that pagan].[38]

For Cervantes, however, the surname *Saavedra* refers not to an ancestral home on a large estate or extension of land but rather to a heroic feat, such as that achieved by the legendary Saavedra of the *Romancero*. Indeed, the surname *Saavedra* proclaims Cervantes's membership in the clan of the Saavedra, thus evoking the bravery and audacity of the *soldados fronterizos*. It also adumbrates a symbolic lineage that connects the writer with the valiant hero of the wars with Granada. The celebrated Saavedra was also a captive, seized in a clean fight, like Cervantes, but more importantly, he was a soldier who resisted the threats and temptations of Islam even in the face of death. By taking *Saavedra* as a surname, Cervantes was recognizing their shared fate. *Saavedra*, then, as recapitulated in this chapter, is an incarnation of limit: both the limit-experience of the captive who survived the encounter with death and the limits set by the cultural and geographical frontiers between Christians and Muslims, often crossed by individuals who met new horizons there, including death.

Through his adoption of the surname *Saavedra*, Cervantes was assuming the sequence of three names reserved for the gentry: Miguel de Cervantes Saavedra. In his new denomination, *Miguel* stands as his baptismal name, *Cervantes* is his patronymic, and *Saavedra* is his *apellido*—his lineage. For these reasons, I propose that *Saavedra* is an *apellido* in the medieval sense explicated by Covarrubias: It functions as a war cry that identifies Cervantes with the host brought together by the surname *Saavedra*. If this *apellido* hails the heroic deeds of Lepanto and Algiers, at both the individual and collective levels, it mourns, at the same time, the catastrophic experience of captivity.

The surname *Saavedra* thus delineates a signature, a geography, a body, and a bleeding scar in Cervantes. In addition, it represents the fluctuating limit between biography and literary production, a border where the biological and the biographical cross each other in Cervantes. *Saavedra* in-carnates the limit-experience from which life is recited, the oscillating bor-der between the body and the corpus of fiction that emerges from it. In the borderline between the biological and the biographical, the name *Saavedra* seems to vindicate new paternities, such as those assumed by Cer-vantes in his prologue to his *Novelas ejemplares*: *"Estas [novelas] son mías propias [. . .]; mi ingenio las engendró y las parió mi pluma"* [these novels are my very own (. . .); they were conceived in my imagination, given birth by my pen].[39] No other phrase illustrates better the problematic question of the boundary between the biological and the biographical in Cervan-tes.

Bodies: Real and Imagined

The problematic nature of this border has been emphasized by Didier Anzieu, who shed light on the connections between the body and its cre-ations. Anzieu claimed that to create is to let oneself be worked by one's conscious, preconscious, and unconscious thoughts but also by one's body, or at least by one's corporeal ego *("son Moi corporel")*, as well as by their problematic junction, dissociation, and reunification (*Le corps*, 44). The artist's body, his or her real, imaginary, or fantasized body, is always present throughout the corpus of his or her work. He or she weaves the traces of this body, of its figures in the plot (the weave) of his or her own oeuvre. The metaphors of dreamwork and of the work of mourning speak of a complement, an analogical counterpart with corporeal activities in the psy-chic register (*Le corps*, 44). There is in the creation of a work of art or of intellect, as Anzieu eloquently argued, a travail of labor, of expulsion, of defecation, of vomiting. One also finds a similitude with the torturer's work, because "the torturer works the body of the victim with insistence, preci-sion, and variety," just as the creator engages in hand-to-hand combat *("travaille au corps à corps")* with the material he or she has chosen. Like-wise, creation makes the artist suffer, extracts confessions from him or her, and disarticulates his or her joints. In these rapports between the body and its creations, there is, finally, what popular parlance calls toil *("la besogne"):* The pleasure of the text in the reader responds, as Anzieu sug-gested, to that pleasure or joy felt by the author as he or she engages in an amorous relation with his or her creation (*Le corps*, 44). These lines seem particularly appropriate to describe Cervantes's relation with his fictions. Numerous Cervantine narratives, such as the episode of Dorotea in *Don Quijote*, the story of the beautiful Zoraida (examined below), the scene of the lion recounted in *Don Quijote* II, and the novella *La gitanilla*, are ani-mated by a special gaiety that infects the reader. Such mirth suggests the existence of a genuine love affair between Cervantes and his creations.[40]

The relations between the book and the body, the body and its fictions, have been emphasized by Derrida in his moving eulogy for Sarah
Kofman: "A book always comes to take the place of the body, insofar as it
has always tended to replace the proper body, and the sexed body, to become its name even, and occupy its place, to serve in place of this occu-
pant, [. . .] following its paradoxical desire, its impossible desire" ("Sarah
Kofman," 169). These relations between the book and the body, the body
and its fictions evoke the radiant body of the Algerian woman Zoraida,
whose presence is announced in *La historia del cautivo* immediately after
the intrusion of the surname *Saavedra*. The signs of Zoraida's imminent
apparition surface after this allusion to Cervantes's name in the fiction he
is writing, as if the nearness to the dangerous vortex of trauma—represented by Saavedra and the scenario of Cervantes's captivity—would engender the fabulous story of Zoraida, one of the most charming creations
of the Cervantine corpus. The mention of Saavedra in the scenario of
Cervantes's captivity introduces the legendary second part of the tale, presided over by fantasy. In this way, as Michel Moner has suggested, *La
historia del cautivo* begins like a tale and ends like a legend: Between these
fantastic textual extremes, "like a sandwich, lies 'une tranche de vie' [a slice,
a cross-section of life]," notes the French Hispanist.[41] Such a reading of
the relations between autobiography and fiction in the Captive's tale inadvertently points to the configurations of trauma and, specifically, to the
way that Cervantes engenders fictions from/in the very maelstrom of his
captivity.

This brings us face-to-face with the body of the legendary Algerian
beauty whose appearance cuts in two the story recounted by Captain Ruy
Pérez de Viedma. From this moment on, autobiography turns into legend, as Moner and others have emphasized (Márquez Villanueva, *Personajes*,
92–140).[42] After mapping the points of contact between *La historia del
cautivo* and *Don Quijote*, I will focus in this section on the legendary aspects of the tale, including its covert eroticism. Related to the notion of
the frontier, discussed in the first part of this chapter, these questions also
allude to the frontier between history and fiction and particularly to the
frontier between life and death. As I will show in the following pages, the
encounter with death subtends this tale. Death appears here under the guise
of the veil, a veil that also distinguishes Muslim convert Zoraida.

Cervantes's Veiled Woman

Let us recall Zoraida's entrance in *Don Quijote*. A veiled woman in Arab
guise arrives, astride a donkey, at Juan Palomeque's inn, accompanied by
a man in the attire of those recently returned from Barbary. The mysterious veiled woman and her older male companion seek lodgings for the

night. When she hears her name described as *lela Zoraida*, she exclaims *"No, no Zoraida: María, María"* to which she hastily adds, *"Sí, sí, María; Zoraida macange"*—which in Arabic means "not Zoraida" (I, 37).[43] We will later learn that this Algerian beauty has decided to abandon her Arabic name and culture to adopt a new name and religion under the name of María. Her gesture recalls other name changes in Cervantes, a pattern significantly highlighted by his addition of the surname *Saavedra* in 1586.

Certainly, the change of name and identity is a recurring paradigm in Cervantes's fictions. In *Don Quijote, hidalgo* Alonso Quijada, or Quesada, becomes Don Quijote de la Mancha, then the Knight of the Sad Countenance, and, finally, the Knight of the Lions. Many *Novelas ejemplares* revolve, as well, around the adoption of a new name and a new identity: Tomás Rodaja is metamorphosed into the Licenciado Vidriera [the Glass Graduate] in the novel by the same name; Carriazo and Avendaño turn into Lope el Asturiano and Tomás Pedro in *La ilustre fregona [The Illustrious Kitchen-Maid]*; Pedro del Rincón and Diego Cortado are baptized by lowlife Monipodio with the nicknames Rinconete and Cortadillo in the novella *Rinconete and Cortadillo;* Don Juan de Cárcamo is transformed into Andrés Caballero, and gypsy-girl Preciosa is converted into Doña Constanza de Meneses in *La gitanilla.*[44] Countless illustrations speak of this obsession with name changes and transformations of identities in Cervantes, even in *Persiles*, where the protagonists alter their names at the very beginning of the novel.

Another conversion in *Don Quijote*, however, virtually parallels that of beautiful Zoraida. This is the previous metamorphosis of charming Dorotea, who is transformed by the intervention of the priest and the art of her storytelling into Princess Micomicona, *"heredera por línea recta de varón, del gran reino de Micomicón"* [heiress in the direct male line from the great kingdom of Micomicón] (I, 29–30). As we may recall, the allegorical tale of Princess Micomicona recapitulates the true story of Dorotea's seduction and later abandonment by nobleman Don Fernando. Paradoxically, it is double-faced Dorotea/Micomicona who asks the Captive to answer whether the veiled lady *"¿es cristiana o mora? Porque el traje y el silencio nos hace pensar que es lo que no querríamos que fuese"* [is a Christian or a Moor? Because by her clothing and her silence we have been led to believe that she is, in fact, what we wish she were not] (*DQ* I, 37). Dorotea's ambiguous question regarding her Moorish counterpart Zoraida speaks to an important issue explored in this chapter: the question of the frontier, with its simultaneous affirmation of and oscillation between two conflicting cultural and religious codes.

The character of Zoraida in *La historia del cautivo* (I, 37–41) and her motives vis-à-vis the Captive have long baffled the critics, so I will briefly summarize here the most relevant perspectives adopted by various readings. Regarding this Cervantine creation, scholars are generally divided into two bands: on the one hand, the advocates of a love story, and on the other, the believers in a Christian conversion. In the first group are Américo Castro, who states that Zoraida "wants to become a Christian, but through the love of the Captive," and Ciriaco Morón Arroyo, who argues that this is an authentic love story between the Captive and a *conversa*, whose conversion justified the break of family ties.[45] In opposition, Leo Spitzer claims that this is "a drama of Divine Grace" where "religion is the kernel, love the envelopment" ("Linguistic," 29). Zoraida's behavior vis-à-vis her father has been severely criticized by Spitzer and others.[46] Along this line, Louis Combet relates Zoraida to the cold, maternal woman who stands as an intermediate figure between the hetaira and the sadic heroines of Sader-Masoch.[47] In turn, Helena Percas de Ponsetti emphasizes the ambiguity of Zoraida's character and the deception and charm of her *"demonio feme-nino"* [feminine demons], while Allison Weber views Cervantes's tale as a reflection on the painful dissolution of the endogamic, affective bonds that link Zoraida to her father.[48] I have examined elsewhere the representation of Zoraida by captive Ruy Pérez de Viedma and the metaphor of the veil in relation to feminist and psychoanalytic perspectives.[49] For the purpose of my arguments in this chapter, I will review my earlier discussion on the connections between Zoraida's story and *Don Quijote*.

La historia del cautivo is divided into three sections, the last of which relates the Captive's liberation at the hands of his Moorish savior Zoraida, their marvelous adventures, and final deliverance onto Spanish soil. Zoraida's story reveals a similar threefold organization: Enclosed between the Moorish narrator's description of the couple's arrival at the inn, the story is concluded by his remarks on the resolution of the interpolated episodes that crisscross each other in the novel, sutured, as it were, by the Captive's tale (I, 46). In earlier articles on this subject, I argued that the body of a Moorish woman—a foreign text, read by a Christian soldier—lies wedged between the preamble and the concluding observations of Arab historian Cide Hamete Benengeli ("Zoraida's Veil," 67). This would turn Zoraida's story, and even Zoraida herself, into a frontier, a borderline between the Christian and the Muslim worlds.

A metaphorical captive in her father's house, Zoraida is also a writer who has recapped the story of her life in the three letters addressed to the Spanish Captain, a prisoner in Hasan Pasha's *baño*. Her three letters, composed in Arabic, which the Captain cannot read, are finally translated by a Spanish renegade from Murcia who offers to render their meaning word by word (*DQ* I, 40). As I mentioned in chapter 2, this character may evoke the historical Maltrapillo or Morat *ra'is*, a renegade from Murcia who was one of the principal corsairs of Algiers in 1580. Maltrapillo, in effect, probably saved Cervantes's life after his fourth escape attempt by interceding before the *bey* Hasan Veneciano. On the other hand, the pattern of translations and retranslations that surfaces in the Captive's tale regarding Arabic and the languages spoken by the renegades highlights the connections between Zoraida's story and *Don Quijote*. The structure of this story not only recalls that of *Don Quijote* but also functions as an anticipation of the famous Cervantine paradigm.

Scholars have signaled the conspicuous repetition of *Don Quijote*'s opening phrase, *"en un lugar de"* [in a village of], at the outset of the Captive's tale (I, 39). The famous inaugural phrase reemerges with respect to the Oidor [the judge] in the episode that follows the story of the escapees Ruy Pérez de Viedma and Zoraida (I, 42).[50] This significant iteration speaks to the crucial place occupied by this narrative among Cervantes's fictions. As we may remember, various critics have proposed that *La historia del cautivo* was composed in 1589–1600 and later incorporated into *Don Quijote*. As such, it would be the "seed" of *Don Quijote*, the *Ur-Quijote*, as Murillo labeled it. I would stress, in the context of this study, that it is precisely the tale that evokes Cervantes's captivity in Algiers that is at the core of the great Cervantine novel. Yet the parallels between the tale and the novel extend further, for Zoraida's story recalls the complex underlying structure of *Don Quijote*. Her story, which stands as a Spanish translation of an Arabic text, retold by the captive Captain as part of the "true discourse" of his life, strikingly repeats the pattern of translations and interpretations that constitute *Don Quijote*. In Zoraida's case, diverse Christian legends recounted by various "authors," such as the Christian slave who taught the Moorish girl to pray, are later collected and reconstructed in Arabic by Zoraida herself, who composes the letters delivered to the Christian captive. These messages are deciphered and rendered into Castilian by a bilingual Spanish renegade—an inversion of *Don Quijote* I, 9—and reinterpreted and edited by the Christian soldier, who presents Zoraida's story woven into his own story to the audience at the inn. Not only are these similarities between the tale and the novel quite suggestive, but they also seem to speak to the place this tale of captivity held among Cervantes's affections.

The Captive, as we know, begins the tale of his miraculous rescue immediately after mentioning the presence of "a Spanish soldier, named Saavedra" in the reenactment of Cervantes's captivity (I, 40). Significantly, Zoraida makes her entrance into the story after this authorial intrusion, as if the very hand that signed Cervantes's name in the text were magically transformed into the enigmatic female hand that appears and disappears at the window that overlooks the courtyard of Hasan Pasha's *baño*. The evocation of this specific window in Cervantes's Algiers seems to open another window onto the scenario of his captivity, one that functions as a fantastic flight into fiction. Zoraida's window, then, is a metaphor for fiction, as suggested by the ending verses of the play *Los baños de Argel*: *"Dura en Argel ese cuento/de amor y dulce memoria [. . .]./Y aún hoy se hallarán en él [en Argel]/la ventana y el jardín"* [This story of love and sweet memories/still lingers in Algiers (. . .)./And even today one may find there, *the window* and the garden] (*Baños* III. 3086–91; emphasis mine).

On the other hand, even before she materializes in the story, Zoraida is portrayed in terms of an ambiguous frontier between history and fiction, and between the Spanish and the Maghribi cultures, as best expressed by Dorotea's question to the Captive: "Is this lady a Christian or a Moor?" This is the question that haunts Cervantes's text, a question embodied by the symbols that mark Zoraida's appearance at the window that overlooks Hasan Pasha's prison. Such symbols, like the small cross made of reeds, which was briefly shown and withdrawn from the latticework, and the ten *cianiís*, or coins used in Barbary, which were dropped in a bundle at the Captain's feet (*DQ* I, 40), arise as images of conflicting cultural and political systems that are simultaneously maintained by the text. In turn, the vacillation between divergent ethnic groups and cultures is emphasized by the Captive's description of the hand showing through the window, a white hand that seems to be at first that of a Christian slave but then, according to the *ajorcas* [bracelets] that adorn it, that of an Algerian woman. This uncertainty is transposed onto the first letter delivered to the Captive, a letter written in Arabic characters yet signed with a Christian cross. The contradictory signatures turn into an escalating confusion of signs that reaches its apex in the scene where the veiled Zoraida is transformed into María. In fact, the preoccupation with the borderline between the Christian and the Muslim worlds is insistently highlighted by this text. Its constant oscillation between the Arabic and the Castilian languages and, specifically, between Allah, Lela Marién, and the "Christian prayers" recited in Arabic by Zoraida, underline the fluctuating movements of the narrative from one cultural code to another.

No other episode exemplifies better the function of Zoraida as an emblem of shifting allegiances than the scene at Agi Morato's [Ḥājjī Murād's] garden, where the Captive sees the beautiful Algerian woman face-to-face for the first time (I, 41). In this rural scenario, with her father acting as interpreter, Zoraida speaks to the Captive in the lingua franca of Algiers, even while punctuating her dialogue with sign language (*DQ* I, 41). Her voluble conversation with the Spaniard in her father's presence exposes not only her discursive abilities but also the clever double entendres with which she questions the Captive about his plans to leave Barbary. Let us recall her histrionic response when her father surprises her embracing the Spanish slave—we might note at this point that Zoraida has already organized the plot of their joint escape from Algiers.

Hājjī Murād's Daughter

In her first letter to the captive, Zoraida states that when she was a child, her father had a slave who taught her to say the *"zalá cristianesca"* [Christian prayers] in Arabic and to worship Lela Marién [the Virgin Mary], whom she wants to see in Spain. Zoraida's background, described by her letters, as well as the questions elicited by her character compels me to examine the historical personages who inspired Cervantes's famous tale. Let us look more closely at Hājjī Murād, whose garden, on the outskirts of Algiers, serves as the scenario of the first encounter between the lovers. We already met the historical Agi Morato, or Hājjī Murād, in chapter 1, when we studied Cervantes's third escape attempt, an endeavor that involved smuggling a letter out of Hasan Pasha's *baño*, addressed to the governor of Orán, Don Martín de Córdoba. As we may recall, the Moor who carried the letter was captured at the doors of Orán and returned to Algiers to Hasan Pasha, who had him impaled. Hasan then ordered Cervantes to receive two thousand blows, which would have meant death. The intervention of a mysterious and powerful mediator in this moment saved Cervantes's life, an ordeal tacitly evoked in the Captive's tale.

When speaking of a "certain Saavedra," the Captive states that although this soldier had done things that would stay in the memories of the Algerians for many years, things done solely to gain his freedom, his master Hasan *"jamás le dio palo, ni se lo mandó dar, ni le dijo mala palabra; y por la menor cosa de muchas que hizo temíamos todos que* había de ser empalado, *y así lo temió él más de una vez"* [never gave him a blow, nor ordered another to strike him, nor said a bad word to him, though for just the least of the things he did we all feared that *he would be impaled*—and more than once even he was afraid exactly of that] (I, 40). I have emphasized the textual allusion to the punishment usually meted out to rebel captives in Algiers: *Empalar* [to impale] was a form of torture or capital punishment that consisted in transfixing a man with a stake and letting him suffer out in the open, until he died. Such was the torture inflicted on the Moor who carried Cervantes's letter to Orán, a man who, according to Cervantes and other witnesses, died courageously, without saying a word (*Información*, 54–55, 80). Antonio de Sosa refers to impalement as a capital punishment imposed by the Algerians, and many early modern European accounts of captivity in Barbary graphically depict these gory scenes. In Cervantes's tale, the allusion to the death sentence suffered by the Moor surfaces in the phrase *"había de ser empalado,"* a punishment Cervantes himself must have feared on this occasion, as the significant reiteration of the verb *empalar*, applied to himself in the text, suggests. The death imprint is thus clearly present in the passage that surrounds Saavedra's name.

It is precisely at this point that Algerian beauty Zoraida surfaces in the tale, followed by her father Hājjī Murād, just as the historical Hājjī Murād probably intervened at a critical juncture of Cervantes's life. Some critics, following the love story between the Captive and Zoraida, have supposed that a Moorish woman, perhaps even the historical Zoraida, interceded with the pasha on behalf of Cervantes. As Canavaggio and other literary historians have proposed, it was probably the influential Hājjī Murād, the diplomatic envoy of the Grand Turk in Algiers, who saved Cervantes from death on this occasion (*Cervantes*, 88; Sola and de la Peña, 236). In chapter 2, we discussed the possibility that Cervantes was an unofficial informer to Hājjī Murād, who maintained ambiguous relations with the Spaniards. Quite conceivably, Hājjī Murād intervened before the pasha to save a captive who had friends in Orán, one who, presumably, also had connections within the Spanish circles of power.

A renegade from Ragusa (now known as Dubrovnik), Hājjī Murād was one of the most respected *alcaides* of Algiers in the last third of the sixteenth century, at the time of Cervantes's and Sosa's enslavement in the city.[51] The *alcaides* were the governors of the territories or jurisdictions attached to the province of Algiers, and their wealth derived from tribute levied on the rural *moros* and *alarbes* (Berber tribes) subject to the *beylerbey* of Algiers (*Topografía*, I: 57). According to Sosa, Hājjī Murād was the first and the richest of the *alcaides* living in Algiers in 1581; his house was one of the most luxurious of the city (*Topografía*, I: 57–58, 194). Since 1572, in the aftermath of the Battle of Lepanto, Hājjī Murād had been engaged in secret negotiations with the Spaniards regarding a truce with the Turks. A year later, when Spanish agent Juan Pexón traveled to Algiers to interview him, Hājjī Murād was around 50 years old: *"hombre muy principal entre ellos, y rico, y de quien se hace mucha cuenta en Argel"* [a very principal man, and rich, highly regarded in Algiers]. He was also deemed to be "a man of good judgment and very good manners in their own [Moorish] way" (quoted by Canavaggio, *"Le 'vrai' visage,"* 26–27).[52]

Regarding Hājjī Murād, the Captive states: *"[era] riquísimo por todo estremo, el cual tenía una sola hija, heredera de toda su hacienda, y [. . .] era común opinión en toda la ciudad ser la más hermosa mujer de la Berbería"* [fabulously rich, he had an only daughter, the heiress to all his wealth. And it was the general opinion throughout the city that she was the most beautiful woman in Barbary] (I, 40). In *Los baños de Argel*, renegade Hazén repeats these epithets, calling Hājjī Murād *"rico en estremo grado"* [rich in extreme degree] and stating, in reference to his daughter: *"sobretodo, le ha dado/el cielo una hija tal/que de belleza el caudal/todo en ella está cifrado"* [particularly, heaven has given him such a daughter, that her beauty constitutes his richest asset] (*Baño*, I.427–31). The same renegade claims that Hājjī Murād: *"[es] un moro de buena masa,/principal y hombre de bien"* [is a rich Moor, a distinguished personage and a good man] (*Baños*, III.425–26). Coming from the mouth of a repentant renegade, or from that of a former captive who suffered the rigors of enslavement in Barbary, this depiction of Hājjī Murād is significant. Other accounts by Christian slaves and spies in the 1570s and 1580s confirm that Hājjī Murād maintained friendly relations with a number of elite captives, as well as with foreign diplomats and merchants, such as the famous Gasparo Corso brothers mentioned in chapter 2. His intimate convictions regarding the Turks and the Islamic religion, privately expressed to various captives, and his leadership of the Moorish faction of Algiers perhaps won Hājjī Murād the respect of the Christian slaves and renegades, who regarded him as "*hombre de bien.*"

His daughter, immortalized by Cervantes in *La historia del cautivo*, reappears in *Los baños de Argel* with the name *Zahara*.[53] As pointed out earlier, Zoraida recounts that when she was a child, a female slave in her father's household taught her Christian prayers and instilled in her a profound love for the Virgin Mary, or Lela Marién (1, 40). In *Los baños de Argel*, Zoraida's double, Zahara, expands these details: The female slave not only breast-fed Zahara ("*me dio leche*") but also taught her everything related to the Christians, including "*las cuatro oraciones*" [the four prayers—that is, the Hail Mary, the Our Father, the Credo, and the Salve Regina] (*Baños, OC*, 14: 47). Zahara's nurse is later identified as Juana de Rentería, a matron who had been esteemed by all in Algiers for her piety and proverbial charity.

As it turns out, the historical underpinnings of these Cervantine fictions are impressive. Antonio de Sosa recounts that the grandmother of Hājjī Murād's daughter—whom we know as Zoraida—was a Christian slave, captured in Barbarossa's attack against the Peñón of Algiers in 1529. Two of the three valiant women who survived this bloody assault were still alive in Algiers when Sosa was writing his notable work around 1580. One of these women, from Majorca, says Sosa, "*es la suegra de Agi Morato, y agüela de la mujer de Muley Maluco, Rey que fue de Fez y de Marruecos*" [is the mother-in-law of Hājjī Murād, and the grandmother of the wife of Muley Maluco ('Abd al-Malik), who was the King of Fez and of Morocco] (*Topografía*, 1: 257). The historical Algerian beauty who inspired Cervantes's fictions was thus the granddaughter of Christians on both her father's and her mother's sides.

Other female slaves in Barbary, including the wives of a few Maghribi rulers, were known for their piety and Christian faith. Fray Jerónimo Gracián de la Madre de Dios, Santa Teresa's confessor, recounts that, during his captivity in Tunis (1593–1595), he met with many female slaves who practiced their religion in secret. Female captives from the pasha's harem, for instance, including the mother and mother-in-law of the pasha himself, sent the priest clean linen shirts, fresh bread, and other presents, such as money, on several occasions. The priest often celebrated clandestine masses for the women of the harem and for renegades, men and women alike (*Obras de Santa Teresa*, II: 460–62). In Algiers, as Sosa recounts, numerous women, such as the pampered wives of certain rich men, prayed regularly to "Christ Our Lord and to his blessed Mother" and "had many masses said, and sent oil for the lamps, and candles for the altars" (*Topografía*, I: 165). In like manner, Hājjī Murād's daughter grew up with a Christian grandmother, and perhaps a Christian mother, among female slaves who were probably Christian. The Algerians, as we know, permitted the practice of the Christian religion, so that masses and other Christian ceremonies were regularly celebrated in the *baños*. In the previous lines, I have attempted to evoke the conceivable atmosphere of Hājjī Murād's household in Algiers, as inferred from historical data. Cervantes knew very well who Hājjī Murād was, yet by refashioning the adventures of captive Ruy Pérez de Viedma, he transposed his dramatic Algerian experience into a semilegendary frame, as I will demonstrate in this chapter.

Let us focus now on the way Cervantes reinscribed the historical events that punctuated his Algerian experiences. The daughter of Hājjī Murād first married 'Abd al-Malik, the aspirant to the Moroccan throne who lived as an exile in Algiers in the 1570s. In chapter 2, we studied the fascinating figure of this sophisticated sultan who established amicable relations with various European rulers. Although Hājjī Murād's daughter was already married to 'Abd al-Malik in 1574, a year before Cervantes arrived in Algiers, the writer refers to 'Abd al-Malik, in *Los baños de Argel*, as engaged to Zahara.[54] In this play, which closely follows the plot of *La historia del cautivo*, Cervantes separates 'Abd al-Malik from his bride and has Zahara refuse her important suitor on the very day of the wedding. The wedding is nevertheless celebrated with great fanfare in the drama, but the veiled woman carried on shoulders in the nuptial cortege is not Hājjī Murād's daughter but her friend, the married Halima. The lavish staging of this wedding allows Cervantes to portray the marriage customs of Algiers, which coincide with the detailed information provided by Sosa about these nuptial feasts (*Topografía*, I: 118–24). At any rate, the alteration of history in *Los baños de Argel* permits the development of the plot, including the love affair between Zahara and Christian captive Lope, with whom she finally escapes.

When 'Abd al-Malik acceded to the Moroccan throne in 1576, his wife and child stayed behind as hostages of the Algerian Turks, who feared that the Sādi sultan was engaging in secret negotiations with the Spaniards. Cervantes might have met the legendary beauty at this time, during his outings from the *baños*, or during his visits to Hājjī Murād's inner sanctum. After the sultan's death in the Battle of Alcazarquivir in 1578, Hājjī Murād's daughter married none other than Hasan Pasha, who became Cervantes's master in 1579. Consequently, these historical personages were not only con-nected with one another but also peculiarly associated with the captive Cer-vantes. Such are the historic lineaments behind the characters of Zoraida, in *La historia del cautivo*, and her double Zahara, in *Los baños de Argel*. One plot, indeed, seems to be a reelaboration of the other. In both the tale and the play, a Christian captive is saved by an Algerian beauty edu-cated in the Christian faith, a young woman who is identified as the daugh-ter of the historical Hājjī Murād. By inscribing this tale in the backdrop of the Mediterranean wars against the Turks, and by reconstructing his greatest vicissitude around an enigmatic personage whose very name evoked the give-and-take between the cross and the crescent in Algiers, Cervantes was able to confer a tantalizing yet convincing atmosphere on his fiction.

"Nuestra estrella" [Our Star]

If Agi Morato or Hājjī Murād plays a significant role in *La historia del cautivo*, it is Zoraida, after all, who is at the core of this tale: She is both its legendary heroine and a striking symbol of freedom. We first met the veiled Zoraida at the scenario of the inn, wavering flirtatiously between the limits set by her two names: *Zoraida* and *María*. The ambiguity of her position on the borderline between two religions and cultural codes illu-minates the Captive's answer to Dorotea: *"Mora es en el traje y en el cuerpo; pero en el alma es muy grande cristiana, porque tiene grandísimos deseos de serlo"* [She is dressed like a Moor, and her body is that of a Moor, but her soul is that of a very genuine Christian, for she has an immense desire to be one] (I, 37). Formulating the Algerian woman's identity within a Chris-tian framework, however, is crucial for the former captive, for his own sta-tus as a Christian would be contested by his experiences in Barbary. Like the men who returned to Spain after a long period of captivity, he would be suspected, along the lines of Zoraida, of belonging to the "other side."

The conflict regarding Zoraida-María's true identity recalls the enig-mas posed by certain Cervantine characters who live on the frontier be-tween two cultures. Don Fernando de Saavedra, the hero of *El gallardo español* studied earlier, exemplifies this equivocal position. In the fashion of the mysterious Algerian beauty who accompanies the Captive, Don Fernando de Saavedra is dressed like a Moor, although at heart, he is a true Christian. The name *Saavedra*, a fundamental symbol of the frontier, flashes at this point like a neon sign. As I argued earlier, the surname *Saavedra* in Cervantes invokes a cluster of significations, such as the trauma of captivity, the death imprint, and the problematic borderline between cultures. As it turns out, Saavedra in *La historia del cautivo* is associated not only with the death scene, signified by Zoraida's apparition, but also with the conflict that Zoraida represents for the audience at the inn. What is apparently intolerable to all, in this scene, is Zoraida's oscillation between cultural boundaries.

The Captain's evocation of the garden scene in Algiers, when he encounters "the most beautiful woman in all Barbary" (I, 40) for the first time, focuses on other questions. His description preferably highlights the nonrepresentable nature of Zoraida's beauty, whose excess is symbolized by the cascade of jewels that adorn her. The quasi-mythical aura emanating from this description calls for a close reading of the passage:

> Demasiada cosa sería decir yo agora la mucha hermosura, la gentileza, el gallardo y rico adorno com que mi querida Zoraida se mostró a mis ojos. Solo diré que más perlas pendían de su hermosísimo cuello, orejas y cabellos que cabellos tenía en la cabeza. En las gargantas de los sus pies, que descubiertas a su usanza, traía, traía dos carcajes (que así se llamaban las mantillas o ajorcas de los pies en morisco) de purísimo oro, con tantos diamantes engastados, que ella me dijo después que su padre los estimaba en diez mil doblas, y las que traía en las muñecas de las manos valían otro tanto. Las perlas eran de gran cantidad y muy buenas porque la mayor gala y bizarría de las moras es adornarse de ricas perlas y aljófar [. . .]; el padre de Zoraida tenía fama de tener muchas y de las mejores que en Argel había, y de tener asimismo más de doscientos mil escudos españoles, de todo lo cual era señora ésta que ahora lo es mía (I, 41).

> [How can I tell you now, with what beauty, what elegance, and wearing what magnificent, rich jewels my beloved Zoraida first showed herself to my eyes? All I can say is that more pearls hung from her lovely neck, her ears, and her hair than she had hairs on her head. On her ankles—bare, in the Moorish style—she wore two *carcajes* (which is what they call ankle bracelets or bangles) of the purest gold, set with so many diamonds that she told me, afterwards, her father had said they were valued at ten thousand doubloons, and the ones she had on her wrists were worth as much more. She wore many, many pearls, and very fine ones, because Moorish women take special pride and pleasure in adorning themselves with all kinds of pearls, big and small (. . .). And Zoraida's father was famous for having not only a great many, but also some of the very best pearls in Algiers, as he was also renowned for the possession of more than two hundred thousand Spanish doubloons, all of which were at the command of her who, now, commands only me.]
>
> (*DQ* I, 41)

What first comes to mind in this spectacular vision is the almost indescribable beauty and radiance of the Algerian woman, a topic to which I shall return shortly. There is no question, moreover, that money is an obsessive and all-pervading theme in this text. The Captive's description turns Zoraida into a commodity, a net worth of the most rigorous kind: The jewels on her body are explicitly assessed in terms of their market value in sixteenth-century Spain. The mere diamonds on Zoraida's gold *carcajes* are appraised in ten thousand *doblas* [doubloons], a sum duplicated by the price of the bracelets that adorn her wrists. Even the diamonds that embellish Zoraida's anklets and the bracelets that grace her wrists are gauged by the Captive according to their approximate market value. This avalanche of riches, however, also extends to Zoraida's father. Hājjī Murād was apparently in possession of the finest collection of pearls in Algiers—not to speak of the finest pearl of all, Zoraida—as well as more than two hundred thousand gold *escudos* in cash. In a time in which cash was scarce and its buying power much greater than its actual worth, these sums must have seemed astronomical.

Certainly, above and beyond the description of Zoraida's jewels, the obsession with money in this tale is striking. Coins and monetary units of all kinds, both Algerian and Spanish, constantly appear in the text, and money is continually added, divided, and counted by the narrator. No details are spared, in the preliminary phase of the tale, regarding the meticulous transactions that have to do with the inheritance of the three brothers. In turn, no sooner has the Captain been captured than the question of the ransom erupts and remains in the foreground, resurfacing continuously from one adventure to the next. We know that the money for this ransom is provided by Zoraida in "miraculous" little bundles, delivered to the captive from the window above. The counting of the coins included in these packets, as well as the detailed numbers provided by the Captive in regard to his ransom and the purchase of the vessel that would lead them to Spain, raises disturbing questions concerning the status of money in this tale.

Is it necessary to evoke, in this context, Cervantes's ransom, fixed in 1580 at 500 *escudos*? Let us consider, once more, the long and agonizing efforts of Cervantes's parents to collect, by means of different loans, the ransom money that was to free their son. As discussed in chapter 2, the sum was finally gathered after five years with the help of the Trinitarian monks who, at the last moment, advanced 220 *escudos* from their general funds to pay for Cervantes's freedom (Canavaggio, *Cervantes*, 94–95).[55] If it is obviously difficult to give precise equivalents of the sixteenth-century Spanish coins mentioned in the text according to today's prices, one thing remains certain: Both Zoraida and Zoraida's father are inordinately rich. The obsession with money in this tale, and its complex relation with the ordeals of Cervantes's own captivity, would thus point again to the intertextual crossings between life and literature in Cervantes. Even so, the insistent materiality of Zoraida's first depiction is soon eclipsed by the Captive's reiteration of Zoraida's indescribable beauty and its effects on his senses. Recalling his first vision of the Algerian woman, the Captive claims that Zoraida *"llegó en todo estremo aderezada y en todo estremo hermosa o, a lo menos a mí me pareció serlo la mas que hasta entonces había visto; y con esto, viendo las obligaciones que me había puesto, me parecía que tenía delante*

a una deidad del cielo, venida a la tierra para mi gusto y para mi remedio"
[was beautifully adorned and fantastically beautiful—or at least so it seemed
to me—the loveliest woman I had ever seen. And if you add to her loveli-
ness my awareness of all I owed her, you can understand that she appeared
before me like some heavenly goddess, descending to earth to aid and delight me] (*DQ* I, 41). Zoraida is, indeed, elevated to the realm of a divin-
ity in this passage. The radiant and inexpressible power of this reverie recalls Romeo's phrase "Juliet is the sun," a loving metaphor that transfers
onto Juliet the blaze Romeo experiences in the state of love. In like manner, the Captive's attempts to describe "the most beautiful woman in Barbary" evoke an image of striking brilliance, one that speaks to the nonrepresentable nature of this desired other. This luminous vision recalls the
symbolism of Zoraida's name: pleiad, cluster of stars.

Throughout the narrative, in effect, Zoraida is often referred to as *"la
estrella de la caña"* [the star of the cane] or *"nuestra estrella"* [our star]
(*DQ* I, 41), a metaphor insistently used in *Los baños de Argel* to allude to
Zahara. Here the term *metaphor* should not be understood in the sense of
the classic rhetorical trope (figuration) but instead, as Julia Kristeva has
reminded us, as "an indefinite jamming of semantic features crowding one
into the other, a meaning being acted out."[56] Let us recall at this point
the connections made by Freud between symptom and metaphor—that is,
his discovery that symptom is metaphor, namely, condensation, of fantasy
(SE, 14: 339–40). His arguments lead me to look more closely at Zoraida
as a fantasy, a notion I shall discuss in the next sections.

"A Woman Clothed in the Sun"

The brilliant chain of metaphors employed by the Captive to describe his
legendary savior establishes the connections between Zoraida's representation and the image of Mary, Queen of Heaven, in the Apocalypse: "A
great wonder in heaven; a woman clothed with the sun, and the moon
under her feet, and upon her head a crown of twelve stars" (Revelations
12:1). This perception of the Virgin, adorned with gold, pearls, and price-
less gems, was especially popular in the Spain of the Counter-Reformation, where a new form of veneration for Mary's Immaculate Conception
emerged.[57] Like Athene, the Virgin also presided over peace and war. From
the sixth century on, her image was often paraded in battles against the
heathens, Turks and Calvinists alike (Warner, 303–08). The fact that Pope
Pius V instituted the feast of Our Lady of Victory in 1573 to celebrate the
Christian defeat of the Turks at the Battle of Lepanto (1571) illustrates these
notions about Mary's powers.

The associations between the cult of the Virgin and the victory of
Lepanto by the Christian armies bring to mind the numerous references

to the Virgin that traverse both *La historia del cautivo* and *El trato de Argel*, among other Cervantine works. Let us evoke, in this sense, the desperate appeal addressed to the Virgin Mary by fugitive Per Álvarez, and the prayers and songs to the Virgin recited by a chorus of captives in the last scene of *El trato*. Constant allusions to Lela Marién or the Virgin Mary traverse the Captive's tale as well, especially regarding the beauty and Christian qualities of Zoraida. Indeed, even before the Captive's tale begins, Zoraida's identification with the Virgin Mary is suggested by the image of the couple's arrival at the inn, the Moorish woman mounted on a donkey and the Captive at her side, playing the role of St. Joseph, an identification reiterated by Zoraida herself when she pronounces her new name: María. Zoraida is later transformed into the very incarnation of the Virgin when the Captive calls her *"señora de nuestra libertad"* [lady of our liberty] (I, 41).

This appellation evokes one of the titles given to Mary as the protector of the captives held by the Turks: "Nuestra Señora de la Libertad" [Our Lady of Liberty]. A significant passage from *Persiles,* which describes the Monastery of Guadalupe, in Spain, confirms my assertions: Its walls enclose *"la santísima imagen de la emperadora de los cielos; la santísima imagen,* otra vez, que es libertad de los cautivos, *lima de sus hierros y alivio de sus pasiones"* [the most holy image of the Empress of Heaven; the saintly image, *I repeat, that means freedom for captives,* a file for their chains, and relief from their suffering] (III, 5: 305/216; emphasis mine).[58] The connection between the phrase *"la santísima imagen"* and the freedom of captives is redoubled by the copula *otra vez,* which forcefully reiterates the links between the Virgin and the suffering captives. Likewise, in *Los baños de Argel,* child-captive Francisquito makes the association between the Virgin Mary and captivity: *"Tengo yo el Ave María/clavada en el corazón, y es la estrella que me guía/en este mar de aflicción"* [I have the *Hail Mary/* hammered into my heart/and she is the star that guides me/in this sea of affliction] (II. 1922–25). Again, in these verses, the Virgin appears as a star that guides the young captive.

No other creature in the Cervantine world, except for the mythic Dulcinea, has been portrayed in such lofty terms, with such brilliance as Zoraida. Her exalted image in *La historia del cautivo* accentuates her symbolic transformation into a bastion of purity as removed from a mortal's touch as her poetic name: star. For these reasons, Zoraida would be evoking the Virgin herself, an argument that falls into place when we consider the numerous *"milagros"* that plague the Captive's tale, such as the literal *"milagro de la caña"* [miracle of the cane] (*DQ* I, 42), which would guide the captives to freedom. The phrase *"el milagro de la caña"* was used by the Captive's brother, the Oidor, when referring to the fantastic manner in which his sibling was freed from captivity. Likewise, when the fugitives arrive in Vélez Málaga after their dramatic escape from Barbary, a horseman who meets them alludes to their liberation in terms of *"milagrosa libertad"* [miraculous liberty] (*DQ* I, 41). Zoraida's clear connections with fantasy, and her miraculous interventions that bring about the freedom of the captives, lead me to suggest, paraphrasing Jacqueline Rose in another context, that as the place onto which lack is projected, and through which it is simultaneously disavowed, Zoraida is a "symptom" for the Captive.[59]

The Paths of Desire

The uncanny representation of Zoraida in terms of an object of fantasy—a fantasy that finds its subtext in the register of the imaginary—transports us into the realm of desire. Zoraida's phantasmatic depiction and her inscription in a legendary frame that evokes the image of the Virgin Mary situate the Captive's imaginary construction in an economy of the unconscious. That there is another scene to language through which we most commonly identify and recognize ourselves is the basic tenet of Freudian psychoanalysis.[60] Desire is certainly at the heart of the psychic apparatus and of psychoanalysis, which tries to account for it. It appears in the constitution of fantasy, of the symptom, the conflict; and the dream, as Freud has illustrated, expresses its workings. In turn, the concept of desire is crucial to Lacan's account of sexuality. He considered that the failure to grasp its implications leads invariably to a reduction of sexuality to need—something, therefore, which could be satisfied. Against this, he quoted Freud's statement: "We must reckon with the possibility that something in the nature of the sexual instinct itself is unfavorable to the realization of complete satisfaction" (SE, II: 188–89). Following Lacan, I am appealing to a notion of sexuality that finds its register in the complex network of fantasies and symbolizations that constitute the human subject.[61]

The representation of Zoraida as an object of desire that evokes the virginal body of Maria Regina—the Virgin Mother who is called on by Christianity to represent supreme earthly power—speaks to the realm of the Other, the imaginary place of "identity" and "wholeness." In her classic essay "Stabat Mater," Kristeva has argued that Mary represents a "totality made of woman and God," an earthly conception of the human mother that embodies the avoidance of death—Mary does not die, but she is transported toward the other world in an Assumption.[62] Paradoxically, even though Christianity postulates that immortality is mainly that of the name of the Father, it relies on a feminine representation of an immortal biology to impose its symbolic revolution. Mary defying death is the theme transmitted to us through the numerous variations of the *Stabat Mater*, which still enchant us in this day and age through the music of Palestrina, Pergolesi, Haydn, and Rossini ("Stabat Mater," 251–52). Men and women, as Kristeva has contended, overcome "the unthinkable of death by postulating maternal love in its place—in the place and stead of death and thought" (252). This love, of which divine love is a paltry derivation, psychologically is probably a recollection of the near side of early identifications, or the primal shelter that ensured the survival of the newborn. In adults, such love usually appears in a surge of anguish at the very moment when the identity of thought and living body collapses ("Stabat Mater," 252). Through the cult of the Virgin Mary, as Cervantes demonstrates in his work, the image of the mother is preserved as an ultimate shield against death.

To illustrate, in the play *El trato de Argel*, the dereliction of the Captive, who is at the verge of madness and death, brings about the desperate prayer to the Virgin Mary, which, in turn, elicits the fantasy of the miraculous lion. This fantasy of salvation, as we saw, allows the writer to escape the scene of trauma through figuration. I suggested earlier that Zoraida is a figure of the Divine Mother. She is, in effect, the marvelous initiator and the guide who, from the onset, has the keys that literally lead to another world—to freedom. In addition, Zoraida appears as an apotropaic defense against death: She emerges in the very moment that the Captive recounts the worst ordeals of his captivity, the cruelties that his master Hasan Pasha (Cervantes's master) inflicted on his Christian slaves. As the Captive claims, the hunger and lack of clothing of the prisoners were nothing compared to Hasan's tortures: *"cada día [Hasan] ahorcaba el suyo [el de cada día], empalaba a éste, desorejaba a aquel"* [every day Hasan hanged a man, impaled one, cut off the ears of another].[63]

In *La historia del cautivo,* moreover, Cervantes evokes the torments and terrible death of the Moor who was impaled for attempting to help him in his third escape attempt. This passage is permeated by images of death, whose presence in the text is symbolized by the notorious phrase *"había de ser empalado"* [he would be impaled]. The phrase, which retains the image of this impalement and of the guilt associated with it, reveals that this horrifying death cannot be enacted nor set aside: It returns in the haunting phrase *"había de ser empalado."* Such a phrase not only invokes the former's captive's terror at the prospect of being impaled and his guilt for the messenger's death but also brings to mind the death sentence decreed for Cervantes on this occasion through the two thousand blows ordered by Hasan Pasha.

I propose that Zoraida is a symptom for the captive: She is the miraculous apparition that transforms this scene of death into a fantasy of escape. In this sense, Zoraida represents a shield against death, a maternal protection from the terrible menace that erupts in the phrase *"había de ser empalado."* As a symptom for the Captive, Zoraida stands for the place onto which lack is projected and through which it is simultaneously disavowed. What is both projected and disavowed in this passage is the reality of the horrifying experience that returns as a haunting nightmare that can neither be enacted nor cast aside. The splitting of the subject, represented by the doubling of Ruy Pérez de Viedma and Saavedra, is replayed in this scenario by the simultaneous invocation and disavowal of the ordeals of captivity, whose other side is the fantasy of salvation, incarnated by Zoraida. The fact that Zoraida is a symptom—that is, a metaphor, a condensation of fantasy—sheds light on these issues. We have known, since Lacan, that a symptom is a screen through which one detects the workings of *signifiance* (the process of formation and de-formation of meaning in the subject). These coextend with the speaking being as such (Kristeva, "Freud and Love," 23). [64] Lacan's view of the symptom as a screen that hides the workings of *significance* illustrates Zoraida's function in this tale: She is the screen that veils the scene of death in the reenactment of trauma by Cervantes.

As I noted earlier, the impulse to bear witness in the survivor is connected to the need to recreate the traumatic images or to create others that may help to symbolize and work through the traumatic event.[65] In these repetitions, there is also the possibility of finding something like an alternative enactment for the images that torment us, of undergoing personal transformation around that image. This is what Cervantes does through his creation, which is also an act of testimony. As a metaphor, Zoraida represents a unifying agency, a point of identification in the zero degree of subjectivity of the narrator, the Captive, and of the author, Cervantes. Metaphor should be understood here as a move toward the discernible, a journey toward the visible, as Kristeva postulates in her essay "Freud and Love" (30). And certainly this marvelous vision that dazzles and enamors the Captive is also an object of love for Cervantes.

The object of love *is* a metaphor for the subject: It is its constitutive metaphor, its "unitary feature," which permits the subject to position or to represent an adored part of the loved one within the symbolic order of which this feature is a part, as Kristeva has remarked ("Freud and Love," 30). The metaphoric object of love not only outlines the crystallization of fantasy, as we have seen with the image of Zoraida, but also adumbrates the poetic nature of the discourse of love. This is why we can speak of an eroticization of the imaginary in *La historia del cautivo*, in other words, of an "erotics of creation" in Cervantes. This is evoked by the tantalizing representation of Zoraida in the tale, by the extraordinary inventions that follow one another in the text, like a chain of fantasies, and, finally, by the gaiety or joie de vivre—the love—that permeates the narrative in which Zoraida moves.

The apparition of Zoraida, then, speaks not only to the reenactment and reelaboration of the traumatic experiences in Cervantes's fiction but also to fantastic and salvific images that open the window of creation. This is why Zoraida can be fairly called *"señora de nuestra libertad,"* as the Captive names her, for, truly, she is the veiled Lady—the fantastic creation—that emancipates the former captive from the bonds of captivity. That this image was liberating in various ways is suggested by the vision of Zoraida's double, Zahara, in *Los baños de Argel*. In this reenactment of *La historia del cautivo*, Don Lope states that Zahara represents freedom from his chains: *"de mi prisión libertad,/de mi muerte alegre vida"* [Liberty from my prison, happy life in the midst of my death] (III.2667–68). For these reasons I propose that *La historia del cautivo* represents a turning point in Cervantes's literary production, a testimonial to the moment in which the former captive turns into a true creator. In the borderline between life and literature, this remarkable mixture of autobiography and fiction opens the way for Cervantes's great invention, *Don Quijote*. In agreement with Murillo, who regards *La historia del cautivo* as the *Ur-Quijote*, I suggest that the second part of this tale, which recounts the story of Zoraida, already contains the fabulous imagery and the splendid artistry that characterize the great novel.

In the end, Zoraida remains veiled, a metaphor in the chain of desire that perpetually oscillates between one and another signified. Like the starred cane that signaled her presence at the window of Hājjī Murād's house, Zoraida inhabits both the tremulous frontier between autobiography and fiction and the borderline between the Christian and the Muslim worlds, which would remain an inexhaustible fountain of creation for Cervantes. As a fantasy bridging Christianity–Islam, a savior who is a mixture of both, Cervantes would be evoking a fantasy of peace—in other words, a fantasy that would undo the war between Christians and Muslims, a war that thrust him into captivity. I have suggested elsewhere that Zoraida represents the "other scene": the place where *it* speaks (*ça parle*) ("Zoraida's Veil," 89). Zoraida, indeed, is a fantasy that evokes the unconscious workings of desire. As we have seen in this chapter, Zoraida's idealized presentation evokes the figure of the mother as a mainstay of love, as well as the identification of the author-narrator with this love. Consequently, it is not fortuitous that Zoraida should be deployed under the metaphor of the veil. The implementation of maternal love, symbolized by Zoraida's presence in this tale, functions as a veil over death. And most certainly, if *La historia del cautivo* emphasizes the semantic richness of the "veil," it also evokes its intimate relation with death, as discussed in the next section, where I examine the poems on the fall of Tunis and La Goleta, included in the Captive's tale.

The Fall of Tunis and La Goleta

I return now to the earlier part of this tale, which focuses on the Mediterranean battles between the Spaniards and the Turks in which Cervantes participated. Describing the leading actors on both sides of these conflicts, this section of the tale starts with the Battle of Lepanto in 1571 and ends with the Captive's report on the fall of Tunis and La Goleta to the Turks in 1574. The narrative is thus framed by the historical events that inaugurated and closed Cervantes's military career in the Mediterranean. After November 1574, indeed, *soldado aventajado* Cervantes would start preparing his return to Spain, a return that, as we know, would be thwarted by his capture aboard the galley *Sol*, in September 1575, by Algerian corsairs.

In this context, Cervantes's account of the fall of Tunis and La Goleta evokes a constellation of annihilation and destruction, which is reiterated by the sonnets written by soldier Pedro de Aguilar, inserted in *La historia del cautivo*. The haunting presence of death in these scenes is stressed both by the Captive's narration and by the sonnets that praise the valor of the soldiers who gave their lives for their king in Tunis and La Goleta. Interrupting the Captive's soliloquy, the allusion to soldier-poet Pedro de Aguilar leads to the intrusion of another voice that effects a break in the narrative sequence of *Don Quijote*. In effect, Pedro de Aguilar's sonnets, recited by one of the guests at the inn, inaugurate a new chapter of the novel, one that includes the Algerian section of this tale, marked by the surname *Saavedra* and the apparition of the legendary Zoraida (*DQ* I, 40). The poems that mourn the fall of Tunis and La Goleta in *La historia del cautivo* thus point to the frontier between autobiography and fiction, a frontier highlighted by a structural break in the narrative. These cuts also speak to the break in the lifeline, the "cut" that severs life, leaving the survivor with a sense of being tainted by death. Represented by the narrative and the poems that mourn the fall of Tunis and La Goleta, this encounter with death is connected, as it turns out, with the metaphor of the veil, which serves as an emblem for Zoraida in this tale.

These historical events are recounted with precision by the Captive's tale. In July 1574, the Ottoman armada appeared before the port of Tunis and the presidio of La Goleta with a force between two hundred fifty and three hundred ships, carrying around seventy-five thousand troops. The Turks, commanded by Sinān Pasha and Alūj Ali, joined the contingents of troops led overland by the governors of Algiers, Tripoli, and Tunis. The impressive Ottoman armada, constituted by a force perhaps as large as one hundred thousand men, launched simultaneous attacks on Tunis and La Goleta, from both land and sea, taking the presidio of La Goleta, defended by seven thousand soldiers, on August 24, 1574.[66] After repeated assaults, the remaining Christian soldiers in the small fort opposite Tunis surrendered on September 13 (Hess, 95). Awaiting the arrival of reinforcements from Italy and Sicily, the besieged Christian soldiers fought heroically yet in vain. In spite of Don Juan de Austria's insistent requests for assistance from Granvelle, the king was in no condition to grant this help, owing to the financial crisis affecting Spain. Notwithstanding, Don Juan attempted to come to the rescue of La Goleta with a contingent of galleys and troops from Naples and Sicily, but his fleet was repeatedly diverted from the coasts of Africa by furious storms that forced him to return to the port of Trapani, in Sicily. On August 23, 1574, while Don Juan sailed for the third time for Tunis, determined to succor the besieged at all costs, La Goleta had already fallen, after a heroic resistance in which thousands of men died or were taken captive by the Turks (Astrana Marín, II: 411–15). Philip II's tepid response to this new challenge from Barbary is explained by the war in the Low Countries, which had utterly drained the Spanish treasury, and by the enormous cost of maintaining a Mediterranean navy, factors that would plunge the Spanish state into bankruptcy a year later, on September 1, 1575. In 1574, however, because Tunis was too far from Spain, the Ottoman forces devastated the imperial garrisons and even returned later, as the Captive tells us, to destroy the fortifications of La Goleta (*DQ* I, 40).

In a laconic reference to these events, included in his 1590 *Memorial* to the Spanish crown, Cervantes clearly states that after Navarino (1572), he was present at Tunis and La Goleta (Sliwa, 225–26). What this phrase exactly means will be clarified below. It is in *La historia del cautivo*, however, that the writer shows himself at his most eloquent, telling us what happened between Don Juan de Austria's October 1573 expedition to Tunis and the catastrophe of August and September 1574. Even more, Cervantes devotes two sonnets to the fall of the fortresses at Tunis and La Goleta, mourning the heavy losses suffered by the soldiers who defended the imperial garrisons. From the Captive's detailed narration of these episodes, we can surmise that Cervantes the soldier probably disembarked with the Christian troops in La Goleta in October 1573, when Don Juan took the fort and the city of Tunis, placing a puppet ruler, Muley Muhammad, in charge of the Moorish and Berber population. Since Charles V's conquest of Tunis in 1535, the fort of La Goleta had remained under imperial control. Fortunately, Cervantes did not remain behind with the garrison in La Goleta after Don Juan de Austria's 1573 offensive. Instead, he would embark with Don Lope de Figueroa's soldiers and would probably spend part of the winter in Sardinia. Escaping misfortune, he missed this encounter with death.

Through the Captive's words, Cervantes praises the heroic defense of Tunis and La Goleta by its soldiers, even while implicitly denouncing the Spanish state for not coming to the aid of the besieged. Alluding to the criticisms that arose in Spain in response to this shocking defeat, the Captive asks: *"Si en La Goleta y en el fuerte apenas había siete mil soldados, ¿cómo podía tan poco número, aunque más esforzados fuesen, salir a la campaña y quedar en las fuerzas contra tanto como era el enemigo? ¿Y cómo es posible dejar de perderse fuerza que no es socorrida, y más cuando la cercan enemigos muchos y porfiados, y en su mesma tierra?"* [If La Goleta and the fort, put together, held barely seven thousand soldiers, how could such a small force, however resolute, come out and hold its own against so huge an enemy army? And how can you help losing a stronghold that is not relieved, and especially when it's surrounded by a stubborn and very numerous army, and on its own ground?] (*DQ* I, 39; translation slightly modified). Highlighting the intrepid resistance of the soldiers who guarded these North African citadels, Cervantes claims that in the twenty-two Ottoman assaults against the fort of Tunis, its small contingent of Spanish and Italian soldiers managed to kill twenty-five thousand enemies; only three hundred men in this fort survived the attacks of the Turks (*DQ* I, 39). Cervantes was among the troops of Don Juan of Austria, which tried to arrive in vain to help the assailed men of La Goleta.

The Captive's information regarding these Mediterranean battles is historical and exact, down to the trench warfare employed by the Turks and the names of the most important personages in these campaigns. On the imperial side: Don Juan Zanoguera, a valiant captain from Valencia; Don Pedro Portocarerro, the general of La Goleta who died of grief on the way to Constantinople, where he was being taken as a captive; and Gabrio Cervellón, the general of the Fort of Tunis, a *"valentísimo soldado"* [very valorous soldier]. Mentioning the great losses suffered among the highborn military leaders, the Captive underscores the death of Pagán Doria—a Knight of St. John and the brother of naval commander Giovanni Andrea Doria—treacherously decapitated by the Arabs and Berbers who were helping him to escape.[67]

Among those lost or captured in this disaster, the Captive tells us, was a soldier named Don Pedro de Aguilar, who was a galley slave, like him, on a Turkish galleon. A native of a village in Andalucía, *"había sido alférez en el fuerte [de Túnez], soldado de mucha cuenta y de raro entendimiento; especialmente tenía especial gracia en lo que llaman poesía* [he had been an ensign in the fort of Tunis and was a soldier of great account and rare intelligence, being specially gifted in what they call poetry] (I, 39). This slave apparently composed poems while rowing, and the Captive, who shared his bench as a galley slave, has memorized two of these sonnets dedicated to the defeat of Tunis and La Goleta.

Against the backdrop of the Mediterranean wars with the Turks, the Captive's reminiscences are rigorously historical. Both Astrana Marín and Jaime Oliver Asín have identified Pedro de Aguilar as an authentic soldier who fought in Tunis. A lieutenant in the company commanded by Cap-

tain Lope Hurtado de Mendoza, Pedro de Aguilar appears in a register of
"[la] gente que se perdió en el fuerte de Túnez" [the soldiers who were lost
in the fort of Tunis], either because they were dead or because they were
captured and made slaves (Astrana Marín, II: 419; Oliver Asín, 309).[68] Because an anonymous report on the fall of La Goleta that includes this listing also contains a collection of poems, Pascual de Gayangos has attributed it to soldier Pedro de Aguilar, mentioned by Cervantes in his tale. Be
that as it may, the poems inserted in the Captive's tale were surely composed by Cervantes himself and ascribed to an alter ego, following the custom inaugurated by Cide Hamete Benengeli in his texts.

The Captive's lyrical description of the fall of Tunis and La Goleta is,
in fact, marked by the insistent repetition of the verb *perderse* [to be defeated, to lose, to disappear], which emphasizes the overwhelming dimension of these defeats:

> *Perdióse*, en fin, La Goleta, *perdióse* el fuerte [. . .]. *Perdióse* primero la Goleta,
> tenida hasta entonces por inexpugnable, y no *se perdió* por culpa de sus
> defensores [. . .]. Y ¿cómo es posible *dejar de perderse* fuerza que no es
> socorrida? [. . .]. *Perdióse* también el fuerte [. . .]. *Rindióse* a partido un
> pequeño fuerte o torre que estaba en mitad del estaño. . . .

> [La Goleta *fell*, in the end, and the fort *fell* (. . .). The first *to fall* was La
> Goleta, until then considered impregnable, and *it fell*, not by any fault of its
> defenders (. . .). And, how is it possible *to help losing* a stronghold that is not
> relieved (. . .)? The fort also *fell* (. . .). A small fort or tower which was in
> the middle of the lake *surrendered* after bartering for terms.]
>
> (*DQ* I, 39; emphasis mine)

There is a close relation between this ominous passage and the phrase with
which the Captive later introduces the presumed author of the sonnets to
the fall of La Goleta: *"entre los cristianos que en el fuerte se perdieron fue
uno llamado don Pedro de Aguilar."* The verb *perderse* is applied here both
to the soldiers lost in war and to those taken prisoner by the Turks, captives who were juridically and spiritually dead, as Cervantes and Sosa claim.
Like the earlier prose account on the fall of Tunis and La Goleta, the
phantasmatic figure of Pedro de Aguilar seems to be tainted by the image
of defeat and disappearance, namely, by the imprint of death.

Referring to the episode of La Goleta in *La historia del cautivo*, Américo
Castro notes: *"de cerca vio entonces nuestro gran escritor la desgracia y la
desventura"* [our great writer thus saw disaster and misfortune closely].[69]
Evidently, the lyrical description and denunciation of the fall of La Goleta
are inspired by the personal experiences of Cervantes, experiences that touch
his most intimate fibers. Although Cervantes was not an eyewitness to the
fall of La Goleta and Tunis, his geographical nearness to these fortresses,
both before and after the 1574 Turkish expedition, his presumable relations

with some of the soldiers who lost their lives there, and his friendship with
a number of survivors of this defeat, explain his impulse to bear witness to
these shocking deaths. His response to this catastrophe leads me to ask,
with Caruth, whether trauma is the encounter with death or the ongoing
experience of having survived it—the shock, the guilt of surviving (*Unclaimed Experience*, 7). Caruth finds a kind of double telling at the core of
the stories of trauma, the oscillation between "a *crisis of death* and the cor-
relative *crisis of life*." Such swaying moves between "the story of the unbearable nature of the event and the story of the unbearable nature of its
survival" (7). In addition, let us consider Cervantes's identification with
the soldiers who guarded the Spanish presidios in North Africa, soldiers
who, like Cervantes, fought in Philip II's armies, presumably advancing
the cause of Christianity across the Mediterranean. Such factors, as well as
the guilt of surviving in the dramatic fall of La Goleta, might have led
Cervantes to seek a measure of insight that would justify these deaths.

Instead, the author draws a bitter lesson from the botched operation
of Tunis and La Goleta. Certain people, he tells us, still believe that the
defense of La Goleta was badly planned, and that it would have been possible to save the fortress even if it had not received help:

> Pero a muchos les pareció, y así me pareció a mí, que fue particular gracia y
> merced que el cielo hizo a España en permitir que se asolase esa oficina y
> capa de maldades, y aquella gomia o esponja y polilla de la infinidad de dineros
> que allá sin provechos se gastaban, sin servir de otra cosa que de conservar la
> memoria de haberla ganado la felicísima del invictísimo Carlos Quinto, como
> si fuera menester para hacerla eterna, como lo es y será, que aquellas piedras
> le sustentaran.

> [But many thought, and I thought so too, that it was a special mercy and
> good favor which Heaven showed to Spain in permitting the destruction of
> that source and hiding place of mischief, that devourer, sponge, and moth
> of incalculable sums, uselessly wasted there to no other purpose except pre-
> serving the memory of its capture by the invincible Charles V. As if to make
> that eternal, as it is and it will be, these stones were needed to support it!]
>
> (*DQ* I, 39)

Cervantes's response to the useless deaths of thousands of Spanish and Italian soldiers in these garrisons is understandable. As a former soldier and a
captive, he probably identified with the men sent to the presidios in North
Africa, who suffered almost as much as the captives in Barbary. Like the
captives, the *soldados fronterizos* were liminal personae, characterized by
their dramatic deprivation. Virtually excluded from the commercial routes
of the Maghrib, the presidios, as discussed earlier, were inhospitable fortresses surrounded by enemy territories, where men could hope at best to
stay alive. Braudel reminds us that life was miserable in these garrisons:

"so near the water, rations rotted and men died of fever" (*Mediterranean*, II: 860). Like the Barbary captives, the soldiers were hungry all year round. Supplies came only by sea, and usually in winter, when the corsairs were presumably at bay. Orán was an exception to this rule, because it obtained meat and grain from the countryside around the citadel. The fate of La Goleta was no different from that of the other presidios, despite its apparently favorable location near the abundant supplies of bread, wine, cheese, and chickpeas of Naples and Sicily. According to Braudel, when Don Alonso Pimentel took command of La Goleta in 1569, the garrison was living on its reserves of cheese—without either bread or wine (*Mediterranean*, II: 861).

Soldiers in these garrisons were supplied with rations by the storekeepers at the price fixed on the shipping labels, and often on credit, through which the troops could amass frightful debts, as they bought food, on credit also, from passing merchants. The problem was aggravated by the fact that pay was lower in the presidios than in Italy—one more reason, when troops were being embarked for the presidios, not to let them know beforehand of their destination, and, once they were there, never to repatriate them. Diego Suárez spent twenty-seven years in Orán, in spite of several attempts to flee as a stowaway on galleys. Only the sick were able to escape the horror of the North African presidios—and then, not always—by being sent to the hospitals of Sicily and Spain.[70]

In sum, the presidios were virtually places of deportation, a fact that Cervantes knew well. Its soldiers, as Cervantes probably intuited, had a fate similar to that of the Barbary captives. Like the captives, these soldiers lived on the borderline between two cultures, often snatching a livelihood from both sides of the border. I argued in this chapter that the oppressive life of the presidios led to multiple escapes of Spanish soldiers who deserted and went over to Islam. As we have seen in this study, Cervantes was both attracted by and preoccupied with the status of the *soldados fronterizos* on the borderland. Perhaps because the presidios were places of banishment and exile, he was sympathetic with the fate of these soldiers who put their lives on the line for the Spanish crown. That the presidios were places of expatriation is verified by the fact that nobles and rich men would be sent there as a punishment. Such was the case of the grandson of Columbus, Luis Colón, who was arrested at Valladolid for trigamy. Condemned to ten years' exile, he arrived in Orán in 1563 and was to die there on February 3, 1573, as confirmed by Braudel (*Mediterranean* II: 861–62).[71]

On the other hand, let us recall that Cervantes shared his captivity with Bartholomeo Ruffino de Chiambery, a survivor of the fall of Tunis and La Goleta who authored an account of this disaster while in prison with Cervantes in Algiers. Ruffino de Chiambery was the auditor in the infantry regimen commanded by the unfortunate Pagán Doria, whose death Cervantes described earlier. Cervantes probably read the lengthy report composed by Ruffino de Chiambery, for he wrote the laudatory sonnets that grace this work: *"Verdad, orden, estilo claro y llano,/qual a perfecto historiador conviene,/en esta breve summa está çifrado"* [Truth, order, clear and straightforward style,/as suits the perfect historian,/in this brief compendium is ciphered]. These are some of the verses dedicated by soldier-poet Cervantes to the historian of La Goleta (Astrana Marín, III: 528).[72] Many conversations probably transpired among these captives who not only partook of a common fate as prisoners in the *baño* but also suffered various close encounters with death. In addition, Cervantes knew and befriended other survivors from Tunis and La Goleta, such as Gabriel de Castañeda and Francisco de Meneses, who testified for him in the *Información de Argel*. Like these Spanish soldiers, Ruffino de Chiambiery was made prisoner in the fall of Tunis, taken to Constantinople as a captive, and finally transferred to Algiers. If his long journey through the Turkish and Algerian *baños* is similar to that of the Captive in *Don Quijote*, his friendship with Cervantes may have also inspired the poems on the fall of La Goleta and the fort of Tunis, ascribed by Cervantes to Pedro de Aguilar.

"El mortal velo" [The Mortal Veil]

The two poems attributed to soldier-poet Pedro de Aguilar are central to *La historia del cautivo*. As we know, the Captive's discourse is a long soliloquy, with only one interruption, caused by the allusion to Don Pedro de Aguilar, the author of two sonnets that lament the fall of Tunis and La Goleta. At the mention of his name, Don Fernando, one of the guests at the inn, interrupts the Captive's tale and confides that Aguilar is his brother who has since been liberated and now lives in their hometown with his family. The sonnets are thus recited by Don Fernando, who knows them by heart. With this change of voice, the floor is taken by one of the narratees, who authorizes, with his intervention, the veracity of the Captive's discourse. At the same time, another type of literary genre—heroic poetry—is introduced in the narrative. Pedro de Aguilar's poems, moreover, appear precisely between chapters 39 and 40 of *Don Quijote* I, inaugurating a new chapter in the novel. Cervantes's doubling game thus joins two pairs of brothers in this scene, on the one hand, Fernando and Pedro de Aguilar from Andalucía, and, on the other, Ruy and Juan Pérez de Viedma from León, who represent the couple *armas y letras* [arms and letters], which this autobiographical narrative is clearly evoking.

The irruption of the sonnets to the fall of Tunis and La Goleta in the midst of the Captive's report on the Mediterranean campaigns of the 1570s not only prefigures the intrusion of the name *Saavedra* in the tale but also exemplifies the "cut" produced by the presence of death in Cervantes's

fictions. The two sonnets mourn the heavy losses incurred in these defeats, even while revealing Cervantes's intimate thoughts on the subject.
Appropriately, the Captive calls these poems epitaphs, for they are literary
epitaphs to the soldiers who gave their lives for their king in North Africa.
The first quatrain of the sonnet to the fall of La Goleta reads:

> Almas dichosas que del *mortal velo*
> Libres y esentas, por el bien que obrastes,
> Desde la baja tierra os levantastes,
> A lo más alto y lo mejor del cielo.

> [Blessed souls, that, from this *mortal veil* set free,
> In guerdon of brave deeds beatified,
> Above this lowly orb of ours abide
> Made heirs of heaven and immortality.]
>   (*DQ* I, 40; emphasis mine)

The first line of this poem explicitly intimates the connection between the
veil and death. Here the veil covers the face of death, separating (mortal)
humans from "the other scene." Emerging as separator, the veil insinuates
that "cut" *[corte]* which is related to death. A verse from *El trato de Argel*,
which refers to the death of Don Juan de Austria, alludes to the cut that
severs life: *"quiso el hado* cortar el hilo de su dulce vida/*y arrebatar el alma
al alto cielo"* [destiny wished *to cut the thread of his sweet life*/and snatch
his soul from the high Heavens] (III, vv. 1517–19; emphasis mine). The character Marandro, in *La Numancia*, also claims *"que la estambre/de mi vida
corta el hado"* [that the twine of my life is *cut* by destiny] (vv. 1842–43;
emphasis mine). Such references to the broken thread of life are often used
by Cervantes, as we shall see in the next chapter. As an epitaph to the
soldados fronterizos who lost their lives in these African citadels, the sonnet
speaks to the imprint of death that marked Cervantes the survivor. The
last tercets of the sonnet enact a symbolic death encounter that recalls what
this experience entailed:

> Primero que el valor faltó la vida
> en los cansados brazos, que, muriendo,
> con ser vencidos, llevan la victoria.
> Y esta vuestra mortal, triste caída
> entre el muro y el hierro, os va adquiriendo
> fama que el mundo os da, y el cielo gloria.

> [Your life, not your valor, was first to fail
> in those your weary arms. And as you died,
> defeated, you carried the victor's hail.
> And this sad fall, your own mortality

between the wall and sword augments the fame
this world gives you and heaven its glory (immortality).]

(*DQ* I, 40)

Recalling a topic dear to Cervantes, exemplified in *El trato de Argel* and,
specifically, in *La Numancia*, the poem endeavors to prove that victory
belongs to the vanquished. Death emerges here as the ineluctable destiny
of these soldiers, trapped between the walls of the fortresses and the swords,
harquebus, and cannons of the enemy hosts. Yet even though the sonnet
attempts to justify the futile deaths of these soldiers in the name of fame
and immortality, Cervantes had condemned, a few lines above, the existence of the North African presidios. As monuments to pride, these fortresses revealed a lack of discernment on the part of the Spanish rulers and,
implicitly, a crass indifference toward the soldiers who defended the Spanish frontiers. In spite of such contradictions, the poems on the fall of Tunis
and La Goleta represent the survivor's recreation of these death scenes,
including his confrontation of excruciating truths. Cervantes's testimony,
in turn, leads to a renewal of imagery—in other words, to the emancipa-
tion from bondage to the deceased that opens the door to creation.

A Turning Point in Cervantes's Literary Production

The veil that masks death in the opening lines of the sonnet to the fall of
La Goleta is also connected to the borderline between life and death,
namely, to the tenuous line that cuts across the frontier between autobiography and fiction in Cervantes. This is the borderland from which life is
recited, the line where the wound, the scar, and the signature *Saavedra*
join each other to acclaim the heroic deeds of the Battle of Lepanto, even
while mourning the catastrophic experiences suffered by Cervantes in
Algiers. The encounter with death, evoked by the narrative and the sonnets on the fall of Tunis and La Goleta, prepares the way for the impossible reenactment of death, which surfaces with the name *Saavedra* in this
text. Betraying the impact of events that history cannot assimilate or integrate as knowledge, the poems on the fall of Tunis and La Goleta announce
the encounter with the Real, which keeps returning through rhythm and
cadence, through poetry and literary creation.

In this way, both the narrative and the poems on the fall of Tunis and
La Goleta open the way for an "erotics of creation" in Cervantes that is
personified by veiled Zoraida in this tale. As a symptom for the Captive,
Zoraida, as I have argued, is the screen that veils the scene of death in the
reenactment of the trauma by Cervantes. Yet this veil also alludes to the
advent of desire, represented by the creation of Zoraida in *La historia del
cautivo*, whose fantastic and salvific images open the way for creation. In

this way, this testimonial narrative illustrates a turning point in Cervantes's literary production, the somersault that carries the former captive across the abyss of trauma and turns him into a creator.[73] At the crossroads of fantasy and history, Zoraida's fiction speaks to the indescribable void, the maelstrom, and the creative fountain symbolized by the surname *Saavedra* in Cervantes.

Algerian Woman at Home. The legend reads: "This deshabille is comfortable, / And quite appropriate for the house; / Since it is the fashion of the country, / I very much approve of its style." This intimate portrait of an Algerian woman and her child shows her wearing a short-sleeved bodice and *gonila* [long vest] and the elaborate embroidered skirt made of colored wool, silk, or satin worn by Turkish and renegade women in Algiers. Her headdress was woven from red, yellow, or green silk, on top of which came a thin cloth braid with the ends finished with a border of gold. While most women in Algiers went barefoot at home, they often wore open slippers made of gold leather. *Right:* the woman carries a steaming plate of couscous. According to Cervantes and Sosa, Algerian women did not cover their faces in the presence of Christian captives.

SOURCE: Henri Bonnart: *Femme d'Alger en déshabillé* [An Algerian Woman in Deshabille] (Bibliothèque Nationale, Paris). Reprinted from Gabriel Esquer, *Iconographie historique de l'Algérie depuis le XVIe siècle jusqu'à 1871* (Paris: Plon, 1929), Vol 1, Plate XXX, no. 80.

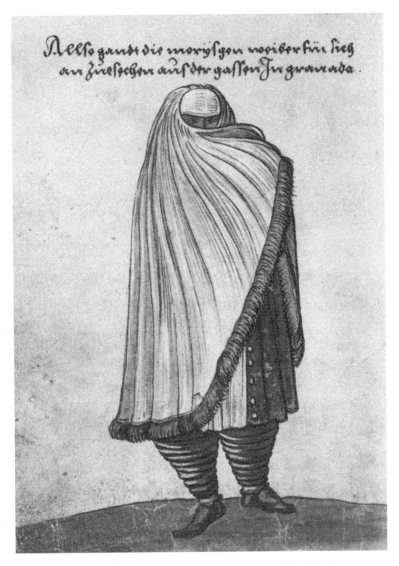

A Moorish Woman from Granada. The legend reads: "The Morisco women look like this in the streets of Granada." The German engraver and illustrator Weiditz travelled to Spain between 1529 and 1532. He was one of the first Europeans to draw the Moorish women of Granada who had been compelled to abandon the traditional face coverings worn on the streets. As this drawing shows, they had substituted for it a broad mantle that made it possible to cover their faces entirely. The woman wears a white band over her forehead, a white mantle, and short red stockings, both embossed with silver.

SOURCE: *A Moorish Woman from Granada* (1514) by Cristoph Weiditz, from *Das Trachtenbuch des Cristoph Weiditz von seinen Reisen nach Spanien* (1529), plate 54, reprinted from the facsimile edition by Theodore Hamper (Berlin: W. de Gruyere & Co., 1927).

Algiers: XVIIth Century. Framed by a stylized couple facing each other, this view of Algiers emphasizes its strong fortifications and military aspect. The map depicts two tall mosques and the Peñón of Algiers, attached to the city by a dam. Three corsair galleons are anchored in the port. While the dress of the man corresponds to a Europeanized view of Barbary fashions, the woman wears an elaborate Turkish headdress and ornate garments with very wide sleeves and pearls.

SOURCE: *Algiers* (XVIIth Century). *Carolus Allard Excudit cum privilegio ordinum Hollandie et Westfrisie N. . . . udiger fecit* (Bibliothèque Nationale, Algiers). Reprinted from Gabriel Esquer, *Iconographie historique de l'Algérie depuis le XVIe siècle jusqu'à 1871* (Paris: Plon, 1929), Vol 1, Plate XXXI, no. 81.

5

"Anudando este roto hilo"
[Tying up this Broken Thread]

Tiempo vendrá, quizá, donde, anudando este roto hilo,
diga lo que aquí me falta y lo que se convenía.
—Cervantes, Prologue to *Persiles.*[1]

IN A BOOK PUBLISHED a year before his death, Primo Levi remarked that
"it has been observed by psychologists that survivors of traumatic events
are divided into two well-defined groups: those who repress their past *en
bloc*, and those whose memory of the offense persists, as though carved in
stone, prevailing over all previous or subsequent experiences. Now," says
Levi, "not by choice, but by nature, I belong to the second group."[2] The
writer then adds that of his two years of life in the Lager, he has not forgotten anything: "Without any deliberate effort, memory continues to re-
store to me events, faces, words, sensations, as if at that time my mind
had gone through a period of exalted receptivity, during which not a detail was lost" (*Moment*, 10–11). One encounters a similar phrase in *La
historia del cautivo*, when, referring to the extraordinary events of his captivity in Algiers, the Captive states: *"De todos los sucesos sustanciales que en
este suceso me acontecieron, ninguno se me ha ido de la memoria, ni aún se
me irá en tanto que tuviere vida"* [Of all the important points which happened to me throughout this event not one has slipped from my memory,
nor will ever do so, as long as I live] (*DQ* I: 40).

Like Levi, Cervantes belongs to the group of survivors to whom the
memory of the catastrophic event returns until the end. Starting with the
Información de Argel, composed in Algiers in 1580, the writer began a compelling testimonial process that would be inexorably repeated until his
death. Through an astonishing diversity of media, from drama and poetry
to official letters and documents that altered his name and identity, to increasingly complex fictions that intertwined the history of the sixteenth-
century Mediterranean with traumatic images and fantasies, Cervantes
insistently reelaborated his Algerian experience. Central to the writer's
inventions is the name *Saavedra*, which inaugurated his (pro)creation: both
his literary offspring and his biological issue, represented by his daughter

Isabel. Yet *Saavedra* also symbolizes the limit-experience of the survivor—the scar, the vortex, the death imprint—even while signaling the beginning of a healing process, the soldering of the shattered selves splintered by trauma. The surname *Saavedra*, fully assumed by Cervantes in *La historia del cautivo* (1589) and in the related *Memorial* requesting a post in the Indies (1590), is the biographical rubric of the man who fought in Lepanto and suffered the trauma of captivity in Algiers. Apparently, the staging of this signature—an event related to other crucial experiences occurring at this time of Cervantes's life—had immensely liberating effects for the creative energy of the writer. After 1589, when *La historia del cautivo* was composed, Cervantes initiated a period of extraordinary productivity that would end only on his deathbed, with the moving farewell to his readers delivered in *Persiles*.

Referring to victims of the Holocaust, Dori Laub has affirmed that "survivors did not only need to survive so they could tell their stories; they also needed to tell their story in order to survive."[3] Laub speaks of the imperative to *tell* that exists in each survivor, the need to *know* his or her own story, which can become a consuming life task. No amount of telling, or narrating, however, seems to appease this inner compulsion: "there are never enough words or the right words, and never enough time listening or the right listening to articulate the story that cannot be fully captured in *thought, memory,* and *speech* ("Trauma," 63). Other writers, such as Primo Levi, have spoken of this burning obsession with recounting the traumatic story. Levi stresses this point in a poignant passage from *Survival in Auschwitz*. He describes his need to tell his story to "the rest," to make "the rest" participate in it: "[this need] had taken on for us, before our liberation and after, the character of an immediate and violent impulse, to the point of competing with our other elementary needs. The book has been written to satisfy this need: first and foremost, therefore, as an interior liberation" (15).

We can read Cervantes through this lens. From his earliest testimony of captivity redacted in 1580 Algiers to his posthumous *Persiles*—signed thirty-five years later at death's door in April 1616—the writings of Cervantes reveal this need to achieve internal liberation through the testimony to, and the reenactment of, his traumatic experience. If his first testimony can be read as a form of action that had to be undertaken so that he could continue the process of survival after liberation, his ensuing literary production—the collection of plays, interludes, novels, poems, and short fictions that populate his long life—speaks to an erotics of creation that springs from the vortex of trauma at the center of Cervantes's fictions. This chapter rehearses the textual itinerary traced by certain recurring images and figures in Cervantes, from the first works written after his release from prison, such as *El trato de Argel* (1581–1583) and *La Galatea* (1585), to his novella *La española inglesa* and his play *Los baños de Argel*, to his posthumous novel *Los trabajos de Persiles y Sigismunda* (1617). Focusing on the gradual evolution of these testimonies, which tend to become more diffused and increasingly intertwined with fiction as they are repeated over and over again, I aim to explore the relationship of words and trauma in Cervantes. By reading "the wound" with the aid of literature, I will examine the relations between trauma and the work of creation, specifically, the therapeutic effects that literary creation seemed to have for Cervantes.

The Recurrent Storm

In an effort to study these complex issues, let us trace a cursory story of a textual itinerary in Cervantes's fictions, one marked by the images that insistently reappear in his literary universe. In chapter 4, I explored some of the complexities of *La historia del cautivo*, such as the extraordinary autobiographical creation that puts the name *Saavedra* on the line, even while hinting at the undulating thread that connects the reenactment of trauma with the paths of desire in Cervantes. This chapter examines a number of Cervantine fictions that relive the experience of capture on the galley *Sol* and the fearful storm associated with that experience, a scene repeated, like a fugue and its variations, in a sequence of works by Cervantes.

The initial passage comes from *La Galatea* (1585), the first novel published by Cervantes after his return to Spain. Timbrio, a gentleman from Jerez whose reality has nothing in common with the life of the shepherds described in this pastoral novel, recreates the horrendous storm that inaugurates his adventures as he sailed from Naples on his way to Spain:

> Salí de la ciudad, y al cabo de los pocos días llegué a la fuerte Gaeta, donde hallé una nave que quería despegar las velas al viento para partirse a España. Embarqueme en ella [. . .]; mas apenas los diligentes marineros zarparon los ferros y descogieron las velas, [. . .] cuando se levantó una [. . .] súbita borrasca, y una ráfaga de viento imbistió [embistió] las velas del navío con tal furia, que rompió el árbol del trinquete y la vela mesana se abrió de arriba a bajo [. . .]. La borrasca crecía, y la mar comenzaba a alterarse, y el cielo daba muestras de durable y espantosa fortuna [. . .]. Era el maestral el viento que soplaba [. . .]. Y así comenzó la nave, llevada de su furia, a correr por el levantado mar con tanta ligereza, que en dos días que duró el maestral, discurrimos por todas las islas de aquel derecho, sin poder en ninguna tomar abrigo.

> [I left the city, and after a few days I arrived at strong Gaeta, where I found a ship that was just about to sail for Spain. I embarked on it (. . .). But, as soon as the diligent sailors weighed anchor and spread the sails, (. . .) there arose an (. . .) unexpected and sudden tempest, and a squall of wind pounded against the ship's sails with such fury that it broke the foremast and the mizzen

sail from top to bottom (. . .). The tempest grew, and the sea began to rise, and the sky was giving signs of a fearful and horrendous storm (. . .). The wind that blew was the mistral (. . .). And so the ship, driven by its fury, began to run with such speed over the stormy sea, that in the two days that the mistral lasted, we sped by all the islands on that course without being able to take shelter on any.]

(*Galatea*, V, 484–85)

The story of the ship swept out to sea by a violent storm recalls Cervantes's own crossing as he sailed on the galley *Sol* from Naples to Barcelona in September 1575. In an enlightening article entitled *"La captura de Cervantes,"* Juan Bautista Avalle-Arce has shown that Cervantes left Naples on September 6 or 7, 1575. Soon after, on September 18, the flotilla, composed of four Spanish galleons, which had been hugging the coast of Italy and Provence, was dispersed by a storm off Port-de-Bouc. The *Sol* was probably swept toward Corsica and other Mediterranean islands by a violent mistral, perhaps as described in the passage from *La Galatea*: *"Y así comenzó la nave, llevada de su furia, a correr por el levantado mar con tanta ligereza, que en dos días que duró el maestral, discurrimos por todas las islas de aquel derecho, sin poder en ninguna tomar abrigo"* [And so the ship, driven by its fury, began to run with such speed over the stormy sea, that in the two days that the mistral lasted, we sped by all the islands on that course without being able to take shelter on any] (*Galatea*, V, 484–85). On September 26, as the *Sol* approached the Catalan coast, not far from Cadaqués or Palamós, it was attacked by Algerian corsairs. After significant resistance, in which the captain and many crew members were killed, the surviving passengers were tied up and taken to Algiers as captives (Avalle-Arce, "La captura," 237–60; Canavaggio, *Cervantes*, 76–77).

In *La Galatea*, the storm takes the ship back to the Port of Gaeta, near Naples, where the exhausted passengers repose for a few days, while the galley is repaired. Sailing again toward Genoa, Timbrio discovers that his beloved Nísida, whom he believed dead, has boarded the ship, dressed as a pilgrim, with her sister Blanca. The lovers' happy encounter, set against the backdrop of a clear and fresh night, is suddenly perturbed by *"la mayor desventura que imaginarse pudiera"* [the worst misfortune that one could possibly imagine] (*Galatea*, 491). What follows is the reenactment of the corsair attack on the *Sol*, which returns to the text like a haunting dream. By the light of the moon, a sailor sights four vessels rapidly approaching the galley: *"Al momento conoció ser de contrarios, y con grandes voces comenzó a gritar: '¡Arma, arma, que bajeles turquescos se descubren!'"* [He immediately recognized them as enemies, and with loud cries he started to shout: "To arms! To arms! For Turkish vessels are in sight!"] (491).

From now on, it is Cervantes who speaks, or better, "cries out" through the narrator's shouts: *"Esa voz y súbito alarido puso tanto sobresalto en todos los de la nave que sin saber darse maña en el cercano peligro, unos a otros se miraban"* [This *cry* and the sudden shrieks caused such panic in the whole crew that, without being able to think about the imminent danger, they all looked at one another] (*Galatea*, 491; emphasis mine). Amid the utter confusion and cries of the passengers, each man takes his place next to the arms. Collapsed with the narrator's voice, however, is the writer's voice that evokes the anguish caused by the recurrence of these images: *"Paso y [mal] punto fue éste que desmaya la imaginación cuando de él se acuerda la memoria"* [This was the situation that makes the imagination faint when memory recalls it] (*Galatea*, 492).

The Spanish captain now discovers fifteen enemy vessels surrounding his ship. The commander of the corsair squadron, Arnaut Mamí—the same corsair who captured Cervantes—asks the Spanish captain to surrender. His denial provokes the ferocious attack of the Turkish-Algerian corsairs, who charge at the Spanish galleon four times in four hours, with great losses and wounds on both sides. The results of this combat are summarized by the narrator: *"Después de habernos combatido dieciséis horas, y después de haber muerto a nuestro capitán y toda la más gente del navío, después de nueve asaltos que nos dieron, los turcos entraron furiosamente en el navío"* [After we had fought for sixteen hours, and after the captain and nearly all the crew of the ship had perished, at the end of nine assaults, the Turks furiously boarded the ship] (493).

The narrative now shifts from a third-person narrator to an *I* who speaks from inside the fray: "Yo *me arrojé por medio de las bárbaras espadas deseoso de morir [. . .] antes de ver a* mis *ojos lo que esperaba. Pero sucedióme al revés* mi *pensamiento, porque abrazándose conmigo tres membrudos turcos y* yo *forcejeando con ellos, de tropel vinimos a dar todos en la puerta de la cámara donde Nísida y Blanca estaban"* [*I* threw myself unarmed amidst the barbarous swords hoping to die [. . .] rather than to see with *my* own eyes what I expected. But things came to pass differently from what *I* had thought, for, as three stalwart Turks grappled with *me*, and *I* was struggling with them, we all fell confusedly up against the door of the cabin where Nísida and Blanca were] (*Galatea*, 494; emphasis mine). This *yo* continues to speak through the voice of Timbrio, who recounts how he killed one of the Turks and was in turn struck twice with two great wounds, whereupon Nísida threw herself on his wounded body, *"con lamentables voces"* [with terrible *cries*] and begged the Turks to kill her (*Galatea*, 494; emphasis mine). Throughout the violent description of this combat, Cervantes and his narrator have been talking *"a una sola voz"*—that is, unanimously. The marked repetition of the term *voces* [cries] in this passage suggests the presence of an Other voice that cries out through the wound, through trauma:

Atraído de las *voces* y lamentos [. . .] acudió a aquella estancia Arnaute [Arnaut Mamí], el general de los bajeles [. . .] e hizo llevar a Nísida y Blanca a su galera, y [. . .] mandó que también a mí me llevasen, pues no estaba aún muerto. De esta manera [. . .], me llevaron a la enemiga galera capitana, donde fui luego curado con alguna diligencia, porque Nísida había dicho al capitán que yo era hombre principal y de gran rescate, con intención que, cebados de la codicia y del dinero que de mí podrían haber, [. . .] mirasen por la salud mía.

[Drawn by the *cries* and laments (. . .) Arnaut Mamí, the general of the vessels, hurried up to the cabin (. . .) and had Nísida and Blanca carried to his galley, and (. . .) he also gave orders for them to carry me there, since I was not dead yet. In this manner (. . .), they transported me to the enemy's flagship, where I was then cured with some diligence, for Nísida had told the captain that I was a man of rank and great ransom, with the intention that, if they were tempted by the bait of greed and of the money they might get from me, (. . .) they would look after my health.]

(*Galatea*, 494; emphasis mine)

If the autobiographical reminiscences of this passage are striking, the eloquence and brutal realism of the scene recall the raw testimony offered by *El trato de Argel*, a play composed at the same time as *La Galatea*. Nevertheless, beyond the clear autobiographical reminiscences of this episode, what surfaces in the text are the "*voces y lamentos*" [cries and lamentations] that reveal a truth impossible to assimilate. This is the story of a wound that *cries out*, that addresses us in an attempt to express an indescribable reality. As Cathy Caruth has argued, trauma is not localizable in an original or violent event situated in the past, but rather in the form in which it returns—unassimilated—to haunt the survivor. What returns to haunt the victim, as Timbrio's story tells us, is "not only the reality of the violent event, but also the reality of the way this violence has not yet been fully known" (*Unclaimed Experience*, 4–6).

"*Voces comencé a dar*" [I Started to Shout]

The cries reappear in *Los baños de Argel*, in the context of a corsair attack on a village on the coast of Spain, where Constanza is abducted in the middle of the night, among many families with children. Her lover Don Fernando recounts his desperation as he watches Constanza being carried away on the enemy galliots. Shouting at the top of his voice from a rock where he has climbed to make himself heard by the corsairs, he cries out to them and offers to ransom her:

Subí, cual digo, aquella peña, adonde
las fustas vi que ya a la mar se hacían.
Voces comencé a dar, mas no responde

ninguno, aunque muy bien todos me oían.
[. . .]
Las voces reforcé; hice las señas
que el brazo y un pañuelo me ofrecía;
Eco tornaba, y de las mismas peñas
los amargos acentos repetía.

[I climbed, like I said, upon that rock, from where
I saw the corsair vessels already setting sail,
I started to shout; but no one responds
although I know that they all heard me.
(. . .)
I cried again at the top of my voice; I made all the signals
that I could muster with my arm and a handkerchief;
Eco returned, and from the same rocks,
repeated my bitter lamentations.]

(*Baños*, II.1726–30, 1736–39)

The poem emphasizes the links between Don Fernando's cries and the shocking reality of the corsair attack, which he cannot oppose. His cries appear in two temporal registers: in the past, as he recalls his former cries (*"voces comencé a dar"*) and, in the present, as he revives the indifference of the corsairs in an actual present: *"mas no responde ninguno."* As these verses show, the traumatic event is not relegated to the past but rather points to an atemporal present where all temporality seems to collapse. Don Fernando's cries, repeated by the echo rebounding from rock to rock, speak to the traumatic reality that affirms itself in its compulsive insistence: His cries hit the deaf rocks only to return muted in the echo reverberated by the cliffs. This scene illustrates the nature of the wound that cries through Don Fernando's *voces*: His cries speak of an other within the self that retains the memory of the traumatic events, a memory that returns to haunt the victim. The moving stanzas of this poem illustrate the way that trauma repeats itself, exactly and incessantly, through the acts, words, or dreams of the survivor.

Another scene in *El trato de Argel* elaborates these ideas. This is the episode in which Algerian beauty Zahara recounts the capture of the galley *San Pablo*, where Antonio de Sosa was abducted. We discussed this scene in chapter 3, showing that the attempts to evade these violent images through a flight into fantasy by the poetic voice (or by the writer behind it) are nevertheless subverted by the crisis at the core of the poem. Let us note here that these lines revive the storm that frequently resurfaces in Cervantes's fiction, followed by the attack of the Algerian corsairs:

Las levantadas hondas, el ruido
del atrevido viento detenía
los corsarios bajeles [. . .]

sin dejarles salir al mar abierto
y en otra parte [. . .]
mostrando su braveza, fatigaba
una galera de christiana gente
y de riquezas llena que, corr[ía] [. . .]
por el hinchado mar sin remo alguno.

[The high waves, the sound
of the furious wind halted
the advance of the corsair vessels (. . .)
stopping them from coming out into the open sea
and in another place (. . .)
showing its bravery, and drained of forces,
a galley full of Christians
and riches ran through
the stormy sea without any oars.]

(*Trato*, II.1245–54)

This depiction stresses a twofold vision: on the one hand, the image of the heavy galleon swept through the stormy sea by the force of the mistral, and, on the other, that of the corsair vessels, harbored in a safe haven, waiting to fall on the disabled galley full of Christians and riches. Such a representation, however, goes beyond the cyclic versions of the ominous storm in Cervantes, for his account of the storm that wrecked the *San Pablo*, as well as that of the ensuing attack of the corsairs, is rigorously and historically accurate. I have found in the Archivo General de Simancas (Spain) relevant documents related to the loss of the *San Pablo*, in May 1577, to Algerian corsairs commanded by Arnaut Mamí. The testimony of pilot Pedro Griego and other sailors who escaped from the galley by jumping overboard in the confusion of the fray confirms Zahara's/Cervantes's account.[4] The capture of the *San Pablo* is also recounted by Portuguese galley slave Domingo Sponto, who was chained to one of the benches on an Algerian galliot. In the turmoil of the assault, Sponto shook off his chains and escaped by swimming to the island of San Pedro, where he encountered the other escapees from the *San Pablo*.[5]

As it turns out, the scene described by Zahara corresponds almost word for word to the fate of the *San Pablo* as ascertained by the testimonies of these sailors. Destroyed by the mistral, the *San Pablo*, in effect, had lost its oars and most of its artillery in its wild course over the embattled sea. Pedro Griego states in his affidavit that the oars were thrown overboard in an attempt to relieve some of the weight of the ship during its mad race (AGS, Estado, leg. 1073, doc. 82–83). Zahara's story ends with the death of the Portuguese captain and of numerous Christians who fell under the enemy bullets, a vision completed by the witnesses who testify that the name of their captain, a Portuguese Knight of Malta, was Captain Botello.

We know now that Cervantes had access to firsthand information regarding this event from his friend Antonio de Sosa, which explains why Zahara's poetic account of this event coincides almost literally with the testimonies of the sailors who escaped the corsair's attack. At the same time, Cervantes's capture, a year and a half before, was strikingly similar to that of Sosa. Both ships were detoured by a mistral or strong west wind that turned into a storm, sweeping the devastated galleys across the ocean until they were overtaken by the corsairs. In his affidavit, Sponto confirmed that the commander of the corsair squadron that took the *San Pablo* was Arnaut Mamí—the same man who captured Cervantes (AGS, Guerra Antigua, 84).

In light of these historical and biographical details, let us discuss this scene from *El trato de Argel* as a way of pulling together various aspects of the creative aftermath of trauma. It is Zahara, an Algerian predecessor of the legendary Zoraida, who speaks for Cervantes in this scenario, which recalls that of his own capture in 1575. Indeed, Zahara recounts the story of the Christian captive Aurelio—an alter ego of Cervantes—who lost his freedom in this attack:

> El robo, las riquezas, los cautivos
> que los turcos hallaron en el seno
> de la triste galera, me ha contado
> un cristiano que allí perdió la dulce
> y amada libertad.

> [The story of the looting, the riches, the captives,
> that the Turks found in the bosom
> of the sad galley has been told to me
> by a Christian who lost there sweet
> and beloved liberty.]

> (*Trato*, II.1256–67)

As we can see in these verses, the depression and melancholy of the captive are projected onto the galley where he was captured, which becomes *"la triste galera"* [the sad galley], and onto the personified image of his lost freedom, now transformed into *"la dulce y amada libertad"* [sweet and beloved liberty]. In the reenactment of grief and mourning dramatized by Zahara's soliloquy, freedom is presented in terms of a lost love object, an image that stresses the interrelationship of separation, loss, and yearning for the lost object—here not only the dead people but also the lost freedom. If the historical Christian captive who recounts his dramatic experience through Zahara's eloquent verses is Dr. Antonio de Sosa, who surely recited the story of his capture to Cervantes, Zahara's verses also function as a screen memory that veils the ordeal of Cervantes's own capture, which possessed almost the same characteristics.

In *Beyond the Pleasure Principle*, Freud suggests that in traumatic neurosis, the compulsion to repeat arises from an earlier inability to experience the feeling that should have corresponded to the trauma. Repetitive dreams about the trauma—or repeated reenactments of the traumatic scene—would be "endeavoring to master the stimulus retrospectively, by developing the anxiety whose omission was the cause of the trauma neurosis" (SE, 18: 32). Even before the turning point represented by the composition of *La historia del cautivo* among Cervantes's works, the iterative restaging of the storm and the scene of his own capture permitted the writer to formulate new inner forms that included not only the traumatic event proper but also a renewal of images that propelled the creator toward the future. The scene in which Zahara describes the capture of the *San Pablo* illustrates, in effect, how the reenactment of the traumatic event leads to a duplication and liberation of images through a fidelity to the traumatic experience—in the sense of remembering what the catastrophic experience entailed—and a simultaneous search for new modes of being and creation. The significant doubling that marks the creation of new selves in Cervantes's fictions is implicitly highlighted by Zahara's words: *"el robo, las riquezas, los cautivos/que los turcos hallaron en el seno/de la triste galera,* me ha contado un cristiano que allí perdió su dulce y amada libertad*"* [emphasis mine].

As one traverses the corpus of Cervantes's works, the phantoms of Algiers reappear in countless fictions, from *El trato de Argel* (1581–1583) and *La Galatea* (1585) to *La historia del cautivo*, to *La española inglesa* and *El amante liberal*, to *Los baños de Argel* and *Persiles*. The phantasmatic recollections acquire a mythical quality in Cervantes's later literary production, emphasizing the point at which historicization reaches its limit. At the same time, the diffusion and mythicization of these images suggest a gradual liberation of the chains of captivity in Cervantes, through "working-off" mechanisms, such as those described by Daniel Lagache in his account of the resolution of defensive conflict, especially in the cure. As opposed to "working through," a sort of psychic work evolving during analysis that follows an interpretation and allows the subject to overcome resistances and to free him- or herself from the grip of repetition, the working-off mechanisms gradually allow the subject to free him- or herself from repetition and from alienating identifications through recollection by thought and word, a process that includes familiarization with the traumatic and fantasy-dominated situation, and the transition from dissociation to integration.[6]

A Story True to the Life of Cervantes

Among the *Novelas ejemplares*, *La española inglesa* represents an intense probing of the subject of captivity, where one captivity remits to another, in a fantastic outburst of invention that seems to have no end. The scenario of the capture returns to this novella in circular patterns that reiterate, through literal fugue and variations, the flashbacks of Algiers. In the first scene, English Catholic Recaredo, sent on a privateering expedition by Queen Elizabeth I, discovers three galleys with Turkish flags in the Strait of Gibraltar and proceeds to attack them. The determined assault of the English ships, camouflaged under Spanish flags, entices the Christian captives on the Turkish galleys to break off their chains and join the melee in favor of the attackers: *"Y así, con el calor que les daba a los cristianos pensar que los navíos ingleses eran españoles, hicieron por su libertad maravillas"* [And so, on fire with the idea that the English ships were Spanish, the galley slaves fought desperately for their freedom].[7]

This encounter with the Turkish-Algerian fleet announces the reappearance of the phantoms of Algiers. The Spaniards who board the English ship relate that while returning from Portuguese India, their galley, which carried a millionaire cargo of pearls, diamonds, and spices, had been caught by a terrible storm, *"y que con tormenta había arribado a aquella parte, toda destruida y sin artillería, por haberla echado a la mar la gente, enferma y casi muerta de sed y de hambre"* [and that they had been driven to that area by the storm, half-wrecked and with no heavy nor light artillery, because the crew, sick and almost dead of hunger and thirst had thrown them overboard] (*EI*, I: 254; *ES*, II: 19). Precisely at this moment, Algerian corsair Arnaut Mamí fell on the crippled Portuguese galleon, whose half-dead crew posed no resistance to the corsairs. Replaying the story of Cervantes's capture, the familiar tale also recalls details from Sosa's seizure aboard the galley *San Pablo*, whose crew, as we may remember, had thrown its artillery overboard. We should note, however, that the description of the storm and the ensuing capture by the Algerians, including the mention of Arnaut Mamí, is now limited to a few lines that open the way for other fictions. After this overture, one of the Spaniards who came on board with the rest of the freed captives declares that he had been captured in a previous attack of the Algerian corsairs, six days after leaving Cádiz, on a ship that was sailing for the Indies. He thus became a witness to the successive assault of the Portuguese galleon by the Barbary corsairs. His daughter, who happens to be Recaredo's beloved Isabela, had been captured, in turn, in the sack of Cádiz by the English in 1596. Since her capture by Recaredo's father Clotaldo, Isabela has been living in his London household. The infinite sequence of captures in this tale, as we can see, leads to a chain of adventures, each more suggestive than the other.

The memories of Algiers reappear again toward the end of *La española inglesa*, when Isabela, who has returned to Spain with her parents, learns that Recaredo has been killed, news that impels her to abandon the world and take her vows as a nun. Among the crowd of onlookers gathered in Seville to admire the beautiful novice on the day of her profession, a familiar Cervantine image appears. Advancing through the throng is *"un hombre vestido en hábito de los que vienen rescatados de cautivos, con una insignia de la Trinidad en el pecho, en señal de que ha sido rescatado por la limosna de los redentores"* [a man dressed in the smock of a ransomed captive, with a badge of the Order of Trinity on his breast, which they wear as a sign that they have been ransomed by the charity collected by the Fathers] (*EI*, I: 277; *ES*, II: 49). The former captive, recognized as Recaredo, admonishes Isabela to stop, because she cannot be a nun while he is alive. Cervantes thus makes his entrance into his own tale in the guise of freed captive Recaredo, only to vanish immediately into his own fiction. The move recalls the apparition of the name *Saavedra* in *La historia del cautivo*, but in *La española inglesa*, instead of the signature of Cervantes's name, the author presents a visual image of captivity in the man clothed in the attire of the ransomed Barbary slaves.

The story of Recaredo's capture, recounted later by Recaredo himself, clearly resembles that of Cervantes. After a pilgrimage to Rome, where he suffered an assassination attempt, Recaredo left Genova in two launches on his way to Spain. He was captured by Algerian corsairs around the Three Marías, a small port near Marseille, and was taken as a captive to Algiers. Remaining there for a year, he was finally ransomed by the Trinitarians, the same order that ransomed Cervantes in 1580. Recaredo's story not only reenacts Cervantes's return to Spain in November 1580 but also offers one of the fullest accounts of his repatriation, including the general procession made by the former captives in Valencia as a sign of devotion and gratitude for their release. Reduced to a few lines, the allusion to Cervantes's capture ushers in other autobiographical reminiscences, such as the visual images of the captive's return to Spain, the involvement of the Trinitarian order in his ransom, and the imminent danger of being killed in Algiers and of being sent to Constantinople as a slave, which would have been fatal for Cervantes, as his spokesman Recaredo claims: *"y de presentarme al Gran Señor redundara en no tener libertad"* [and if I had been sent to the Sultan, the result would have been that I would have never been freed] (*EI*, I: 282; *ES*, II: 55).

Traumatic truth, then, is increasingly diffused and mixed with fiction in this novella, which rehearses the story of Cervantes's capture and other Algerian reminiscences, even while opening the doors to new inventions. In this way, *La española inglesa* seems to confirm the truth of its Cervantine closing remarks: *"Esta novela nos podrá enseñar [. . .] de cómo sabe el cielo sacar de las mayores adversidades nuestras, nuestros mayores provechos"* [This novel can teach us (. . .) how heaven can draw out of our greatest adversities the greatest blessings for us] (*EI*, I: 283; *ES*, II: 56). As the late Ruth El Saffar remarked, this reflection seems to have a meaning for Recaredo, Isabela, and Cervantes, since at the end the characters inherit the author's role and narrate a story true to the life of Cervantes himself.[8] This is the most abstract formulation of the idea, developed in *El casamiento engañoso* and *El coloquio de los perros*, that writing can transform one's disgraces into good fortune. Certainly, when Cervantes observes that *"las mayores adversidades nuestras"* [our greatest adversities] are linked to *"nuestros mayores provechos"* [our greatest blessings], the latter include his creations.

The episodes explored in this novella signal the point of *décolage* or takeoff of creation in Cervantes, a nodule that, as we have seen, often originates in the nucleus of reminiscences related to his capture and enslavement in Barbary. In like manner, these passages speak to the three forms of psychic work described by Anzieu in his book *Le corps de l'oeuvre*: dreamwork, the work of mourning, and the work of creation (19). Like dreamwork, the fantasies that the writer produces with his eyes open, later crystallized into a creation, transform a difficult reality into a horizon of marvelous inventions, an alternative presented by life to the lethal components of a crisis. Furthermore, through the figure of the captive who returns from Barbary, alluding to his ordeals and his reasonable fears of never returning to his country, Cervantes's fiction exposes the operations of the work of mourning. The representation of lack, loss, exile, and pain, and the identification with the loved and lost object (his former self)—revived in the figure of Recaredo—speak to the mourning effected in the very weaving of creation. Indeed, the work of mourning not only entails the acceptance of a cruel reality, as demonstrated by Cervantes's text, but also ushers in the third form of psychic work, the work of creation, through the activation of dormant sectors of the libido, an activation revealed by the extraordinary fantasies staged by Cervantes's fictions.

"Una lición de las cosas de Argel" [A Lesson on Things about Algiers]

As this cursory review shows, the image of his capture returns obsessively to Cervantes's texts, gradually evolving into shorter, more faded testimonies, which are complexly intertwined with his fiction. The last reference to his capture occurs in Cervantes's last novel, *Persiles*, a novel the writer signed on his deathbed. As Avalle-Arce has noted, the literary production of Cervantes opens and closes with the memory of his most painful experience (*"La captura,"* 269). Following the pattern displayed by *La historia del cautivo* and *La española inglesa*, among other Cervantine fictions, the episode of the false captives in *Persiles* emphasizes the reenactment of, and simultaneous evasion from, the ordeal of captivity. In this novel, the lies that turn out to be intimate truths point to the evasive insistence of trauma, to its links with forgetting. It is through this semivoluntary oblivion that trauma seems to be experienced in this narrative.

A phantasmagoric scene in *Persiles,* in effect, speaks to the problematic question of remembering and forgetting in trauma. Concomitantly, it is not fortuitous that questions of memory and forgetting should arise in *Persiles,* a narrative that, Aurora Egido has reminded us, represents a constant variation on the exercise of memory and its function in the art of writing novels.[9] This episode that interests us in *Persiles* is the tale of the false captives who appear among a crowd of pilgrims, "*[en] un lugar, no muy pequeño ni muy grande, de cuyo nombre no me acuerdo*" [in a town, neither very small nor very large, whose name I don't remember], as the third-person narrator claims (*Persiles,* 343/247). The Cervantine formula par excellence—"*en un lugar de La Mancha de cuyo nombre no quiero acordarme*" [in a village of La Mancha, whose name I don't want to remember]—should alert us to the import of this text. The meaningful phrase connects the episode of *Persiles* not only with the opening words of *Don Quijote* but also with other pivotal Cervantine fictions, such as *La historia del cautivo,* where this expression is reiterated.[10] More important, the question of remembering and not remembering stressed by this passage of *Persiles*—"*un lugar [. . .] de cuyo nombre no me acuerdo*"—is connected with the problem of looking and not looking back that marks the appearance of the name *Saavedra* in the Captive's tale. The implicit testimonial "I don't remember," or "I don't want to remember," which subtends the episode of the counterfeit captives in *Persiles,* clearly points to the associations between trauma and forgetting. As explained by Caruth, "it is not just that the experience of trauma is repeated after its forgetting, but that it is only through its inherent forgetting that it is first experienced" (*Unclaimed Experience,* 17).

The following passage from *Persiles* proclaims the return of the phantoms of Algiers, even while alluding to the problematic question of traumatic memory. This episode opens with an introductory excursus full of resonances, an exordium related by an unnamed first-person narrator who refers to the relation between truth and lies, history and fiction:

> Las peregrinaciones largas siempre traen consigo diversos acontecimientos [. . .]. Bien nos lo muestra esta historia, cuyos acontecimientos nos cortan el hilo, poniéndonos en duda donde será bien anudarle; porque no todas las cosas que suceden son buenas para contarlas [. . .]; acciones hay que, por grandes, deben de callarse, y otras que, por bajas, no deben decirse [. . .]; puesto que es excelencia de la historia, que cualquier cosa que en ella se escribía puede pasar al sabor de la verdad que trae consigo; lo que no tiene

la fábula, a quien conviene guisar sus acciones con tanta puntualidad y gusto, y con tanta verisimilitud, que a despecho y a pesar de la mentira, que hace disonancia con el entendimiento, forme una verdadera armonía.

(*Persiles*, III, 10, 343)

[Long pilgrimages always bring with them a variety of events (. . .). This history is a good example, for the thread is cut off by certain events, leaving us unsure as to where it will be best to tie it back together again. Not everything that happens makes good telling (. . .); there are acts that precisely because of their great consequence ought to be passed over in silence, and others, so base (or insignificant) they should not be mentioned (. . .). The outstanding thing about history is that anything written in it is made palatable by the taste of truth it brings with it. Fiction does not have that advantage, and its actions must be prepared with such accurate details and good taste, and with such an appearance of fact, so that notwithstanding and despite its untruth, which unavoidably generates some dissonance in the mind, its structure may be truly harmonious.]

(*Persiles* 246; translation slightly modified)[11]

The curious passage, which heralds the story of the false captives, appears to justify and clarify the author's inclusion of the next episode, even while accentuating a number of significant concerns on his part. I will underline here, in order of appearance, the motif of the "cut thread" and of its possible attachment at some later time, a theme followed by the question of the events that ought to be silenced because of their unspeakable consequences or their gross nature. In addition, the parenthetical commentary of the narrator touches on the question of historical truth, a question eloquently underscored by the complex oscillations between truth and fiction that mark the ensuing story of counterfeit captivity. Finally, the narrator refers to the problem of fiction, which, despite its untruth, must have an appearance of fact—that is, a verisimilar plot—in which the author must harmoniously mingle the historical and the fictional to capture the belief of his audience. Some of these questions, as it turns out, are related to the trauma of captivity.

The image of the "cut thread" evokes other passages associated with death in Cervantes, such as the verses that mourn the death of Don Juan de Austria in *El trato de Argel*, quoted in chapter 4: "*quiso el hado* cortar el hilo *de su dulce vida*" [destiny wished *to cut the thread* of his sweet life] (III. 1517–19; emphasis mine). In like manner, the relevant story recounted in *Persiles*—"*historia cuyos acontecimientos* nos cortan el hilo" [a history, the events of which *cut off our thread*]—is implicitly related to the break that severs the line of vitalizing experience, a feeling connected with the death imprint that marks traumatic experience. These fictions allude to the "break in the lifeline" caused by trauma, the "broken connection," as Robert Jay Lifton called his study on death and the continuity of life. Although

Cervantes often refers to the "cut" or the "broken thread of life," it is in *Persiles*, a novel that reveals the perception of impending death in Cervantes, where this metaphor takes a poignant turn.

The allusion to the "cut thread" (of life? of the narrative?) introduces the episode of the two former captives, who wear the garments used by those who have recently returned from Barbary. Displaying a large canvas depicting their adventures, the former captives recite the tale of their suffering in Algiers, expecting to collect a fee from their sympathetic audience. As Periandro and Auristela arrive with their group of pilgrims to the mythical town whose name has been silenced by the narrator, the two strangers in their early twenties, dressed as rescued captives, are in the process of explaining a large painting of Algiers to the crowd in the town's square. Two large chains next to them are a testimony to their past misfortune. One of the strangers, who has a clear voice and a skilled tongue, from time to time cracks a whip held in his hand, a noise that resounds through the air, piercing everyone's ears and recalling the ignominies suffered by the galley slaves. The former captive begins his speech by saying: *"Ésta, señores, que veis aquí pintada es la ciudad de Argel, gomia y tarasca de todas las riberas del mar Mediterráneo, puerto universal de cosarios, y amparo y refugio de ladrones, que desde este pequeñuelo puerto que aquí va pintado, salen con sus bajeles a inquietar el mundo"* [Señores, you see painted here the city of Algiers, the most insatiable glutton on all the shores of the Mediterranean, a universal haven for pirates and a shelter and refuge for thieves who, from this little harbor here, set out in their ships to trouble the world] (*Persiles*, 344/247).

This description of Algiers unfolds into minute details, as the freed captive–narrator follows the particulars of the painting, beginning with the picture of a corsair galliot with twenty-two benches, then with the image of a Turk who is standing between the two lines of oarsmen, holding in his hand the arm of a Christian he has just cut off. Likewise, the gifted storyteller presents four Christian galleons that are chasing and closing in on the Turkish vessel; he later zeroes on a captive stained by the blood of the amputated arm with which he has been beaten; and finally, points to the galley's captain by the historical name of Dragut, *"corsario tan famoso como cruel"* [a pirate as famous as he was cruel] (*Persiles*, 345/247). The narrator now focuses on the first captive on the first bench, whose face is stained by the blood of the amputated arm, and claims that this is a picture of himself, who was the stroke of that galley, while the man next to him on the bench is his companion here, who was not so beaten. Recounting the shouts of the Turk to the galley slaves, the storyteller peppers his performance with appropriate Turkish insults: *"rospeni"* [son of a bitch], *"manahora"* [watch out, you . . .], and *"denimaniyoc"* [atheist infidel]!

One of the town's mayors, an old man who had been a captive for many years in Algiers, recognizes the corsair vessel, for he had rowed in it as a galley slave. He decides to test the storytellers to see whether they are "false captives" and thus asks them whose galleys were those chasing the corsair's ship. The freed captive answers: *"las galeras eran de Don Sancho de Leiva; la libertad no la conseguimos porque no nos alcanzaron"* [the galleys belonged to Don Sancho de Leiva. We didn't gain our liberty because they did not overtake us] (*Persiles* 345/248). The mayor's questions become more and more incisive, now turning to the gates and to the freshwater fountains of Algiers, which the impostor cannot identify, claiming that these ordeals have erased his memory: *"los trabajos que en él [Argel] he pasado me han quitado la memoria de mí mismo"* [the trials I have undergone there (in Algiers) have even taken my memory away] (346/248). Denouncing *"[las] mentiras y embelecos"* [lies and inventions] of these false captives, the mayor threatens to parade them through the streets and have them flogged by the town crier, and, additionally, send them to the galleys. Then the mayor exclaims: *"Yo he estado en Argel cinco años esclavo y sé que no me dais señas dél en ninguna de las cosas de cuantas habéis dicho"* [I was a slave in Algiers for five years and know full well that you haven't described it to me accurately in any of the things you've said] (*Persiles* 347/249). Unmasked by the old man, the impostors confess they are not captives at all, but students from Salamanca who want to see the world.[12]

The enormous painting of Algiers with its infinite details, as well as the false captives' depiction of the North African city—its marina, its galliots, and its tortures—can be obviously read as a magnificent and dizzying *mise en abyme* for the corpus of Cervantes's works, a corpus that emanates from the recollections of his Algerian experiences. As it turns out, in spite of its constant oscillation between truth and fiction, this passage alludes to specific historical events related to the capture of Cervantes. In this dazzling whirlwind of lies and truths that seem to revolve around a bottomless vortex, the author's capture appears in the persona of Don Sancho de Leiva, the historical commander of the flotilla to which the galley *Sol* was attached when it set sail for Spain in September 1575. It also emerges in the description of the four Spanish galleons that comprised the flotilla, and in the exact number of galleons (three) that did chase the corsairs without being able to overtake them, after Cervantes and his companions were seized by the Algerians. And it finally surfaces in the visceral cry of the old mayor: *"Yo he estado en Argel cinco años esclavo"* [I was a captive in Algiers for five years]. In a surreptitious way, then, the familiar theme of Cervantes's capture by Barbary corsairs has returned to the text. The emphasis, however, has been displaced to the slippage between remembering and not remembering, between historical truth and fiction, and between traumatic experience and creation.

The story now takes a curious turn, for the spurious captives are ulti-

mately not punished, owing to various farcical mishaps, such as the fact
that the town crier could not find any donkeys in town on which to parade the impostors as they are flogged.[13] In addition, the spirited defense
of their ploy and their art by one of the false captives manages to placate
both city mayors. As a result, the compassionate first mayor, who had testified to his long captivity in Algiers, ends by inviting the young men to
his house, *"donde les quiero dar una lición de las cosas de Argel tal que de
aquí en adelante nadie les coja en mal latín, en cuanto a su fingida historia"*
[where I'll give him a lesson on things about Algiers, so that from now on
no one will catch them making mistakes in their Latin, I mean, in their
made-up story] (*Persiles* 350/251). The significant Cervantine phrases ut-
tered by the mayor of this mythical city *"de cuyo nombre no me acuerdo,"*
as well as his true knowledge about Algiers, identify this old man with Cervantes, who reappears in his own text as a fountain of information on the
North African city and as a skillful narrator willing to pass on to others his
literary skills.

At the same time, let us note the complexities of this text that simultaneously advances and retreats from the images of Algiers in an intricate
game of hide-and-seek enacted around the vortex of trauma. This episode
opens up a kind of writing that traces the negatives and residues of the
traumatic experience, a writing that begins with "I don't remember" and
later playfully stresses the problem of forgetting in the context of the ordeal of human bondage. In an earlier passage of *Persiles*, also marked by
the appearance of a terrible storm, Cervantes confirms that *"las desdichas y
afliciones turban las memorias de quien las padece"* [misfortunes and afflictions confuse the memory of those who suffer from them] (77/37). The
fact that the false captives, who paradoxically relate a profoundly true story,
appeared in a town whose name cannot be remembered by the narrator—
"de cuyo nombre no me acuerdo"—sheds light on this passage, constructed
from phantasmatic shards and recollections. From the perspective of trauma,
moreover, this passage marks the difficulty of catching "the real thing"—
the nucleus of trauma itself—which in this episode keeps slipping away amid
the tangled web of truths, lies, and fiction woven by Cervantes. As we may
recall, the story of the false captives was introduced by the mention of the
"cut thread" of life, which the narrator was attempting to reattach in the
allusive excursus that announces this travel adventure, with its accidents
and diversity of events: *"bien nos lo muestra esta historia, cuyos acontecimientos nos cortan su hilo, poniéndonos en duda dónde será bien anudarle."*
Indeed, beyond the extraordinary maze of masks, historical truths, and fictions deployed by this episode, the story of the "false captives" refers to
the break that severs the line of vitalizing experience, a feeling connected
with the death imprint and an inner perception of death undergone in
trauma.

If the references to Cervantes's captivity reemerge now in increasingly stealthy manner, reworked and camouflaged through Cervantes's literary production, they are also connected with the question of lies and truths in fiction, an abiding preoccupation in Cervantes. It is not fortuitous, then, that after the false-captives episode, the old mayor of the mythical city would greet Periandro and his group with the following words: *"Vosotros, señores peregrinos, ¿traéis algún lienzo que enseñarnos? ¿Traéis otra historia que hacernos creer por verdadera, aunque la haya compuesto la misma mentira?"* [Do you too, my good pilgrims, have some canvas with you to show us? Did you also bring with you some story you'll want us to believe is true, even though it may have been made up by Falsehood itself?] (*Persiles*, 350/ 251). Indeed, the vertiginous amalgamation of facts and fiction described in this chapter suggests that Cervantes used the false-captives adventure to illustrate the art of properly constructing a *fábula*—a verisimilar plot— as exemplified by his dictum, cited earlier, regarding his poetics of fiction: "[The] actions [of fiction] must be prepared with such accurate details and good taste, and with such an appearance of fact, so that notwithstanding and despite its untruth, which unavoidably generates some dissonance in the mind, its structure may be truly harmonious" (*Persiles*, 343/246). The tale of the false captives, then, is a skillful Cervantine demonstration of the mingling of the historical and the invented according to the major principles underlined by *Persiles*: the pleasure of variety, the travel narrative as a medium of diversity, the complex mixture of history and fiction, and the need for verisimilitude in fiction.[14]

In addition, beyond the fundamental concepts concerning the verisimilar —that is, beyond its masterly "untruths"—the episode of the pseudocaptives demonstrates the persistence of image memories that come to index the belated effects of the past on Cervantes's narratives. It also confirms the writer's familiarization and convergence with the traumatic events, which allows him to play with and to reinscribe the motif of captivity in his fiction by means of his art. The captivity motif, it bears remembering, is bound up with the dialectic of life and death—that is, with "dying" and "being reborn" through creation. This interpretation may shed light on the allusion to the cut thread of life—of narrative—that has to be retied by the writer, the creator.

"El hilo roto" [The Broken Thread]

The metaphor of the "cut thread" in Cervantes acquires a special connotation in the light of the postmodern discussion on trauma and its aftereffects on its victims. Indeed, when Donald W. Winnicott fittingly referred to trauma as a "break in the lifeline" or as a "snapping in the thread of continuity of life," he came close to voicing not only the spirit of our times but also our reason for using the traumatic syndrome to illustrate all psychiatric disorder.[15] In the light of the traumatic events of September 11, 2001, in New York City and Washington, DC, I must say that never has an expression been so close to expressing the tragic mark of the twentieth and twenty-first centuries as this phrase by Winnicott: "a break in the lifeline." What is broken—shattered in this break—is the experience of life, the construction of vitality, as Lifton proposed (*Broken Connection*, 179). In one way or another, Lifton reminds us, this break takes place in all psychiatric disturbance. The definition of the traumatic experience as one in which "the individual is threatened with his death or the destruction of a part of his body," then, has reverberations for every expression of mental disturbance. The place of death and death anxiety are essential to the traumatic syndrome, where death is so close, as we have seen. Earlier in this study, we defined the survivor as one who has encountered death in some bodily or psychic fashion and has remained alive. He or she has experienced that cut or break in his or her lifeline of which Cervantes clearly speaks in his work, a break that can leave one permanently engaged in either repair or the acquisition of new twine, as Cervantes implicitly suggests in the farewell to his readers that inaugurates *Persiles*.

The episode of the false captives in *Persiles* both retells the story that the author had been recounting for about thirty years, since he was ransomed in 1580, and closes Cervantes's literary testimonies on his Algerian captivity. Probably soon after he finished this chapter, Cervantes would compose the prologue to his beloved *Persiles*.[16] Concomitantly, at the end of his life, *"puesto ya el pie en el estribo"* [with his foot on the stirrup], as he wrote the Count of Lemos in his dedication of *Persiles*, signed on April 16, 1616, Cervantes attempted again to tie the thread cut by history. He would refer, once more, to the metaphor of the cut thread in his prologue-farewell to *Persiles*, where he says good-bye to his *"lector amantísimo"* [dearest reader]: *"Tiempo vendrá, quizá, donde,* anudando este roto hilo, *diga lo que aquí me falta y lo que se convenía"* [A time may come, perhaps, when I *shall tie up this broken thread* and say what I failed to here and what would have been fitting (emphasis mine)]. The metaphor of the "cut thread," in effect, also alludes to the thread of creation, cut or broken by traumatic events. In the prologue to *Persiles*, the author enacts his last literary tour de force as a symbolic farewell to his readers, even while returning one more time to the motif of the cut thread, now in reference to his impending death and his creations.

As we know, Cervantes's prologues perform a true subversion of the prologue as canonical form.[17] If the prologue to *Don Quijote*—an anti-prologue—emerges from the narrator's reticence about the requisites of the genre, the prologue to *Persiles* evolves as a narrative of a retrospective personal event, one that again performs a radical break with canonical precepts. In this prologue, Cervantes represents his close encounter between Esquivias and Madrid with a drab student *"todo vestido de pardo, antiparras, zapato redondo y espada con contera, valona bruñida, trenzas iguales"* [dressed all in rustic brown with leggings, round-toed shoes, a sword in a chapped scabbard, and a starched lace collar with its matching ties] (*Persiles*, 47/15). As Canavaggio has suggested, the figure of this student invokes the fortunes and adversities—the military career, the wounds, the captivity—that constitute Cervantes's past (*"Cervantes en primera persona,"* 70). The self-irony with which Cervantes reviews his past in this episode extends to his humorous acceptance of his belated success as a writer, obliquely revealed by the words of the student-soldier who salutes him: *"¡Éste es el manco sano, el famoso todo, el escritor alegre y, finalmente, el regocijo de las Musas!"* [This is the wholesome cripple, the completely famous and gay writer, and, finally, the delight of the muses!]. His effusive words, however, are soberly rebuked by the narrator, who answers: *"Yo señor, soy Cervantes, pero no el regocijo de las Musas, ni ninguna de las demás baratijas que ha dicho"* [I, sir, am Cervantes, but not the delight of the muses, nor any of the other foolish things that you mentioned] (*Persiles*, 48/15). In this encounter with a younger self that recalls Borges's story *"El otro"* in *El libro de arena*, Cervantes institutes his literary *yo* [I] as the thread that weaves through his different texts. To paraphrase Canavaggio, this authorial *I* confirms the remarkable coherence of the personal myth imposed by Cervantes, through which the author reveals and conceals himself at the same time (*"Cervantes en primera persona,"* 71).

Cervantes's parting embrace of the student who represents his past life introduces his celebrated farewell to his readers, a farewell that comes out of the metaphor of the cut thread: *"Tiempo vendrá, quizá, donde, anudando este roto hilo, diga lo que aquí me falta y lo que se convenía. ¡Adiós gracias; adiós donaires; adiós regocijados amigos; que yo me voy muriendo, y deseando veros presto contentos en la otra vida!"* [A time may come, perhaps, when I shall tie up this broken thread and say what I failed to here and what would have been fitting. Goodbye, humor; goodbye, wit; goodbye, merry friends; for I am dying and hope to see you soon, happy in the life to come!]. Bidding farewell, too, to the wit, humor, and invention that marked his creations—as confirmed by the author himself and by the student's sly greeting—the final words of this prologue signal the connections between the metaphor of the cut thread (or threads) and his literary creation, emphasized by the writer's moving *adiós* to his readers (*Persiles*, 49/16).

That this "broken thread" is associated with Cervantes's literary production is confirmed by the juncture of traumatic reenactments and fantastic inventions studied in this book, and, specifically, by the splendid adventure of the false captives, discussed above. In addition, the associations between the broken thread of the narrative and the corpus of Cervantes's works are underlined by the phrase that describes the writer's closing *adiós* to the student who parts from him at the Toledo bridge, a bridge that evokes the symbolic break between life and death: *"Dejóme tan mal dispuesto como él iba caballero en su burra, a quien había dado gran ocasión a mi pluma para escribir donaires [. . .]. Tiempo vendrá, quizá, donde, anudando este roto hilo, diga lo que aquí me falta y lo que se convenía"* [He left me just as ill at ease as he was trying to be a gentlemen on that ass. He had afforded my pen the opportunity to be witty (. . .). A time may come, perhaps, when I shall tie up this broken thread and say what I failed to here and what would have been fitting] (*Persiles*, 49/15). In this last farewell to his past, Cervantes corroborates that the metaphor of the broken thread— the thread broken by traumatic events—is also firmly tied to his writing.

As he faced death, then, Cervantes attempted to connect the broken thread of his life, of his narrative, which is inextricably intertwined with his literary invention. Cervantes's fictions, in effect, obsessively return to this metaphor to allude to the vicissitudes of narration: Among other Cervantine characters, Cardenio alludes in *Don Quijote* to *"el roto hilo de mi desdichada historia"* [the broken thread of my miserable story] (*DQ* I, 27); Cide Hamete speaks in the same novel of *"[el] rastrillado, torcido y aspado hilo [de la historia]"* [the twisted, spun, and crisscrossing thread of history] (*DQ* I, 28); and Berganza refers in *El coloquio de los perros* to *"el roto hilo de mi cuento"* [the broken thread of my tale] (*Novelas ejemplares*, II: 307). Woven with the events "que nos cortan el hilo," these threads are part of the extraordinary tapestry created by Cervantes over his lifetime with the shards and reminiscences of his Algerian captivity. This broken thread, however, will never be connected: instead, it will join *"el hilo de su dulce vida"* [the thread of his sweet life] (*Trato* III. 1517–18), which will be soon cut by "the inexorable Fates," as Margarita asserts in *El gallardo español* (II. 2088–89).[18] These stories can only be told in a literary language, a language that claims and, at the same time, defies our understanding.

Chronology

1453	Conquest of Constantinople by the Ottoman Turks.
1469	Marriage of Ferdinand of Aragon and Isabella of Castile.
1474	Castile under the control of Isabella. Accession of Ferdinand to the crown of Aragon. Unification of the kingdoms of Castile and Aragon.
1491	Siege of Granada by the forces of the Catholic monarchs, Ferdinand and Isabella.
1492	Conquest of the Nasrid Kingdom of Granada by the Catholic monarchs. On January 2, the deposed ruler Boabdil presents to Ferdinand the keys of the Alhambra, and the crucifix and the royal standard are raised above the highest tower.
1493	Boabdil and some six thousand Muslims from Granada leave Spain for Africa.
1494	Papal blessing to an African crusade against Islam given by Pope Alexander VI. Pope authorizes the tax known as the *cruzada* to pay for it.
1499	Policy of forced conversion and mass baptism of the Muslim population of Granada initiated by Cardinal Cisneros.
1499–1501	First revolt of the Alpujarras led by the Muslim population of Granada.
1500–1501	Rebellion of the Alpujarras suppressed.
1501–1502	Choice between emigration or conversion given to Muslim population as a whole, first in Granada and shortly afterwards in Castile.
1504	Death of Isabella of Castile. On her deathbed, she requests her husband to devote himself "unremittingly to the conquest of Africa and to the war against Islam."
1505	Conquest of Mers-el-Kebir by Spanish forces led by Cardinal Cisneros.
1509	Crusade and conquest of Orán by Cardinal Cisneros and Pedro Navarro.
1510	Capture of Bougie and Tripoli by the Spaniards.
1516	Death of Ferdinand of Aragon. Arūj Barbarossa conquers Algiers and kills its ruler Selim ben Tumi.
1518	Death of Arūj Barbarossa at the siege of Tlemcen by the Spaniards.
1519	Charles I of Spain, the grandson of the Catholic monarchs Ferdinand and Isabella, is elected Emperor of the Holy Roman Empire.
1521	Capture of Belgrade by Süleymān the Magnificent.

1526	Süleymān invades Hungary and destroys the Hungarian army.
1529	Siege of Vienna by Süleymān.
	Khair ad-Dīn Barbarossa captures the Peñón de Argel, the key to Algiers, and founds the Algerian state under Ottoman protection.
1530	Knights of St. John of Jerusalem established in Malta and Tripoli by Charles V.
1534	Khair ad-Dīn Barbarossa becomes *kapudan pasha* of the Turkish armada. Conquest of Tunis by the Ottoman armada led by Khair ad-Dīn Barbarossa.
1534–1541	Khair ad-Dīn Barbarossa and his armada devastate the Italian coasts, taking many prisoners.
1541	Third attack against Algiers launched by Charles V. The imperial fleet is completely destroyed by a tempest. The surviving crews are massacred by the Berber tribes of Algiers.
1547	Miguel de Cervantes born in Alcalá de Henares, probably on September 29, the fourth child of Leonor de Cortinas and the surgeon Rodrigo de Cervantes.
1551	Capture of Tripoli from the Knights of Malta by the Ottoman armada.
1556	Abdication of Charles V. Accession of Philip II to the Spanish throne.
1557	The Moriscos are forbidden from writing or speaking in Arabic, wearing their traditional costume, using their surnames, public bathing, celebrating matrimonial rites, or listening to traditional music.
1558	Death of Charles V.
	Death of the Count of Alcaudete, governor of Orán, in the defeat of Mostaganem by Barbary armies. Thousands of Spanish soldiers are captured by the Algerians.
	Miguel de Cervantes studies under Juan López de Hoyos in Madrid.
1568–1570	Second revolt of the Alpujarras in Granada. The Morisco leaders seek the help of the Ottoman and of the Turkish-Algerian rulers.
1569	Three poems composed by Miguel de Cervantes are published in a collection edited by Juan López de Hoyos mourning the death of Isabel de Valois.
	Miguel de Cervantes is accused of having wounded a certain Antonio de Sigura. He arrives in Rome in September and enters the service of Julius Acquaviva, who will be made Cardinal in 1570.
1569–1570	Alūj Ali Pasha, *beylerbey* of Algiers, sends soldiers and arms to the rebels of Granada.
1570	Don Juan de Austria and his armies crush the Morisco rebellion in the Alpujarras. The Moriscos are expelled from Granada and disseminated throughout Spain.
	Conquest of Cyprus by the Turks.
1571	Holy League, constituted by Venice, Spain, and the Holy See, under the command of Don Juan de Austria. Soldier Miguel de Cervantes embarks on the galley *Marquesa* that belongs to the Christian armada led by Don Juan de Austria.
	Battle of Lepanto takes place on October 7, in the gulf of Lepanto

(Greece). The Christian armies obtain victory over the Ottoman forces, led by Ali Pasha.

Cervantes is wounded at Lepanto and convalesces at Messina.

1572   Cervantes ascends to *soldado aventajado*. Takes part in the Mediterranean campaigns against the Turks led by Don Juan de Austria.

1573   Cervantes takes part in Don Juan de Austria's expeditions against the Turks in North Africa. Don Juan captures Tunis. Cervantes among the Imperial troops.

1574   Fall of La Goleta and Tunis to the Turkish-Algerian forces led by Alūj Ali Pasha.

1575   On their return to Spain, soldier Miguel de Cervantes and his brother Rodrigo are captured by Barbary corsairs near the coast of Catalonia. The brothers begin their captivity in Algiers.

1576   Cervantes's first escape attempt by land. Deserted by the Moorish guide who was leading them to Orán, the fugitives are forced to return to the Algerian *baño*. Cervantes is beaten and put in chains.

1577   Cervantes writes the laudatory poems for Bartholomeo Ruffino de Chiambery's history of the fall of La Goleta and Tunis, composed in the *baños*.

The galley *San Pablo* of the Order of Malta attacked by Algerian corsairs on April 1. Dr. Antonio de Sosa and various Knights of St. John captured aboard.

Hasan Pasha becomes *beylerbey* of Algiers.

Rodrigo, Miguel's brother, is ransomed by the Mercederian order in August.

Miguel's second escape attempt, known as the episode of the cave. Miguel is captured, taken before Hasan Pasha, and put in chains in the *baño*.

1578   Cervantes's third escape attempt: He smuggles a letter out of the *baño*, directed to the governor of Orán, Don Martín de Córdoba. The Moor who takes the letter to Orán is caught and impaled, and Hasan Pasha orders Cervantes "to be given two thousand blows." Cervantes is probably saved though the intervention of the influential Hājjī Murād.

1579   Cervantes's fourth escape attempt, involving sixty fugitives and an armed vessel bought through a Valencian merchant. The plotters are denounced by Dr. Juan Blanco de Paz. Cervantes is imprisoned in Hasan Pasha's prison for Moors.

On November 6, Cervantes sends a letter and some poems composed in prison to fellow captive Antonio Veneziano, who is confined in the *baño*.

1580   Cervantes ransomed by the Trinitarian order on September 19. Notarized affidavit known as *Información de Argel* presented between October 10 and 22 in Algiers. Dr. Antonio de Sosa testifies that Cervantes often wrote poetry during his confinement and showed him his works. Cervantes returns to Spain via Valencia. Philip II becomes king of Portugal.

1581   Cervantes at Philip II's court in Lisbon. Secret mission to Orán. Request for exchange of corsair Arnaut, imprisoned in Castilnovo

(Naples), for Dr. Antonio de Sosa, a captive in Algiers, denied by Viceroy of Naples.

Dr. Antonio de Sosa is finally liberated in October.

1582   Cervantes in Madrid. First attempt to find a post in the Indies. Writes *El trato de Argel* (?), even while composing *La Galatea*. Dr. Antonio de Sosa in Madrid.

1583   *Numancia* (?).

1584   Love affair with Ana Franca de Rojas. Birth of their daughter Isabel de Saavedra.

On December 12, Cervantes marries Catalina de Salazar in Esquivias.

1585   First part of *La Galatea* appears. Miguel's father Rodrigo dies.

1586   Cervantes starts using surname Saavedra in legal documents.

1587   Departure for Seville. Works as the new commissary officer for the supply of Philip II's Armada.

1588   Defeat of the Spanish Armada.

1590   Cervantes requests for the second time a post in the Indies, which is again denied. Writes *Historia del cautivo* [*The Captive's Tale*], later included in *Don Quijote*.

1592   Cervantes jailed at Castro del Río for a short period of time.

1594   End of Cervantes's Andalusian commissions. Begins work as a tax collector in the kingdom of Granada.

1596   Sack of Cadiz by Howard and Essex.

1597   Cervantes jailed in Seville for having deposited state moneys with a banker who fled after going bankrupt.

1598   Death of Ana Franca, mother of Cervantes's daughter Isabel de Saavedra.

Death of Phillip II. Accession of Phillip III. Government of the duke of Lerma.

1600   Miguel's brother Rodrigo dies in the Battle of the Dunes in Flanders. Miguel initiates a period of fertile literary creation in Toledo and Madrid.

1601   Court moves to Valladolid.

1602   Cervantes at Esquivias. Writes *Don Quijote*.

1604   Cervantes at Valladolid. Finishes *Don Quijote*.

1605   First part of *Don Quijote* appears. The book is an instant success. A new edition appears in the next year, as well as four pirate editions.

1606   Isabel de Saavedra marries Diego Sanz.

Court returns to Madrid, and Cervantes follows with his family.

1608   Diego Sanz dies. Isabel de Cervantes Saavedra marries Luis de Molina.

1609   Expulsion of the Moriscos begins.

1612   Miguel attends literary salons in Madrid.

Diego de Haedo edits and publishes Dr. Antonio de Sosa's *Topographia, e historia general de Argel* in Valladolid.

1613   *Novelas ejemplares*.

Return to the captivity motif in *El amante liberal* and *La española inglesa*.

1614   *Viaje del Parnaso*.

Second part of *El ingenioso hidalgo Don Quijote de La Mancha*, composed by Fernández de Avellaneda, appears in Tarragona.

1615   *Ocho comedias y ocho entremeses.*

Return to the captivity motif in the plays *Los baños de Argel, El gallardo español,* and *La gran sultana.*

Second part of *Don Quijote* appears in Madrid, printed by Juan de la Cuesta.

1616   Dedication of *Persiles* to Count of Lemos, signed on April 16.

Final return to the motif of captivity in *Persiles.*

Cervantes dies in Madrid on April 22.

1617   Posthumous publication of *Persiles.*

Notes

Abbreviations:

AGS   Archivo General de Simancas

BAE   *Biblioteca de autores españoles*

CODOIN   *Colección de documentos inéditos para la historia de España*, 112 vols (Madrid: 1842-90).

SE   *The Standard Edition of the Complete Psychological Works of Sigmund Freud*. Ed. James Strachey. 24 vols. (London: The Hogarth Press, 1974).

EI-2   *Encyclopedia of Islam*, 2nd edition (1960-)

SIHM   Sources inédites de l'histoire du Maroc

Introduction

1. Antonio de Sosa's great work, *Topographia, e historia general de Argel*, was edited and published thirty years later by Fray Diego de Haedo, a nephew of the bishop by the same name, to whom Sosa had given his manuscript after being released from slavery in 1581. See chapter 2 for information on Sosa and his friendship with Cervantes.

2. Emanuel d'Aranda, *Relation de la captivité & liberté du sieur d'Aranda, jadis esclave à Alger* [. . .] (Bruxelles: Chez Jean Mommart, 1662), recently reedited as *Les Captifs d'Alger*, ed. Latifa Z'Rari (Paris: Editions Jean Paul Rocher, 1997), 23. This popular work had six new editions, as well as various English and Flemish translations in the seventeenth and eighteenth centuries.

3. Risa Rodi, "An Interview with Primo Levi," *Partisan Review* 3 (1987): 355–66; the citation is from 366.

4. Álvaro Mutis, *Diario de Lecumberri* (México: Alfaguara, 1997), 10–11.

5. Geoffrey Hartman, "On Traumatic Knowledge and Literary Studies," *New Literary History* 26 (1995): 537–63.

6. Juan Goytisolo, *Crónicas sarracinas* (Barcelona: Ibérica, 1982), 60–61; see also Diana de Armas Wilson's pioneering book, *Cervantes, the Novel, and the New World* (New York: Oxford University Press, 2001). Wilson rightly argues that "the cross-cultural contacts that Columbus inaugurated in the Indies–exploration, conquest, and colonization–resonate throughout Cervantes's two long novels, *Don Quijote* (1605, 1615) and *Persiles* (1617)" (3). If Cervantes's great novels were indeed

stimulated by the geographical excitement of an unfamiliar new world, the five years he spent as a captive in multicultural Algiers, where twenty-two languages were spoken, according to Flemish captive Emanuel d'Aranda, must have opened Cervantes's spirit to new visions, new languages, and new worlds, long before he attempted to leave for the Indies.

7. The reinvigorated interest in trauma fueled by the cycle of violence in the Balkans and other tragic events in the United States have led to the creation of trauma study centers in various universities, such as the International Trauma Studies Program at New York University, the first to combine academic research on trauma with mental health programs developed in wartime. Similarly, Florida State University now offers a Ph.D. in systemic traumatology, which studies effective methods of assessment and treatment of interpersonal relationships following traumatic events. These programs join other efforts, like the monthly trauma studies workshop for professionals, scholars, and survivors sponsored by the University of Illinois at Chicago and the program that Yale University has established for Holocaust studies. More trauma centers have recently opened across the country, offering help to the survivors and families affected by the disasters of New York City and Washington, DC.

8. Jacques Lacan, *The Four Fundamental Concepts of Psychoanalysis*, ed. Jacques-Allain Miller, trans. Alan Sheridan (New York: Norton, 1978), 41. See also Dylan Evans, *An Introductory Dictionary of Lacanian Psychoanalysis* (New York: Routledge, 1966), especially 159–61.

9. Caruth, *Unclaimed Experience: Trauma, Narrative, and History* (Baltimore: Johns Hopkins University Press, 1996).

10. María Antonia Garcés, letter to Octavio Paz, 28 October 1983, *El laberinto de la soledad*, Edición conmemorativa: 50 Aniversario, ed. Enrico Mario Santí, 2 vols. (México: Fondo de Cultura Económica, 2000), II: 54–59.

11. This, of course, refers to slips of the tongue, blunders, or parapraxis, as well as to the workings of the repetition-compulsion that reveal the sway of the unconscious on the subject.

12. Malcolm Bowie, *Lacan* (Cambridge, MA: Harvard University Press, 1991), especially 94–95, 102–3, and 109–13. The citation is from page 94.

13. Primo Levi, *If This Is a Man* and *The Truce*, trans Stuart Woolf (London: Abacus, 1987). *La tregua [The Truce]* has also been translated as *The Reawakening*.

14. Dori Laub, "Bearing Witness or the Vicissitudes of Listening," *Testimony: Crises of Witnessing in Literature, Psychoanalysis and History*, ed. Shoshana Felman and Dori Laub (New York: Routledge, 1992) 57–74. The quotation comes from page 69.

15. Primo Levi, *The Periodic Table*, trans. Raymond Rosenthal (New York: Shocken Books, 1984), 151.

16. See Louise Fothergill-Payne, "*Los tratos de Argel, Los cautivos de Argel* y *Los baños de Argel: tres 'trasuntos' de un 'asunto,'*" *El mundo el teatro español en el Siglo de Oro: ensayos dedicados a John E. Varey*, ed. José María Ruano de la Haza (Ottawa: Dovehouse 1989), 181. The voluminous number of Christian captives, which constituted 20 to 25 percent of the population of Algiers, calculated at approximately 125,000 people in the 1570s, emphasizes the thriving business of the Barbary slave markets with their cruel traffic in human lives.

17. Carroll Johnson, unpublished paper, entitled "¿Cervantes coyote?," delivered at the XIIIth Congress of the Asociación Internacional de Hispanistas, Madrid,

11 July 1998. Johnson rightly argues that the long statement of the *Información de Argel* is Cervantes's first prose work, a coherent autobiographical account "organized in episodes or 'chapters' " (5). I thank Professor Johnson for kindly furnishing a copy of his paper.

Chapter 1

1. [When I arrived a captive, and saw this land,/Ill-famed in all the world, whose bosom conceals,/Protects, embraces such a throng of pirates,/I could not keep from weeping] (Saavedra, *El trato de Argel* 1, 396–99).

2. Américo Castro, *El pensamiento de Cervantes* (Madrid: Imprenta de la Librería y Casa Editorial Hernando, 1925), 386; Juan Bautista Avalle-Arce, "La captura de Cervantes," *Boletín de la Real Academia Española* (1968): 237–80. Likewise, Astrana Marín claims that the "fixed memory" of the Algerian captivity recurs in numerous Cervantine works; *Vida ejemplar y heroica de Miguel de Cervantes Saavedra,* 7 vols. (Madrid: Instituto Editorial Reus, 1949–1952), II, 465, n. 1. See also Alonso Zamora Vicente, "El cautiverio en la obra de Cervantes," *Homenaje a Cervantes,* ed. Francisco Sánchez-Castañer, 2 vols. (Madrid: Mediterráneo, 1950), II: 239. Unless otherwise noted, all translations are mine.

3. Juan Goytisolo, *Crónicas sarracinas* (Barcelona: Ibérica, 1982), 60.

4. On trauma, see also Cathy Caruth, *Unclaimed Experience: Trauma, Narrative, and History* (Baltimore: Johns Hopkins University Press, 1996), 3–4.

5. George Camamis, *Estudios sobre el cautiverio en el Siglo de Oro* (Madrid: Gredos, 1977), 53 and 57–59. E. González-López also signaled that the *Captive's Tale* inaugurated the Spanish historical novel: "Cervantes, maestro de la novela histórica contemporánea: la *Historia del cautivo,*" in *Homenaje a Casalduero,* Madrid, 1972, 179-87. That the theme of captivity was a constant in Cervantes, as well as one of the great literary finds of his time, is stressed by Mercedes García-Arenal and Miguel Ángel de Bunes in *Los españoles en el Norte de África: siglos XV–XVIII* (Madrid: Editorial MAPFRE, 1992), 103–04.

6. Luis Rosales, *Cervantes y la libertad,* 2 vols. (Madrid: Sociedad de Estudios y Publicaciones, 1960), II: 555–56.

7. The earliest biography containing an account of Cervantes's military service and of his Algerian captivity is that of Martín Fernández de Navarrete, *Vida de Miguel de Cervantes Saavedra* (Madrid: Imprenta Real, 1819).

8. Jean Canavaggio, *Cervantes,* trans. J. R. Jones (New York: Norton, 1990), and Spanish trans., *Cervantes: en busca del perfil perdido,* 2nd ed., expanded (Madrid: Espasa-Calpe, 1992). Further references to the English work appear parenthetically in the text as *Cervantes,* indicating page number. I also often refer to the expanded Spanish version of Canavaggio's book, *En busca del perfil.* See also William Byron's extensive *Cervantes, A Biography* (New York: Doubleday, 1978), although Byron often extrapolates from Cervantes's fictions to fill gaps in the author's life. On Cervantes's captivity, consult Donald P. McCrory's introduction to his translation of *Historia del cautivo,* Cervantes, *The Captive's Tale (Historia del cautivo), Don Quixote, Part One, Chapters 39–41* (Warminster, England: Aris & Philips, 1994), 1–58.

9. See, among others, Ahmed Abi-Ayad, "El cautiverio argelino de Miguel de Cervantes," *Notas y estudios filológicos* 9 (1994): 12–17; Daniel Eisenberg, "Por qué

volvió Cervantes de Argel?" in *Ingeniosa invención: Essays on Golden Age Literature Presented to Geoffrey Stagg on his Eighty-Fifth Birthday*, ed. Ellen Anderson and Amy Williamsen (Newark, DE: Juan de la Cuesta, 1998), 241–53; Ottmar Hegyi, "Algerian Babble Reflected in *Persiles*," in *Ingeniosa invención: Essays on Golden Age Spanish Literature*, ed. Ellen Anderson and Amy Williamsen (Newark, DE: Juan de la Cuesta, 1998), 225–39; Michael McGaha, "Hacia la verdadera historia del cautivo de Cervantes," *Revista Canadiense de Estudios Hispánicos* XX, 3 (1996): 540–46; Helena Percas de Ponseti, "¿Quién era Belerma?," *Revista Hispánica Moderna* 49 (1996): 375–92; and Françoise Zmantar, "Miguel de Cervantes y sus fantasmas de Argel," *Quimera* (December 2, 1980): 31–37. For a rich study of the Barbary world and its relation to Cervantes, see Emilio Sola y José F. de la Peña, *Cervantes y la Berbería: Cervantes, mundo turco-berberisco y servicios secretos en la época de Felipe II* (México: Fondo de Cultura Económica, 1995). The interest in Cervantes's captivity is attested to by the proceedings of a colloquium entitled *La huella del cautiverio en el pensamiento y en la obra de Cervantes*, ed. Ángela Monleón (Madrid: Fundación Cultural Banesto, 1994). See also Alberto Sánchez's review of the critical works on Cervantes's captivity, "Revisión del cautiverio cervantino en Argel," *Cervantes* XVII, 1 (1997): 7–24, and, by the same author, "Nuevas orientaciones en el planteamiento de la biografía de Cervantes," in *Cervantes* (Madrid: Centro de Estudios Cervantinos, 1995), 19–40. On the relation between "truths" and fiction surrounding Cervantes's life, see Eduardo Urbina, "Historias verdaderas y la verdad de la historia: Fernando Arrabal vs. Stephen Marlowe," *Cervantes* 18 (1998): 158–69. On Cervantes and the Turks, consult Albert Mas, *Les turcs dans la littérature espagnole du Siècle d'Or*, 2 vols. (Paris: Centre de Recherches Hispaniques, 1967), 1: 280-283, and Ottmar Hegyi, *Cervantes and the Turks: Historical Reality versus Literary Fiction in* La Gran Sultana *and* El amante liberal (Newark, DE: Juan de la Cuesta, 1992).

10. See Canavaggio, *Cervantes*, 82, 96; Goytisolo, *Crónicas sarracinas*; Michael McGaha, "Don Quixote as Arabesque," *Cervantes: Estudios en la víspera de su centenario*, ed. Kurt & Roswitha Reichenberger, 2 vols. (Kassel: Reichenberger, 1994), 1: 163–71; Donald McCrory, Introduction to *The Captive's Tale*, 9; Sola and de la Peña, *Cervantes y la Berbería*, 187–275; Alberto Sánchez, "Libertad, humano tesoro," *Anales Cervantinos* 23 (1994): 9–21; and Zamora Vicente, "El cautiverio," in *Homenaje a Cervantes*, II: 239–56.

11. Fernand Braudel, "Imperio y monarquía en el Siglo XVI," *En torno al Mediterráneo* (Barcelona: Paidós, 1997), 181. This is a compilation and translation of various articles by Braudel, such as his classic study, "Les espagnols et l'Afrique du Nord, 1492–1598," *Revue africaine* 69 (1928): 84–233 and 351–428. See also Leopold Von Ranke, *Die Osmanen und die Spanische Monarchie im* 16. *und* 17. *Jahrhundert*, 4th ed. (1837; repr. Leipzig, 1877); English translation by Walter K. Kelly, *The Ottoman and the Spanish Empires in the Sixteenth and Seventeenth Centuries* (London, 1843).

12. *The Maghrib* shall be used throughout this work as a collective name for the North African region that extends from present-day Morocco to the west of Egypt, a region that now encompasses the four countries of Morocco, Algeria, Tunisia, and Libya. I also refer to these territories as *Barbary* [Berbería], which is the name given by the Europeans to the region, especially when looking at the area from an early modern European perspective.

13. Two Papal Bulls by Alexander VI, from 1493 and 1494, sanctioned the Afri-

can crusade while offering Spain legal titles of possession (Braudel, *En torno*, 49). The text of the 1494 Latin Bull, with its Spanish translation, appears in the Appendix to José M. Dousinague, *La política internacional de Fernando el Católico* (Madrid: Espasa-Calpe, 1944), 521–24. On the Spanish North African campaigns, see Andrew C. Hess, *The Forgotten Frontier: A History of the Sixteenth-Century Ibero-African Frontier* (Chicago: University of Chicago Press, 1978), 26–43, and John B. Wolf, *The Barbary Coast: Algiers under the Turks, 1500 to 1830* (New York: Norton, 1979), 5–16.

14. Dousinague, *La política internacional*, 128–38, 154–67, 184–229, 344–71, and *Testamentaria de Isabel la Católica*, ed. Antonio de la Torre y del Cerro (Valladolid: Instituto "Isabel la Católica" de Historia Eclesiástica, 1968), 445–75. In August 1505, barely six months after Isabella's death, Ferdinand prepared an army of seven thousand soldiers and one hundred ninety vessels to attack Mazalquivir "to make war on the Moors"; see Andrés Bernáldez, *Memorias del reinado de los reyes católicos* (Madrid: Real Academia de la Historia and Consejo Superior de Investigaciones Científicas, 1962), 490–94. See also Mohamed Ibn Azzuz Hakim, "El testamento de Isabel la Católica y sus consecuencias funestas sobre las relaciones hispano-marroquíes," *Huellas comunes y miradas cruzadas: Mundos árabe, ibérico e iberoamericano*, ed. Mohamed Salhi (Rabat: Facultad de Letras y de Ciencias Humanas, 1995), 27–35.

15. Navarro's refusal to invade the interior of the Maghrib provoked serious imputations from Cardinal Cisneros, who accused him of wanting to raid the coastal cities of North Africa with no other objective than booty. See *Cartas del Cardenal Don Fray Francisco Jiménez de Cisneros dirigidas a don Diego López de Ayala*, ed. Pascual Gayangos and Vicente de la Fuente (Madrid: Imprenta del Colegio de Sordomudos y de Ciegos, 1867), 50–58; on Pedro Navarro's African conquests, see Cesáreo Fernández Duro, *Armada española desde la unión de los Reinos de Castilla y de León 1476–1664*, 4 vols. (Madrid: Establecimiento Tipográfico "Sucesores de Rivadeneira," 1895–1897), I: 77–89; Martín de los Heros, *Historia del Conde Pedro Navarro* in *Colección de documentos inéditos para la Historia de España* [CODOIN], 112 vols. (Madrid: Imprenta de la viuda de Calero, 1854), XXV: 106–45. This collection of documents will be hereafter cited as CODOIN in the notes.

16. Fernández Duro, *Armada Española desde la unión de los reinos de Castilla y Aragón, 1476–1664*, I: 65–66. Ferdinand's pragmatic against privateering, dated January 12, 1489, is reproduced in the Appendix to *Armada*, I: 347–48. In succeeding warrants, signed in Zaragoza on June 30, 1498, Ferdinand authorized the Basque and Guipuscoan peoples to embark on privateering expeditions, which were also allowed in the Italian seas (*Armada* I: 64). See also Geoffrey Fischer, *Barbary Legend* (Oxford: Clarendon Press, 1957), 30–33, and Enrique Otero Lana, *Los corsarios españoles durante la decadencia de los Austrias: El corso español del Atlántico peninsular en el siglo XVIII (1621–1697)* (Madrid: Editorial Naval, 1992), 43. As Fernand Braudel demonstrates, similar raids were carried out in the Mediterranean by Christian corsairs, such as the Knights of Malta. See Braudel's classic work, *The Mediterranean and the Mediterranean World in the Age of Philip II*, trans. Siân Reynolds, 2 vols. (New York: Harper & Row, 1972), II: 865–91; trans. of *La Méditerranée et le monde Méditerranéen à l'époque de Philippe II* (1949; rev. ed. Paris, 1966).

17. Francisco López de Gómara, *Crónica de los muy nombrados Omiche y Haradin Barbarrojas* [sic], included in *Memorial histórico español de la Real Academia de Historia* (Madrid: Real Academia de Historia, 1853), VI: 331–439. Written after Charles

V's defeat in Algiers (1541), this chronicle never saw light until the nineteenth century. For a résumé of the Barbarossa brothers' activities in the Maghrib, see Hess, 61–65. See also Antonio de Sosa's detailed account of the Barbarossa brothers' government in Diego de Haedo, ed., *Epítome de los reyes de Argel, Topografía e historia general de Argel*, 3 vols., ed. Ignacio Lauer y Landauer (Madrid: Sociedad de Bibliófilos Españoles, 1927–1929), I: 213–77. A rich view of the Barbarossas' carrier in the Mediterranean is offered by Emilio Sola in the four consecutive articles published in *Historia 16*; Sola, "La saga de los Barbarroja," *Historia 16* (1989): XIV.158 (1989): 8–16; XIV.159 (1989): 82–90; XIV.160 (1989): 73–81; and XIV.161 (1989): 91–98. By the same author, see *Un Mediterráneo de piratas: Corsarios, renegados y cautivos* (Madrid: Tecnos, 1988). The sixteenth-century Ottoman manuscript on Barbarossa's life, written by Seyid Murad and entitled *Gazavat-i Hayreddin Pasa* [*The Holy War of Hayreddin Pasha*], was found on the principal Ottoman galley captured at Lepanto in 1571. Conserved in the Library of El Escorial, it was translated in 1578 as *Crónica del guerrero de la fe Hayreddin Barbarroja*. This work has been recently edited by Miguel Ángel de Bunes and Emilio Sola as *La vida, y historia de Hayradin, llamado Barbarroja* (Granada: Universidad de Granada, 1997).

18. Two excellent books study the history of these émigrés and their settlement in North Africa: Míkel de Epalza, *Los moriscos antes y después de la expulsión* (Madrid: Editorial MAPFRE, 1992), and Mercedes García-Arenal and Miguel Ángel de Bunes, *Los españoles y el Norte de África. Siglos XV-XVIII* (Madrid: Editorial MAPFRE, 1992).

19. See Letter 574, dated July 31, 1516, in Pietro Martire's Latin *Epistolarium*, trans. José López Toro, 4 vols. (Madrid: Imprenta Góngora, 1956), III: 234–35.

20. The slayer of Barbarossa, Ensign García Fernández de la Plaza, was rewarded for this feat by Charles V with a coat of arms bearing the head and crown of Barbarossa. See the privilege and description of this coat of arms in the Appendix to Lopez de Gómara, *Crónica de los Barbarroja, Memorial histórico español* VI, 487–88.

21. Barbarossa left Constantinople on May 28, 1534, with approximately eighty galleons and one thousand two hundred thirty-three Christian slaves on board, as reported by a Spanish espionage agent: "Memoria de la orden que tiene la armada de Barbarroja. Año 1534," in the Appendix to López de Gómara, *Crónica de los Barbarroja, Memorial histórico español*, IV: 521–23. Khair ad-Dīn's army, composed of some eight thousand Albanians, Anatolians, Greeks, and Christian renegades, landed in Tunis on August 16, 1534, and met little opposition (Wolf, 19). Charles V reconquered Tunis in 1535, yet the memory of Barbarossa's exploits remained with the Spaniards for a long time.

22. Castilnovo was the Italian name for the Imperial enclave of Hersegnovi, on the Dalmatian coast, which was devastated by Barbarossa's armada in 1539. López de Gómara describes this catastrophe in his *Guerra del mar del Emperador Carlos V*, 198-205. This defeat was lamented by Spanish and Italians poets alike, as sung by the poet Luigi Tansillo: "in lode di quei tre mila soldati spagnuoli, che/furono morti da turchi a Castel Nuovo della Bosna" [in praise of those three thousand Spanish soldiers who were killed by the Turks at Castelnuovo of Bosnia] (cited by Manuel González Álvarez in "Carlos V y Europa: el legado del Emperador," *(cervantesvirtual. com/historia/CarlosV/presentacion.shtml))*.

23. See the letters written by Andrea Doria, Viceroy Fernando Gonzaga, and Gallego, accountant to the emperor, regarding the negotiations with Barbarossa, as well as an answer composed in Spanish by the corsair himself, in the Appendix to

Gómara's *Crónica de los Barbarroja, Memorial histórico español*, VI: 530–39. Barbarossa kept the sultan constantly informed of the negotiations with Charles V, as stated by a Spanish spy in Constantinople in a letter to Count Doria. See E. Watleb and Dr. Monnereau, "Negotiations entre Charles-Quint et Keir-ed-din (1538–1540)," *Revue africaine* 15 (1871): 138–48.

24. According to Spanish sources, the force included twenty-four thousand German, Italian, and Spanish troops, twelve thousand marines, and over two thousand horses, plus cannons and siege equipment. The fleet included sixty-five galleys and four hundred fifty transport vessels of all sizes (Wolf, 27; Hess, 74). See López de Gómara, *Guerras de mar del Emperador Carlos V*, ed. Miguel Ángel de Bunes Ibarra and Nora Edith Jiménez (Madrid: Sociedad Estatal para la Conmemoración de los Centenarios de Felipe II y Carlos V, 2000), 211–23, and Prudencio de Sandoval, *Historia de la vida y hechos del Emperador Carlos V*, ed. Carlos Seco Serrano, 3 vols. (Madrid: Atlas, 1955), III: 103–14. Sandoval's account of these wars was based on Gómara's unpublished manuscript, which he copied.

25. *Beylerbey* [*beylerbeyi*] or *beglerbeg* [*beglerbegi*; "commander of the commanders"] originally designated a commander-in-chief of the army, but it came to mean a provincial governor at the time of the regency of Algiers. I will use the term *beylerbey* when speaking of the "kings" of Algiers, as Sosa calls the governors of the province of Algiers under Ottoman suzerainty.

26. *Gazavat*, ms. 942, Bibliothèque-Musée d'Alger, translated into French as "L'expédition espagnole de 1541 contre Alger," *Revue africaine* 202 (1891): 177–206. The citations come from pages 184 and 194–95; also S. Murad Çelebi, *Gazavat-i* 145, cited in Gómara's *Guerras del Emperador*, ed. de Bunes Ibarra and Jiménez, 220, n. 425.

27. See Brantôme, "Charles Le Quint," in *Oeuvres complètes de Pierre de Bourdeilles, abbé et seigneur de Brantôme*, ed. Prosper Merimée, 13 vols. (Paris: P. Janet, 1858), I: 132–33. Although Wolf (27–30) gives a succinct account of the emperor's defeat, he misunderstands Brantôme's French text and attributes the question allegedly asked by Brantôme to Charles V himself. The emperor's serene report on the disaster, recounted in a letter to Cardinal Tavera, is summarized by José A. Yaque Laurel, "La expedición de Carlos V a Argel: El relato imperial," *África* 199 (1958): 13–15.

28. Nicholas Durand de Villegagnon, *Carlo V Emperatoris Expeditio in Africam ad Algeriam*, trans. Ricardus Grafton (1542). The pamphlet is included in Vol. 4 of *Harleian Miscellany: A Collection of Scarce, Curious, and Entertaining Pamphlets and Tracts as well as Manuscript and in Print. Selected from the Library of Edward Harley, second Earl of Oxford*, 10 vols. (London, 1809–1813), IV: 532–43.

29. For a detailed description of Cervantes's role in the Battle of Lepanto and of his military career in the Mediterranean, see Canavaggio, *Cervantes*, 48–77, as well as the revised Spanish edition, *Cervantes: En busca del perfil perdido*, 55–75. On the Battle of Lepanto, see Braudel, *Mediterranean* II: 1027–1103; John Lynch, *Spain: 1516–1598* (Oxford, UK, and Cambridge, MA: Basil Blackwell, 1991), 327–41; Luciano Serrano, *La Liga de Lepanto entre España, Venecia y la Santa Sede (1570–1573)*, 2 vols. (Madrid: Imprenta de Archivos, 1918–1920), I: 68–101, 124–42. Also by Serrano, *España en Lepanto* (Barcelona: Editorial Labor, 1935; repr. Madrid: Editora Nacional, 1975), as well as a series of contemporary accounts in CODOIN III: 184–360.

30. Testimony delivered by Ensign Mateo de Santistebán, a companion of Cervantes in Lepanto, Madrid, March 20, 1578. See *Información de Miguel de Cervantes*

de lo que ha servido a S.M. y de lo que ha hecho estando captivo en Argel [. . .], transcripción de Pedro Torres Lanzas (Madrid: Ediciones El Árbol, 1981), 29. Most of the known yet scattered documents regarding Cervantes have been collected and impeccably edited by K. Sliwa, *Documentos de Miguel de Cervantes Saavedra* (Pamplona: EUNSA, Ediciones Universidad de Navarra, 1999), 50–51. This collection of documents shall be hereafter cited as Sliwa, plus page number (Sliwa, 50-51).

31. Cervantes, Prologue to his *Novelas ejemplares*, ed. Harry Sieber, 2 vols. (Madrid: Cátedra, 1988), 1: 51. For the English translation, see Cervantes, *Exemplary Novels (Novelas ejemplares)*, 4 vols., trans. B.W. Ife (Warminster, England: Aris & Philips, 1992), 1: 3.

32. The number of casualties differs slightly in Braudel and Canavaggio, among others. Braudel claims the Christians lost ten galleys and had eight thousand men killed and twenty-one thousand wounded (*Mediterranean*, II: 1102). Spanish testimonies of the time generally minimize the losses endured by the Christians. See the report of Don Juan de Austria's confessor, Fray Miguel Servia, *Relación de los sucesos de la Armada de la Santa Liga y entre ellos el de la Batalla de Lepanto*, included in CODOIN XI: 359–71; on these data, see Serrano, *La Liga de Lepanto*, 137–38.

33. Miguel de Cervantes, *Historia del cautivo*, in *Don Quijote de la Mancha*, ed. Luis Andrés Murillo, 2 vols. (Madrid: Castalia, 1978), 1: 477. I shall use Donald McCrory's English translation of *The Captive's Tale*, hereafter cited parenthetically in the text. Unless otherwise noted, the English translation of *Don Quijote* (cited parenthetically in text as *DQ*) refers to the Norton Critical Edition, trans. Burton Raffel, ed. Diana de Armas Wilson (New York, Norton, 1999).

34. In *Cervantes: En busca del perfil perdido*, Canavaggio suggests that the Battle of Lepanto implied a deceptive triumph: Europe was unable to capitalize on the advantages derived from its victory. The Turkish withdrawal attributed to Lepanto did not really occur until ten years later, when the Ottoman Empire turned against Persia (67; see also his English *Cervantes*, 58–59).

35. His promotion to *soldado aventajado* is first mentioned in the pay order of November 15, 1574, signed at Palermo by the duke of Sessa, assigning the soldier pay of twenty-five *escudos* (Canavaggio, *Cervantes*, 65; Sliwa, 44).

36. *El trato de Argel*, in Miguel de Cervantes Saavedra, *Obra completa*, ed. Florencio Sevilla Arroyo and Antonio Rey Hazas, 18 vols. (Madrid: Alianza Editorial, 1996), 2: 1.396–99, hereafter cited as *Trato* plus act and verse numbers (*Trato*, 1.396–99).

37. Alberto Guglielmotti, *Storia de la marina pontificia*, 10 vols. (Roma: Tipografia Vaticana, 1886–1893), III: 49; quoted by Salvatore Bono, *Il corsari barbareschi* (Roma: Eri-Edisioni Radiotelevisione Italiana, 1964), 12–13.

38. The success of these expeditions leads Grand Master Pietro del Monte (1568–1572) to grant a license for the fitting of corsair ships under the flag of the order, subject to a tax of nine percent on the booty captured (Cassar, 141). Corsair activity in Malta included a complex system of distribution that reserved eleven percent of the booty for the victorious captain, ten percent for the grand master of the Order of Malta, and so on, down to a small proportion for the nuns of St. Ursula in Valletta.

39. On the Knights of St. John of Jerusalem of the Order of Malta, see Joseph Attard, *The Knights of Malta* (San Gwan, Malta: Publishers Enterprise Group [PEG], 1992), and Peter Earle, *Corsairs of Malta and Barbary* (Annapolis, MD: United States Naval Institute, 1970). See also Ettore Rossi, *Storia della Marina dell'Ordine*

di S. Giovanni di Gerusalemme di Rodi e di Malta (Rome & Milan: Societa Editrice D'Arte Illustrata, 1926); Jaime Salvá, *La Orden de Malta y las acciones contra turcos y berberiscos en los siglos XVI y XVII* (Madrid: Instituto Histórico de la Marina, 1944); H.J.A. Sire, *The Knights of Malta* (New Haven & London: Yale University Press, 1994), which provides useful information; Ubaldino Mori Ubaldini, *La marina del Sovrano Militare Ordine de San Giovanni de Gerusalemme di Rodi e di Malta* (Roma: Regionale Editrice, 1971); and Joseph M. Wismayer, *The Fleet of the Order of St. John, 1530–1798* (Valletta: Midsea Books Ltd., 1997). The highly accessible narrative on the Knights of St. John by Claire-Éliane Engel, *Histoire de l'Ordre de Malte* (Genève-Paris: Nagel, 1968), is greatly fictionalized and deficient as a work of history.

40. Antonio de Sosa, *Diálogo de los mártires de Argel*, ed. Emilio Sola and José María Parreño (Madrid: Hiperión, 1990), 94–98; see also *Diálogo de los mártires de Argel* in Diego de Haedo, *Topografía e historia general de Argel*, ed. Ignacio Bauer y Landauer, 3 vols. (Madrid: Sociedad de Bibliófilos Españoles, 1927–1929), III: 48–55. This work will be parenthetically cited in the text by both editions: *Mártires* (1990), followed by the edition included in *Topografía* (1929).

41. "La description de la ville d'Alger" in Nicholas de Nicolay, *Les navigations, pérégrinations et voyages faits en la Turquie* (Lyons, 1567), recently published as *Dans l'empire de Soliman le Magnifique*, ed. Marie-Christine Gomez-Géraud and Stéphane Yérasimos (Paris: Presses du CNRS, 1989), 64–65.

42. When foreign ships anchored in Algiers, the corsairs would place severe restrictions on the city and its slaves for fear that the Christian captives would try to flee. This is illustrated by Nicholas de Nicolay's daunting description of the pursuit of his ships and maltreatment of his entourage in 1551 by the Algerians, who accused the Frenchmen of hiding a number of Christian slaves on board (61–64); see also Salvatore Bono, *Il corsari barbareschi*, 340–41.

43. Antonio de Sosa, now identified as the author of *Topographia, e historia general de Argel*, attributed to Diego de Haedo (1612), claims that in the 1570s there were more than twenty-five thousand Christian slaves in Algiers; see Diego de Haedo, ed., *Topografía e historia general de Argel*, I: 47. This work will be cited parenthetically in the text as *Topografía* plus volume and page number.

44. *Ra'is* [Turkish *re'is*] means "head, leader of a recognizable group." It was the name given to the captain of a small vessel, and, in Algiers, to a corsair who owned various vessels. On the corso or corsair activity of the Algerians, see H.-D. de Grammont's classic article in two parts: "La course, l'esclavage et la rédemption à Alger," "Première partie: La course," *Revue historique* 26 (1884): 1–42; and "Seconde partie: L'esclavage," *Revue historique* 27 (1884): 1–44. See also Hipólito Sancho de Sopranis, "Cádiz y la piratería turco-berberisca en el siglo XVI," *Archivos del Instituto de Estudios Africanos* 26 (1953): 7–77.

45. Camamis, *Estudios sobre el cautiverio en el siglo de oro* (Madrid: Gredos, 1977), 124–50, especially 140–43.

46. French historian Ferdinand Denis, who supposed that Haedo traveled to Algiers in 1605, found questionable that this elaborate treatise could have been composed from accounts given by former slaves; see his "Haedo," in *Nouvelle biographie générale* (Paris: Firmin Didot, 1853). See also H.-D. de Grammont, *Histoire d'Alger sous las domination turque, 1515–1830* (Paris, 1887), which owes much to *Topographia*. De Grammont translated the *Epítome de los reyes de Argel*, included in *Topographia*,

into French, as *Histoire des rois d'Alger* (Algiers: Revue Africaine, 1881; reprinted 1998).

47. Pérez Pastor, *Documentos cervantinos hasta ahora inéditos*, 2 vols. (Madrid: Establecimiento Tipográfico de Fortanet, 1897–1902), I: 235, n. 1.

48. On Antonio de Sosa, see Emilio Sola, "Antonio de Sosa: Un clásico inédito amigo de Cervantes (historia y literatura)," *Actas del Primer Coloquio Internacional de la Asociación de Cervantistas, Alcalá de Henares 29/30 nov.–1/2 dic. 1988* (Barcelona: Anthropos, 1990); Vol. 1, 409-12 (by the same author, "Miguel de Cervantes, Antonio de Sosa y África," *Actas del Primer Encuentro de Historiadores del Valle de Henares* (Guadalajara-Alcalá de Henares, 1988), 617–23; consult also the two forewords in Antonio de Sosa, *Diálogo de los mártires de Argel*, ed. Emilio Sola and José M. Parreño (Madrid: Hiperión, 1990), by Parreño (9–23) and Sola (26–52); as well as Emilio Sola and José F. de la Peña, *Cervantes y la Berbería*, 277–91.

49. Henri-Delmas de Grammont, trans., *Histoire des rois d'Alger* (Alger: A. Jourdan, 1881). This translation had appeared in installment in *Revue africaine* (1880–1881). Historian de Grammont argues that the *Epítome* is "the capital part of Haedo's work, and its knowledge is indispensable [. . .] since it is the only book that gives the account of the events that occurred during the XVI century. Without it, the most obscure night would reign over this period." See *Histoire des rois d'Alger* (Saint-Denis, France: Editions Bouchène, 1998), 15.

50. Daniel Eisenberg's proposition that Cervantes is the author of *Topografía* is untenable; "Cervantes, autor de la *Topografía e historia general de Argel*, publicada por Diego de Haedo," *Cervantes* XVI, 3 (1996): 32–53. Eisenberg's thesis that the work was written in Spain because there was no access to books in Algiers fails to take into account Sosa's commentaries, in his *Dialogues*, on the text he is constantly writing and rewriting in Algiers, and the books he is reading, or citing by heart. In addition, Sosa's diatribes against the Muslims, his religious fanaticism, and his obsession with the tortures imposed on Christian slaves are incompatible with Cervantes's views. Finally, Sosa's formidable erudition, which covers the classics and the fathers of the church, is not consistent with Cervantes's intellectual background.

51. See the excellent discussion on early modern captives and renegades in García-Arenal and de Bunes, *Los españoles y el Norte de África*, 209–25.

52. The actual Turkish word was *banyol*, meaning "royal prison." There are discrepancies as to the origin of this term. Covarrubias, in his *Tesoro de la lengua castellana o española* (1611), claims that its source is the Latin *balneum*, which he translates as "corral, yard." It was in such "yards" that the Algerians kept their captives, especially those held for ransom.

53. Fray Melchor de Zúñiga O.S.F., "Descripción de la República de la ciudad de Argel," ms. 3227, fol. 136 v° –141 r°, Biblioteca Nacional, Madrid.

54. Juan de Balcázar remembers the names of some of Cervantes's companions in this venture: "Don Francisco de Meneses, who was a Captain in la Goleta for his Majesty; don Beltrán; Ensign Ríos; sergeant Navarrete; and another gentleman called Osorio, and another gentleman whose name was Castañeda" (*Información de Argel*, 102).

55. *Topografía* II: 91–92, 101–06, 123–25, 173–87ff. The horrible tortures suffered by the Christian captives in Algiers are described by Sosa in *Diálogo de los mártires de Argel* (1990), included in *Topografía*, III: 27–192.

56. André Zysberg, "Les galères de France sous le règne de Louis XIV. Essai de

comptabilité globale," in *Les marines de guerre européennes (XVIe–XVIIIe siècles)*, ed. Martine Acerra, José Merino and Jean Meyer (Paris: Presses de l'Université de Paris–Sorbonne, 1985), 403–36. For an excellent synthesis of this question, see García-Arenal and de Bunes, *Los españoles*, 220–45.

57. This is the first biography of Cervantes in Algiers, which includes a detailed description of his second escape attempt and a summary of the rest, all recapitulated in Sosa's *Diálogo de los mártires*.

58. The fact that the work was not published until 1612, although it had carried the license for publication since 1604, implies that Haedo Jr. waited until the death of his uncle in 1608 to publish Sosa's treatise, to represent it as a work authored by both uncle and nephew (Camamis, 148–49).

59. Francisco Navarro Ledesma, *Cervantes*, trans. Don and Gabriela Bliss (New York: Charter-house, 1973), 93, 108, and Michael MacGaha, "Hacia la verdadera historia," among others.

60. Back in Orán by October 2, 1577, Fresneda recounted that he was first captured at sea but later released and taken to Algiers when it was found out that he was a negotiator sent by Don Martín de Córdoba. On the conversations between Fresneda and Hājjī Murād, see Don Martín de Córdoba, "To Philip II," 9 and 10 October 1577. The coded letters are included in Chantal de la Véronne, ed., *Les sources inédites de l'histoire du Maroc*, 1ère série, dynastie sa'dienne (1539–1560), archives et bibliothèques d' Espagne, 3 vols. (Paris: Paul Geuthner, 1961), t. III (1560–1578), III: 327–35. This series will be hereafter cited in the text as SIHM, followed by the series, country of the archives, volume, and page number.

61. The report, written by the Commander Fray François Lanfreducci and Fray Jean Othon Bosio, has been published as "Costa e discorsi di Barberia," *Rapport maritime, militaire et politique sur la Côte d'Afrique, depuis le Nil jusqu'à Cherchell par deux membres de l'Ordre de Malte (1er Septembre 1587)*, French trans. Pierre Granchamp, *Revue africaine* 66 (1925): 419–549.

62. Auguste Cour, *L'établissement des dynasties des chérifs au Maroc: Et leur rivalité avec les turcs de la régence d'Alger, 1509–1830* (Paris: Ernest Leroux, 1904), and Mercedes García Arenal, "Mahdí, murabit, sharif: d'avènement de la dynastie sa'dienne," *Studia islamica* 71 (1990): 77–114.

63. Bartolomé and Lucile Benassar, *Los cristianos de Alá: La fascinante aventura de los renegados*, trans. José Luis Gil Aristu (Madrid: Nerea, 1989); trans. from the French, *Les Chrétiens d'Allah: L'histoire extraordinaire des renégats, XVI et XVII siècles* (Paris: Perrin, 1989). See also Miguel Ángel de Bunes Ibarra, "Reflexiones sobre la conversión al islam de los renegados en los siglos XVI y XVII," *Hispania Sacra* 42 (1990):181–98; Mercedes García Arenal, "Les conversions d'européens a l'islam dans l'historie: Esquisse générale," *Social Compass* 46 (3) (1999): 273–81; Bartolomé Benassar, "La vida de los renegados españoles y portugueses en Fez (hacia 1580–1615)," *Relaciones de la Península Ibérica con el Magreb, siglos XIII–XVI. Actas del Coloquio (Madrid, 17–18 diciembre, 1987)*, ed. Mercedes García Arenal and María J. Viguera (Madrid: CSIC, 1988), 665–67; and Bernard Rosenberg, "Mouriscos et Elches: Conversions au Maroc au début du XVIe siècle," *Relaciones de la Península Ibérica con el Magreb, siglos XIII–XVI, Actas del Coloquio (Madrid, 17–18 diciembre, 1987)*, ed. García Arenal and Viguera, 621–77.

Chapter 2

1. [To my mind there is no happiness on earth to compare with recovering lost liberty] *The Captive's Tale, Don Quijote* I, 39.

2. On Antonio Veneziano, see Salvatore Bono, *I corsari barbareschi*, 392–96; Gaetano Millunzi, "Antonio Veneziano," in *Archivio storico siciliano* XIX (Palermo: Tipografia "Lo Statuto," 1894) 18–198; and Eugenio Mele, "Miguel de Cervantes y Antonio Veneziano," *Revista de archivos, bibliotecas y museos* 29 (Madrid, 1913): 82–90.

3. Astrana Marín offers a detailed account of these findings, which coincided with the work of Juan Antonio Pellicer, *Noticias literarias para la vida de Cervantes* (1778), I: 217–23.

4. *Información de Argel,* in *Información de Miguel de Cervantes de lo que ha servido á S.M. y de lo que ha hecho estando captivo en Argel, y por la certificación que aquí presenta del duque de Sesa se verá como cuando le captivaron se le perdieron muchas informaciones, fees y recados que tenia de lo que había servido á S.M. (Documentos),* Transcripción de Pedro Torres Lanzas (Madrid: Ediciones El Árbol, 1988), 47–170.

5. I shall sometimes refer to Antonio de Sosa as Dr. Sosa, especially when mentioning letters or legal documents of the period, which always include his title.

6. Katherine Elliot Van Liere, "Humanism and Scholasticism in Sixteenth-Century Academe: Five Student Orations from the University of Salamanca," *Renaissance Quarterly* 53 (2000): 57–107, especially 65–66. Literary references to the prohibitive costs of a doctoral degree in Salamanca are abundant. For one amusing example, see Juan Huarte de San Juan, *Examen de ingenios para las ciencias,* ed. Guillermo Serés (Madrid: Cátedra, 1989), 551ff. The universities that conferred law and canon law degrees in early modern Spain and Portugal were Salamanca and Valladolid, the University of Coimbra, and the Spanish College at Bologna. On Salamanca, see Antonio García y García, "Los difíciles inicios (siglos XIII–XIV)," and "Consolidaciones del siglo XV," in *La Universidad de Salamanca: Historia y proyecciones,* ed. Manuel Fernández Álvarez et al., 2 vols. (Salamanca: Universidad de Salamanca, 1989), I: 13–34 and 35–58. On the University of Salamanca in the sixteenth century, see the excellent article by Manuel Fernández Álvarez, "Etapa renacentista," *La Universidad de Salamanca,* I: 59–101.

7. For the prevalence of law, specially canon law, in Salamanca, see García y García, 55; also Mariano Peset and Enrique González González, "Las facultades de leyes y cánones" in *La Universidad de Salamanca,* II: 9–61. On the Portuguese students at Salamanca in the sixteenth and seventeenth centuries, see Ángel Marcos de Dios, "Área Lusa," in "Estado de la cuestión: Trayectoria histórica," *La Universidad de Salamanca,* I: 425–44.

8. Pilot Pedro Griego and some of the sailors and soldiers who escaped by jumping overboard claimed the corsairs fell on the ship with such swiftness that she was immediately subdued by the attackers (Archivo General de Simancas [AGS], Estado, leg. 1073, doc. 82–83). Another view is provided by galley slave Domingo Sponto, who escaped from the Algerian galleys at the moment of the attack (AGS, Guerra Antigua, leg. 83, doc. 84). See chapter 5 on these questions.

9. Fabricated in Algiers, the galliot was smaller than a galleon, swift, with fourteen to twenty-five benches. Light and rounded in front and in back, the galliot surpassed the galleon in performance. While Christian galleons had six to eight

rowers per bench, often recruited in prisons, Algerian galliots had ten oarsmen per bench, all of them experienced seamen. See Moulay Belhamissi, *Histoire de la marine algérienne (1516–1830)* (Alger: Entreprise Nationale du Livre, 1983), 60.

10. Some of these knights, such as Fray Antonio de Toledo and Fray Francisco de Valencia, were imprisoned with Cervantes in the *beylerbey*'s *baño*. Cervantes mentions them in *El trato de Argel*. On the capture of the *San Pablo*, see Fra Bartolomeo Dal Pozzo, *Historia della sacra religione di Malta*, 2 vols. (Verona, 1702), I: 130. I thank Maltese historian Joseph Muscat for this data regarding the *San Paolo* or *San Pablo*. The loss of the galley *San Pablo* is registered in the *Liber conciliorum Magni Magistri Johannis Levesque de la Cassière* Ann. 1574–77ff., 4v. and 5, in *Records of the Order of St. John of Jerusalem of Malta* (National Library of Malta, Archives 95–96).

11. Sosa's three dialogues appear in volumes II and III of Haedo, *Topografía e historia general de Argel*, ed. Ignacio Lauer and Landauer, 3 vols. (Madrid: Sociedad de Bibliófilos Españoles, 1927–1929). See also Antonio de Sosa, *Diálogo de los mártires de Argel*, ed. Emilio Sola and José M. Parreño (Madrid: Hiperión, 1990). I shall refer to both editions of *Diálogo de los mártires*: the 1990 edition (*Mártires*) and the one included in *Topografía* II.

12. In his French translation of *Epítome de los reyes de Argel*, H.-D. de Grammont notes that after 1581, "when Haedo left Algiers, History (l'Histoire) is replaced by anecdotes on captivity and privateering [. . .], the reason being that, at this time Haedo returned to Messina, to his uncle, the Bishop of this city [. . .]. But this does not detract from the high historical value of this book, whose allegations are almost always in accordance with the official documents," *Histoire des rois d'Alger*, trans. Henri-Delmas de Grammont (Saint-Denis: Bouchène, 1998), 230, n.1.

13. John Morgan, *A Complete History of Algiers: To which is prefixed, an epitome of the general history of Barbary, from the earliest times: Interspersed with many curious remarks and passages, not touched on by any writer whatever* (London: J. Bettenham, 1728–1729).

14. Diego de Haedo, *Topographia, e historia general de Argel, repartida en cinco tratados, do se veran casos estraños, muertes espantosas, y tormentos exquisitos, que conviene se entiendan en la Christiandad* . . . (En Valladolid: Por Diego Fernández de Córdoba y Oviedo, a costa de Antonio Coello, 1612). As mentioned above, the work was edited by Ignacio Lauer y Landauer, *Topografía e historia general de Argel*, 3 vols. (Madrid: Sociedad de Bibliófilos Españoles, 1927–1929). Both the princeps edition and the 1927–1929 reprint are extremely difficult to find. A scholarly edition of these works is thus urgently needed. *Topografía* was translated into French by Dr. Monnereau and published in installments in *Revue africaine* nos. 82-90 (1870-1871). *Epítome de los reyes de Argel* was translated by H.-D. de Grammont as *Histoire des rois d'Alger*, *Revue africaine* (1880–1881), and later appeared in one volume: Diego de Haedo, *Histoire des rois d'Alger* (Algiers: Adolphe Jourdan, 1881). Both works have recently been reprinted as Diego de Haedo, *Histoire des rois d'Alger* (Saint-Denis: Editions Bouchène, 1998) and Diego de Haedo, *Topographie et histoire générale d'Alger* (Saint-Denis: Editions Bouchène, 1998).

15. Cristóbal Pérez Pastor, *Documentos cervantinos hasta ahora inéditos*, 2 vols. (Madrid: Establecimiento Tipográfico de Fortanet, 1897–1902) II: 235, n. 6.

16. Mohamed Mounir Salah studies in his dissertation the correspondences between various passages of the *Dialogues* and the first and second parts of *Topografía e historia general de Argel*; "El Doctor Sosa y la *Topografía e Historia general de Argel*," dissertation Universitat Autònoma de Barcelona, 1991.

17. Luis del Mármol Carvajal, *Descripción general de África*, 3 vols. (Granada, 1573), II: fol. 91. Sosa offers a detailed description of the Jews in sixteenth-century Algiers (*Topografía*, I: 111–14). For the seventeenth-century Jewish quarters in Algiers, see Pancracio Celdrán Gomariz, "La judería de Argel según un manuscrito inédito del primer tercio del siglo XVII: El 3227 de la Biblioteca Nacional de Madrid," *Sefarad* 42 (1982): 327–55. On the Jews of Morocco, see Enrique Gozalbes Gravioto, "Los judíos de Marruecos en el siglo XVII según los viajeros europeos de la época," *El siglo XVII Hispano-Marroquí*, ed. Mohammed Salhi (Rabat: Facultad de Letras y Ciencias Humanas, 1997), 293–310.

18. On the Jewish-Muslim sociocultural dialogue in the Maghrib, especially in Fez and Algiers, see Haïm Zafrani, *Juifs d'Andalousie et du Maghreb* (Paris: Maisonneuve et Larose, 1996), and Michel Abitbol, "Juifs d'Afrique du Nord et expulsés d'Espagne après 1492," *Revue d'histoire des religions* (1993): 49–90. Many ordinances (*Taqqanot*) of the Sephardi in Fez and Algiers were composed in Spanish. See Simón Levy, "Arabófonos e hispanófolos (bəldiyin y 'azmiyin') en la Judería de Fez, dos siglos después de la expulsión," *El siglo XVII Hispano-Marroquí*, 333–51.

19. Sosa gives a detailed description of the abuses committed by Hasan Veneciano during his first government in *Epítome de los reyes de Argel* (*Topografía*, I: 377–90). See also de Grammont's translation, *Histoire des rois d'Alger* (Saint-Denis: Bouchène, 1998) 178–88.

20. Helen G. Friedman, *Spanish Captives in North Africa in the Early Modern Age* (Madison: University of Wisconsin Press, 1983), especially 71–72.

21. These Langues constituted the basis for the communal life and military organization of the Order. Each Langue was divided into various Grand Priories and these into Commanderies to which several knights were attached under the authority of the Commanders (Sire, 92).

22. After the epic victory of the Knights of Malta in the terrible siege of the island by the Ottomans and their allies (1564–1565), the popularity of the Knights of St. John soared in Europe. Various English plays attest to their historical importance, such as Marlowe's *The Jew of Malta* (1589), Kyd's *Soleman and Perseda* (1590), Webster's *The White Devil* (1612) and *The Devil's Law Case* (1617), and Fletcher's *The Knight of Malta* (1618), a collaborative effort with Massinger and Field. See Peter F. Mullany, "The Knights of Malta in Renaissance Drama," *Neuphilologische Mitteilungen* 2, 74 (1978): 297–310. In Spain, Lope de Vega, among others, wrote various plays about the Knights of Malta, such as *La pérdida honrosa y caballeros de San Juan*, and *El valor de Malta*; see Ch. Faliu and J. P. Lasalle, "'El Valor de Malta' de Lope de Vega (?): Traitement dramatique et référent historique," *Las órdenes militares en el Mediterráneo Occidental (S. XII–XVIII)*, Coloquio Las Órdenes Militares en el Mediterráneo Occidental, Madrid, 4–6 May 1983 (Madrid: Casa de Velásquez, 1989), 341–58, and Juan Manuel Rozas, "Lope de Vega y las órdenes militares (notas sobre el sentido histórico de su teatro)" *Las órdenes militares en el Mediterráneo Occidental (S. XII–XVIII)*, Coloquio Las Órdenes Militares en el Mediterráneo Occidental, Madrid, 4–6 May 1983 (Madrid: Casa de Velásquez, 1989) 359–67. In 1626, Lope requested admittance into the Order of St. John of Malta from Pope Urbanus VIII, obtaining the titles of Frey and Doctor as an old man.

23. Antonio González de Torres, *"captivi et in manibus infidelium"* [a captive and in hands of the infidel], was still in Algiers in 1582, when Andreas de Saosa [sic] (Sosa or Sousa), liberated in March 1581, became his curator in Valletta. See folios

4v, 5, 31 f. 32v, 74, 166 v, 243 r., and 282 r. in the *Liber conciliorum Jean l' Evêque de la Cassière, Catalog of the Order of St. John*, compiled by Rev. J. Mizzi, 2 vols., II, Part 5, Archives 95–96 (Valletta: Malta National Library, 1979).

24. So far, there seem to be two Antonio*s* de Sosa or Sousa, related to the Order of St. John of Malta: a Frei [Fray] Antonio de Sousa, admitted as a knight on December 22, 1540, and another Antonio de Sosa apparently admitted in 1577, a name that seems to refer, however, to Emanuel de Sosa Coutinho. His brother Frei André, or Andreas de Sousa, was admitted as a knight on or before August 21, 1580. See Frei D. Manoel Pinto da Fonseca Teixeira de Souza, Pello Cavalheiro, and Joao Fereira de Sà Sarmento, Procurador anciano do Illm. Priorado de Portugal, *Lista/ alfabetica,/e memoria/dos/nomes, e appellidos dos cavalheiros/portugueses, que se a chao descritos no anti-/go livro de rodes, que principiou nadi-/ta ilha, e convento aos 30 de novem-/bro de 1503, e acabou nesta de Malta/aos 27. de novembro de 1599* (Malta: Anno 1747). I thank Comm. Frá John Edward Critien from the Order of Malta in Rome for his kind help in looking through these archives. On the Sosa Coutinho brothers, see Manoel Jozé da Costa Felgueiras Gayo, *Nobiliário de famílias de Portugal*, 12 vols. (Braga: Carvalhos de Basto, 1989; fac. da 1 ed. 1938), IX. 2: 244.

25. The mistaken notion that Dr. Sosa was from Córdoba derives from a document composed by the Trinitarians, which mentions a certain Antonio de Sosa from Córdoba among the Christian slaves who could not be ransomed in 1580 because of their death, absence, or apostasy (Pérez Pastor, I: 74–80). Pérez Pastor, however, does not confuse this man with Dr. Antonio de Sosa. He lists them separately and gives Dr. Sosa a Portuguese origin, according to his name (I: 235–36).

26. This letter, composed by Dr. Antonio de Sosa, was signed by Dr. Sosa and twenty-eight other captives, including Miguel de Cervantes Saavedra. It is included in Fray Bernardo de Vargas, *Cronica sacri/et militaris ordinis/B. Mariae de Mercede,/ redemptionis captivorum* (Panormi, 1622) II: 106–09. Its Spanish translation appears in Fray Francisco de Neyla, *Gloriosa/fecundidad/de Maria/en el campo de la/católica iglesia* (Barcelona: Rafael Figueró, 1698), 190–95. I thank María Concepción Lois Cabello from the Biblioteca Nacional de Madrid for her help in getting copies of these letters. For a modern reproduction of this memorial, see Cristóbal Pérez Pastor, *Documentos cervantinos*, II: 379–80.

27. A letter dated May 8, 1577, written by Jean l'Evesque de la Cassière to the viceroy of Sicily, congratulates him on his appointment and mentions the loss of the galley *San Pablo* (Archivo General de Simancas, Estado, leg. 1.147, doc. 85).

28. Zuñiga "to the King," Naples, 9 June 158, AGS, Estado, legajo 1.084; quoted by Sola and de la Peña, 182.

29. See Emanuel d'Aranda, *Relation de la captivité et liberté du sievr Emanuel d'Aranda, iadis esclaue à Alger. Où se trouuent plusieurs particularitez de l'Affrique, dignes de remarque* (Paris: Par la Compagnie des Libraires du Palais, 1665), now reedited as Emanuel d'Aranda, *Les captifs d'Alger*, ed. Latifa Z'Rari (Paris: J.-P Rocher, 1997). There were numerous editions and translations of this work. I have also consulted the English translation, *The History of Algiers and Its Slavery: with Many Remarkable Particularities of Africk, Written by the Sieur Emanuel d'Aranda, Sometime a Slave There; English'd by John Davies* . . . (London: Printed for John Starkey, 1666).

30. This man should not be confused with Cristóbal de Villalón, author of *El Crotalón* and the *Diálogo de las transformaciones de Pitágoras*, who was born in 1505 (Astrana Marín, III: 48–51). Apparently, various writers in early modern Spain con-

cealed themselves under this name. *Maestro* Cristobal de Villalón, who testifies on behalf of Cervantes in 1580, claims that he was born in 1535 and met Cervantes in 1576; his title reveals he was a doctor of theology.

31. Miguel de Cervantes, Prólogo, *Novelas ejemplares*, ed. Harry Sieber, 2 vols. (Madrid: Cátedra, 1988), I: 52. For the English translation, see Miguel de Cervantes, Prologue to his *Exemplary Novels*, trans. B.W. Ife, 4 vols. (Warminster, UK: Aris & Phillips Ltd., 1992), I: 5.

32. For the representation of the Islamic Other, especially in England, see Samuel C. Chew's classic work, *The Crescent and the Rose: Islam and England during the Renaissance* (New York: Oxford University Press, 1937), especially 100–49, and William Montgomery Watt, *Muslim–Christian Encounters: Perceptions and Misperceptions* (London: Routledge, 1991). Daniel J. Vitkus provides an excellent synthesis of the Western demonization of the Turks in his Introduction to *Three Turk Plays from Early Modern England:* Selimus, A Christian Turned Turk, *and* The Renegado (New York: Columbia University Press, 2000), 1–53.

33. Pierre Dan, *Histoire de Barbarie, et de ses corsaires. Des royavmes, et des villes d'Alger, de Tvnis, de Salé, & de Tripoly. Divisée en six livres. Ov il est traitté de leur governement, de leurs moeurs, de leur cruautez, de leur brigandages, de leur sortilèges, et plusieurs autres particularitez remarquables. Ensemble des grandes misères et de crvels tourmens qu'enduren les Chrestiens captifs parmy ces infidels*, 2. Ed. Reueuë & augm. de plusieurs pieces, par le mesme autheur (Paris: Chez P. Rocolet, 1649).

34. Chantal de la Véronne, "Les frères Gasparo Corso," in *Les sources inédites de l'histoire du Maroc de 1530 à 1845* [SIHM], Première série, dynastie sa'dienne (1539–1560), archives et bibliothèques d'Espagne, ed. Chantal de la Véronne, 3 vols. (Paris: Paul Geuthner, 1961), t. III (1560–1578), III: 157–65, and several letters and reports by Francisco and Andrea Gasparo Corso, in SIHM, Première série, dynastie sa'dienne, Espagne, III: 166*ff.* A fascinating view of the Gasparo Corsos' activities in the Maghrib and Spain is offered by Dahiru Yahya, *Morocco in the Sixteenth Century: Problems of Patterns in African Foreign Policy* (Atlantic Highlands, NJ: Humanities Press, 1981), 46–55.

35. In *El trato de Argel*, the unnamed "king" [*beylerbey*] of Algiers appears as a money-grubbing, irascible man who orders the death by *bastinado* of a Christian captive caught while attempting to escape (*Trato*, IV.2338–53).

36. The lavish wedding is described by Cervantes in Act III of *Los baños de Argel*. See *Los baños de Argel*, in Miguel de Cervantes, *Obras completas*, ed. Florencio Sevilla Arroyo and Antonio Rey Hazas, 18 vols. (Madrid: Alianza, 1998), 14. On the relations between the historical character of Zoraida and Cervantes's *La historia del cautivo* and *Los baños de Argel*, see the classic article by Jaime Oliver Asín, "La hija de Agi Morato en la obra de Cervantes," *Boletín de la Real Academia Española* 27 (1947–1948): 245–39.

37. See Fray Luis Nieto's account of the conflicts and combats between the Sharifs, *Relación de las Guerras de Berbería* (1578), in *Colección de documentos inéditos para la historia de España* [CODOIN] (Madrid: 1891), 100: 411–58. The anonymous French translation of this manuscript, entitled *Histoire véritable des dernières guerres advenues en Barbarie*, was published in Paris in 1579 and reprinted in Henry de Castries et al. (eds.), SIHM, Première série, dynastie sa'dienne (1530–1660), archives et bibliothèques de France, 2 vols., t. I, Paris: 1905; t. II, Paris, 1908, I: 436–505.

38. 'Abd al-Malik left Algiers in December 1575, with six thousand Turkish riflemen, one thousand soldiers, subjects to the king of Kuko [Kabylia], and eight hun-

dred cavalry forces, and he was joined by an additional sixty thousand Berbers and Moors who adhered to his cause (*Topografía*, I: 368).

39. French medic Guillaume Bérard, who saved 'Abd al-Malik's life during an epidemic in Constantinople, later became his friend. When 'Abd al-Malik acceded to the throne, Bérard was appointed consul of France in Morocco. See "Provisions de l'office de consul de France au Maroc en faveur de Guillaume Bérard," in SIHM, ed. Henry de Castries et al, France, Première série, dynastie sa'dienne (1530–1660), I: 367–69.

40. See Mercedes García Arenal, "Textos españoles sobre Marruecos en el siglo XVI: Fray Juan Bautista y la *Crónica [. . .] de Mulley Abdelmelec*," *Al-Qantara* II (1981): 168–92. For 'Abd al-Malik's early career and short reign, see Yahya, 46–91; on the ruler's exile in Algiers, see Sola and de la Peña, 100–34. Various documents and letters of the Moroccan sultan have been reproduced by Chantal de la Véronne, ed., SIHM, Première série, dynastie sa'dienne (1539–1560), archives et bibliothèques d' Espagne, 3 vols. (Paris: Paul Geuthner, 1961), t. III (1560–1578), III: 166–89.

41. On Pīrī Re'īs's extraordinary achievements as a cartographer and a scientist of navigation, see *The Encyclopedia of Islam*, new edition, 9 vols. (Leiden: E.J. Brill, 1995), VIII: 308–9, hereafter cited parenthetically in the text as *EI-2*. Copies of Pīrī Re'īs's world maps are to be found in the Topkapi Palace library in Istanbul. See *EI-2* IX: 535–36.

42. *EI-2*, I: 832–42; see also "Suleiman the magnificent" in Will Durant, *The Reformation: A History of European Civilization from Wycliff to Calvin: 1300–1564*, vol. 6 of *The Story of Civilization*, 10 vols. (New York: Simon and Schuster, 1957), VI: 714.

43. Faruk Bilici, "Les bibliothèques vakif-s à Istanbul au XVIe siècle," *Livres et lectures dans le monde Ottoman, Revue des mondes musulmans et de la Méditerranée* 87–88, Séries Histoire (Aix-en-Provence, 1999): 39–59; Lale Uluç, "Ottoman Book Collecting and Illustrated Sixteenth Century Shiraz Manuscripts," *Livres et lectures*, 85–107. In the seventeenth century, public libraries opened in Turkey, almost at the same time as in England, France, and Italy, with permanent funds with free access to the public (Hitzel, "Manuscrits, livres" 24–25).

44. Ibrâhîm Peçevi, *Peçevi Tarihi*, ed. Murat Uraz, 2 vols. (Istanbul: Nesriyat Yrudu, 1968–1969); quoted by Frédéric Hitzel, "Manuscrits, livres," 19–38. Hitzel discusses the literature read by Ottoman society from the sixteenth to the nineteenth century, including the popular poetry that coexisted alongside classic literature and "learned" poetry ("Manuscrits, livres," 32–36).

45. Published originally in Italian, as *Della descritione dell'Africa/et dell cose notabili/che quivi sono/per Giovanni Lioni Africano* (Venice, 1550), Leo Africanus's work was reedited again in 1554 by Giovanni Baptista Ramusio, in his *Navigazioni e viaggi*. See Jean-Léon l'Africain, *Description de l'Afrique*, trans. and ed. Alexis Epaulard et al., 2 vols. (Paris: Librairie d'Amérique et d'Orient Adrien-Maisonneuve, 1956). For the English translation, see *The History/and/Description of Africa/and/of the Notable Things Therein Contained,/written by/Al-Hassan Ibn-Mohammed Al-Wezaz Al-Fasi,/a Moor, Baptised as Giovanni Leone, but Better Known as/Leo Africanus,/Done into English in the Year 1600,/by/John Pory*, ed. Robert Brown, 3 vols. (London: Hakluyt Society, 1846). I shall cite both translations in the text. For Giovanni Batista Ramusio's *Navigazioni e viaggi*, see *Navigationi et viaggi*, Venice, 1563–1606, introd. R. A. Skelton and ed. George B. Parks (Amsterdam: Theatrum Orbis Terrarum, 1967–1970).

46. Around these theological colleges erected around the al-Karwiyyīn mosque, in this city of religion and learning, flourished what Jacques Berque has called "the School of Fās"; see his article, "Ville et Université. Aperçu sur l'histoire de l'École de Fās," in *Revue historique de droit français et étranger* 27 (1949): 64–117.

47. Nicolas Clénard "to Jacques Latomus," 9 April 1541, in *Correspondance de Nicolas Clénard*, ed. and trans. Alphonse Roersch, 3 vols. (Bruxelles: Palais des Académies, 1946), I: 171–82; for the French translation of this Latin letter, see *Correspondance* III: 118–31.

48. Defensive feelings regarding Koranic texts were still prevalent in 1846, when John Brown, the English editor of Leo's *Africa*, claimed that the authorities in Fez and other towns of Morocco "even object to the Christian visitors being allowed to buy any object in the bazaars which may happen to have a verse of the Koran on it" (*Africa*, III: 508).

49. On the theft of the sultan's library, see Mercedes García Arenal and Gerard Wiegers, *Entre el Islam y Occidente: Vida de Samuel Palache, judío de Fez* (Madrid: Siglo XXI, 1999), 112.

50. "*[La Valette] estoit un très bel homme,* [. . .] *parlant très bien en plusieurs langues, comme le* [. . .] *français, l'espagnol, grec, arabe, et turc* [. . .]. *Je l'ai vu parler toutes ces langues sans aucun truchement*" [La Valette was a very handsome man, (. . .) speaking various languages very well, such as (. . .) French, Spanish, Greek, Arabic and Turkish (. . .). I saw him speak all of these languages without any interpreter] (Brantôme, *Oeuvres complètes*, VI: 248).

51. In *Los baños de Argel*, where this plot is repeated, Don Lope is able to read the letter sent by the Moorish Zahara—the play does not specify whether it is written in Spanish or Arabic.

52. Bartholomeo Ruffino de Chiambery's account of the defeat of La Goleta and Tunis by the Turks, entitled *Sopra la desolatione della Goletta e forte di Tunisi: Insieme la conquista fatta de Turchi, de Regni di Fezza, e di Marocco*, remained unpublished. The work was dedicated to Duke of Savoy Filiberto Emanuele on 3 February 1577, and Cervantes wrote the laudatory sonnets for it (Astrana Marín, II: 527–28). *Sopra la desolatione* has been translated into French by Paul Sebag, "Une relation inédite sur la prise de Tunis par les turcs, en 1574," *Cahiers de la Tunisie* 16–18 (61-64, 71-72) (1968–1970): 8–250. For Cervantes's sonnets, see Miguel de Cervantes, *Poesías completas*, ed. Vicente Gaos, 2 vols. (Madrid: Castalia, 1981), II: 336–37.

53. On this custom, see Agustín G. de Amezúa, introduction to *Descripción general de África* by Luis del Mármol Carvajal (1573–1599), (Madrid: Consejo Superior de Investigaciones Científicas, 1953), I: 14–15. The cases cited above are discussed in *Noticias y documentos relativos a la historia y literatura recogidos por don Cristóbal Pérez Pastor*, vol. 10 of *Memorias de la Real Academia Española*, 13 vols. (Madrid: Imprenta y Estereotipia de Rivadeneira-Imprenta de la Revista de Legislación, 1870–1910), X : 353–54, 356–57, 366–68.

54. The renegades who returned to their country of origin, voluntarily or through capture by the Christians, would have to open an inquest before the Inquisition, giving a detailed account of their conversion to Islam and life in Barbary. See Benassar and Benassar, *Los cristianos de Allah*.

55. Carroll B. Johnson views Cervantes's statements in the *Información de Argel* as a construction, where one finds "the first character invented by Cervantes." See "La construcción del personaje en Cervantes," *Cervantes* 15 (1995): 8–31.

56. I am indebted in these pages to Emilio Sola and José F. de la Peña's sensitive discussion of the testimonies consigned in the *Información de Argel* (*Cervantes y la Berbería*, 227–59).

57. The testimonies collected by Sliwa in *Documentos de Miguel de Cervantes Saavedra* offer a revealing picture of the activities carried out by Leonor de Cortinas between 1575 and 1580 on behalf of her two sons (*Documentos*, 45–66).

58. The deed of ransom is in the Archivo Histórico Nacional, Madrid, AHN, *Libro de la redempçion*, fols. 182v-183r; see Astrana Marín, III: 89–91.

59. We can cite the case of Rodrigo Chaves, who stated on December 19, 1580, in Madrid that he had been a slave for six years in Constantinople and Algiers and that he owed two thousand three hundred *reales* to certain merchants who loaned him the money so that he could ransom himself (Sliwa, 115–16). In Algiers, Chaves found some merchants who financed his ransom.

60. *Los trabajos de Persiles y Sigismunda*, ed. Juan Bautista Avalle-Arce (Madrid: Castalia, 1970) Bk. IV, Ch. 14, 474. I shall hereafter refer to this edition parenthetically in the text, citing book, chapter, and page number (*Persiles*, IV, 14, 74).

61. Martha Lucia Aristizábal, "Aspectos psicológicos del secuestro," Unpublished paper, Fundación País Libre, Bogotá, Colombia, 23 November 1994.

62. Cervantes's ransom was completed with an individual donation of fifty *escudos* and by an additional fifty *escudos* spared by the Trinitarians. The ransomed captive undertook to pay the rest of the money (one thousand three hundred forty *doblas*) to the Order of the Holy Trinity (Astrana Marín, III: 89–91).

63. *The Inflation Calculator*, ed. S. Morgan Friedman, *www.westegg.com/inflation/infl.cgi/*, February 18, 2002.

64. See also Miguel Ángel de Bunes, *La imagen de los musulmanes y del Norte de África en la España de los siglos XVI y XVII: Los caracteres de una hostilidad* (Madrid: Hiperión, 1989), and García Arenal and de Bunes, *Los españoles y el Norte de África, siglos XV–XVIII*, 249.

65. Fray Prudencio de Sandoval, *Historia de la vida y hechos del Emperador Carlos V*, 3 vols. (Madrid: Atlas, 1955–1956), Book XXV, ch. 32, III: 208.

66. See Louis Combet, *Cervantès et les incertitudes du désir* (Lyon: Presses Universitaires de Lyon, 1980); Françoise Zmantar, "Cervantes y sus fantasmas de Argel," *Quimera*, 2 noviembre 1980, 31–37; by Zmantar also, "Qui es-tu Azán, Azán ou es-tu?," *Les personnages en question*, IV Colloque du S.E.L, Toulouse, 1–3 Décembre 1983 (Université de Tolouse-Le-Mirail: Service de Publications, 1984), 165–73; and Rosa Rossi, *Escuchar a Cervantes: Un ensayo biográfico* (Valladolid: Ámbito, 1988) and *Sulle trace di Cervantes: profilo inedito dell'autore del Chisciotte* (Roma: Editori Riunti, 1997); as well as Fernando Arrabal, *Un esclavo llamado Cervantes* (Madrid: Espasa-Calpe, 1996). Eduardo Urbina reviews Arrabal's book in "Historias verdaderas y la verdad de la historia: Fernando Arrabal vs. Stephen Marlowe," *Cervantes* 18 (1998): 158–69. Adrienne Martin discusses the "splendors and miseries" of the biographies of Cervantes published after Canavaggio (1986), in particular those of Arrabal (1996) and Rossi (1988), in "Hacia el Cervantes del siglo que termina," *Estudios de literatura española de los siglos XIX y XX: Homenaje a Juan María Díez Taboada* (Madrid: C.S.I.C., 1998), 617–22.

67. Ciriaco Morón Arroyo, *Nuevas meditaciones del Quijote* (Madrid: Gredos, 1976), 139.

Chapter 3

1. [To get rid of or to mitigate the cruel/weight of reality, he hid his head in dreams]. This is one of the many poems by Borges on soldier-creator Cervantes; "Un soldado de Urbina," in *El otro, el mismo, Jorge Luis Borges: Obra poética, 1923–1977*, ed. Carlos V. Frías (Buenos Aires: Emecé Editores, 1977), 193. For its English translation, see "A Soldier of Urbina," trans. Alaistair Reid, in *Jorge Luis Borges, Selected Poems*, ed. Alexander Coleman (New York: Viking Penguin, 1999), 79.

2. This chapter is a greatly expanded version of an earlier essay, "'Cuando llegué cautivo': Trauma and Testimony in *El trato de Argel*," in *Cervantes para el Siglo XXI/Cervantes for the 21st Century*, Commemorative Collection in Honor of Professor Edward Dudley, ed. Francisco LaRubia-Prado (Newark, DE): Juan de la Cuesta, 2001), 79–105.

3. Alberto Sánchez, "Aproximación al teatro de Cervantes," *Cervantes y el teatro*, Special issue of *Teatro: Cuadernos* 7 (1992): 11–30, especially 15.

4. Evidence of Cervantes's keen interest in the theater is found in the debate between the priest and the Canon of Toledo in *Don Quijote* I, 48; in Canto IV of *Viaje del Parnaso*, in the dialogue between Cervantes and Pancracio de Roncesvalles in *Adjunta al Parnaso*; and, above all, in the prologue to Cervantes's *Ocho comedias y entremeses* (1615).

5. The company of Angulo el Malo, called "Angulo y los *Corteses*," acted in Madrid in November 1582. Cervantes must have met this play manager in his endeavors around the stage. Originally from Córdoba, Angulo el Malo must be differentiated from Angulo el Bueno, cited in *El coloquio de los perros*, who was an actor [*representante*], "*el más gracioso que entonces tuvieron y ahora tienen las comedias*" [the funniest there ever was and now the plays have] (*Novelas ejemplares* II: 353); on these issues, see Astrana Marín, III: 299–300.

6. Vicente Gaos, Introduction to Cervantes, *Viaje del Parnaso*, in Cervantes, *Poesías Completas*, 2 vols., ed. V. Gaos (Madrid: Castalia, 1973), I: 38–42; see also Elias L. Rivers, *Suma cervantina*, ed. Juan Bautista Avalle-Arce (London: Támesis Books, 1973), 424–26; and by Rivers also, "Cervantes's *Journey to Parnassus*," *Modern Language Notes* 85 (1970): 243–48; on the autobiographical and burlesque dimensions of *Viaje del Parnaso*, see Jean Canavaggio, "La dimensión autobiográfica del *Viaje del Parnaso*," *Cervantes* 1.1 (1981): 29–41.

7. Portuguese dramatist Juan de Matos Fragoso (1608–1669) mentions the play *La bizarra Arsinda* "del ingenioso Cervantes" in his own drama *La corsaria catalana* [*The Female Corsair from Catalonia*]; quoted by Manuel Serrano y Sanz, *Apuntes para una biblioteca de escritoras españolas desde el año 1401 al 1883*, 4 vols., Biblioteca de Autores Españoles, 268–71 (Madrid: M. Rivadeneira, 1975), I: 169. Because Matos Fragoso often reworked earlier plays, he might have seen the text of Cervantes's drama or heard about it from people who saw it staged.

8. Geoffrey Stagg, "The Date and Form of *El Trato de Argel*," *Bulletin of Hispanic Studies* 30.120 (1953): 181–92; Franco Meregalli, "De *Los tratos de Argel* a *Los baños de Argel*," in *Homenaje a Casalduero*, ed. Rizel Pincus and Gonzalo Sobejano (Madrid: Gredos, 1972), 395–409. On the dating of *El trato* in 1583, see Astrana Marín, VII: 778–79 and Wardropper, who argued that regarding the dating of Cervantes's works, "each *Cervantista* has his favorite theories, almost never verifiable" (152); "Comedias," in Juan Bautista Avalle-Arce and Edward C. Riley, eds., *Suma cervantina* (London: Tamesis, 1973), 147–69.

9. See the affidavits subscribed in Madrid on 19 December 1580, in K. Sliwa, *Documentos de Miguel de Cervantes Saavedra* (Pamplona: Eunsa, 1999), 114–15, and Pérez Pastor, 1: 65–73.

10. Jean Canavaggio, *Cervantès dramaturge: Un théâtre à naître* (Paris: Presses Universitaires de France, 1977), 20–21.

11. On the early Spanish theater, including that of Cervantes, see Manuel Sito Alba, "El teatro en el siglo XVI," *Historia del teatro en España*, ed. José María Borque et al., 2 vols. (Madrid: Taurus, 1983), 1: 341–66; J.E. Varey, "El teatro en la época de Cervantes," *Cosmovisión y escenografía: El teatro español en el Siglo de Oro* (Madrid: Castalia, 1987), 205–16; and Bruce Wardropper, "Cervantes's Theory of the Drama," *Modern Philology* 52.4 (1955): 212–21. On the *Corrales*, see John J. Allen, "El corral de la Cruz: Hacia la reconstrucción del primer corral de comedias de Madrid," *El mundo del teatro español en el Siglo de Oro: Ensayos dedicados a John E. Varey*, ed. José María Ruano de la Haza, *Ottawa Hispanic Studies* 3 (Ottawa: Dovehouse, 1989), 21–34, and especially Allen's classic work, *El Corral del Príncipe, 1583–1744* (Gainesville: University Presses of Florida, 1983).

12. Prologue to *Ocho comedias y ocho entremeses nunca representados*, in Miguel de Cervantes, *Obra completa*, ed. Florencio Sevilla Arrollo and Antonio Rey Hazas, 18 vols. (Madrid: Alianza, 1998), 14: 12; hereafter cited in the text as *OC*, plus volume and page number. See also *Viaje del Parnaso*, in Cervantes, *Poseías completas*, ed. Vicente Gaos, 1: 182–83. Cervantes's drama *La Jerusalén* is probably the play entitled *La conquista de Jerusalén por Godofre de Bullón*, found by Stefano Arata; see his "Edición de textos y problemas de autoría: el descubrimiento de una comedia olvidada," in *La comedia*, ed. Jean Canavaggio (Madrid: Casa de Velázquez, 1995), 51–75. The play has been edited and published by Arata in *Criticón* 54 (1992): 9–112.

13. "Sus *Tratos de Argel*/Cervantes/hizo" [His *Life in Algiers*/Cervantes wrote]; Agustín de Rojas, *El viaje entretenido*, ed. J. Ressot (Madrid: Castalia, 1972), 152.

14. The play is mentioned both as *El trato de Argel* and *Los tratos de Argel*. The extant manuscript of the play found in Madrid's Biblioteca Nacional is entitled *Comedia llamada trato de Argel hecha por Miguel de Cervantes [. . .]* (MS 14630, BN). The text found by Antonio Sancha, included in his edition of *Viaje del Parnaso* (1784), is also entitled *El trato de Argel*. See Canavaggio, "A propos de deux 'Comedias' de Cervantès: Quelques remarques sur un manuscrit récemment retrouvé," *Bulletin hispanique* 68 (1966): 5–29.

15. Miguel de Cervantes, *Los trabajos de Persiles y Sigismunda*, ed. Juan Francisco Avalle-Arce (Madrid: Castalia, 1970), hereafter cited parenthetically in the text with book, chapter, and page numbers. See also the erudite edition of *Persiles* by Carlos Romero Muñoz (Madrid: Cátedra, 1997). For the English translation, see Cervantes, *The Trials of Persiles and Sigismunda*, trans. Celia Richmond Weller and Clark A. Colahan (Berkeley: University of California Press, 1989).

16. Sevilla Arroyo and Rey Hazas, Introduction to *Los baños de Argel*, in Miguel de Cervantes, *Obra completa*, *OC*, 14: xv. For the relationship between Cervantes and Lope, see Louise Fothergill-Payne, "*Los tratos de Argel*, *Los cautivos de Argel* y *Los baños de Argel*: Tres 'trasuntos' de un 'asunto,'" *El mundo del teatro español en el Siglo de Oro: Ensayos dedicados a John E. Varey*, ed. José María Ruano de la Haza, *Ottawa Hispanic Studies* 3 (Ottawa: Dovehouse, 1989), 177–96.

17. On the adaptation and staging of *Los baños de Argel* by Francisco Nieva, see the articles included in *Los baños de Argel de Miguel de Cervantes, un trabajo teatral de Francisco Nieva, música de Tomás Marco*, ed. José Monleón (Madrid: Centro

Dramático Nacional, 1980). For the production of and response to *La gran sultana*, see the appendix to *Cervantes y el teatro*, special edition of *Cuadernos de teatro cásico* 7 (1992): 197–231; also Luciano García Lorenzo "'La gran sultana' de Miguel de Cervantes: Adaptación del texto y puesta en escena," *Cervantes: Estudios en la víspera de su centenario*, 2 vols. (Kassel: Reichenberger, 1994), II: 401–32; and Susana Hernández Araico, "Estreno de *La gran sultana*: Teatro de lo otro, amor y humor," *Cervantes* 14.2 (1994): 155–65. Manuel Muñoz Carabantes studies the twentieth-century staging of Cervantes's plays in "El teatro de Cervantes a la escena española entre 1939 y 1991," *Cervantes y el teatro*, special edition of *Cuadernos de teatro cásico* 7 (1992): 140–95. On *La gran sultana*, see also George Mariscal's provocative article, "*La gran sultana* and the Issue of Cervantes's Modernity," *Revista de estudios hispánicos* 28.2 (1994): 185–211.

18. Adolfo Marsillac, Introduction to *La gran sultana*, in *Cervantes y el teatro*, *Cuadernos de teatro clásico* 7 (1992): 201–02. This same volume includes a series of articles on Cervantes's theater and ample information on the staging of *La gran sultana*.

19. See Ruano de la Haza's outstanding study, *La puesta en escena en los teatros comerciales del Siglo de Oro* (Madrid: Castalia, 2000), 31.

20. Teresa J. Kirschner, "Desarrollo de la puesta en escena en el teatro histórico de Lope de Vega," *Revista canadiense de estudios hispánicos* 15.3 (1991): 453–63. See also Victor Dixon, "La comedia de corral de Lope como género visual," *Edad de Oro* 5 (1986): 35–58; Aurora Egido, ed., *La escenografía en el teatro barroco* (Salamanca: Universidad de Salamanca, 1989); José Lara Garrido, "Texto y espacio escénico en Lope de Vega (La primera comedia: 1579-1597)," *La escenografía en el teatro barroco*, 91–126; J.E. Varey, *Cosmografía y escenografía: El teatro español en el Siglo de Oro* (Madrid: Castalia, 1987); and Ignacio Arellano, *Convención y recepción: Estudios sobre el teatro del Siglo de Oro* (Madrid: Gredos, 1999).

21. Cervantes's dramatic monologues or dialogues often let the actor know where he or she is supposed to be at the time, as illustrated by these lines for fugitive Per Álvarez: *"Entre estas matas quiero/asconderme, porque es entrado el día"* [I want to hide among these bushes, because it is already high day] (*Trato*, IV, 1986–1987).

22. Antonio Rey Hazas, "Las comedias de cautivos de Cervantes," *Los imperios orientales en el teatro del Siglo de Oro, Actas de las XVI Jornadas de Teatro Clásico, Almagro, julio de 1993*, ed. Felipe B. Pedraza Jiménez and Rafael González Cañal (Almagro: Universidad Castilla-La Mancha y Festival de Almagro, 1994), 29–56, especially 34.

23. Armando Cotarello y Valledor, *El teatro de Cervantes: Estudio crítico* (Madrid: Tipografía de la *Revista de archivos, bibliotecas y museos*, 1915): 188. On *Los tratos*, see also Francisco Induráin's Introduction to *Obras completas de Cervantes* (Madrid: Atlas, 1962), xxiii; and Zamora Vicente, "El cautiverio en la obra de Cervantes," *Homenaje a Cervantes*, II: 239–55.

24. André Green, *The Tragic Effect: The Oedipus Complex in Tragedy*, trans. Alan Sheridan (New York: Cambridge University Press, 1979); trans. of *Un oeil en trop, le complexe d'Oedipe dans la tragédie* (Paris: Éditions de Minuit, 1969).

25. *El trato de Argel*, in Miguel de Cervantes, *Obra completa*, eds. Florencio Sevilla Arroyo and Antonio Rey Hazas, *OC*, 2: 9–104, hereafter cited parenthetically as *Trato*, followed by act and verse number.

26. Plays began at 2 P.M. between October 1 and March 31 and at 4 P.M. the rest

of the year, and they lasted until the end of the day (Ruano de la Haza, *La puesta*, 38).

27. The anonymous author of *Viaje de Turquía [Journey to Turkey]* (c. 1550) confirms that only the Turks who were very zealous regarding their beliefs upheld this law. See the excellent scholarly edition of *Viaje de Turquía*, ed. Marie-Sol Ortola (Madrid: Castalia, 2000), as well as the revised edition by Fernando García Salinero (Madrid: Cátedra, 2000).

28. Alfonso X, el Sabio, *Las siete partidas*, ed. Santos Alfaro y Lafuente. Leyes Españolas (Madrid: Imprenta de LA LEY, 1867). See also J. E. Cirlot, *A Dictionary of Symbols*, trans. Jack Sage (New York: Philosophical Library, 1983); and on the number as a philosophical system, Vincent Foster Hopper, *Medieval Number Symbolism* (New York: Columbia University Press, 1938).

29. See the survey of late medieval and Renaissance doctrines on purgatory in Henry Sullivan's suggestive study, *Grotesque Purgatory: A Study of Cervantes's Don Quijote, Part II* (University Park, PA: Pennsylvania State University Press, 1996), 67–101. Sullivan demonstrates Cervantes's preoccupation with purgatory at the end of his life, as revealed in *Don Quijote* II.

30. Whether Cervantes read Dante is unknown. Besides the allusions to Dante's *Inferno* in *El trato*, there is a brief reference to "the famous Dante" in section 6 of *La Galatea*, and Friedrich finds "a distinct borrowing from the *Inferno* (or from the *Aeneid*)" in *Don Quijote* II, chap. 69 (quoted by Sullivan, 75).

31. Primo Levi, *If This Is a Man* and *The Truce*, trans. Stuart Woolf (London: Abacus, 1987); trans. of *Se questo e un uomo* (Turin: Einaudi, 1958); on Primo Levi, see *Reason and Light: Essays on Primo Levi*, ed. Susan R. Tarrow, Western Societies Program Occasional Paper No. 25 (Cornell University: Center for International Studies, 1990); and Myriam Anissimov, *Primo Levi: Tragedy of an Optimist*, trans. Steve Cox (Woodstock, NY: Overlook Press, 1999).

32. The lines recited by Aurelio in his soliloquy on the Golden Age (*Trato*, III.1331–36), seem to allude to Dante's *Inferno*. While canto XI of the *Inferno* portrays the usurers, cantos XXI–XIII revolve around the sin of fraud, described in these verses by Cervantes.

33. Angel G. Loureiro, *The Ethics of Autobiography: Replacing the Subject in Modern Spain* (Nashville: Vanderbilt University Press, 2000); Jorge Semprún, *L'écriture et la vie* (Paris: Gallimard, 1994), 34, translated as *Literature or Life*, trans. Linda Coverdale (New York: Viking, 1996).

34. Theodor Adorno, *Prism*, trans. Samuel Weber and Shierry Weber (London: Neville Spearman, 1967), 34. Other voices have joined Adorno, stressing different lines of thought. Following suit, Elie Wiesel states: "there is no such thing as literature of the Holocaust, nor can there be," *A Jew Today*, trans. Marion Wiesel (New York: Random House, 1978), 197–98. Among other exegeses of Adorno's remark, see Irving Howe, "Writing and the Holocaust," *New Republic* (October 27, 1986), 28–30; Sander Gilman, *Jewish Self-Hatred* (Baltimore: Johns Hopkins University Press, 1986), 319; Sidra DeKoven Ezrahi, *By Words Alone* (Chicago: Chicago University Press, 1980), xi; Ernst van Alphen, *Caught by History: Holocaust Effects in Contemporary Art, Literature, and Theory* (Stanford, CA: Stanford University Press, 1997); and Berel Lang, *Holocaust Representation: Art within the Limits of History and Ethics* (Baltimore: Johns Hopkins University Press, 2000).

35. Juan F. Sanz Sampleyano, "La demografía histórica en Andalucía," in *Demografía histórica en España*, ed. Vicente Pérez Moreda y David-Sven Reher

(Orán: El Arquero, 1988), 181–91; for the population of the Crowns of Castile and Aragon, see the chapters in this book; see also Jordi Nadal, *La población española (Siglos XVI a XX)* (Barcelona: Ariel, 1984); A. Moliné-Bertrand, *Au Siècle d'Or: L'Espagne et ses hommes. La population du Royaume de Castile au XVIe siècle* (Paris: Economica, 1985); I.A.A. Thompson and Bartolomé Yun Casalilla, eds., *The Castilian Crisis of the Seventeenth Century: New Perspectives on the Economic and Social History of Seventeenth-Century Spain* (Cambridge: Cambridge University Press, 1994).

36. Other allusions to the lingua franca in Cervantes appear in the novella *El amante liberal* (*OC*, 6: 543) and in his play *La gran sultana* (1.179–81).

37. Baltasar Fra Molinero, *La imagen del negro en el teatro del Siglo de Oro* (Madrid: Siglo XXI, 1995).

38. See Leo Spitzer's brilliant essay, "Linguistic Perspectivism in *Don Quijote,*" *Leo Spitzer: Representative Essays*, ed. Alban Forcione et al. (Stanford, CA: Stanford University Press, 1988), 225–71. Spitzer notes the difference between Turkish and Arabic words in Cervantes, the latter being nearly always connected with religion, specifically, with "things Christian" (257). Albert Mas stresses the contrast between the representations of Muslims by Cervantes and those of other early modern authors who launched virulent attacks and insults against Islam. Cervantes rejects Islam but never describes it in undignified terms. The Turks, however, are painted in a crude way. Cervantes particularly criticizes their attraction for young boys, which becomes a leitmotif in his work; Albert Mas, *Les turcs dans la littérature espagnole du Siècle d'Or*, 2 vols. (Paris: Centres de Recherches Hispaniques, 1967), I: 287–335, especially 319, 334–35.

39. *I sommersi e i salvati* (Turin: Enaudi, 1986) was completed shortly before Primo Levi's tragic death; see Primo Levi, *Los hundidos y los salvados*, trans. Pilar Gómez Bedate (Barcelona: Muchnik, 1995), and its English translation, *The Drowned and the Saved*, trans. Raymond Rosenthal (New York: Summit Books, 1988).

40. I am indebted in these lines to Luce López-Baralt's splendid article, "El cálamo supremo (al-qalam al-'Alà) de Cide Hamete Benengeli," *Mélanges María Soledad Carrasco Urgoiti*, ed. Abdeljelil Temimi, 2 vols. (Zagouan: Foundation Temimi pour la Recherche Scientifique et l'Information, 1999), II: 343–61. Annemarie Schimmel explains that "a central theme of Koranic mythology is the concept of the *lawh al-mafūz*, the Well-Preserved Tablet, on which the destinies of men have been engraved since the beginning of time"; *Mystical Dimensions of Islam* (Chapel Hill: University of North Carolina Press, 1975), 414.

41. Jerónimo Gracián de la Madre de Dios was Santa Teresa's confessor and close collaborator. Captured by Barbary corsairs during a trip to Italy, he remained captive in Tunis for two years (1593–1595). He recounted his captivity in *Peregrinación de Anastasio*, in *Escritos de Santa Teresa, añadidos e ilustrados por Don Vicente de la Fuente*, ed. Vicente de la Fuente, 2 vol. (Madrid: M. Ribadeneira, 1861–1862), II: 452–74. See also Robert Ricard, "Le père Jérome Gratien de la Mère de Dieu et sa captivité à Tunis (1593–1595)," *Revue africaine* 89 (1945): 190–200.

42. Pedro Calderón de la Barca, *El príncipe constante*, ed. Alberto Porqueras Mayo (Madrid: Espasa-Calpe, 1975); the play was staged in Madrid around 1629.

43. Philippe Lacoue-Labarthe, *La poésie comme expérience* (Paris: Bourgois, 1986), 30; see also his etymology of *expérience*, from the Latin *experiri*, "to undergo"; the radical is *periri*, which one encounters in *peril*, "danger," and its relation to *per*, "crossing" (30, n. 6).

44. The list is staggering, but see, among others, Robert J. Lifton, *The Broken Connection: On Death and the Continuity of Life* (New York: Basic Books, 1983); Roger S. Gotlieb, ed., *Thinking the Unthinkable: Meanings of the Holocaust* (New York: Paulist Press, 1990); Geoffrey H. Hartman, "On Traumatic Knowledge and Literary Studies," *New Literary History* (1995): 537–63; Cathy Caruth, ed., *Trauma: Explorations in Memory* (1995), and by Caruth also, *Unclaimed Experience: Trauma, Narrative, and History* (1996); Shoshana Felman and Dori Laub, *Testimony: Crises of Witnessing in Literature, Psychoanalysis, and History* (1992); and Dominick LaCapra, *Writing History, Writing Trauma* (Baltimore: Johns Hopkins University Press, 2001).

45. On the splitting of the ego, see Freud, "Fetishism" (1927), *The Standard Edition of the Complete Psychological Works of Sigmund Freud* [*SE*], trans. and ed. James Strachey, 24 vols. (London: Hogarth Press, 1974), XXI: 149–57; "The Splitting of the Ego in the Process of Defense" (1940), *SE* XXIII: 271–78; and *An Outline of Psychoanalysis* (1940), *SE* XXIII: 141–207, especially 201. See also J. Laplanche and J.-B. Pontalis, *The Language of Psychoanalysis*, trans. Donald Nicholson-Smith (New York: Norton, 1973).

46. See Melanie Klein, "Notes on some Schizoid Mechanisms" (1946), *The Selected Melanie Klein*, ed. Juliet Mitchell (New York: Free Press, 1986), 175–200.

47. Juan de Balcázar recalls the names of some of Cervantes's companions in this venture: "Don Francisco de Meneses, who was a Captain in la Goleta for his Majesty; don Beltrán; Ensign Ríos; Sergeant Navarrete; and another gentleman called Osorio, and another gentleman whose name was Castañeda" (*Información de Argel*, 102).

48. *Topografía*, II: 91–92, 101–06, 123–25, 173–87. The third part of this work, entitled *Diálogo de los Mártires de Argel*, describes the tortures suffered by Christian captives at the hands of the Algerians; see Antonio de Sosa, *Diálogo de los mártires de Argel*, ed. Parreño and Sola, and the same work in *Topografía*, III: 27–192.

49. *El "informe secreto" de Mateo Alemán sobre el trabajo forzado en las minas de Almadén*, ed. Germán Bleiberg (London: Tamesis, 1985); and also by Bleiberg, "Mateo Alemán y los galeotes," *Revista de Occidente* 39 (1966): 330–63.

50. Vicente Graullera Sanz, *La esclavitud en Valencia en los siglos XVI y XVII* (Valencia: Instituto Valenciano de Estudios Históricos, Institución Alfonso el Magnánimo, Diputación Provincial, Consejo Superior de Investigaciones Científicas, 1978). See also Luis Fernández Martín, S.J., *Comediantes, esclavos y moriscos en Valladolid, Siglos XVI y XVII* (Valladolid: Universidad de Valladolid, Caja de Ahorros y M. P. de Salamanca, 1988).

51. *Relación* de Miguel de Cuneo, *Cartas de particulares a Colón y relaciones coetáneas*, ed. Juan Gil and Consuelo Varela (Madrid: Alianza, 1984), 235–60, especially 245.

52. Paul Bamford, *Fighting Ships and Prisons: The Mediterranean Galleys of France in the Age of Louis XIV* (Minneapolis: University of Minnesota Press, 1973), 178.

53. Mármol Carvajal, *De la descripción del África*, I: 23; the story of Androcles by Aulus Gelius is told by Seneca, *De beneficiis* 2.19.1, in Seneca, *Works: English & Latin Selections*, trans. John W. Basore, 3 vols., Loeb Classical Library (Cambridge, MA: Harvard University Press, 1928–1935), vol. 3. Pedro Mexía recounts other classic legends about lions in his *Silva de varia lección*, ed. Antonio Castro, 2 vols.

(Madrid: Cátedra, 1989) 1: 541–51. Mexía's *Silva*, Part II, probably inspired the love story in Cervantes's play *Los baños de Argel*. See Dámaso Alonso, "*Los baños de Argel* y la *Comedia del degollado*," *Revista de filología española* 24 (1937): 213–18.

54. Sturgis E. Leavitt, "Lions in Early Spanish Literature and on the Spanish Stage," *Hispania* 44.2 (1961): 272–76.

55. See Ruano de la Haza's excellent chapter on "Los animales en los corrales de comedias," in *La puesta en escena de los teatros comerciales del Siglo de Oro*, 271–85.

56. Cervantes was aware of the presence of lions in chivalric literature, as proven by the "Adventure of the Lions" in *Don Quijote* II, 17). His allusion to the legend of Manuel de León reinforces this point. The historic Manuel de León became famous at the time of the Catholic monarchs for entering a lion's cage to pick up a glove thrown by a lady, a feat mentioned in *Don Quijote*, I, 49, and recounted in various ballads, such as in Juan de Timoneda's *Rosa gentil* (1573).

57. Shemaryahu Talmon, "Daniel," *The Literary Guide to the Bible*, ed. Robert Alter and Frank Kermode (Cambridge, MA: Harvard University Press,1987), 343–46.

58. San Isidoro de Sevilla, *Etimologías*, Edición bilingüe, trans. José Oroz Reta and Manuel-A. Marcos Casquero, 2 vols. (Madrid: Biblioteca de Autores Cristianos, 1993), XII, 2, 5; see also Cesáreo Bandera Gómez, "El sueño del Cid en el episodio del león," in *El "Poema de Mio Cid": poesía, historia, mito* (Madrid: Gredos, 1969), 82–114.

59. Quintilian's classic definition of allegory is from his *Institutio oratoria* VIII, vi, 44, trans. H.E. Butler, 4 vols., Loeb's Classical Library (Cambridge, MA: Harvard University Press, 1980), III: 400; Sebastián de Covarrubias follows Quintilian's definition in his *Tesoro de la lengua castellana o española* (Madrid, 1611); see also Heinrich Lausberg, *Manual de retórica literaria: Fundamentos de una ciencia de la literatura*, trans. José Pérez Rico, 3 vols. (Madrid: Gredos, 1980), II: § 895, 285. For allegory in the Spanish tradition, see Louise Fothergille-Payne, *La alegoría en los autos y farsas anteriores a Calderón* (London: Tamesis, 1977).

60. Angus Fletcher, *Allegory: The Theory of a Symbolic Mode* (Ithaca: Cornell University Press, 1964); see also Edwin Honing, *Dark Conceit: The Making of Allegory* (London: Faber and Faber, 1959); Stephen J. Greenblatt, ed., *Allegory and Representation* (Baltimore: Johns Hopkins University Press, 1981); Paul de Man, "Pascal's Allegory of Persuasion," in *Allegory and Representation*, ed. Stephen J. Greenblatt, 1–23; Joel Fineman, "The Structure of Allegorical Desire," in *Allegory and Representation*, ed. Stephen J. Greenblatt, 26–60; and Carolyne Van Dyke, *The Fiction of Truth: Structures of Meaning and Dramatic Allegory* (Ithaca: Cornell University Press, 1985).

61. Mieke Bal, *Reading Rembrandt: Beyond the Word–Image Opposition* (Cambridge: Cambridge University Press, 1991), 83.

62. For the connections between trauma and Freud's article "Creative Writers and Day-Dreaming," see Monique Schneider, *Le trauma et la filiation paradoxale* (Paris: Ramsay, 1988), 58. Schneider's splendid study has influenced my reading of trauma in these pages.

63. J.B. Pontalis, *Entre le rêve et la douleur* (Paris: Gallimard,1977), 261–62. See also Michèle Bertrand, *La pensée et le trauma: Entre psychanalyse et philosophie* (Paris: Editions L'Harmattan, 1990).

64. Dori Laub and Nanette Auerhahn, "Knowing and Not Knowing: Massive Psychic Traumatic Memory," Fortunoff Video Archives for Holocaust Testimonies,

Yale University, *Bulletin trimestriel de la Foundation Auschwitz* 44–45 (1994): 69–95. The inability of trauma victims to form narratives of traumatic experience is studied by Jodie Wigren, "Narrative Completion in the Treatment of Trauma," *Psychotherapy* 31.3 (1994): 415–23.

65. Sandor Ferenczi, "Réflexions sur le traumatisme," *Oeuvres complètes* IV: 1927–1933, trans. Coq Héron et al., 4 vols, *Psychanalyse* 4 (Paris: Payot, 1982), IV: 139–47; see also his thoughts on trauma and fantasy in "Notes et fragments," *Psychanalyse* 4, IV: 287–89.

66. For this double motif in *El trato*, see Edward Friedman's fine study "Cervantes's Dramatic Development: From *Los tratos de Argel* to *Los baños de Argel*," *The Unifying Concept: Approaches to the Structure of Cervantes's* Comedias (York, SC: Spanish Literature Publication Company, 1981), 61–79.

67. On the renegade in Cervantes as a marginal frontier figure associated with deviant sexuality, see Paul Julian Smith, "'The Captive's Tale': Race, Text, Gender," *Quixotic Desire: Psychoanalytic Perspectives on Cervantes*, ed. Ruth El Saffar and Diana de Armas Wilson (Ithaca: Cornell University Press, 1993), 227–35.

68. Edward C. Riley, "*Los pensamientos escondidos* and *figuras morales* of Cervantes," *Homenaje a William L. Fitcher*, ed. A. David Kossov and José Amor y Vázquez (Madrid: Castalia, 1971), 623–31.

69. Fray Melchor de Zúñiga O.S.F., *Descripción de la República de la ciudad de Argel*, Madrid, Biblioteca Nacional, ms. 3227, fol 136, v°–141 r°; reproduced in *Judeoconversos y moriscos en la literatura del Siglo de Oro, Actas del "Grand Séminaire" de Neuchâtel, Neuchâtel, 26 a 27 de mayo de 1994*, ed. Irene Andres-Suárez (Paris: Diffusion Les Belles Lettres, 1995), 184–86.

70. On conversion to Islam, see Mercedes García Arenal, "Les conversions d'européens à l'islam dans l'histoire: Esquisse générale," and Miguel Ángel de Bunes Ibarra, "Reflexiones sobre la conversión de los renegados en los siglos XVI y XVII," cited in chapter 2. On homosexuality in Cervantes's Algerian plays *El trato de Argel* and *Los baños de Argel*, see Adrienne Martin, "Images of Deviance in Cervantes's Algiers," *Cervantes* 15 (1995): 5–15.

71. Casalduero speaks of the "spiritual unity" of the play in his *Sentido y forma del teatro de Cervantes* (Madrid: Gredos, 1966), 220.

72. Enrique Fernández has recently studied the testimonial and therapeutic aspects of Cervantes's play; "*Los tratos de Argel*: Obra testimonial, denuncia política y literatura terapéutica," *Cervantes* 20.1 (2000): 7–26.

73. Anne Uberfeld, *Lire le théâtre*, 2 vols., 2nd ed. (1977–1981; reprinted Paris: Belin, 1996), I: 41; translated as *Reading Theater*, trans. Frank Collins, ed. Paul Perron and Patrick Debbèche (Toronto: University of Toronto Press, 1999).

74. Nelly Furman, "The Language of Pain in *Shoah*," *Auschwitz and After: Race, Culture, and the "Jewish Question" in France*, ed. Lawrence D. Kritzman (New York: Routledge, 1995), 299–312, especially 299.

75. For the significance of the name *Saavedra* in relation to Algiers, see Françoise Zmantar, "Miguel de Cervantes y sus fantasmas de Argel," *Quimera* 2 (Barcelona, 1980): 31–37, and the expanded version of this article, "Saavedra et les captifs du *Trato de Argel* de Miguel de Cervantes," *L'autobiographie dans le monde hispanique, Actes du Colloque International de la Baume-lès-Aix, 11-13 Mai, 1979* (Aix-en-Provence: Université de Provence, 1980), 185–203.

76. Cathy Caruth, "An Interview with Robert Jay Lifton," in Cathy Caruth, ed., *Trauma: Explorations in Memory* (Baltimore: Johns Hopkins University Press,

1995), 128–47, especially 137; on trauma and splitting of the ego, see also Lifton, "Survivor Experience and Traumatic Syndrome," *The Broken Connection: Death and the Continuity of Life* (New York: Basic, 1983), 163–78.

77. On Cervantes's admiration for Garcilaso, see José Manuel Blecua, "Garcilaso y Cervantes," *Sobre Poesía de la Edad de Oro* (Madrid: Gredos, 1970), 151–60.

Chapter 4

1. [Nothing of importance that took place in this affair has escaped my memory or ever will, so long as I live] *The Captive's Tale* (*DQ* I, 40).

2. See, among others, Luis Andrés Murillo, *The Golden Dial: Temporal Configuration in Don Quijote* (Oxford: Dolphin Book Co., 1975), 76; for the relations of this phrase with Cervantes's imprisonment in Seville, see Francisco Rodríguez Marín, "La cárcel donde se engendró el *Quijote*," *Estudios cervantinos* (Madrid: Atlas, 1947), 65–92; Astrana Marín, V: 226–42; and Emilio Orozco Diaz, *Cervantes y la novella de barroco*, 119-21.

3. Miguel de Cervantes, *Los trabajos de Persiles y Sigismunda*, ed. Juan Bautista Avalle-Arce (Madrid: Castalia, 1970), book I, chapter I, 51. For the translation, see Cervantes, *The Trials of Persiles and Sigismunda*, trans. Celia Richmond Weller and Clark A. Colahan (Berkeley: University of California Press, 1989), 17. I shall cite parenthetically in the text the page of the Spanish edition first, followed by that of its English translation (51–52/17).

4. John J. Allen, "Autobiografía y ficción: El relato del Capitán Cautivo (*Don Quijote* I, 39–41)," *Anales Cervantinos* 15 (1976): 149–55.

5. Jacques Derrida, *Otobiographies: L'enseignement de Nietzsche et la politique du nom propre* (Paris: Galilée, 1984). Its English translation, *The Ear of the Other,* is a new ed. of this text, followed by two round-table discussions on autobiography and translation. See *The Ear of the Other: Otobiography, Transference, Translation,* ed. Christie McDonald, trans. Peggy Kamuf (Lincoln: University of Nebraska Press, 1988). The following pages closely follow Derrida's lineaments.

6. Geoffrey Bennington and Jacques Derrida, *Jacques Derrida*, trans. Geoffrey Bennington (Chicago: University of Chicago Press, 1999), 148.

7. Derrida, "Coming into One's Own," in Geoffrey Hartman, ed., *Psychoanalysis and the Question of the Text* (Baltimore: Johns Hopkins University Press, 1985), 144–48.

8. Christopher Norris, *Derrida* (Cambridge, MA: Harvard University Press, 1987), 211.

9. Francisco Márquez Villanueva, *Personajes y temas del Quijote* (Madrid: Tauros, 1975), 98–99.

10. On these dates, see Allen, "Autobiografía," 2; *El ingenioso hidalgo Don Quijote de la Mancha*, ed. Francisco Rodríguez Marín, 10 vol. (Madrid: Atlas, 1947–1949), III: 171, n. 3; Astrana Marín, II: 387–88; and Francisco Ayala, "La invención del Quijote," *Los Ensayos: Teoría y Crítica Literaria* (Madrid: Aguilar, 1972), 654. On *La historia del cautivo*, see Allen, "Autobiografía"; Edward C. Riley, "Episodio, novela, y aventura en *Don Quijote*," *Anales Cervantinos* 5 (1955–1956): 209–30; Márquez Villanueva, *Personajes y temas*, 92–140; Juergen Hahn, *"El capitán cautivo*: The Soldier's Truth and Literary Precept in *Don Quijote*, Part I," *Journal of His-*

panic Philology 3 (1979): 269–73; and Luis Andrés Murillo, "Cervantes's *Tale* of the Captive Captain," *Florilegium Hispanicum: Medieval and Golden Age Studies Presented to Dorothy Clotelle Stark*, ed. J.S. Geary et al. (Madison, WI: Hispanic Seminary of Medieval Studies, 1983), 229–43. Jaime Oliver Asín discusses the historicity of *The Captive's Tale* in his classic article "La hija de Agi Morato," *Boletín de la Real Academia Española* 27 (1947–1948): 245–339.

11. Luis Andrés Murillo, "El *Ur-Quijote*: Nueva hipótesis, " *Cervantes* 1 (1981): 43–50; see also by Murillo, "The Chronology of Composition," in *The Golden Dial: Temporal Configuration in Don Quijote* (Oxford: Dolphin Book Co., 1975), especially 72–98.

12. Miguel might have met Gonzalo Cervantes Saavedra in the Battle of Lepanto. Astrana Marín suggests that Cervantes and Gonzalo de Cervantes Saavedra might have gone to school together in Córdoba during the 1550s (1: 331–35); see also Francisco Rodríguez Marín, "Los Cervantes cordobeses que no son parientes del autor del 'Quijote,' lo son en grado lejano," *Estudios Cervantinos* (Madrid: Atlas, 1947), 158–64.

13. On this mission, see Jean Cazanave, "Cervantès à Oran, 1581," *Société de géographie et d'archéologie d' Oran* 43 (1923): 215–42.

14. Augustin Redondo, "Moros y moriscos en la literatura española de los años 1550–1580," *Judeoconversos y moriscos en la literatura del Siglo de Oro, Actas del "Grand Séminaire" de Neuchâtel, Neuchâtel, 26 a 27 de mayo de 1994*, ed. Irene Andres-Suárez (Paris: Diffusion Les Belles Lettres, 1995), 51–83; the phrase quoted is from 59.

15. See the classic articles by Jean Cazanave, "*El gallardo español* de Cervantes (1)" *Langues néo-latines* 126 (1953): 5–17, and "*El gallardo español* de Cervantes (2)," *Langues néo-latines* 127 (1953): 3–14; also Frederick A. de Armas, "Los excesos de Venus y Marte en *El gallardo español*," *Cervantes: Su obra y su mundo, Actas sobre el I Congreso Internacional sobre Cervantes*, ed. Manuel Criado de Val (Madrid: Edi 6, 1978), 249–59; William A. Stapp, "*El gallardo español*: La fama como arbitrio de la realidad," *Cervantes: Su obra y su mundo, Actas sobre el I Congreso Internacional sobre Cervantes*, ed. Manuel Criado de Val (Madrid: Edi 6, 1978), 261–72; Stanislav Zimic, "*El gallardo español*," in *El teatro de Cervantes* (Madrid: Castalia, 1992), 87–117; Gethin Hughes, "*El gallardo español*: A Case of Misplaced Honor," *Cervantes* 13 (1993): 65–75; E. Michael Gerli, "Aristotle in Africa: History, Fiction and Truth in *El gallardo español*," *Cervantes* 15 (1995): 43–57; and María Soledad Carrasco Urgoiti, "*El gallardo español* como héroe fronterizo," *Actas del Tercer Congreso Internacional de Cervantistas, Gala Galdana, Menorca, 20–25 de octubre de 1997* (Palma: Unversitat de Islas Baleares, 1998), 571–81.

16. See Mercedes García Arenal and Miguel Ángel de Bunes, *Los españoles en el norte de África, siglos XV–XVIII* (Madrid: Editorial Mapfre, 1992), 238–55 and 257–74, and Beatriz Alonso Acero, *Orán-Mazalquivir, 1589–1639: Una sociedad española en la frontera de Berbería* (Madrid: Consejo Superior de Investigaciones Científicas, 2000).

17. Ginés Pérez de Hita, *Guerras Civiles de Granada*, ed. Shasta Bryant (Newark, DE: Juan de la Cuesta, 1982), 308–11; "Romance de Sayavedra," *Romancero viejo*, ed. Mercedes Díaz Roig (Madrid: Cátedra, 1988), 75. Ramón Menéndez Pidal's study of this ballad is still essential; *Estudios sobre el Romancero español* (Madrid: Espasa-Calpe, 1970), 155–63 and 463–88.

18. On the Saavedra family, consult the outstanding article by Rafael Sánchez

Saus, "Los Saavedra y la frontera con el reino de Granada en el siglo XV," *Estudios sobre Málaga y el reino de Granada en el V centenario de la conquista* (Málaga: Servicio de Publicaciones, Diputación Provincial de Málaga, 1987), 163–82.

19. Victor Turner, "Betwixt and Between: The Liminal Period in Rites of Passage," in *The Forest of Symbols: Aspects of Ndembu Ritual* (Ithaca, NY: Cornell University Press, 1967), 93–230, especially 93–95.

20. Cervantes probably used the surname *Saavedra* for the first time in Algiers, in a letter written in Latin by Antonio de Sosa to Pope Gregory XIII and various European rulers in 1580. Among the twenty-nine signatures of captives from various nations is that of Miguel Cervantes *Saavedra*. This *Memorial*, which attested to the heroic behavior of ransomer monk Jorge de Olivar, was reproduced by Pérez Pastor II: 379–80; see Antonio de Sosa "to Gregorio XIII," in Fray Bernardo de Vargas, *Cronica sacri et militare ordinis B. Mariae de Mercede, redemptionis captivorvm* [. . .] (Panormi, 1622), 107–09; also included in Fray Francisco de Neyla, *Gloriosa fecundidad de la Virgen María en el campo de la Católica Iglesia* [. . .] (Barcelona, 1698), 191–95.

21. See the documents collected by Pérez Pastor for 1587, 1588, and 1589, where the author is called *Cervantes de Saavedra, Cervantes de Sayavedra,* and/or *Cervantes Saavedra* (Pérez Pastor II: 98-110*ff;* Sliwa, 147*ff*). Curiously, when Cervantes's sister Magdalena becomes the curator of his natural daughter Isabel, after her mother's death in 1599, Magdalena states that she is the daughter of the *"licenciado Cervantes de Saavedra,"* deceased (Pérez Pastor I: 136). Because surgeon Rodrigo de Cervantes did not bear the surname *Saavedra,* an explanation for this slip of the pen could be that Miguel de Cervantes himself was now regularly using the name Saavedra as his second last name or that Magdalena was trying to protect the illegitimate child's name by suggesting that *Saavedra* was a family name. On Saavedra, consult Françoise Zmantar, "Miguel de Cervantes y sus fantasmas de Argel," *Quimera,* 2 December 1980: 31–37.

22. Cervantes calls Vélez de Guevara *"quitapesares"* [trouble-soother] and speaks affectionately of him: *"Topé a Luis Vélez, lustre y alegría/y discreción del trato cortesano,/y abracéle, en la calle, a medio día"* [I ran into Luis Vélez/glory and delight/and pattern of courteous manners,/and I embraced him, in the street, at noon] (vv. 394–96); *Viaje del Parnaso,* ed. Vicente Gaos, I: 175. See also Forrest Eugene Spencer and Rudolph Schevill, *The Dramatic Works of Luis Vélez de Guevara: Their Plots, Sources, and Bibliographies,* University of California Publications in Modern Philology, vol. 19 (Berkeley: University of California Press, 1937).

23. *Sotomayor* was a surname used by members of the Cervantes branch from Córdoba: it belonged to Alonso Cervantes de Sotomayor, a brother of Gonzalo Cervantes Saavedra. Cervantes's sister Luisa changed her name to Luisa de Belén in February 1565, when she entered the Carmelite convent in Alcalá de Henares (Astrana Marín, I: 25, 443–52) and Magdalena became Magdalena de Jesús (Canavaggio, *Cervantes,* 117).

24. Like many others in his family, Nicolás de Ovando took the name of his ancestor, the famous Governor of Hispaniola (1502–1509). Ovando's father, jurist Luis Carrillo, was a Knight of Santiago and a member of the King's Council. He had received the surname of his mother Catalina Carrillo, who was the daughter of Captain Bernal Francés, a celebrated captain in the armies of the Catholic monarchs (Astrana Marín, II: 44–45). On Spanish surnames, see Ángel de los Ríos's classic

study, *Ensayo histórico etimológico y filológico sobre los apellidos castellanos desde el siglo X hasta nuestra edad* (Madrid: Imprenta de M. Tello, 1871).

25. Isabel was the daughter of actress Ana Franca. The letter-contract of dowry was signed on August 28, 1608, and Isabel's marriage was celebrated on September 8. Isabel was probably never legitimized, although subsequently, she would identify herself in official documents with her two patronymics, Isabel de Cervantes y Saavedra; Pérez Pastor, *Documentos cervantinos*, I: 131–37, 147–55, 164–68ff. For her testament (1631), see Pérez Pastor, I: 199–210.

26. Sigmund Freud, prologue to the second edition of *The Interpretation of Dreams*, SE IV: xxvi.

27. On the death of Freud's father and its effect on his creations, see Didier Anzieu's admirable work, *Freud's Self-Analysis*, trans. Peter Graham (Madison, CT: International Universities Press, 1986), 160–74.

28. Eliott Jaques, "Death and the Mid-Life Crisis," *International Journal of Psycho-Analysis* 46 (1965): 502–14; Didier Anzieu, *Le corps de l'oeuvre* (Paris: Gallimard, 1981), 30–31.

29. See Mary Douglas's classic work, *Purity and Danger: An Analysis of Concepts of Pollution and Taboo* (New York: Praeger, 1966).

30. Robert Jay Lifton, *The Future of Immortality and Other Essays for a Nuclear World* (New York: Basic Books, 1987), 200.

31. Between 1597 and 1590, Cervantes's work took him near Córdoba and Montilla, where he could have met Inca Garcilaso. In September 1587, following royal orders, the king's purveyor, Miguel de Cervantes Saavedra, seized stock of bread and grain belonging to the Church of Écija, for which he was excommunicated (Canavaggio, *Cervantes*, 144–47). In Montilla, the Cabildo had previously opposed the sending of another commissioner from Córdoba who was to recruit forces for the armada. On July 19, 1587, the Cabildo chose Garcilaso de la Vega to represent them before the king and requested the commissioner be forbidden from entering Montilla. See Raúl Porras Barrenechea, *El Inca Garcilaso en Montilla (1561–1614)* (Lima: San Marcos, 1955), and John Varner, *El Inca: The Life and Times of Inca Garcilaso* (Austin: University of Texas Press, 1968), 292–94.

32. Max Hernández, *Memoria del bien perdido: Conflicto, identidad y nostalgia en el Inca Garcilaso de la Vega* (Lima: Instituto de Estudios Peruanos, 1993), 99–111.

33. When some of these *solares* became towns, the families whose surnames came from them were careful to establish the seniority of the *solar* in rapport to the town. See Alonso de Ercilla: "los anchos muros del solar de Ercilla; solar antes fundado que villa" [the thick walls of the ancestral home of Ercilla; founded before it became a villa]; *La Araucana*, ed. Marcos Morínigo and Isaías Lerner, 2 vols. (Madrid: Castalia, 1987), Canto 27, II: 228.

34. Cervantes, "El retablo de las maravilla," in Miguel de Cervantes, *Entremeses*, ed. Eugenio Ascension (Madrid: Castalia, 1980), 176–82.

35. *El amante liberal*, in Miguel de Cervantes, *Novelas ejemplares*, ed. Harry Sieber, 2 vol. (Madrid: Cátedra, 1998), I: 135–88; for the scene described here, see especially 181.

36. See Miguel de Cervantes Saavedra, *L'ingénieux hidalgo don Quichotte de la Manche*, Trad. de Louis Viardot, avec des déssins de Gustave Dorée, gravés par H. Pisan, 2 v. (Paris: Librairie de L. Hachette et cie, 1863).

37. Diego Pérez de Vargas was a historical personage from the times of Fernando III el Santo (1199–1252). The story recounted by Don Quijote appears in Diego

Rodríguez de Almela, *Valerio de las historias escolásticas y de España*, and in a ballad by Lorenzo de Sepúlveda; see *Don Quijote*, I, ed. Murillo, I: 131, n. 12.

38. Ginés Pérez de Hita, *Historia de los zegríes y abencerrajes (Primera parte de las Guerras civiles de Granada)*, ed. Paula Blanchard-Demouge (Madrid: Imprenta de E. Bailly-Baillière, 1913); reprint, ed. Pedro Correa (Granada: Universidad de Granada, 1999), 283. The legendary story is retold by Lope de Vega in his early play *Los hechos de Garcilaso de la Vega* (1579–1583) and restaged in his play *El cerco de Santa Fe e ilustre hazaña de Garcilaso*, where the mythical duel between Garcilaso and the Moor Tarfe is reenacted. The legend, however, may be significant only as an indication of the reverence this family commanded in the kingdom of Castile. See Bernard Giovate, *Garcilaso de la Vega* (Boston: Twayne Publishers, 1975).

39. Prologue to the *Novelas ejemplares*, ed. Harry Sieber, 2 vols. (Madrid: Cátedra, 1988), I: 52.

40. The poetic and festive nature of Cervantes's language in *La Gitanilla* is studied in my article, "Poetic Language and the Dissolution of the Subject in *La Gitanilla* and *El licenciado Vidriera*," *Caliope* 2 (1996): 85–104.

41. Michel Moner, "Du conte merveilleux a la pseudo-autobiographie: Le récit du Captif (*Don Quichotte*, I, 39–41)," *Écrire sur soi en Espagne: Modèles et écarts: Actes du XII Colloque International d'Aix-en-Provence (4-5-6 décembre 1986)* (Aix-en-Provence: Université de Provence, 1988), 57–71. Moner sees the Captive's tale as a fragmented story refracted in a broken mirror (59–60).

42. See Georges Cirot, "Le cautivo de Cervantès et Notre Dame de Liesse," *Bulletin hispanique* 38 (1936): 378–83.

43. Unless otherwise noted, I will refer to *El ingenioso hidalgo Don Quijote de la Mancha*, ed. Luis Andrés Murillo, 2 vol. (Madrid: Castalia 1978). For the English translation, see Miguel de Cervantes Saavedra, *The History of That Ingenious Gentleman Don Quijote de la Mancha*, trans. Burton Raffel, introduction by Diana de Armas Wilson (New York: Norton, 1995).

44. Another example of these name changes: In the play *El rufián dichoso* [*The Happy Ruffian*], Cristóbal de Lugo takes the name of Padre de la Cruz after embracing monastic life, while his valet Lagartija [Wall Lizard] becomes Fray Antonio.

45. Américo Castro, *El pensamiento de Cervantes* (Barcelona: Noguer, 1972), 143. Ruth El Saffar interprets *La historia del cautivo* as a "love story" in which the characters "are able to interact creatively" (*Beyond Fiction*, 77); see also Franco Meregalli, "De los *Tratos de Argel* a *Los baños de Argel*," in *Homenaje a Casualdero: Crítica y poesía, ofrecido por sus discípulos* (Madrid: Gredos, 1972), 395–409; E. González López "Cervantes, maestro de la novela histórica contemporánea: La *Historia del Cautivo*," *Homenaje a Casalduero*, 183–84.

46. For other adverse criticism of Zoraida, see Cirot, "Le Cautivo de Cervantès et Notre Dame de Liesse," 381–82; and Márquez Villanueva, *Personajes y temas*, 115–34.

47. Louis Combet, *Cervantès ou les incertitudes du désir* (Lyon: Presses Universitaires de Lyon, 1980), 133 and 176. See also E. Michael Gerli, "Rewriting Myth and History: Discourses of Race, Marginality and Resistance in *The Captive's Tale* (*Don Quijote*, I, 37–42)," *Refiguring Authority: Reading and Writing, and Rewriting in Cervantes*, Studies in Romance Languages 39 (Lexington, Kentucky: University Press of Kentucky, 1995), 40–60.

48. Helena Percas de Ponsetti, *Cervantes y su concepto del Arte* (Madrid: Gredos, 1975), 243–57; Ciriaco Morón Arroyo, "La historia del cautivo y el sentido del *Quijote*," *Iberoromania* 18 (1983): 91–105; Alison Weber, "Padres e hijas: Una lectura

intertextual de *La historia del cautivo*," Actas del Segundo Coloquio International de la Asociación de Cervantistas, Alcalá de Henares 6–9 nov. 1989 (II-CIAC) (Barcelona: Anthropos, 1991): 425–31.

49. María Antonia Garcés, "Zoraida's Veil: The 'Other' Scene of *The Captive's Tale*," *Revista de estudios hispánicos* 23.1 (1989): 65–98; see also by Garcés the revised version of this article, "Cervantes's Veiled Woman," *The New Norton Critical Edition of Don Quijote*, trans. Burton Raffel, ed. Diana de Armas Wilson (New York: Norton, 1998), 821–30.

50. Karl-Ludwig Selig, "Cervantes: 'En un lugar de . . .'," *Modern Language Notes* 86 (1971): 266–68.

51. On Hājjī Murād and his daughter, see Jaime Oliver Asín's essential study, "La hija de Agi Morato," *Boletín de la Real Academia Española* 27 (1947–1948): 245–339.

52. See also Canavaggio, "Agi Morato entre historia y ficción," *Cervantes: Entre vida y creación* (Alcalá de Henares: Biblioteca de Estudios Cervantinos, 2000), 39–44.

53. While Oliver Asín and Márquez Villanueva consider *Los baños de Argel* to have been written in 1588 as a draft of *La historia del cautivo*, others, such as Astrana Marín, Aldo Ruffinato, and Canavaggio, situate the piece after 1608, because it follows Lope's play *Los cautivos de Argel* (1599) and includes events that occurred between 1601 and 1608 (Canavaggio, *Cervantès dramaturge*, 21–23). On the female captive in Cervantes, see Jean Canavaggio, "La captive chrétienne, des *Tratos de Argel* aux *Baños de Argel*: Traditions et récréation cervantine," *Images de la femme en Espagne au XV et XVII siècles: Des traditions aux renouvellements et à l'émergence d'images nouvelles, Colloque International (Sorbonne et Collège d'Espagne, 28–30 septembre 1992)*, ed. Augustin Redondo (Paris: Publications de la Sorbonne, 1994), 213–25.

54. Their only child, called Muley Ismā'il, was born in March 1575. The news arrived in Philip II's court through a letter from Francisco Gasparo Corso, written on March 23, 1575. Gasparo Corso informed the king that 'Abd al-Malik had just had a son (Oliver Asín, 265).

55. Canavaggio calculates that the 500 gold *escudos* paid for Cervantes's liberation would have been equivalent, in 1989 moneys, to U.S. $17,000 (*Cervantes*, 315–16). This amount would be approximately U.S. $24,500 for the year 2001.

56. Julia Kristeva, "Freud and Love: Treatment and its Discontents," *Tales of Love*, trans. Leon S. Roudiez (New York: Columbia University Press, 1987), 21–56, especially 37.

57. Marina Warner, *Alone of All Her Sex: The Myth and Cult of the Virgin Mary* (New York: Knopf, 1976), 236–54. Works by painters in early modern Spain, such as Velázquez, El Greco, Zurbarán, and Murillo, attest to the efforts to depict Mary as the heavenly apparition that transcends death, as illustrated by Velázquez's painting *La inmaculada concepción*.

58. On Cervantes's special devotion to the Virgin, see Américo Castro, *El pensamiento de Cervantes*, 245–328; Agustín G. de Amezúa y Mayo, *Cervantes: Creador de la novela corta española*, 2 vols. (Madrid: Consejo Superior de Investigaciones Científicas, 1957), I: 122–26; Alban Forcione, *Cervantes and the Humanist Vision: A Study of Four Exemplary Novels* (Princeton, NJ: Princeton University Press, 1982), 327–33; and Ángel Valbuena Prat, "Cervantes, escritor católico," *Estudios de literatura religiosa española* (Madrid, 1964): 127–42.

59. Jacqueline Rose, "Feminine Sexuality—Jacques Lacan and the *école*

freudienne," Sexuality in the Field of Vision (London: Verso, 1986), 49–81, especially 72.

60. On the role of the *Other* in the constitution of the subject, see Bruce Fink, *The Lacanian Subject* (Princeton, NJ: Princeton University Press, 1995), 1–23.

61. On the status of the woman as fantasy in relation to the desire of the man, see Jacques Lacan, *Encore*, in *Feminine Sexuality*, ed. Juliet Mitchell and Jacqueline Rose, trans. Jacqueline Rose (New York: Norton, 1983), especially 136–48 and 149–61.

62. Julia Kristeva, "Stabat Mater," *Tales of Love*, trans. Leon S. Roudiez (New York: Columbia University Press, 1987), 234–63.

63. This autobiographical passage reiterates Cervantes's testimony in *La información de Argel*: *"el rei Haçan hera tan cruel que por solo huirse un cristiano, é porque alguno le encubriese ó le favoresciese en la huida, mandaua ahorcar vn hombre, ó por lo menos cortarle las orejas y las narices"* [the king Hasan was so cruel that, merely because a Christian tried to escape, and because someone might cover up for him or help him in this escape, he would order a man to be hanged, or, at least, he would have his ears and nose cut off] (*Información*, 53).

64. *Signifiance* can be translated as "significance," especially since this term carries the connotation of covert rather than ostensible meaning. I have retained the French *signifiance*, nevertheless, in part to avoid other connotations. *Signifiance*, as Kristeva uses this term, alludes to operations that are both fluid and archaic, in the sense Freud gave to this latter word in his *Introductory Lectures to Psychoanalysis* (Lecture 13). To paraphrase Leon S. Roudiez, *signifiance* refers to work performed in language (through the miscellaneous articulation of semiotic and symbolic dispositions) that permits a text to signify what representative and communicative speech does not express; see his introduction to Julia Kristeva, *Desire in Language: A Semiotic Approach to Literature and Art*, ed. Leon S. Roudiez (New York: Columbia University Press, 1980), 18.

65. In *Beyond the Pleasure Principle*, Freud suggests that in traumatic neurosis, the compulsion to repeat arises from an earlier inability to experience the feeling that should have corresponded to the trauma. Repetitive dreams about, or repetitive reenactments of, the trauma, then, are "endeavoring to master the stimulus retrospectively, by developing the anxiety whose omission was the cause of the trauma neurosis" (SE, 18: 32); this is what Lifton calls "failed enactment," an incapacity to feel what should have been but was not experienced (*Broken Connection*, 174).

66. Situated in the inlet by that name, La Goleta was the fortress that protected the port of Tunis, considered inexpugnable once Charles V took the city in 1535. The Arab and Berber land forces were calculated by Cervantes to be about four hundred thousand troops, obviously an error. Sosa stated that in July 1574, Ramadān Pasha sent Ottoman commander Alūj Ali nine galleys packed with troops, artillery, and munitions for the assault of Tunis and La Goleta (*Topografía*, 1: 367–68).

67. On these defeats, see the letter addressed by Don Juan de Austria to Cardinal Granvelle on August 3, 1574, lamenting Don Pedro Puertocarrero's poor defense of these positions, and the reports by Don Juan de Zanoguera on the defeats of La Goleta and the fort of Tunis; these documents are reproduced by Francisco Rodríguez Marín in "La pérdida de la Goleta y el fuerte," Apéndice XVIII, *El ingenioso hidalgo Don Quijote de la Mancha*, ed. Rodríguez Marín, 10 vols. (Madrid: Atlas, 1949), IX: 240–42, 242–61; Archivo General de Simancas (AGS), Secretaría de Estado, legajo 450.

68. Pedro De Aguilar's name is listed in the *Memorias del cautivo en la Goleta de Túnez*, ed. Pascual de Gayángos (Madrid: Sociedad de Bibliófilos Españoles, 1875). Astrana Marín alluded to other men with the same name, such as a certain Pedro de Aguilar who witnessed Isabel de Cervantes or Isabel de Saavedra's last testament on September 19, 1652 (II: 419).

69. Americo Castro, *Cervantès* (Paris, 1931), 18; cited by Oliver Asín, 314.

70. A letter from the marquis of Pescara and Viceroy of Sicily to Philip II, written on December 24, 1570, states that the hospitals in Palermo were crowded with the sick from La Goleta (cited by Braudel, *Mediterranean*, II: 861).

71. Some other famous *desterrados* were Felipe de Borja, the natural brother of Maestro de Montesa; the Duke of Veraguas, Almirante de las Indias; and Don Gabriel de la Cueva (1555), all named by Diego Suárez in his memoirs of Orán (cited by Braudel, *Mediterranean*, II: 862).

72. As mentioned in chapter 2, Bartholomeo Ruffino de Chiambery wrote a history of the fall of La Goleta and Tunis, entitled *Sopra la desolatione della Goletta e forte di Tunisi: Insieme la conquista fatta de Turchi, de Regni di Fezza, e di Marocco*, which remained unpublished in Italian. This work, however, was translated into French and published by Paul Sebag, "Une relation inédite sur la prise de Tunis par les turcs, en 1574," *Cahiers de la Tunisie* 16–18 (61-64, 71-72) (1968–1970): 8–250. Cervantes's sonnets are included in Miguel de Cervantes, *Poesías completas*, ed. Vicente Gaos, 2 vols. (Madrid: Castalia, 1981), II: 336–37.

73. The phallus signifies this mark where language is joined to desire. See Lacan, "The Signification of the Phallus," *Ecrits*, 287–88.

Chapter 5

1. [A time may come, perhaps, when I shall tie up this broken thread and say what I failed to here and what would have been fitting.] Miguel de Cervantes, *Los trabajos de Persiles y Sigismunda*, ed. Juan Bautista Avalle-Arce (Madrid: Castalia, 1970); for the English translation, see Cervantes, *The Trials of Persiles and Sigismunda*, trans. Celia Richmond Weller and Clark A. Colahan (Berkeley: University of California Press, 1989). I shall parenthetically cite the original Spanish by page numbers, followed by the page numbers of the English version. See also the fine edition of *Los trabajos de Persiles y Sigismunda* by Carlos Romero Muñoz (Madrid: Cátedra, 1997).

2. Primo Levi, *Moments of Reprieve* (New York, 1986), 10–11.

3. Dori Laub, "Trauma and Testimony: The Process and the Struggle," in Cathy Caruth, *Trauma: Explorations in Memory*, 61–99; the quotation is from 63. I acknowledge my debt to Dori Laub, whose work has deeply touched me. In addition, I have been influenced by the work of Cathy Caruth, *Unclaimed Experience: Trauma, Narrative, and History* (Johns Hopkins University Press, 1996).

4. Testimony of pilot Pedro Griego and other sailors from the galley *San Pablo*, Archivo General de Simancas (AGS), Estado, leg. 1073, doc. 82–83.

5. Testimony of Domingo Sponto, AGS, Guerra Antigua, doc. 84.

6. See "Working-off Mechanisms" in *The Language of Psychoanalysis*, ed. Jean Laplanche and J.-B. Pontalis, trans. Donald Nicholson-Smith (New York: Norton, 1973), 486–87, and Daniel Lagache, "La psychanalyse et la structure de la personalité," *La psychanalyse* VI (1961): 5–54. In the long process of his literary testimonies to,

and reelaboration of, his captivity, Cervantes might have approximated the mechanisms of working off.

7. *La española inglesa*, in Cervantes, *Novelas ejemplares*, ed. Harry Sieber, 2 vols. (Madrid: Cátedra, 1988), I: 253–54; for its English translation, see Cervantes, *The English Spanish Girl*, in Cervantes, *Exemplary Novels*, trans. R. M. Price, ed. B.W. Ife, 4 vols. (Warminster: Aris & Phillips Ltd., 1992), II: 19. I shall parenthetically cite the original Spanish with its initials *EI* (*Española inglesa*), citing the volume (I) and page number, followed by its English version, identified as *ES* (*English Spanish-Girl*), with its volume (II) and page numbers.

8. Ruth El Saffar, *Novel to Romance: A Study of Cervantes's* Novelas ejemplares (Baltimore: Johns Hopkins University Press, 1974), 161; for El Saffar's study of *La española inglesa*, see 150–62.

9. Aurora Egido, "La memoria y el arte narrativo del *Persiles*," *Nueva revista de filología hispánica* 2 (1990): 621–41; see also her book *Cervantes y las puertas del sueño: Estudios sobre* La Galatea, El Quijote *y* El Persiles (Barcelona: Promociones y Publicaciones Universitarias, 1994), where this article is reproduced (285–06).

10. As Avalle-Arce notes, the famous initial lines of *Don Quijote* are a parody of early modern notarial language, such as *"Diversas personas viejas e antiguas de cuyos nombres no se acuerda"* [Diverse old and ancient persons, whose names he does not remember], used in affidavits and notarized documents. See Avalle-Arce, "Tres comienzos de la novela," *Papeles de Son Armadans* 110 (1965): 181–214.

11. These words recall those of El Pinciano: *"la materia es larga para el poeta, porque en tantos años de peregrinación se pueden ingerir muchos y muy largos episodios"* [The matter is long for the poet, because in so many years of travel (peregrinations) many and very long episodes can occur]; Alonso López Pinciano, *Philosofía antigua poética*, ed. Alfredo Carballo Picazo, 3 vols. (Madrid: Consejo Superior de Investigaciones Científicas, 1953), II: 357.

12. The "false captives" constituted a plague in early modern Spain; their aim was to collect alms or donations to pay for their fake ransom. The problem is discussed by contemporary literary works, such as the anonymous *Viaje de Turquía*, ed. Fernando García Salinero (Madrid: Cátedra, 2000); Cristóbal Pérez de Herrera, *Amparo de los pobres*, ed. Michel Cavillac (Madrid: Espasa-Calpe, 1975), 34; and Diego Galán, *Cautiverio y trabajos de Diego Galán*, ed. Manuel Serrano y Sanz (Madrid: Sociedad de Bibliófilos Españoles, 1913), 435–36.

13. Those sentenced to public disgrace were paraded, half-naked and on donkeys, through the Spanish towns while the executioner or town crier beat them with lashes.

14. For the discussion of literary precepts in *Persiles*, see Alban Forcione, *Cervantes, Aristotle and the Persiles* (Princeton, NJ: Princeton University Press, 1970), especially 276–77; also by Forcione, *Cervantes's Christian Romance: A Study of Persiles y Sigismunda* (Princeton, NJ: Princeton University Press, 1972), especially 136–37. On *Persiles*, see also Diana de Armas Wilson's classic work, *Allegories of Love: Cervantes's Persiles and Sigismunda* (Princeton, NJ: Princeton University Press, 1991).

15. Donald W. Winnicott, "The Location of Cultural Experience," in *Playing and Reality* (London: Routledge, 1971), 95–103, especially 97; see also by Winnicott, "The Concept of Trauma in Relation to the Development of the Individual within the Family," in *Psycho-Analytic Explorations*, ed. Claire Winnicott et al. (Cambridge,

MA: Harvard University Press, 1989), 130–48; and, by the same author, "Fear of Breakdown," in *Psycho-Analytic Explorations*, 87–95.

16. The dating of this work has elicited many hypotheses: Among other critics, Avalle-Arce proposes that books I and II of *Persiles* were composed between 1599 and 1605, and books III and IV between 1612 and 1616; see his Introduction to *Persiles* (Madrid, 1973), 14–20. For his part, Carlos Romero Muñoz has suggested that this novel was initiated in Seville after the publication of the *Filosofía antigua poética* by El Pinciano (1596), that book II was composed around 1598–1599, the last two books after 1614, and the conclusion of *Persiles,* written in the last months of Cervantes's life; see Romero Muñoz's Introduction to *Persiles* (1997), 17–31. For an overview of these critical positions, consult Isabel Lozano Renieblas, *Cervantes y el mundo del Persiles* (Alcalá de Henares: Biblioteca de Estudios Cervantinos, 1998), 19–49.

17. See Américo Castro, "Los prólogos del *Quijote*," *Hacia Cervantes* (Madrid: Taurus, 1967), 262–301; Elias Rivers, "Cervantes's Art of the Prologue," *Estudios literarios de hispanistas norteamericanos dedicados a Helmut Hatzfeld*, ed. J.M. Solà-Solé et al. (Barcelona: Hispam, 1974), 167–71; and Jean Canavaggio, "Cervantes en primera persona," *Cervantes: Entre vida y creación* (Alcalá de Henares: Centro de Estudios Cervantinos, 2000), 65–83.

18. Of the Three Parcae or Fates, Clotho, Lachesis, and Atropos, the last one was in charge of cutting the thread of life, a topic much favored by Cervantes, who refers to it in his plays *El rufián dichoso* (II, vs. 1651), *El trato de Argel* (III, vs. 1518), and *La Numancia* (II, vs. 874).

Bibliography

"Documentos para la puesta en escena de *La Gran Sultana* de Miguel de Cervantes por la Compañía Nacional de Teatro Clásico en Sevilla, el 6 de Septiembre de 1992." *Cervantes y el teatro. Cuadernos de teatro clásico* 7 (1992): 197–231.

Abi-Ayad, Ahmed. "El cautiverio argelino de Miguel de Cervantes." *Notas y estudios filológicos* 9 (1994): 12–17.

Abitbol, Michel. "Juifs d'Afrique du Nord et expulsés d'Espagne après 1492." *Revue d'histoire des religions* (1993): 49–90.

Abun-Nasr, Jamil M. *A History of the Maghrib in the Islamic Period.* Cambridge: Cambridge University Press, 1987.

Adorno, Theodor. *Prism.* Trans. Samuel Weber and Shierry Weber. London: Neville Spearman, 1967.

Albuquerque, Martim de, et al., eds. *Portugal and the Order of Malta: A European Perspective.* Lisboa: Inapa, 1998.

Alfonso X, el Sabio. *Las siete partidas.* Ed. Santos Alfaro y Lafuente. Madrid: Imprenta de LA LEY, 1867.

Allen, John J. "Autobiografía y ficción: El relato del Capitán cautivo (*Don Quijote* I, 39–41)." *Anales Cervantinos* 15 (1976): 149–55.

———. "El Corral de La Cruz: Hacia la reconstrucción del primer corral de comedias de Madrid." *El mundo del teatro español en el Siglo de Oro: Ensayos dedicados a John E. Varey.* Ed. José María Ruano de la Haza. Ottawa Hispanic Studies 3. Ottawa: Dovehouse, 1989. 21–34.

———. *El Corral del Príncipe, 1583–1744.* Gainesville, FL: University Press of Florida, 1983.

Alonso Acero, Beatriz. *Orán-Mazalquivir, 1589–1639: Una sociedad española en la frontera de Berbería.* Madrid: Consejo Superior de Investigaciones Científicas, 2000.

Alonso, Dámaso. "*Los baños de Argel* y *La comedia del degollado*." *Revista de filología española* 24 (1937): 213–18.

Alphen, Ernst van. *Caught by History: Holocaust Effects in Contemporary Art, Literature, and Theory.* Stanford, CA: Stanford University Press, 1997.

Amezúa y Mayo, Agustín González de. *Cervantes: Creador de la novela corta española.* 2 vols. Madrid: Consejo Superior de Investigaciones Científicas, 1957.

———. "Introducción." *Descripción general de África de Luis del Mármol Carvajal* (1573–1599). Vol. 1. Madrid: Consejo Superior de Investigaciones Científicas, 1953.

Anissimov, Myriam. *Primo Levi: Tragedy of an Optimist.* Trans. Steve Cox. Woodstock, NY: Overlook, 1999.

Anzieu, Didier. *Freud's Self-Analysis.* Trans. Peter Graham. Madison, CT: International Universities Press, 1986.

———. *Le corps de l'oeuvre.* Paris: Gallimard, 1981.

Aranda, Emanuel d'. *The History of Algiers and Its Slavery: With Many Remarkable Particularities of Africk, Written by the Sieur Emanuel D'Aranda, Sometime a Slave There.* Trans. John Davies. London: John Starkey, 1666.

———. *Les captifs d'Alger.* Ed. Latifa Z'Rari. Paris: J.P. Rocher, 1998.

———. *Relation de la captivité et liberté du Sievr Emanuel d'Aranda, iadis esclaue à Alger. Où se trouuent plusieurs particularitez de l'Affrique, dignes de remarque.* Paris: Compagnie des Librairies du Palais, 1665.

———. *Relation de la captivité & liberté du sieur d'Aranda, jadis esclave à Alger* [. . .]. Bruxelles: Chez Jean Mommart, 1662.

Arata, Stefano. "Edición de textos y problemas de autoría: El descubrimiento de una comedia olvidada." *La Comedia.* Ed. Jean Canavaggio. Madrid: Casa de Velázquez, 1995. 51–75.

"Arch. 94. Liber Conciliorum Magni Magistri Iohannis Levesque de la Cassière, Annorum 1574–77." *Catalogue of the Records of the Order of St. John of Jerusalem in the National Library of Malta.* Ed. Rev. J. Mizzi. Vol. 2. Valetta: Malta University Press, 1979.

"Arch. 95. Liber Conciliorum Magni Magistri Iohannis Levesque de la Cassière, Annorum 1577–81." *Catalogue of the Records of the Order of St. John of Jerusalem in the National Library of Malta.* Ed. Rev. J. Mizzi. Vol. 2. Valetta: Malta University Press, 1979.

Arellano, Ignacio. *Convención y recepción: Estudios sobre el teatro del Siglo de Oro.* Madrid: Gredos, 1999.

Aristizábal, Martha Lucía. "Aspectos psicológicos del secuestro." Unpublished paper. Fundación País Libre, Bogotá, Colombia, November 23, 1994.

Arrabal, Fernando. *Un esclavo llamado Cervantes.* Madrid: Espasa-Calpe, 1996.

Astrana Marín, Luis. *Vida ejemplar y heróica de Miguel de Cervantes Saavedra.* 7 vols. Madrid: Instituto Editorial Reus, 1949–1952.

Attard, Joseph. *The Knights of Malta.* San Gwan, Malta: Enterprise Group, 1992.

Avalle-Arce, Juan Bautista. "Introducción." Miguel de Cervantes, *Los trabajos de Persiles y Sigismunda.* Madrid: Castalia, 1970. 14–20.

———. "La captura de Cervantes." *Boletín de la Real Academia Española* 48 (1968): 237–80.

———. "Tres comienzos de la novela." *Papeles de Son Armadans* 110 (1965): 181–214.

Ayala, Francisco. "La invención del Quijote." *Los ensayos: Teoría y crítica literaria.* Madrid: Aguilar, 1972.

Bal, Mieke. *Quoting Caravaggio: Contemporary Art, Preposterous History.* Chicago: University of Chicago Press, 1999.

———. *Reading Rembrandt: Beyond the Word–Image Opposition.* Cambridge: Cambridge University Press, 1991.

Bamford, Paul. *Fighting Ships and Prisons: The Mediterranean Galleys of France in the Age of Louis XIV.* Minneapolis, MN: University of Minnesota Press, 1973.

Bandera Gómez, Cesáreo. *El Poema de Mio Cid: Poesía, historia, mito.* Madrid: Gredos, 1969.

Barbarroja, Hayradin. "Billete de Barbarroja para Don Fernando Gonzaga." Apéndice a *Crónica de los Barbarroja por Francisco López de Gómara. Memorial histórico español.* Vol. 6. Madrid: Imprenta de Real Academia de Historia, 1853. 539.

Belhamissi, Moulay. *Histoire de la marine algérienne (1516–1830).* Alger: Entreprise Nationale du Livre, 1983.

Benassar, Bartolomé. "La vida de los renegados españoles y portugueses en Fez (hacia 1580–1615)." *Relaciones de la Península Ibérica con El Magreb, Siglos XIII–XVI. Actas del Coloquio (Madrid, 17–18 Diciembre, 1987).* Ed. Mercedes García Arenal and María J. Viguera. Madrid: Consejo Superior de Investigaciones Científicas, 1988. 665–67.

Benassar, Bartolomé, and Lucile Benassar. *Les chrétiens d'Allah: L'histoire extraordinaire des renégats, XVI et XVII siècles.* Paris: Perrin, 1989.

———. *Los cristianos de Alá: La fascinante aventura de los renegados.* Trans. José Luis Aristu. Madrid: Nerea, 1989.

Bennington, Geoffrey, and Jacques Derrida. *Jacques Derrida.* Trans. Geoffrey Bennington. Chicago: University of Chicago Press, 1999.

Bernáldez, Andrés. *Memorias del reinado de los reyes católicos.* Madrid: Real Academia de la Historia y Consejo Superior de Investigaciones Científicas, 1962.

Berque, Jacques. "Ville et Université: Aperçu sur l'histoire de l'École de Fās" in *Revue historique de droit français et étranger* 27 (1949): 64-117.

Bertrand, Michèle. *La pensée et le trauma: Entre psychanalyse et philosophie.* Paris: L'Harmattan, 1990.

Bilici, Faruk. "Les bibliothèques vakif-s à Istanbul au XVIe siècle." *Livres et lecture dans le monde Ottoman.* Ed. Frédéric Hitzel. Special ed. of *Revue des mondes musulmans et de la Méditerranée* 87–88 (1999): 39–59.

Blecua, José Manuel. *Sobre poesía de la Edad de Oro.* Madrid: Gredos, 1970.

Bleiberg, Germán, ed. *El informe secreto de Mateo Alemán sobre el trabajo forzado en las minas de Almadén.* London: Tamesis, 1985.

Bono, Salvatore. *Il corsari barbareschi.* Roma: Eri-Edizion Radiotelevisione Italiana, 1964.

Borges, Jorge Luis. "A Soldier of Urbina." *Selected Poems.* Trans. Alastair Reid. Ed. Alexander Coleman. New York: Viking Penguin, 1999. 179.

———."Un soldado de Urbina." *El otro, el mismo, Jorge Luis Borges: Obra Poética, 1923-1977.* Ed. Carlos V. Frías. Buenos Aires: Emecé Editors, 1977. 193.

Bowie, Malcolm. *Lacan.* Cambridge, MA: Harvard University Press, 1991.

Boyer, P. "Les renégats et la marine de la Régence d'Alger." *Revue de l'Occident Musulman et de la Méditerranée* 39 (1985): 93–107.

Brantôme, Pierre de Bourdeilles, Abbé et seigneur de. "Charles Le Quint." *Oeuvres complètes de Pierre de Bourdeilles, Abbé et Seigneur de Brantôme.* Ed. Prosper Merimée. Vol. 1. Paris: P. Janet, 1858. 132–33.

Braudel, Fernand. *En torno del Mediterráneo.* Trans. Agustín López y María Tabuyo. Ed. Roselyne de Ayala and Paule Braudel. Barcelona: Paidós, 1997.

———. "Imperio y monarquía en el siglo XVI." Trans. Agustín López and María Tabuyo. *En torno al Mediterráneo.* Ed. Roselyne de Ayala and Paul Braudel. Barcelona: Paidós, 1997. 167–218.

———. *La Méditerranée et le monde méditerranéen à l'époque de Philippe II.* 1949. 2 ed. Paris: A. Colin, 1966.

———. "Les espagnols et l'Afrique du Nord, 1492–1577." *Revue africaine* 2 (1928): 84–233.

———. "Les espagnols et l'Afrique du Nord, 1492–1577." *Revue africaine* 3 (1928): 351–428.

———. *The Mediterranean and the Mediterranean World in the Age of Philip II.* Trans. Siân Reynolds. 2 vols. New York: Harper & Row, 1972.

Bunes, Miguel Ángel de, and Mercedes García Arenal, eds. *Los españoles en el Norte de África: Siglos XV-XVIII.* Madrid: MAPFRE, 1992.

Bunes Ibarra, Miguel Ángel de. *La imagen de los musulmanes y del Norte de África en la España de los siglos XVI y XVII: Los caracteres de una hostilidad.* Madrid: Consejo Superior de Investigaciones Científicas, 1989.

———. "Reflexiones sobre la conversión al islam de los renegados en los siglos XVI y XVII." *Hispania sacra* 42 (1990): 181–98.

Bunes Ibarra, Miguel Ángel de, and Emilio Sola, eds. *La vida, y historia de Hayradin, llamado Barbarroja.* Granada: Universidad de Granada, 1997.

Byron, William. *Cervantes: A Biography.* New York: Doubleday, 1978.

Calderón de la Barca, Pedro. *El príncipe constante.* Ed. Alberto Porqueras Mayo. Madrid: Espasa-Calpe, 1975.

Camamis, George. *Estudios sobre el cautiverio en el Siglo de Oro.* Madrid: Gredos, 1977.

Canavaggio, Jean. "Agi Morato entre historia y ficción." *Cervantes: Entre vida y creación.* Alcalá de Henares: Biblioteca de Estudios Cervantinos, 2000. 39–44.

———. *Cervantes.* Trans. J. R. Jones. New York: Norton, 1990.

———. *Cervantès dramaturge: Un théâtre à naître.* Paris: Presses Universitaires de France, 1977.

———. "Cervantes en primera persona." *Cervantes: Entre vida y creación.* Alcalá de Henares: Centro de Estudios Cervantinos, 2000. 65–83.

———. *Cervantes: En busca del perfil perdido.* Trans. Mauro Armiño. 2 ed. Madrid: Espasa-Calpe, 1992.

———. *Cervantes: Entre vida y creación.* Alcalá de Henares: Biblioteca de Estudios Cervantinos, 2000.

———. "La captive chrétienne, des *Tratos de Argel* aux *Baños de Argel*: Traditions et récréation cervantine." *Images de la femme en Espagne au XV et XVII siècles: Des traditions aux renouvellements et à l'émergence d'images nouvelles, Colloque International (Sorbonne et Collège d'Espagne, 28–30 Septembre 1992).* Ed. Augustin Redondo. Paris: Publications de la Sorbonne, 1994. 213–25.

———. "La dimensión autobiográfica del *Viaje del Parnaso*." *Cervantes* 1.1 (1981): 29–41.

———. "Le 'vrai' visage d'Agi Morato." *Hommage à Louis Urrutia. Les langues néo-latines* 239 (1980): 23–38.

———. "A propos de deux 'Comedias' de Cervantès: Quelques remarques sur un manuscrit récemment retrouvé." *Bulletin hispanique* 68 (1966): 5–29.

Carrasco Urgoiti, María Soledad. "*El gallardo español* como héroe fronterizo." *Actas del tercer congreso internacional de cervantistas, Gala Galdana, Menorca, 20–25 de Octubre de 1997.* Palma: Unversitat de Islas Baleares, 1998. 571–81.

Caruth, Cathy. "An Interview with Robert Jay Lifton." *Trauma: Explorations in Memory.* Ed. Cathy Caruth. Baltimore, MD: Johns Hopkins University Press, 1995. 128–47.

_____, ed. *Trauma: Explorations in Memory*. Baltimore, MD: Johns Hopkins University Press, 1995.

_____. *Unclaimed Experience: Trauma, Narrative, and History*. Baltimore: Johns Hopkins University Press, 1996.

Casalduero, Joaquín. *Sentido y forma del teatro de Cervantes*. Madrid: Gredos, 1966.

Cassar, Paul, *Medical History of Malta*. London: Wellcome Historical Medical Library, 1965.

Castries, Henry de, et al., ed. *Les sources inédites pour l'histoire du Maroc de 1530 à 1845, Première série, dynastie saadienne (1530–1660), archives et bibliothèques de France*. 2 vols. Paris: Ernest Leroux, 1905–1908.

Castro, Américo. *El pensamiento de Cervantes*. Madrid: Imprenta de la Librería y Casa Editorial Hernando, 1925.

_____. *El pensamiento de Cervantes*. Barcelona: Noguer, 1972.

_____. "Los Prólogos del Quijote." *Hacia Cervantes*. Madrid: Taurus, 1967. 262–301.

Cazenave, Jean. "Cervantès à Oran, 1581." *Société de géographie et d'archéologie d' Oran* 43 (1923): 215–42.

_____. "*El gallardo español* de Cervantes (1)." *Langues néo-latines* 126 (1953): 5–17.

_____. "*El gallardo español* de Cervantes (2)." *Langues néo-latines* 127 (1953): 3–14.

Celdrán Gomariz, Pancracio. "La judería de Argel según un manuscrito inédito del primer tercio del Siglo XVII: El 3227 de la Biblioteca Nacional de Madrid." *Sefarad* 42 (1982): 327–55.

Cervantes, Miguel de. *The Captive's Tale (La historia del cautivo), Don Quixote, Part One, Chapters 39–41*. Trans. Donald McCrory. Warminster, England: Aris and Phillips, 1994.

_____. *Comedia llamada* Trato de Argel *hecha por Miguel de Cervantes*. ms. 14630. Biblioteca Nacional, Madrid.

_____. *Don Quijote*. Trans. Burton Raffel. Ed. Diana de Armas Wilson. New York: Norton, 1999.

_____. *Don Quijote de la Mancha*. Ed. Luis Andrés Murillo. 2 vols. Madrid: Castalia, 1978.

_____. "El amante liberal." Miguel de Cervantes, *Novelas ejemplares*. Ed. Harry Sieber. Vol. 1. Madrid: Cátedra, 1998. 135–88.

_____. *Los baños de Argel*. Ed. Florencio Sevilla Arroyo and Antonio Rey Hazas. Vol. 14 of *Obra completa de Miguel de Cervantes*. 18 vols. Madrid: Alianza, 1998.

_____. "El coloquio de los perros." Miguel de Cervantes, *Novelas ejemplares*. Ed. Harry Sieber. Vol. 2. Madrid: Cátedra, 1985. 299–359.

_____. "La española inglesa." Miguel de Cervantes, *Novelas ejemplares*. Ed. Harry Sieber. Vol. 1. Madrid: Cátedra, 1998. 243–83.

_____. *La Galatea*. Ed. Francisco Estrada and María Teresa Lopez García-Berdoy. Madrid: Catédra, 1995.

_____. *El gallardo español*. Ed. Florencio Sevilla Arroyo and Antonio Rey Hazas. Vol. 13 of *Obra completa de Miguel de Cervantes*. 18 vols. Madrid: Alianza, 1997.

_____. *El ingenioso hidalgo Don Quijote de La Mancha*. Ed. Francisco Rodríguez Marín. 10 vols. Madrid: Atlas, 1947–49.

_____. "El retablo de las maravillas." Miguel de Cervantes. *Entremeses*. Ed. Eugenio Ascensio. Madrid: Castalia, 1980. 176–82.

————. "El Trato de Argel." *Viaje del Parnaso*. Madrid: Antonio Sancha, 1784.

————. *El trato de Argel*. Ed. Florencio Sevilla Arroyo and Antonio Rey Hazas. Vol. 2 of *Obra completa de Miguel de Cervantes*. 18 vols. Madrid: Alianza, 1996.

————. *Exemplary Novels*. Trans. B.W. Ife. 4 vols. Warminster, England: Aris and Philips, 1992.

————. *The History of That Ingenious Gentleman Don Quijote de La Mancha*. Trans. Burton Raffel: New York: Norton, 1995.

————. "Información de Argel." *Información de Miguel de Cervantes de lo que ha servido á S.M. y de lo que ha hecho estando captivo en Argel, y por la certificación que aquí presenta del duque de Sesa se verá como cuando le captivaron se le perdieron muchas informaciones, fees y recados que tenía de lo que había servido á S.M. (Documentos)*. Ed. Pedro Torres Lanzas. Madrid: El Árbol, 1981.

————. "La conquista de Jerusalén por Godofre de Bullón." *Criticón* 54 (1992): 9–112.

————. *Novelas ejemplares*. Ed. Harry Sieber. 2 vols. Madrid: Cátedra, 1988.

————. *La Numancia*. Ed. Florencio Sevilla Arrollo and Antonio Rey Hazas. Vol. 1 of *Obra completa de Cervantes*. 18 vols. Madrid: Alianza, 1996.

————. *Obra completa*. Ed. Florencio Sevilla Arroyo and Antonio Rey Hazas. 18 vols. Madrid: Alianza, 1996–99.

————. *Ocho comedias y ocho entremeses nunca representados*. Ed. Florencio Sevilla Arrollo and Antonio Rey Hazas. Vol. 14 of *Obra completa de Cervantes*. 18 vols. Madrid: Alianza, 1998.

————. *Poesías completas*. Ed. Vicente Gaos. 2 vols. Madrid: Castalia, 1981.

————. "Prólogo." *Ocho comedias y ocho entremeses nunca representados*. Ed. Florencio Sevilla Arroyo and Antonio Rey Hazas. Vol. 14 of *Obra completa de Miguel de Cervantes*. Madrid: Alianza, 1998. 9–15.

————. *The Trials of Persiles and Sigismunda*. Trans. Celia Richmond Weller and Clark A. Colahan. Berkeley, CA: University of California Press, 1989.

————. *Los trabajos de Persiles y Sigismunda*. Ed. Juan Bautista Avalle-Arce. Madrid: Castalia, 1970.

————. *Los trabajos de Persiles y Sigismunda*. Ed. Carlos Romero Muñoz. Madrid: Cátedra, 1997.

————. "Viaje del Parnaso." Miguel de Cervantes, *Poesías completas*. Ed. Vicente Gaos. Vol. 1. Madrid: Castalia, 1974. 182–83.

Chew, Samuel C. *The Crescent and the Rose. Islam and England during the Renaissance*. New York: Oxford University Press, 1937.

Chiambery, Bartholomeo Ruffino de. *Sopra la desolatione della Goletta e forte di Tunisi: Insieme la conquista datta de Turchi, de Regni di Fezza, e di Marocco*, 1577.

————. "Une relation inédite sur la prise de Tunis par les Turcs, en 1574." Trans. Paul Sebag. Vol. 16–18. *Cahiers de la Tunisie*, 1968–70. 8–250.

Cicioni, Mirna. *Primo Levi: Bridges of Knowledge*. Oxford: Berg, 1995.

Cirlot, J.E. *A Dictionary of Symbols*. Trans. Jack Sage. New York: Philosophical Library, 1983.

Cirot, G. "*Le Cautivo* de Cervantès et Notre Dame de Liesse." *Bulletin Hispanique* 38 (1936): 381–82.

Cisneros, Cardenal Fray Francisco Jiménez de. *Cartas del Cardenal Don Fray Francisco Jiménez de Cisneros dirigidas a Don Diego López de Ayala*. Ed. Pascual

Gayangos and Vicente de la Fuente. Madrid: Imprenta del Colegio de Sordomudos y de Ciegos, 1867.

Clénard, Nicolas. *Correspondance de Nicolas Clénard.* Trans. Alphonse Roersch. Ed. Alphonse Roersch. 3 vols. Bruxelles: Palais des Académies, 1946.

Combet, Louis. *Cervantès ou les incertitudes du désir.* Lyon: Presses Universitaires de Lyon, 1980.

Cooper, J.C. *An Illustrated Encyclopaedia of Traditional Symbols.* London: Thames and Hudson, 1978.

Cotarello y Valledor, Armando. *El teatro de Cervantes: Estudio crítico.* Madrid: Tipografía de la Revista de Archivos, Bibliotecas y Museos, 1915.

Cour, Auguste. *L'établissement des dynasties des chérifs au Maroc: Et leur rivalité avec les turcs de la régence d'Alger, 1509-1830.* Paris: Ernest Leroux, 1904.

Covarrubias Horozco, Sebastián de. *Tesoro de la lengua castellana o española.* Ed. Felipe C.R. Maldonado. Madrid: Castalia, 1994.

Covarrubias, Sebastián. *Tesoro de la lengua castellana o española.* Madrid: L. Sánchez, 1611.

Cuneo, Miguel de. *Cartas de particulares a Colón y relaciones coetáneas.* Ed. Juan Gil and Consuelo Varela. Madrid: Alianza, 1984.

Dan, Pierre. "Diego De Haedo." *Les plus illustres captifs ou recueil des actions héroiques d'un grand nombre de guerriers et autres chrétiens réduits en esclavage par les mahométans.* Ed. R.P. Calixte de la Providence. Vol. 2. Lyon: Delhomme et Briguet, 1892. 203–04.

———. *Histoire de Barbarie, et de ses corsaires. Des royavmes, et des villes d'Alger, de Tvnis, de Salé, & de Tripoly. Divisée en six livres. Ov il est traitté de leur govvernement, de leurs moeurs, de leur cruautez, de leur brigandages, de leur sortilèges, et plusieurs autres particularitez remarquables. Ensemble de grandes miseres et de crvuels tourmens qu'endurent les Chrestiens captifs parmy ces infideles.* 2 ed. Paris: P. Rocolet, 1649.

De Armas, Frederick A. "Los excesos de Venus y Marte en *El Gallardo Español.*" *Cervantes: Su obra y su mundo, Actas del I Congreso Internacional sobre Cervantes.* Ed. Manuel Criado de Val. Madrid: Edi 6, 1978. 249–59.

Denis, Ferdinand. "Haedo." *Nouvelle biographie générale.* Paris: Firmin Didot, 1853. 50-51.

Derrida, Jacques. "Coming into One's Own." *Psychoanalysis and the Question of the Text.* Ed. Geoffrey H. Hartman. Baltimore: Johns Hopkins University Press, 1978. 114-148.

———. "The Deaths of Roland Barthes." Jacques Derrida, *The Work of Mourning.* Ed. Pascale-Anne Brault and Michael Naas. Chicago: University of Chicago Press, 2001. 31-67.

———. *The Ear of the Other: Otobiography, Transference, Translation.* Trans. Peggy Kamuf. Ed. Christie McDonald. Lincoln, NE: University of Nebraska Press, 1988.

———. *Otobiographies: L'enseignement de Nietzsche et la politique du nom propre.* Paris: Galilée, 1984.

———. "Sarah Kofman." Jacques Derrida, *The Work of Mourning.* Ed. Pascale-Anne Brault and Michael Naas. Chicago: University of Chicago Press, 2001. 165-188.

Dixon, Victor. "La comedia de corral de Lope como género visual." *Edad de Oro* 5 (1986): 35–58.

Doria, Andrea. "Carta de Andrea Doria al Emperador sobre las cosas de Barbarroja, 2 de octubre de 1539." Apéndice a *Crónica de los Barbarroja por Francisco López de Gómara. Memorial histórico español.* Vol. 6. Madrid: Imprenta de Real Academia de Historia, 1853. 533–34.

———. "Instrucciones dadas por el Príncipe Andrea Doria y Fernando Gonzaga al contador Juan Gallego para tratar con Barbarroja, Mesina a 2 de Septiembre de 1539." Apéndice a *Crónica de los Barbarroja por Francisco López de Gómara. Memorial histórico español* Vol. 6. Madrid: Imprenta de Real Academia de Historia, 1853. 537–38.

Douglas, Mary. *Purity and Danger: An Analysis of Concepts of Pollution and Taboo.* New York: Praeger, 1966.

Dousinague, José M. *La política internacional de Fernando el Católico.* Madrid: Espasa-Calpe, 1944.

———. *Testamentaria de Isabel la Católica.* Ed. Antonio de la Torre y del Cerro. Valladolid: Instituto "Isabel la Católica" de Historia Eclesiástica, 1968.

Durant, Will. *The Reformation: A History of European Civilization from Wycliff to Calvin: 1300–1564.* Vol. 4 of *The Story of Civilization.* 10 vols. New York: Simon and Schuster, 1957.

Dyke, Carolyne van. *The Fiction of Truth: Structures of Meaning and Dramatic Allegory.* Ithaca, NY: Cornell University Press, 1985.

Earle, Peter. *Corsairs of Malta and Barbary.* Annapolis, MD: United States Naval Institute, 1970.

Egido, Aurora. *Cervantes y las puertas del sueño: Estudios sobre* La Galatea, El Quijote *y* El Persiles. Barcelona: Promociones y Publicaciones Universitarias, 1994.

———, ed. *La escenografía en el teatro barroco.* Salamanca: Universidad de Salamanca, 1989.

———. "La memoria y el arte narrativo del Persiles." *Nueva revista de filología hispánica* 2 (1990): 621–41.

Eisenberg, Daniel. "Cervantes, autor de la *Topografía e historia general de Argel,* publicada por Diego de Haedo." *Cervantes* XVI, 3 (1996): 32-53.

———. "¿Por qué volvió Cervantes de Argel?" *Ingeniosa invención: Essays on Golden Age Literature Presented to Geoffrey Stagg on His Eighty-Fifth Birthday.* Ed. Ellen Anderson and Amy Williamsen. Newark, DE: Juan de la Cuesta, 1998. 241–53.

El Saffar, Ruth. *Beyond Fiction: The Recovery of the Feminine in the Novels of Cervantes.* Berkeley, CA: University of California Press, 1984.

———. *Novel to Romance: A Study of Cervantes's* Novelas Ejemplares. Baltimore, MD: Johns Hopkins University Press, 1974.

The Encyclopedia of Islam. 9 vols. Leiden: E.J. Brill, 1995.

Engel, Claire-Éliane. *Histoire de l'Ordre de Malte.* Genève: Nagel, 1968.

Evans, Dylan. *An Introductory Dictionary of Lacanian Psychoanalysis.* New York: Routledge, 1966.

Epalza, Míkel de. *Los moriscos antes y después de la expulsión.* Madrid: MAPFRE, 1992.

Ercilla, Alonso de. *La Araucana.* Ed. Marcos Morínigo and Isaías Lerner. 2 vols. Madrid: Castalia, 1987.

Ezrahi, Sidra DeKoven. *By Words Alone: The Holocaust in Literature.* Chicago: Chicago University Press, 1980.

Faliu, Ch., and J.P. Lasalle. "'El Valor de Malta' de Lope de Vega (?): Traitement dramatique et référent historique." *Las órdenes militares en el Mediterráneo Occidental (S. XII–XVIII), Coloquio Las órdenes militares en el Mediterráneo Occidental, Madrid, 4–6 May 1983*. Madrid: Casa de Velásquez, 1989. 341–58.

Felgueiras Gayo, Manoel José da Costa. *Nobiliário de família de Portugal: Título de Souza*. Vol. 9. 12 vols. 1938. Reprint Braga: Carvalhos de Basto, 1989.

Felman, Shoshana, and Dori Laub. *Testimony: Crises of Witnessing in Literature, Psychoanalysis, and History*. New York: Routledge, 1992.

Ferenczi, Sandor. "Réflexions sur le traumatisme." Trans. Coq Héron et al. *Oeuvres complètes de Sandor Ferenczi, 1927–1933, Psychanalyse 4*. Vol. 4. Paris: Payot, 1982. 139–47.

Fernández Álvarez, Manuel. "Etapa Renacentista." *La Universidad de Salamanca: Historia y proyecciones*. Ed. Manuel Fernández Álvarez et al. Vol. I. Salamanca: Universidad de Salamanca, 1989. 59–101.

Fernández Álvarez, Manuel, et al., ed. *La Universidad de Salamanca: Historia y proyecciones*. 2 vols. Salamanca: Universidad de Salamanca, 1989.

Fernández de Navarrete, Martín. *Vida de Miguel de Cervantes Saavedra*. Madrid: Imprenta Real, 1819.

Fernández Duro, Cesáreo. *Armada española desde la unión de los Reinos de Castilla y de León, 1476–1664*. 4 vols. Madrid: Establecimiento Tipográfico "Sucesores de Rivadeneira," 1895–1897.

Fernández, Enrique. "*Los tratos de Argel*: Obra testimonial, denuncia política y literatura terapéutica." *Cervantes* 20.1 (2000): 7–26.

Fernández Martín, Luis, S.J. *Comediantes, esclavos y moriscos en Valladolid, siglos XVI y XVII*. Valladolid: Universidad de Valladolid, Caja de Ahorros y M. P. De Salamanca, 1988.

Fineman, Joel. "The Structure of Allegorical Desire." *Allegory and Representation*. Ed. Stephen J. Greenblatt. Baltimore, MD: Johns Hopkins University Press, 1981. 26–60.

Fink, Bruce. *The Lacanian Subject*. Princeton, NJ: Princeton University Press, 1995.

Fischer, Geoffrey. *Barbary Legend*. Oxford: Clarendon, 1957.

Fletcher, Angus. *Allegory: The Theory of a Symbolic Mode*. Ithaca Cornell University Press, 1964.

Fontenay, Michel. "Corsaires de la foi ou rentiers du sol? Les Chevaliers de Malte dans le Corso méditerranéen au XVII siècle." *Revue d'histoire moderne et contemporaine* 35 (1988): 361–84.

———. "Le developpement urban du port de Malte du XVIe au XVIIIe siècle." *Revue du monde musulman et de la Méditerranée* 71 (1994): 91–108.

———. "Le Maghreb barbaresque et l'esclavage méditerranéen aux XVIe et XVIIe siècles." *Cahiers de la Tunisie* 44.3–4 (1991): 7–43.

———. "L'empire Ottoman et le risque corsaire au XVIIe siècle." *Revue d'histoire moderne et contemporaine* 32 (1985): 185–208.

Forcione, Alban. *Cervantes and the Humanist Vision: A Study of Four Exemplary Novels*. Princeton, NJ: Princeton University Press, 1982.

———. *Cervantes, Aristotle, and the Persiles*. Princeton, NJ: Princeton University Press, 1970.

———. *Cervantes's Christian Romance: A Study of Persiles y Sigismunda*. Princeton, NJ: Princeton University Press, 1972.

Fothergille-Payne, Louise. *La alegoría en los autos y farsas anteriores a Calderón.* London: Tamesis, 1977.

———. *"Los Tratos de Argel, Los cautivos de Argel* y *Los baños de Argel:* tres 'trasuntos' de un 'asunto.'" *El mundo del teatro español en el Siglo de Oro: Ensayos dedicados a John E. Varey.* Ed. José María Ruano de la Haza. Ottawa Hispanic Studies 3. Ottawa: Dovehouse, 1989. 177–96.

Fra Molinero, Baltasar. *La imagen del negro en el teatro del Siglo de Oro.* Madrid: Siglo XXI, 1995.

Frassica, Pietro, ed. *Primo Levi as Witness: Proceedings of a Symposium Held at Princeton University, April 30–May 2, 1989.* Fiesole: Casalini, 1990.

Freud, Sigmund. "Fetishism." Trans. James Strachey. *The Standard Edition of the Complete Psychological Works of Sigmund Freud.* Ed. James Strachey. Vol. 21. London: The Hogarth Press, 1974. 149–57.

———. *The Interpretation of Dreams.* Trans. James Strachey. *The Standard Edition of the Complete Psychological Works of Sigmund Freud.* Ed. James Strachey. Vol. 4. London: Hogarth, 1974.

———. "On Narcissism: An Introduction." Trans. James Strachey. *The Standard Edition of the Complete Psychological Works of Sigmund Freud.* Ed. James Strachey. Vol. 14. London: The Hogarth Press, 1981. 67–102.

———. *An Outline of Psychoanalysis.* Trans. James Strachey. *The Standard Edition of the Complete Works of Sigmund Freud.* Ed. James Strachey. Vol. 23. London: Hogarth, 1974. 14–207.

———. "The Splitting of the Ego in the Process of Defense." Trans. James Strachey. *The Standard Edition of the Complete Psychological Works of Sigmund Freud.* Ed. James Strachey. Vol. 23. London: The Hogarth Press, 1974. 271–78.

———. *The Standard Edition of the Complete Psychological Works of Sigmund Freud.* Trans. James Strachey. Ed. James Strachey. 24 vols. London: Hogarth, 1974.

Friedman, Edward. *The Unifying Concept: Approaches to the Structure of Cervantes's Comedias.* York, SC: Spanish Literature Publication Company, 1981.

Friedman, Helen G. *Spanish Captives in North Africa in the Early Modern Age.* Madison: University of Wisconsin Press, 1983.

Friedman, S. Morgan, ed. *The Inflation Calculator. www.westegg.com/inflation/infl.cgi/.* February 26, 2001.

Furman, Nelly. "The Language of Pain in *Shoah.*" *Auschwitz and After: Race, Culture, and the "Jewish Question" in France.* Ed. Lawrence D. Kritzman. New York: Routledge, 1995. 299–312.

Galán, Diego. *Cautiverio y trabajos de Diego Galán.* Ed. Manuel Serrano y Sanz. Madrid: Sociedad de Bibliófilos Españoles, 1913.

Gandía, Enrique de. *Del origen de los nombres y apellidos y de la ciencia genealógica.* Buenos Aires: Librería y Editorial "La Facultad," 1930.

Gaos, Vicente. "Introducción a *Viaje del Parnaso.*" *Poesías completas de Miguel de Cervantes.* Ed. Vicente Gaos. Vol. 1. Madrid: Castalia, 1974. 38–42.

Garcés, María Antonia. "Cervantes's Veiled Woman." *The New Norton Critical Edition of Don Quijote.* Trans. Burton Raffel. Ed. Diana de Armas Wilson. New York: Norton, 1998. 821–30.

———. "Carta a Octavio Paz, 28 de octubre de 1983," *El laberinto de la soledad.*

Ed. Enrico Mario Santí. Edición conmemorativa: 50 Aniversario. Vol. 2. México: Fondo de Cultura Económica, 2000. 54–59.

———. "'Cuando llegué cautivo': Trauma and Testimony in *El trato de Argel*." *Cervantes para el Siglo XXI / Cervantes for the 21st Century*, Commemorative Collection in Honor of Professor Edward Dudley, ed. Francisco LaRubia-Prado (Newark, DE: Juan de la Cuesta, 2001), 79–105.

———. "Poetic Language and the Dissolution of the Subject in *La gitanilla* and *El licenciado Vidriera*." *Calíope* 2 (1996): 85–104.

———. "Zoraida's Veil: The 'Other' Scene of the *Captive's Tale*." *Revista de estudios hispánicos* 23.1 (1989): 65–98.

García Lorenzo, Luciano. "*La gran sultana* de Miguel de Cervantes: Adaptación del texto y puesta en escena." *Cervantes: Estudios en la víspera de su centenario.* Vol. 2. Kassel: Reichenberger, 1994. 401–32.

García Salinero, Fernando, ed. *Viaje de Turquía.* Madrid: Cátedra, 2000.

García y García, Antonio. "Consolidaciones del Siglo XV." *La Universidad de Salamanca: Historia y proyecciones.* Ed. Manuel Fernández Álvarez et al. Vol. 1. Salamanca: Universidad de Salamanca, 1989. 35–58.

———. "Los difíciles inicios (siglos XIII–XIV)." *La Universidad de Salamanca: Historia y proyecciones.* Ed. Manuel Fernández Álvarez et al. Vol. 1. Salamanca: Universidad de Salamanca, 1989. 13–34.

García Arenal, Mercedes. "Les conversions d'européens à l'islam dans l'histoire: Esquisse générale." *Social Compass* 46 (1999): 273–81.

———. "Mahdí, Murabit, Sharif: L'avénement de la dynastie sa'dienne." *Studia islamica* 71 (1990): 77–114.

———. "Textos españoles sobre Marruecos en el siglo XVI: Fray Juan Bautista y *La Crónica [. . .] de Mulley Abdelmelec*." *Al-Qantara* 2 (1981): 168–92.

García Arenal, Mercedes, and Gerard Wiegers. *Entre el Islam y Occidente: Vida de Samuel Palache, judío de Fez.* Madrid: Siglo XXI, 1999.

García Arenal, Mercedes, and María J. Viguera, ed. *Relaciones de la Península Ibérica con el Magreb, Siglos XIII–XVI. Actas del Coloquio (Madrid, 17–18 Diciembre, 1987).* Madrid: Consejo Superior de Investigaciones Científicas, 1988.

García Arenal, Mercedes, and Miguel Ángel de Bunes. *Los españoles y el Norte de África: Siglos XV–XVIII.* Madrid: MAPFRE, 1992.

Gayangos, Pascual, ed. *Memorias del cautivo en la Goleta de Túnez.* Madrid: Sociedad de Bibliófilos Españoles, 1875.

Gerli, E. Michael. "Aristotle in Africa: History, Fiction and Truth in *El gallardo español*." *Cervantes* 15 (1995): 43–57.

———. "Rewriting Myth and History: Discourses of Race, Marginality and Resistance in the *Captive's Tale* (*Don Quijote* I, 37–42)." *Refiguring Authority: Reading, Writing, and Rewriting in Cervantes.* Vol. 39. Lexington, KY: University Press of Kentucky, 1995. 40–60.

Ghazavouât. ms. 942 and 774. Bibliothèque d'Alger.

Gilman, Sander. *Jewish Self-Hatred.* Baltimore, MD: Johns Hopkins University Press, 1986.

Giovate, Bernard. *Garcilaso de la Vega.* Boston: Twayne, 1975.

Gomez-Géraud, Marie-Christine, and Stéphane Yérasimos, ed. *Dans l'empire de Soliman le Magnifique/Nicholas de Nicolay.* Paris: Centre National de la Recherche Scientifique, 1989.

Gonzaga, Fernando, Virrey de Sicilia. "Carta de D. Fernando Gonzaga al Emperador sobre las cosas de Barbarroja, 2 de Agosto de 1539." Apéndice a *Crónica de
los Barbarroja por Francisco López De Gómara. Memorial histórico español*. Vol.
6. Madrid: Imprenta de Real Academia de Historia, 1853. 530–33.

González Álvarez, Manuel. "Carlos V y Europa: el legado del Emperador."
(cervantesvirtual.com/historia/CarlosV/presentacion.shtml).

González López, Emilio. "Cervantes, maestro de la novela histórica contemporánea: La *Historia del cautivo*." *Homenaje a Casalduero*. Ed. Rizel Pincus
Sigele and Gonzalo Sobejano. Madrid: Gredos, 1972. 179–87.

Gotlieb, Roger S., ed. *Thinking the Unthinkable: Meanings of the Holocaust*. New
York: Paulist, 1990.

Goytisolo, Juan. *Crónicas sarracinas*. Paris: Ruedo Ibérico; Barcelona: Ibérica de
Ediciones y Publicaciones, 1982.

Gozalbes Gravioto, Enrique. "Los judíos de Marruecos en el siglo XVII según los
viajeros europeos de la época." *El siglo XVII hispano-marroquí*. Ed. Mohammed
Salhi. Rabat: Facultad de Letras y Ciencias Humanas, 1997. 293–310.

Gracián de la Madre de Dios, Jerónimo. "Peregrinación de Anastasio." *Escritos de
Santa Teresa, añadidos e ilustrados por Don Vicente de la Fuente*. Ed. Vicente
de la Fuente. Vol. 2. Madrid: M. Ribadeneira, 1861–1862. 452–74.

———. *Tractado de la redempción de captivos, en que se cuenta las grandes miserias
que padescen los Christianos que están en poder de los infieles, y de la qual sancta
obra sea su rescate, y de algunos medios y apuntamientos para ello*. Roma, 1597.

Gracián de la Madre Dios, Jerónimo. *Peregrinación de Anastasio: Diálogos de las
persecuciones, trabajos, tribulaciones y Cruces que ha padecido el Padre Fray
Gerónimo Gracián de La Madre de Dios desde que tomó el hábito del Carmelita
Descalzo hasta el año 1613, y de muchos consuelos y misericordias de Nuestro Señor
que ha recibido. Pónese su manera de proceder en lo espiritual con algunas luces
que acerca de sus sucesos tuvieron la beata Madre Teresa de Jesús y algunas otras
siervas de Dios que se los pronosticaron . . . /*. Burgos: El Monte Carmelo, 1905.

Gracián, Jerónimo. *Crónica de cautiverio y de misión*. Ed. Luis Rosales. Madrid:
Ediciones FE, 1942.

Grammont, Henry-Delmas de. *Histoire d'Alger sous la domination turque 1515–1830*.
Paris: Ernest Leroux, 1887.

———. "La course, l'esclavage et la rédemption à Alger, Première partie: La
course." *Revue historique* 26 (1884): 1–42.

———. "La course, l'esclavage et la rédemption à Alger, Seconde partie: L'esclavage." *Revue historique* 27 (1884): 1–44.

Graullera Sanz, Vicente. *La esclavitud en Valencia en los siglos XVI y XVII*. Valencia:
Instituto Valenciano de Estudios Históricos, Institución Alfonso el Magnánimo,
Diputación Provincial, Consejo Superior de Investigaciones Científicas, 1978.

Green, André. *The Tragic Effect: The Oedipus Complex in Tragedy*. Trans. Alan
Sheridan. New York: Cambridge University Press, 1979.

———. *Un oeil en trop: Le complexe d'Oedipe dans la tragédie*. Paris: Minuit,
1969.

Greenblatt, Stephen J., ed. *Allegory and Representation*. Baltimore, MD: Johns
Hopkins University Press, 1981.

Guglielmotti, Alberto. *Storia de la marina pontificia*. Vol. 3. Roma: Tipografia
Vaticana, 1886–1893.

Haedo, Diego de. "Epítome de los reyes de Argel." *Topografía e historia general de Argel*. Ed. Ignacio Bauer y Landauer. Vol. 1. Madrid: Sociedad de Bibliófilos Españoles, 1927. 213–426.

———. *Histoire des rois d'Alger*. Trans. Henri-Delmas de Grammont. Saint-Denis: Bouchène, 1998.

———. *Histoire des rois d'Alger*. Trans. Henri-Delmas de Grammont. Alger: Adolphe Jourdan, 1881.

———. *Topografía e historia general de Argel*. Ed. Ignacio Bauer y Landauer. 3 vols. Madrid: Sociedad de Bibliófilos Españoles, 1927–29.

———, ed. *Topographia, e historia general de Argel, repartida en cinco tratados do se verán casos extraños, muertes espantosas y tormentos exquisitos que conviene se entiendan en la Cristiandad* [. . .]. Valladolid: Diego Fernández de Córdova y Oviedo, a costa de Antonio Coello, 1612.

———. "Topographie et histoire générale d'Alger." Trans. Dr. Monnereau and A. Berbrugger. *Revue africaine* 14 (1870): 364–75, 414–43, 490–519.

———. "Topographie et histoire générale d'Alger." Trans. Dr. Monnereau and A. Berbrugger. *Revue africaine* 15 (1871): 41–69, 90–111, 202–37, 307–9, 375–95, 458–73.

———. *Topographie et histoire générale d'Alger*. Trans. Dr. Monnereau and A. Berbrugger. Saint-Denis: Editions Bouchène, 1998.

Hahn, Juergen. "El capitán cautivo: The Soldier's Truth and Literary Precept in *Don Quijote*, Part I." *Journal of Hispanic Philology* 3 (1979): 269–73.

Hakim, Mohamed Ibn Azzuz. "El testamento de Isabel la Católica y sus consecuencias funestas sobre las relaciones hispano-marroquíes." *Huellas comunes y miradas cruzadas: Mundos árabe, ibérico e iberoamericano*. Ed. Mohamed Salhi. Rabat: Facultad de Letras y de Ciencias Humanas, 1995. 27–35.

Hartman, Geoffrey H. "On Traumatic Knowledge and Literary Studies." *New Literary History: A Journal of Theory and Interpretation* 26.3 (1995): 537–63.

———, ed. *Psychoanalysis and the Question of the Text*. Baltimore: The Johns Hopkins University Press, 1978.

Hegyi, Ottmar. "Algerian Babble Reflected in *Persiles*." *Ingeniosa invención: Essays on Golden Age Spanish Presented to Geoffrey Stagg on His Eighty-Fifth Birthday Literature*. Ed. Ellen Anderson and Amy Williamsen. Newark, DE: Juan de la Cuesta, 1998. 225–39.

———. *Cervantes and the Turks: Historical Reality Versus Literary Fiction in* La gran sultana *and* El amante liberal. Newark, DE: Juan de la Cuesta, 1992.

Hernández Araico, Susana. "Estreno de *La gran sultana*: Teatro de lo otro, amor y humor." *Cervantes* 14.2 (1994): 155–65.

Hernández, Max. *Memoria del bien perdido: Conflicto, identidad y nostalgia en el Inca Garcilaso de la Vega*. Lima: Instituto de Estudios Peruanos, 1993.

Heros, Martín de los. "Historia del Conde Pedro Navarro." *Colección de documentos inéditos para la historia de España*. Vol. 25. Madrid: Imprenta de la viuda de Calero, 1854. 106–45.

Hess, Andrew C. *The Forgotten Frontier: A History of the Sixteenth-Century Ibero-African Frontier*. Chicago: University of Chicago Press, 1978.

———. "The Moriscos: An Ottoman Fifth Column in Sixteenth-Century Spain." *American Historical Review* 74 (1968): 1–25.

Hitzel, Frédéric. "Manuscrits, livres, et culture livresque à Istanbul." *Livres et lecture dans le monde ottoman*. Ed. Frédéric Hitzel. Special ed. of *Revue des mondes musulmans et de la Mediterranée* 87-88 (1999): 19-38.

Honing, Edwin. *Dark Conceit: The Making of Allegory.* London: Faber and Faber, 1959.

Hopper, Vincent Foster. *Medieval Number Symbolism.* New York: Columbia University Press, 1938.

Howe, Irving. "Writing and the Holocaust." *New Republic,* October 27, 1986: 28–30.

Huarte de San Juan, Juan. *Examen de ingenios para las ciencias.* Ed. Guillermo Serés. Madrid: Cátedra, 1989.

Hughes, Gethin. "*El gallardo español*: A Case of Misplaced Honor." *Cervantes* 13 (1993): 65–75.

Induráin, Francisco. "Introducción." *Obras completas de Cervantes.* Ed. Francisco Induráin. Biblioteca de Autores Españoles. Madrid: Atlas, 1962.

Isidoro de Sevilla, San. *Etimologías.* Trans. José Oroz Reta and Manuel-A. Marcos Casquero. 2 vols. Madrid: Biblioteca de Autores Cristianos, 1993.

Jaques, Eliott. "Death and the Mid-Life Crisis." *International Journal of Psycho-Analysis* 46 (1965): 502–114.

Johnson, Carroll B. *Cervantes and the Material World.* Chicago: University of Illinois Press, 2000.

———. "¿Cervantes coyote?" Unpublished paper. Delivered at the XIII Congress of the Asociación Internacional de Hispanistas, Madrid, 11 July 1998.

———. "La construcción del personaje en Cervantes." *Cervantes* 15 (1995): 8–31.

Julien, Charles André. *Histoire de l'Afrique du Nord: Tunisie, Algérie, Maroc: Des origines à la conquête arabe (647 ap. J.-C.).* Paris: Payot, 1951.

Kaddache, Mahfoud. *L'Algérie durant la période ottomane.* Alger: Office des Publications Universitaires, 1998.

Kirschner, Teresa J. "Desarrollo de la puesta en escena en el teatro histórico de Lope de Vega." *Revista canadiense de estudios hispánicos* 15.3 (1991): 453–63.

Klein, Melanie. "Notes on Some Schizoid Mechanisms (1946)." *The Selected Melanie Klein.* Ed. Juliet Mitchell. New York: Free Press, 1986. 175–200.

The Koran. Trans. N. J. Dawood. 5th ed. New York: Penguin, 1990.

Kristeva, Julia. *Desire in Language: A Semiotic Approach to Literature and Art.* Ed. Leon S. Roudiez. New York: Columbia University Press, 1980.

———. "Freud and Love: Treatment and its Discontents." *Tales of Love.* Trans. Leon S. Roudiez. New York: Columbia University Press, 1987. 21-56.

———. "Stabat Mater." *Tales of Love.* Trans. Leon S. Roudiez. New York: Columbia University Press, 1987. 234-263.

———. *Tales of Love.* Trans. Leon S. Roudiez. New York: Columbia University Press, 1987.

La Véronne, Chantal de. "Les frères Gasparo Corso et le Chérif Moulay 'Abd El-Malek (1569–1574)." *Les sources inédites de l'histoire du Maroc de 1530 à 1845, Première série, Dynastie saadienne (1539–1560), archives et bibliothèques d' Espagne.* Ed. Chantal de la Véronne. Vol. 3 (1560–1578). Paris: Paul Geuthner, 1961. 157–65.

———, ed. *Les sources inédites de l'histoire du Maroc de 1530 à 1845, Première série, dynastie saadienne (1539–1560), archives et bibliothèques d'Espagne.* 3 vols. Paris: Paul Geuthner, 1961.

Lacan, Jacques. *Écrits: A Selection.* Trans. Alan Sheridan. New York: Norton, 1977.

————. *The Four Fundamental Concepts of Psychoanalysis.* Ed. Jacques-Allain Miller. Trans. Alan Sheridan. New York: Norton, 1978.

————. "God and the *Jouissance* of ~~The~~ Woman. A Love Letter." Trans. Jacqueline Rose. *Feminine Sexuality.* Ed. Juliet Mitchell and Jacqueline Rose. New York: Norton, 1983. 137–48.

————. "A Love Letter (Une lettre d'amour)." Trans. Jacqueline Rose. *Feminine Sexuality.* Ed. Juliet Mitchell and Jacqueline Rose. New York: Norton, 1983, 149-61.

LaCapra, Dominick. *Writing History, Writing Trauma.* Baltimore, MD: Johns Hopkins University Press, 2001.

Lacoue-Labarthe, Philippe. *La poésie comme expérience.* Paris: Bourgois, 1986.

Lagache, Daniel. "La psychanalyse et la structure de la personalité." *La psychanalyse* VI (1958): 5–54.

Lanfreducci Bosio, Fray François, and Fray Jean Othon. "Costa e Discorsi di Barberia, Rapport maritime, militaire et politique sur la côte d'Afrique, depuis le Nil jusqu'à Cherchell par deux membres de l'Ordre de Malte (1er septembre 1587)." *Revue africaine* 66 (1925): 419–549.

Lang, Berel. *Holocaust Representation: Art within the Limits of History and Ethics.* Baltimore, MD: Johns Hopkins University Press, 2000.

Laplanche, Jean, and J.-B. Pontalis. *The Language of Psychoanalysis.* Trans. Donald Nicholson-Smith. New York: Norton, 1973.

Lara Garrido, José. "Texto y espacio escénico en Lope de Vega (la primera comedia: 1579–1597)." *La escenografía en el teatro barroco.* Ed. Aurora Egido. Salamanca: Universidad de Salamanca, 1989. 91–126.

Laub, Dori. "An Event without a Witness: Truth, Testimony and Survival." *Testimony: Crisis of Witnessing in Literature, Psychoanalysis and History.* Ed. Shoshana Felman and Dori Laub. New York: Routledge, 1992. 75–92.

————. "Bearing Witness or the Vicissitudes of Listening." *Testimony: Crises of Witnessing in Literature, Psychoanalysis and History.* Ed. Shoshana Felman and Dori Laub. New York: Routledge, 1992. 57–74.

————. "Trauma and Testimony: The Process and the Struggle." *Trauma: Explorations in Memory.* Ed. Cathy Caruth. Baltimore, MD: Johns Hopkins University Press, 1995. 61–99.

Laub, Dori, and Nanette Auerhahn. "Knowing and Not Knowing: Massive Psychic Traumatic Memory." *Bulletin trimestriel de la Foundation Auschwitz* 44–45 (1994): 69–95.

Lausberg, Heinrich. *Manual de retórica literaria: Fundamentos de una ciencia de la literatura.* Trans. José Pérez Rico. 3 vols. Madrid: Gredos, 1980.

Leavitt, Sturgis E. "Lions in Early Spanish Literature and on the Spanish Stage." *Hispania sacra* 44.2 (1961): 272–76.

Leo, Africanus. *Della descrittione del'Africa/et dell cose notabili/che quivi sono/per Giovanni Lioni Africano. Delle navigationi et Viaggi nel qual si contiene la Descrittione Dell'Africa.* Ed. Giovanni Battista Ramusio. Vol. 1. Venetia: Heredi di Lucantonio Giunti, 1550.

————. *Della descrittione dell'Africa/et dell cose notabili/che quivi sono/per Giovanni Lioni Africano. Delle navigationi et viaggi nel qual si contiene la descrittione dell'Africa.* Primo [-Terzo] Volume, & Terza Editione *Delle Navigationi Et Viaggi Raccolto Gia Da M. Gio. Battista Ramvsio* . . . Ed. Giovanni Battista Ramusio. Vol. 1. 3 vols. Venetia: Stamperia de Givnti, 1563.

————. *Descripción de África y de las cosas notables que en ella se encuentran por Juan León Africano (Al-Hasan-Ben Muh. al-Wazzan al-Fasi)*. Publicaciones del Instituto General Franco de Estudios e Investigación Hispano-Árabe. n.d.: Imperio, 1952.

————. *Description de l'Afrique*. Trans. Alexis Épaulard. Ed. Alexis Épaulard et al. 2 vols. Paris: Librairie d'Amérique et d'Orient Adrien-Maisonneuve, 1956.

————. *The History/and/Description of Africa/and/of the Notable Things Therein Contained,/Written by/Al-Hassan Ibn-Mohammed Al-Wezaz Al-Fasi,/a Moor, Baptised as Giovanni Leone, but Better Known as/Leo Africanus,/Done into English in the Year 1600*. Trans. John Pory. Ed. Robert Brown. 3 vols. London: Hakluyt Society, 1896.

Levi, Primo. *The Drowned and the Saved*. Trans. Raymond Rosenthal. New York: Summit, 1988.

————. *I sommersi e i salvati*. Turin: Enaudi, 1986.

————. *If this Is a Man and the Truce*. Trans. Stuart Woolf. London: Abacus, 1987.

————. *Los hundidos y los salvados*. Trans. Pilar Gómez Bedate. Barcelona: Muchnik, 1995.

————. *Moments of Reprieve*. New York: Summit, 1986.

————. *The Periodic Table*. Trans. Raymond Rosenthal. New York: Shocken, 1984.

————. *Se questo è un uomo*. Turin: Einaudi, 1958.

————. *Survival in Auschwitz: The Nazi Assault on Humanity*. Trans. Stuart Woolf. New York: Maxwell Macmillan International, 1993.

Levy, Simón. "Arabófonos e hispanófolos (Baldiyin y 'azmiyin') en la Judería de Fez, dos siglos después de la expulsión." *El siglo XVII hispano-marroquí*. Ed. Mohammed Salhi. Rabat: Facultad de Letras y Ciencias Humanas, 1997. 333–51.

"L'expédition espagnole de 1541 contre Alger." *Revue africaine* 202 (1891): 177–206.

Liere, Katherine Elliot van. "Humanism and Scholasticism in Sixteenth-Century Academe: Five Student Orations from the University of Salamanca." *Renaissance Quarterly* 53 (2000): 57–107.

Lifton, Robert Jay. *The Broken Connection: On Death and the Continuity of Life*. New York: Basic Books, 1983.

————. *The Future of Immortality and Other Essays for a Nuclear World*. New York: Basic Books, 1987.

López-Baralt, Luce. "El cálamo supremo (Al-Qalam al-'Alà) de Cide Hamete Benengeli." *Mélanges María Soledad Carrasco Urgoiti*. Ed. Abdeljelil Temimi. Vol. 2. Zagouan: Foundation Temimi pour la Recherche Scientifique et l'Information, 1999. 343–61.

————. *Islam in Spanish Literature, from the Middle Ages to the Present*. Trans. Andrea Hurley. New York: Brill, 1992.

López de Coca Castañer, J. E. "Granada y el Magreb: La emigración andalusí (1485–1516)." *Actas del coloquio sobre las relaciones de la Península Ibérica con el Magreb (Siglos XIII–XVI)*. Ed. Mercedes García Arenal and María J. Viguera. Madrid: Consejo Superior de Investigaciones Científicas, 1988. 409–51.

López de Gómara, Francisco. "Crónica de los muy nombrados Omiche y Haradin Barbarrojas," *Memorial histórico español: Colección de documentos, opúsculos y antigüedades que publica la Real Academia de Historia*. Vol. 6. Madrid: Imprenta de Real Academia de Historia, 1853. 327–440.

———. *Guerras de mar del Emperador Carlos V*. Ed. Miguel Ángel de Bunes Ibarra and Nora Edith Jiménez. Madrid: Sociedad Estatal para la Conmemoración de los Centenarios de Felipe II y Carlos V, 2000.

López Pinciano, Alonso. *Philosofía antigua poética*. Ed. Alfredo Carballo Picazo. Madrid: Consejo Superior de Investigaciones Científicas, 1953.

Loureiro, Angel G. *The Ethics of Autobiography: Replacing the Subject in Modern Spain*. Nashville, TN: Vanderbilt University Press, 2000.

Lozano Renieblas, Isabel. *Cervantes y el mundo del Persiles*. Alcalá de Henares: Biblioteca de Estudios Cervantinos, 1998.

Lynch, John. *Spain, 1516–1598: From Nation State to World Empire*. Oxford: Basic Blackwell, 1991.

Man, Paul de. "Pascal's Allegory of Persuasion." *Allegory and Representation*. Ed. Stephen J. Greenblatt. Baltimore, MD: Johns Hopkins University Press. 1–23.

Marcos de Dios, Ángel. "Estado de la cuestión: Trayectoria histórica. Área lusa." *La Universidad de Salamanca: Historia y proyecciones*. Ed. Manuel Fernández Álvarez et al. Vol. 1. Salamanca: Universidad de Salamanca, 1989. 425–44.

Mariscal, George. "*La gran sultana* and the Issue of Cervantes's Modernity." *Revista de estudios hispánicos* 28.2 (1994): 185–211.

Mármol Carvajal, Luis del. *Descripción general de África*. Granada, 1573. Facsim. ed. Vol. 1. Madrid: Consejo Superior de Investigaciones Científicas, 1953.

———. *Primera parte de la Descripción general de Affrica con todos los sucessos de guerras que a auido entre los infieles, y el pueblo Christiano, y entre ellos mesmos desde que Mahoma inueto su secta, hasta el año del señor mil y quinientos y setenta y vno*. Vol. 1. Granada: Rene Rabut, 1573.

———. *Segvnda parte y libro septimo de la Descripcion general de Affrica, donde se contiene las prouincias de Numidia, Libia, la tierra de los negros, la baxa y alta Etiopia, y Egipto, cō todas las cosas memorables della*. Málaga: I. Rene, 1599.

Márquez Villanueva, Francisco. *Personajes y temas del Quijote*. Madrid: Taurus, 1975.

Marrast, Robert. *Miguel de Cervantès, dramaturge*. Paris: L'Arche, 1957.

Marsillac, Adolfo. "*La gran sultana*." *Cuadernos de teatro clásico* 7 (1992): 201–02.

Martin, Adrienne L. "Images of Deviance in Cervantes's Algiers." *Cervantes* 15 (1995): 5–15.

———. "Hacia el Cervantes del siglo que termina." *Estudios de literatura española de los siglos XIX y XX: Homenaje a Juan María Díez Taboada*. Madrid: Centro Superior de Investigaciones Científicas, 1998. 617–22.

Martire d'Anghiera, Pietro. *Epistolario*. Trans. José López de Toro. *Documentos inéditos para la historia de España*, 9–12. Ed. José López de Toro. 4 vols. Madrid: Imprenta Góngora, 1955.

Mas, Albert. *Les turcs dans la littérature espagnole du Siècle d'Or*. 2 vols. Paris: Centre de Recherches Hispaniques, 1967.

Matamoro, Blas. "Sombras cervantinas." *Vuelta*. Feb. 1997: 48–50.

McCrory, Donald P. "Introduction." *The Captive's Tale (La historia del cautivo)*

Don Quixote, Part One, Chapters 39–41. Warminster, England: Aris and Philips, 1994. 1–58.

McGaha, Michael. "Don Quixote as Arabesque." *Cervantes: Estudios en la víspera de su centenario*. Ed. Kurt and Roswitha Reichenberger. Vol. 1. Kassel: Reichenberger, 1994. 163–71.

———. "Hacia la verdadera historia del cautivo Miguel de Cervantes." *Revista canadiense de sstudios hispánicos* 20.3 (1996): 540–46.

Mele, Eugenio. "Miguel de Cervantes y Antonio Veneziano." *Revista de archivos, bibliotecas y museos* 29 (1913): 82–90.

"Memoria de la órden que tiene la armada de Barbarroja. Año 1534." Apéndice a *Crónica de los Barbarroja por Francisco López de Gómara. Memorial histórico español*. Vol. 6. Madrid: Imprenta de Real Academia de Historia, 1853. 521–23.

Menéndez Pidal, Ramón. *Estudios sobre el romancero español*. Madrid: Espasa-Calpe, 1970.

Meregalli, Franco. "De *Los tratos de Argel* a *Los baños de Argel*." *Homenaje a Casalduero*. Ed. Rizel Pincus and Gonzalo Sobejano. Madrid: Gredos, 1972. 395–409.

Mexía, Pedro. *Silva de varia lección*. Ed. Antonio Castro. 2 vols. Madrid: Cátedra, 1989.

Millunzi, Gaetano. "Antonio Veneziano." *Archivio storico siciliano*. Vol. 19. Palermo: Tipografia "Lo Statuto," 1894. 19–198.

Mizzi, Rev. J., ed. *Liber Conciliorum Jean l'Évêque de la Cassière, Catalog of the Order of St. John*. 2 vols. Valletta, 1979.

Moliné-Bertrand, A. *Au Siècle d'Or: L'Espagne et ses hommes: La population du royaume de Castille au XVI Siècle*. Paris: Economica, 1985.

Moner, Michel. "Du conte merveilleux à la pseudo-autobiographie: Le récit du Captif (*Don Quichotte*, I, 39–41)." *Écrire sur soi en Espagne: Modèles et écarts: Actes du XII colloque international d'Aix-en-Provence (4-5-6 Décembre 1986)*. Aix-en-Provence: Université de Provence, 1988. 57–71.

Monleón, Ángela, ed. *La huella del cautiverio en el pensamiento y en la obra de Miguel de Cervantes*. Madrid: Fundación Cultural Banesto, 1994.

Monleón, José, ed. *Los baños de Argel de Miguel de Cervantes, un trabajo teatral de Francisco Nieva, música de Tomás Marco*. Madrid: Centro Dramático Nacional, 1980.

Monnereau Dr., and Watleb, E. "Négociations entre Charles-Quint et Keir-Ed-Din (1538–1540)." *Revue africaine* 15 (1871): 138–48.

Morgan, John. *A Complete History of Algiers: To Which Is Prefixed, an Epitome of the General History of Barbary, from the Earliest Times: Interspersed with Many Curious Remarks and Passages, Not Touched on by Any Writer Whatever*. London: J. Bettenham, 1728–1729.

Mori Ubaldini, Ubaldino. *La marina del Sovrano militare ordine di San Giovanni di Gerusalemme, di Rodi e di Malta*. Roma: Regionale Editrice, 1971.

Morón Arroyo, Ciriaco. "La historia del cautivo y el sentido del *Quijote*." *Iberoromania* 18 (1983): 91–105.

———. *Nuevas meditaciones del* Quijote. Madrid: Gredos, 1976.

Mullany, Peter F. "The Knights of Malta in Renaissance Drama." *Neuphilologische Mitteilungen* 74.2 (1978): 297–310.

Muñoz Carabantes, Manuel. "El teatro de Cervantes a la escena española entre 1939 y 1991." *Cuadernos de teatro clásico* 7 (1992): 140–95.

Murillo, Luis Andrés. "Cervantes's Tale of the Captive Captain." *Florilegium Hispanicum: Medieval and Golden Age Studies Presented to Dorothy Clotelle Stark*. Ed. J.S. Geary et al. Hispanic Seminary of Medieval Studies. Madison, WI, 1983. 229–43.

———. "El Ur-Quijote: Nueva hipótesis." *Cervantes* I (1981): 43–50.

———. *The Golden Dial: Temporal Configuration in* Don Quijote. Oxford: Dolphin, 1975.

Mutis, Álvaro. *Diario de Lecumberri*. México: Alfaguara, 1997.

———. *Siete novelas: Empresas y tribulaciones de Maqroll el Gaviero*. Bogotá: Alfaguara, 2000.

Nadal, Jordi. *La población española (Siglos XVI a XX)*. Barcelona: Ariel, 1984.

Navarro Ledesma, Francisco. *Cervantes, the Man and the Genius*. Trans. Don and Gabriela Bliss. New York: Charter-House, 1973.

Neyla, Fray Francisco de. *Gloriosa fecundidad de la Virgen María en el campo de la Católica Iglesia*. Barcelona: Rafael Figueró, 1698.

Nicolay, Nicolas de. *Dans l'Empire de Soliman le Magnifique*. Ed. Marie-Christine Gomez-Géraud and Stéphane Yérasimos. Paris: Centre National de la Recherche Scientifique, 1989.

———. *Les navigations, peregrinations et voyages, faicts en la Tvrquie*. Anvers: Guillaume Silius, 1577.

———. *Les quatre premiers livres des Navigations et Pérégrinations Orientales, de N. N. Avec les figures au naturel tant d'hommes que de femmes selon la diversité des nations, et de leur port, maintien, et habitz*. Lyon: G. Roville, 1568.

Nieto, Fray Luis. "Histoire véritable des dernières guerres advenues en Barbarie." *Les sources inédites de l'histoire du Maroc de 1530 à 1845, Première série, dynastie saadienne (1530–1660), archives et bibliothèques de France*. 1579. Ed. Henry de Castries et al. Vol. 2. Paris, 1905–1908. 436–505.

———. "Relación de las guerras de Berbería." *Colección de documentos inéditos para la historia de España*. Ed. Don José Sancho Rayón y Don Francisco de Zabálburu. Vol. 100. Colección de documentos inéditos para la historia de España. Madrid: Imprenta de Rafael Marco y Viñas, 1891. 413–58.

Norris, Christopher. *Derrida*. Cambridge, MA: Harvard University Press, 1987.

Oliver Asín, Jaime. "La hija de Agi Morato en la obra de Cervantes." *Boletín de la Real Academia Española* 27 (1947–1948): 245–339.

Olson, Paul. "Symbolic Hierarchy in the Lion Episode of the *Cantar de Mio Cid*." *MLN* 77 (1962): 499–511.

Orozco Díaz, Emilio. *Cervantes y la novela del barroco*. Ed. José Larra Garrido. Granada: Universidad de Granada, 1992.

Ortola, Marie-Sol, ed. *Viaje de Turquía*. Madrid: Castalia, 2000.

Otero Lana, Enrique. *Los corsarios españoles durante la decadencia de los Austrias: El corso español del Atlántico peninsular en el siglo XVII (1621–1697)*. Madrid: Editorial Naval, 1992.

Padilla, Pedro de. *Romancero de Pedro de Padilla*. Madrid: Imprenta de M. Ginesta, 1880.

Patruno, Nicholas. *Understanding Primo Levi*. Columbia, SC: University of South Carolina Press, 1995.

Peçevi, Ibrâhîm. *Peçevi Tarihi*. Ed. Murat Uraz. 2 vols. Istanbul: Nesriyat Yrudu, 1968–1969.

Pellicer y Pilares, Juan Antonio. *Noticias literarias para la vida de Cervantes.* Madrid: D. Gabriel de Sancha, 1800.

Percas de Ponsetti, Helena. *Cervantes y su concepto del arte.* 2 vols. Madrid: Gredos, 1975.

———. "¿Quién Era Belerma?" *Revista hispánica moderna* 49 (1996): 375–92.

Pérez de Herrera, Cristóbal. *Amparo de los pobres.* Ed. Michel Cavillac. Madrid: Espasa-Calpe, 1975.

Pérez de Hita, Ginés. *Guerras civiles de Granada: Primera parte.* Ed. Shasta M. Bryant. Newark, DE: Juan de la Cuesta, 1982.

———. *Historia de los zegríes y abencerrajes (Primera parte de las guerras civiles de Granada).* Ed. Pedro Correa. Granada: Universidad de Granada, 1999.

Pérez Pastor, Cristóbal. *Documentos cervantinos hasta ahora inéditos.* 2 vols. Madrid: Establecimiento Tipográfico de Fortanet, 1897–1902.

_____, ed. *Noticias y documentos relativos a la historia y literatura española.* Vol. 10–13 of *Memorias de la Real Academia Española.* 13 vols. Madrid: Imprenta y Estereotipia de Rivadeneira-Imprenta de la Revista de Legislación, 1870–1910.

Peset, Mariano, and Enrique González González. "Las facultades de leyes y cánones." *La Universidad de Salamanca: Historia y proyecciones.* Ed. Manuel Fernández Álvarez et al. Vol. 2. Salamanca: Universidad de Salamanca, 1989. 9–61.

Pinto da Fonseca Teixeira de Souza, Manoel, and Ioaõ Fereira de Sà Sarmeto. *Lista/Alfabetica,/e Memoria/Dos/Nomes, e Apelidos dos Cavalheiros/Portugueses, que se achaõ descritos no anti/go Libro de Rodes, que principiou na di/ta Ilha, e Convento aos 3. de Novem/bro de 1503, e acabou nesta de Malta/aos 27. de Novem-bro de 1599./Com declaraçaõ das dignidades, comendas,/emais honras, que os ditos Cavalheiros tive/raõ no Illm°: Priorado de Portugal da Sa/grada Religiaõ de S: Ioaõ de Ierusalem./Feita por Ordem/do Eminentiss: e Rev: Monsenhor/Gram Mestre da Sagrada Religiaõ de S: Ioaõ de/Ierusalem.* Malta, 1657.

Pontalis, J.-B. *Entre le rêve et la douleur.* Paris: Gallimard, 1977.

Porras Barrenechea, Raúl. *El Inca Garcilaso en Montilla (1561–1614).* Lima: San Marcos, 1955.

Pozzo, Bartolomeo Fra dal, conte. *Historia della sacra religione militare di S. Giovanni Gerosolimitano detta di Malta.* 2 vols. Verona: G. Berno, 1703–1715.

"Provisions de l'office de consul de France au Maroc en faveur de Guillaume Bérard, Chenonceau, 10 Juin 1577." *Les sources inédites pour l'histoire du Maroc de 1530 à 1845, Première série, dynastie saadienne (1530–1660), archives et bibliothèques de France.* Ed. Henry de Castries et al. Vol. 1. Paris: Ernest Leroux, 1905. 367–69.

Quintilian, Marcus Fabius. *Institutio oratoria.* Trans. H. E. Butler. Loeb's Classical Library. 4 vols. Cambridge: Harvard University Press, 1980.

Ramusio, Gian Batista. *Navigationi et viaggi: Venice, 1563–1606 [di] Gian Batista Ramusio.* Amsterdam: Theatrum Orbis Terrarum, 1967–1970.

Ranke, Leopold von. *Die Osmanen und die spanische Monarchie im 16. und 17. Jahrhundert.* Leipzig: Duncker, 1877.

———. *The Ottoman and the Spanish Empires in the Sixteenth and Seventeenth Centuries: The History of the Popes, Their Churches and State, in the Sixteenth and Seventeenth Centuries.* Trans. Walter K. Kelly. London: Wittaker and Co, 1843.

"Real privilegio del Emperador concedido al Alférez García Fernández de la Plaza el que pueda llevar por armas un escudo con la cabeza de Bar-barroja." Apéndice a *Crónica de los Barbarroja por Francisco López de Gómara. Memo-*

rial histórico español. Vol. 6. Madrid: Imprenta de Real Academia de Historia, 1853. 487–88.

Redondo, Augustin. "Moros y moriscos en la literatura española de los años 1550–1580." *Judeoconversos y moriscos en la literatura del Siglo de Oro, Actas del "Grand Séminaire" de Neuchâtel, Neuchâtel, 26 a 27 de Mayo de 1994*. Ed. Irene Andres-Suárez. Paris: Diffusion Les Belles Lettres, 1995. 51–83.

Rey Hazas, Antonio. "Las comedias de cautivos de Cervantes." *Los imperios orientales en el teatro del Siglo de Oro, Actas de las XVI jornadas de teatro clásico, Almagro, Julio de 1993*. Ed. Felipe B. Pedraza Jiménez and Rafael González Cañal. Almagro: Universidad Castilla-La Mancha y Festival de Almagro, 1994. 29–56.

Ricard, Robert. "Textes espagnoles sur la Berbérie (XV, XVI et XVII siècles)." *Revue africaine* 89 (1945): 26–40.

———. "Le Père Jérome Gratien de la Mère de Dieu et sa captivité à Tunis (1593–1595)." *Revue africaine* 89 (1945): 190–200.

Riley, Edward C. "Episodio, novela, y aventura en *Don Quijote*." *Anales Cervantinos* 5 (1955–1956): 209–30.

———. "*Los pensamientos escondidos* and *figuras morales* of Cervantes." *Homenaje a William L. Fitcher*. Ed. A. David Kossov and José Amor y Vázquez. Madrid: Castalia, 1971. 623–31.

Riley-Smith, Jonathan Simon Christopher. *Hospitallers: The History of the Order of St. John*. London: Hambledon, 1999.

Ríos, Ángel de los. *Ensayo histórico etimológico y filológico sobre los apellidos castellanos desde el Siglo X hasta nuestra Edad*. Madrid: Imprenta de M. Tello, 1871.

Rivers, Elias L. "Cervantes's Art of the Prologue." *Estudios literarios de hispanistas norteamericanos dedicados a Helmut Hatzfeld*. Ed. J.M. Solà-Solé et al. Barcelona: Hispam, 1974. 167–71.

———. "Cervantes's Journey to Parnassus." *MLN* 85 (1970): 243–48.

———. "*Viaje del Parnaso* y poesías sueltas." *Suma cervantina*. Ed. Juan Bautista Avalle-Arce and Edward C. Riley. London: Támesis Books, 1973. 119–46.

Rodi, Risa. "An Interview with Primo Levi." *Partisan Review* 3 (1987): 355–66.

Rodríguez Marín, Francisco, ed. *El ingenioso hidalgo Don Quijote de La Mancha*. 10 vols. Madrid: Atlas, 1947-49.

———. "La cárcel donde se engendró *El Quijote*." *Estudios Cervantinos*. Madrid: Atlas, 1947. 65–92.

———. "Los Cervantes cordobeses que no son parientes del autor del 'Quijote,' lo son en grado lejano." *Estudios Cervantinos*. Madrid: Atlas, 1947. 158–64.

Rojas, Agustín de. *El viaje entretenido*. Ed. J. Ressot. Madrid: Castalia, 1972.

Romancero viejo. Ed. Mercedes Díaz Roig. Madrid: Cátedra, 1988.

Romero Muñoz, Carlos. Introdución. Miguel de Cervantes. *Los trabajos de Persiles y Sigismunda*. Ed. Carlos Romero Muñoz. Madrid: Cátedra, 1997. 17–31.

Rosales, Luis. *Cervantes y la libertad*. 2 vols. Madrid: Sociedad de Estudios y Publicaciones, 1960.

Rose, Jacqueline. *Sexuality in the Field of Vision*. London: Verso, 1986.

Rosenberg, Bernard. "Mouriscos et Elches: Conversions au Maroc au début du XVIe siècle." *Relaciones de la Península Ibérica con el Magreb, siglos XIII–XVI. Actas del Coloquio (Madrid, 17–18 Diciembre, 1987)*. Ed. Mercedes García Arenal and María J. Viguera. Madrid: Consejo Superior de Investigaciones Científicas, 1988. 621–77.

Rossi, Ettore. *Storia della Marina dell'Ordine di S. Giovanni di Gerusalemme di Rodi e di Malta*. Roma: Società Editrice D'Arte Illustrata, 1926.

Rossi, Rosa. *Escuchar a Cervantes: Un ensayo biográfico*. Valladolid: Ámbito, 1988.

———. *Sulle trace di Cervantes: Profilo inedito dell'autore del* Chisciotte. Roma: Riunti, 1997.

Rostagno, Lucia. *Mi faccio turco: Esperienze ed immagini dell'islam nell'Italia moderna*. Roma: Istituto per l'Oriente C. A. Nallino, 1983.

Roudiez, Leon S. Introduction. Julia Kristeva. *Desire in Language: A Semiotic Approach to Literature and Art*. New York: Columbia University Press, 1980. 1-20.

Rozas, Juan Manuel. "Lope de Vega y las órdenes militares (Notas sobre el sentido histórico de su teatro)." *Las órdenes militares en el Mediterráneo Occidental (S. XII–XVIII), Coloquio Las órdenes militares en el Mediterráneo Occidental, Madrid, 4–6 May 1983*. Madrid: Casa de Velásquez, 1989. 359–67.

Ruano de la Haza, José María. *La puesta en escena en los teatros comerciales del Siglo de Oro*. Madrid: Castalia, 2000.

Salah, Mohamed Mounir. "El Doctor Sosa y la *Topografía e historia general de Argel*." Diss. Universitat Autònoma de Barcelona, 1991.

Salhi, Mohammed, ed. *El siglo XVII hispano-marroquí*. Rabat: Facultad de Letras y Ciencias Humanas, 1997.

Salvá, Jaime. *La Orden de Malta y las acciones españolas contra turcos y berberiscos en los siglos XVI y XVII*. Madrid: Instituto Histórico de Marina, 1944.

Sánchez, Alberto. "Aproximación al teatro de Cervantes." *Cervantes y el teatro. Cuadernos de Teatro Clásico* 7 (1992): 11–30.

———. "Libertad, humano tesoro." *Anales Cervantinos* 23 (1994): 9–21.

———. "Nuevas orientaciones en el planteamiento de la biografía de Cervantes." *Cervantes*. Ed. Anthony Close et al. Madrid: Centro de Estudios Cervantinos, 1995. 19–40.

———. "Revisión del cautiverio cervantino en Argel." *Cervantes* 17.1 (1997): 7–24.

Sánchez Saus, Rafael. "Los Saavedra y la frontera con el Reino de Granada en el siglo XV." *Estudios sobre Málaga y el Reino de Granada en el V centenario de la Conquista*. Málaga: Servicio de Publicaciones, Diputación Provincial de Málaga, 1987. 163–82.

Sandoval, Prudencio de. *Historia de la vida y hechos del Emperador Carlos V*. Ed. Carlos Seco Serrano. 3 vols. Madrid: Atlas, 1955–1956.

Sanz Sampleyano, Juan F. "La demografía histórica en Andalucía." *Demografía histórica en España*. Ed. Vicente Pérez Moreda and David-Sven Reher. Orán: El Arquero, 1988.

Schimmel, Annemarie. *Mystical Dimensions of Islam*. Chapel Hill, NC: University of North Carolina Press, 1975.

Schneider, Monique. *Le trauma et la filiation paradoxale*. Paris: Ramsay, 1988.

Sebag, Paul, trans. "Une relation inédite sur la prise de Tunis par les turcs, en 1574." *Cahiers de la Tunisie* 16–18.61-64, 71-72 (1968–1970): 8–250.

Selig, Karl-Ludwig. "Cervantes: 'En un lugar de . . .' " *MLN* 86 (1971): 266–68.

Semprún, Jorge. *L'écriture ou la vie*. Paris: Gallimard, 1994.

————. *Literature or Life.* Trans. Linda Coverdale. New York: Viking, 1996.

Seneca, Lucius Annaeus. *De Beneficiis.* Trans. John W. Basore. Loeb Classical Library. Vol. 3 of *Seneca, Works. English & Latin Selections.* 3 vols. Cambridge: Harvard University Press, 1928–1935.

Serrano, Luciano. *España en Lepanto.* Barcelona: Labor, 1935. Madrid: Editora Nacional, 1975.

————. *La Liga de Lepanto entre España, Venecia y la Santa Sede (1570–1573).* 2 vols. Madrid: Imprenta de Archivos, 1918–1920.

Serrano y Sanz, Manuel. *Apuntes para una biblioteca de escritoras españolas desde el año 1401 al 1883.* Biblioteca De Autores Españoles 268–271. Vol. 1. 4 vols. Madrid: M. Rivadeneira, 1975.

Servia, Fray Miguel. "Relación de los sucesos de la armada de la Santa Liga y entre ellos el de la Batalla De Lepanto." *Colección de documentos inéditos para la historia de España.* Vol. 9. Madrid: Imprenta de la viuda de Calero, 1842–1895. 359–71.

Sevilla Arroyo, Florencio, and Antonio Rey Hazas. "Introducción: 'El teatro de Cervantes: Segunda época.'" *Obra completa: Miguel de Cervantes.* Ed. Florencio Sevilla Arroyo and Antonio Rey Hazas. Vol. 14. Madrid: Alianza, 1998. I–XLIX.

————, eds. *Obra completa de Miguel de Cervantes.* 18 vols. Madrid: Alianza, 1998.

Sire, H.J.A. *The Knights of Malta.* New Haven, CT: Yale University Press, 1994.

Sito Alba, Manuel. "El teatro en el siglo XVI." *Historia del teatro en España.* Ed. José María Borque et al. Vol. 1. Madrid: Taurus, 1983. 341–66.

Sliwa, K., ed. *Documentos de Miguel de Cervantes Saavedra.* Pamplona: EUNSA, Ediciones Universidad de Navarra, 1999.

Smith, Paul Julian. "*The Captive's Tale:* Race, Text, Gender." *Quixotic Desire: Psychoanalytic Perspectives on Cervantes.* Ed. Ruth El Saffar and Diana de Armas Wilson. Ithaca, NY: Cornell University Press, 1993. 227–35.

Sola, Emilio. "Antonio de Sosa: Un clásico inédito amigo de Cervantes (Historia y Literatura)." *Actas del primer coloquio internacional de la Asociación de Cervantistas, Alcalá de Henares, 29/30 Nov.–1/2 Dic. 1988.* Alcalá de Henares: Anthropos, 1990. Vol. 1. 409–12.

————. "La saga de los Barbarroja." *Historia 16* 14.158–161 (1989): 8–16, 82–90, 73–81, 91–8.

————. "Miguel de Cervantes, Antonio de Sosa y África." *Actas del I encuentro de historiadores del Valle de Henares.* Guadalajara: Institución de Estudios Complutenses, Fundación Marqués de Santillana, Centro de Estudios Cervantinos, 1988. 617–23.

————. *Un Mediterráneo de piratas: Corsarios, renegados y cautivos.* Madrid: Tecnos, 1988.

Sola, Emilio, and José F. de la Peña. *Cervantes y la Berbería: Cervantes, mundo turco-berberisco y servicios secretos en la época de Felipe II.* México: Fondo de Cultura Económica, 1995.

Sola, Emilio, and Miguel Ángel de Bunes, eds. *La vida, y historia de Hayradin, llamado Barbarroja: Gazavat-I Hayreddin Pasa (La crónica del guerrero de la Fé Hayreddin Barbarroja).* Granada: Universidad de Granada, 1997.

Sopranis, Hipólito Sancho de. "Cádiz y la piratería turco-berberisca en el siglo XVI." *Archivos del Instituto de Estudios Africanos* 26 (1953): 7–77.

Sosa, Antonio de. "Ad Papam Gregorium XIII." *Chronica Sacri/et Militaris Or-*

dinis/B. Mariae de Mercede,/Redemptionis Captivorum. Ed. Fray Bernardo de Vargas. Vol. 2. Panormi: Apud Ioannem Baptistam Maringum, 1622. 107–09.

———. "Carta a Nuestro Santissimo Papa Gregorio XIII, el Colegio de los Ilustrissimos, y Reverendissimos Señores Cardenales [. . .]" *Gloriosa/Fecundidad/de Maria/en el Campo de la/Catolica Iglesia.* Ed. Fray Francisco de Neyla. Barcelona: Rafael Figueró, 1698. 190–95.

———. *Diálogo de los mártires de Argel.* Ed. Emilio Sola and José M. Parreño. Madrid: Hiperión, 1990.

———. "Diálogo de los mártires de Argel." *Topografía e historia general de Argel.* Ed. Diego de Haedo. Ignacio Bauer y Landauer ed. Vol. 3. Madrid: Sociedad de Bibliófilos Españoles, 1927–1929. 1–274.

———. "Epítome de los reyes de Argel." *Topografía e historia general de Argel.* Ed. Diego de Haedo. Ignacio Bauer y Landauer. Vol. 1. Madrid: Sociedad de Bibliófilos Españoles, 1927. 213–426.

———. *Histoire des rois d'Alger.* Ed. Diego de Haedo. Trans. Henri-Delmas de Grammont. Alger: Adolphe Jourdan, 1881.

———. *Histoire des rois d'Alger.* Trans. Henri-Delmas de Grammont. Saint-Denis: Editions Bouchène, 1998.

———. *Topografía e historia general de Argel.* Ed. Diego de Haedo. Ignacio Bauer y Landauer, ed. 3 vols. Madrid: Sociedad de Bibliófilos Españoles, 1927-29.

———. *Topographia, e historia general de Argel, repartida en cinco tratados do se veran casos extraños, muertes espantosas y tormentos exquisitos que conviene se entiendan en la Cristiandad* [. . .]. Ed. Diego de Haedo. Valladolid: Diego Fernández de Córdova y Oviedo, a costa de Antonio Coello, 1612.

———. *Topographie et histoire générale d'Alger.* Trans. Dr. Monnereau and A. Berbrugger. Saint-Denis: Editions Bouchène, 1998.

———. "Topographie et histoire générale d'Alger." Trans. Dr. Monnereau and A. Berbrugger. *Revue africaine* 82–90 (1870–71).

Sousa, António Caetano de. *História genealógica da casa real portuguesa.* Ed. M. Lopes de Almeida and César Pegado. 12 vols. Coimbra: Atlântida, 1946–54.

Spencer, Forrest Eugene, and Rudolph Schevill. *The Dramatic Works of Luis Vélez de Guevara: Their Plots, Sources, and Bibliographies.* University of California Publications in Modern Philology. Vol. 19. Berkeley, CA: University of California Press, 1937.

Spencer, William. *Algiers in the Age of the Corsairs.* Norman, OK: University of Oklahoma Press, 1976.

Spitzer, Leo. "Linguistic Perspectivisim in *Don Quijote.*" *Leo Spitzer: Representative Essays.* Ed. Alban Forcione et al. Stanford, CA: Stanford University Press, 1988. 225–71.

Stagg, Geoffrey. "The Date and Form of *El trato de Argel.*" *Bulletin of Hispanic Studies* 30.120 (1953): 181–92.

Stapp, William A. "*El gallardo español:* La fama como arbitrio de la realidad." *Cervantes: Su obra y su mundo, Actas del I Congreso internacional sobre Cervantes.* Ed. Manuel Criado de Val. Madrid: Edi 6, 1978. 261–72.

Sullivan, Henry W. *Grotesque Purgatory: A Study of Cervantes's* Don Quixote, Part II. University Park, PA: Pennsylvania State University Press, 1996.

Talmon, Shemaryahu. "Daniel." *The Literary Guide to the Bible.* Ed. Robert Alter and Frank Kermode. Cambridge, MA: Harvard University Press, 1987. 343–46.

Tarrow, Susan, ed. *Reason and Light: Essays on Primo Levi.* Ithaca, NY: Center for

International Studies, Cornell University, 1990.

Thompson, I.A.A., and Bartolomé Yun Casalilla, eds. *The Castilian Crisis of the Seventeenth Century: New Perspectives on the Economic and Social History of Seventeenth-Century Spain.* Cambridge: Cambridge University Press, 1994.

Torre y del Cerro, Antonio de, ed. *Testamentaria de Isabel la Católica.* Valladolid: Instituto "Isabel la Católica" de Historia Eclesiástica, 1968.

Torres, Diego de. *Relación del origen y suceso de los Xarifes y del estado de los reinos de Marruecos, Fez y Tarudante.* Ed. Mercedes García Arenal. Madrid: Siglo XXI, 1980.

Torres Lanzas, Pedro, ed. *Información de Miguel de Cervantes de lo que ha servido a S.M. y de lo que ha hecho estando captivo en Argel[. . .].* Madrid: El Árbol, 1981.

Turbet-Delof, Guy. *Bibliographie critique du Maghreb dans la littérature française, 1532–1715.* Alger: Société nationale d'édition et diffusion, 1976.

Turner, Victor W. "Betwixt and Between: The Liminal Period in Rites of Passage." *The Forest of Symbols: Aspects of Ndembu Ritual.* Ithaca, NY: Cornell University Press, 1967. 93–230.

———. *Dramas, Fields, and Metaphors: Symbolic Action in Human Society.* Ithaca, NY: Cornell University Press, 1974.

Ubersfeld, Anne. *Lire le théâtre.* Paris: Belin, 1996.

———. *Lire le théâtre II. L'école du spectateur.* Paris: Belin, 1996.

———. *Reading Theatre.* Trans. Frank Collins. Ed. Paul Perron and Patrick Debbèche. Toronto: University of Toronto Press, 1999.

Uluç, Lale. "Ottoman Book Collecting and Illustrated Sixteenth-Century Shiraz Manuscripts." *Livres et lecture dans le monde Ottoman.* Ed. Frédéric Hitzel. Special ed. of *Revue des mondes musulmans et de la Méditerranée* 87–88 (1999): 85–107.

Urbina, Eduardo. "Historias verdaderas y la verdad de la historia: Fernando Arrabal vs. Stephen Marlowe." *Cervantes* 18 (1998): 158–69.

Valbuena Prat, Ángel. *Estudios de literatura religiosa española: Época medieval y Siglo de Oro.* Madrid: Gredos, 1964.

Varey, J.E. *Cosmografía y escenografía: El teatro español en el Siglo de Oro.* Madrid: Castalia, 1987.

Vargas, Fray Bernardo de. *Cronica Sacri et militare Ordinis B. Mariae de Mercede, redemptionis captivorvm [. . .].* Panormi: Apud Ioannem Baptistam Maringum, 1622.

Varner, John. *El Inca: The Life and Times of Inca Garcilaso.* Austin: University of Texas Press, 1968.

Vega Carpio, Lope de. "El Valor De Malta." *Obras de Lope de Vega.* Ed. Marcelino Menéndez y Pelayo. Vol. 26 of Biblioteca de Autores Españoles. Madrid: Atlas, 1969. 177–226.

———. "La pérdida honrosa y caballeros de San Juan." *Obras de Lope de Vega.* Ed. Marcelino Menéndez y Pelayo. Vol. 25 of Biblioteca de Autores Españoles. Madrid: Atlas, 1969. 249–300.

Viaje de Turquía. Ed. Marie-Sol Ortola. Madrid: Castalia, 2000.

La vida, y historia de Hayradin, llamado Barbarroja: Gazavat-I Hayreddin Pasa (la crónica del guerrero de la Fé Hayreddin Barbarroja). Ed. Miguel Ángel de Bunes and Emilio Sola. Granada: Universidad de Granada, 1997.

Villegaignon, Nicolas Durand de. "A Lamentableand Piteous Treatise, Verye Necessarye for Everie Christen Manne to Reade: Wherin Is Contayned, Not Onely the High Entreprise and Valeauntnes of Th'emperouor Charles V. And His Army (in His Voyage Mde to the Town of Argier in Affrique, against the Turckes, the Enemyes of the Christen Fayth, Th'inhabitoures of the Same), but also The Myserable Chaunces of Wynde and Wether; with Dyverse Other Adversities, Ahble to Move a Stonye Hearte . . ." Trans. Ricardus Grafton. *Harleian Miscellany: A Collection of Scarce, Curious, and Entertaining Pamphlets and Tracts as Well as Manuscript and in Print. Selected from the Library of Edward Harley, Second Earl of Oxford.* 1542. Ed. William Oldys and Thomas Park. Vol. 4. Harleian Miscellany. London: White and Co., 1809. 532–43.

Villegaignon, Nicolas Durand de. *Carlo V Emperatoris Expeditio in Africam Ad Algeriam: Per Nicolaum Villagagnomem equitem rhodium gallum* . . . Argentorati: Vuendelinum Rihelium, 1542.

Vitkus, Daniel J. Introduction. *Three Turk Plays from Early Modern England: Selimus, A Christian Turned Turk, and* The Renegado. New York: Columbia University Press, 2000. 1–53.

Wardropper, Bruce. "Cervantes's Theory of the Drama." *Modern Philology* 52.4 (1955): 212–21.

———. "Comedias." *Suma cervantina.* Ed. Juan Bautista Avalle-Arce and Edward C. Riley. London: Tamesis, 1973. 147–69.

Warner, Marina. *Alone of All Her Sex: The Myth and Cult of the Virgin Mary.* New York: Knopf, 1976.

Watt, William Montgomery. *Muslim-Christian Encounters: Perceptions and Misperceptions.* London: Routledge, 1991.

Weber, Alison. "Padres e hijas: Una lectura intertextual de la *Historia del cautivo.*" *Actas del segundo coloquio internacional de la Asociación de Cervantistas, Alcalá De Henares 6–9 Nov. 1989 (II-CIAC).* Barcelona: Anthropos, 1991. 425–31.

Wiesel, Elie. *A Jew Today.* Trans. Marion Wiesel. New York: Random House, 1978.

Wigren, Jodie. "Narrative Completion in the Treatment of Trauma." *Psychotherapy* 31.3 (1994): 415–23.

Williams, Henry Smith, ed. *The Historians' History of the World: A Comprehensive Narrative of the Rise and Development of Nations as Recorded by over Two Thousand of the Great Writers of All Ages.* Vol. 25. London: Hooper and Jackson, 1909.

Wilson, Diana de Armas. *Allegories of Love: Cervantes's* Persiles and Sigismunda. Princeton, NJ: Princeton University Press, 1991.

———. *Cervantes, the Novel, and the New World.* New York: Oxford University Press, 2000.

Winnicott, Donald W. "The Concept of Trauma in Relation to the Development of the Individual within the Family." *Psycho-Analytic Explorations.* Ed. Claire Winnicott et al. Cambridge, MA: Harvard University Press, 1989.

———. "Fear of Breakdown." *Psycho-Analytic Explorations.* Ed. Claire Winnicott et al. Cambridge, MA: Harvard University Press, 1989. 87–95.

———. "The Location of Cultural Experience." *Playing and Reality.* London: Routledge, 1971. 95–103.

Wismayer, Joseph M. *The Fleet of the Order of St. John, 1530–1798.* Valletta: Midsea, 1997.

Wolf, John B. *The Barbary Coast: Algiers under the Turks, 1500 to 1830.* New York: Norton, 1979.

Yahya, Dahiru. *Morocco in the Sixteenth Century: Problems of Patterns in African Foreign Policy.* Atlantic Highlands, NJ: Humanities, 1981.

Yaque Laurel, José A. "La expedición de Carlos V a Argel: El relato imperial." *África* 199 (1958): 13–15.

Zafrani, Haïm. *Juifs d'Andalousie et du Maghreb.* Paris: Maisonneuve et Larose, 1996.

Zamora Vicente, Alonso. "El cautiverio en la obra de Cervantes." *Homenaje a Cervantes.* Ed. Francisco Sánchez-Castañer. Vol. 2. Madrid: Mediterráneo, 1950. 384–401.

Zimic, Stanislav. "*El gallardo español.*" *El teatro de Cervantes.* Madrid: Castalia, 1992. 87–117.

———. "*Los tratos de Argel.*" *El teatro de Cervantes.* Madrid: Castalia, 1992. 37–56.

Zmantar, Françoise. "Miguel de Cervantes y sus fantasmas de Argel." *Quimera* 2 nov. 1980: 31–7.

———. "Qui es-tu Azán, Azán où es-tu?" *Les personnages en question, IV colloque du S.E.L, Toulouse, 1–3 décembre 1983.* Université de Tolouse-Le-Mirail, 1984. 165–73.

———. "Saavedra et les captifs du *Trato de Argel* de Miguel de Cervantes." *L'autobiographie dans le monde hispanique, Actes du colloque international de la Baume-lès-Aix, 11–13 mai, 1979.* Aix-en-Provence: Université de Provence, 1980. 185–203.

Zúñiga, Fray Melchor de, O.S.F. *Descripción de la República de la ciudad de Argel.* ms. 3227, fol. 136v–141r. Biblioteca Nacional, Madrid.

———. "Descripción de la República de la ciudad de Argel." *Judeoconversos y moriscos en la literatura del Siglo de Oro, Actas del "Grand Séminaire" de Neuchâtel, Neuchâtel, 26 a 27 de Mayo de 1994.* Ed. Irene Andres-Suárez. Paris: Diffusion Les Belles Lettres, 1995. 184–86.

Zysberg, André. "Les galères de France sous le règne de Louis XIV. Essai de comptabilité globale." *Les marines de guerre européennes (XVIe–XVIIe siècles).* Ed. Martine Acerra et al. Paris: Presses de l'Université de Paris-Sorbonne, 1985. 403–36.

Index

---

* References to *Topographia, e historia general de Argel* (1612) and to the modern edition of *Topografía* (1927–29) are so frequent that they have not been listed separately. They begin on page 2.